NATURAL AWAKENING

An Advanced Guide for Sharing Nondual Awareness

NATURAL
AWAKENING

An Advanced Guide for
Sharing Nondual Awareness

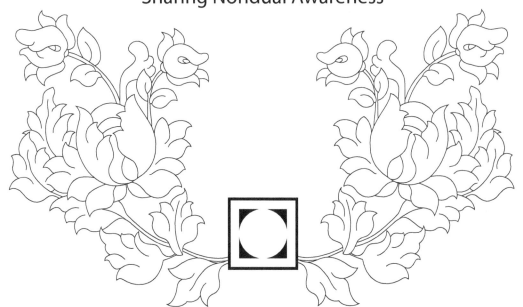

Peter Fenner, Ph.D.

NATURAL AWAKENING
An Advanced Guide for Sharing Nondual Awareness
Peter Fenner

Book design: Karma Yönten Gyatso
Illustrations: Marie Barincou

Published by
The Sumeru Press Inc.
PO Box 2089, Richmond Hill, ON
Canada L4E 1A3

LIBRARY AND ARCHIVES CANADA CATALOGUING IN PUBLICATION

Fenner, Peter G., 1949-, author
  Natural awakening : an advanced guide for sharing nondual awareness /
Peter Fenner, Ph.D.

Includes bibliographical references and index.
Issued in print and electronic formats.
ISBN 978-1-896559-24-7 (pbk.).--ISBN 978-1-896559-25-4 (ebook)

  1. Madhyamika (Buddhism)--Psychological aspects.
2. Awareness--Religious aspects--Buddhism. 3. Spiritual life--Buddhism. I. Title.

BQ7460.F45 2015   294.3'92   C2015-903286-5
                     C2015-903287-3

 For more information about The Sumeru Press
visit us at *www.sumeru-books.com*

*To the masters of awareness
from ancient India and Tibet,
especially Nagarjuna and Longchenpa,
who have given me so much inspiration
and guidance through their timeless wisdom.*

*To my gurus of this life, who have loosened the knots
of my convoluted karma, and showered me
with their infinite love and compassion.*

*May the recognition of nondual awareness
arise this very instant in the mindstreams of all beings
throughout the universe. May it never darken or diminish.*

*May the ultimate medicine of pure awareness manifest
like sunbeams bursting through winter clouds
bringing peace, love and harmony
to this fractious human existence.*

Table of contents

Endorsements

Peter Fenner is one of the leading nonduality teachers of our time. In this generous, comprehensive book, Dr. Fenner offers a complete compendium of the ways he has found to evoke nondual awakening in his students. Here we find the full breadth of his understanding, based on his own realization of nonduality, his extensive knowledge of Buddhist teachings and his compassionate response to human suffering. I highly recommend this book to anyone who wants to open to, and guide others to, this most profound dimension of human experience.

> Judith Blackstone, Ph.D.,
> author of *The Enlightenment Process* and *The Empathic Ground*, New York.

In *Natural Awakening*, Peter Fenner further develops his brilliant postmodern implementation of Buddhist nondual wisdom. Peter has taken the refined deconstructive practices that have liberated tens of thousands of Asian contemplatives and adapted them for effective Western use. I highly recommend it.

> Robert Thurman, Ph.D.,
> Buddhist Scholar, Columbia University, President of Tibet House in New York, NY.

Peter Fenner's exceptional clarity of mind, deep familiarity with Buddhist texts, decades of wonderfully caring teaching experience and his pitch-perfectly worded guidances in *Natural Awakening* untie myriad illusory snares of mental suffering for any reader.

> Stuart Sovatsky, Ph.D.,
> author of *Advanced Spiritual Intimacy and Words From the Soul*, California.

Natural Awakening offers an illuminating look under the hood into Peter Fenner's nondual teacher training program that guides us into not knowing and having authentic, spontaneous, and deeply transformative conversations about nothing. This masterful work—lucid, keenly insightful, and beautifully written—will be of interest to beginning students and experienced teachers alike. A real gem and resource.

> John J. Prendergast, Ph.D.,
> author of *In Touch*, Chief Editor of *The Undivided*, California.

I had the great fortune to experience Peter Fenner's Natural Awakening Training and to immerse myself in this *Guide*. The Training has been a wonderful opportunity to experience a new way of being with my students and as a facilitator. Learning to hold others in a space of unconditional awareness has been a gift both for me and those I come in contact with as a mentor. This *Guide* has become my travel companion and the book that I go back to most frequently. The book organizes the practical teaching in such a systematic and complete way that that it can stand alone and be used independently of the Training. Peter convivially teaches us to dance in the paradoxes of nonduality and utilize participants' cognitive powers to lead us beyond the limits of the conceptual mind. I give Peter Fenner the strongest endorsement possible, as my gratitude to his transmission cannot be expressed in words.

> Mariusz Wirga, M.D.,
> Medical Director, Psychosocial Oncology, Todd Cancer Institute, Long Beach Memorial Medical Center, Long Beach, California.

Peter is a living master of Madhyamika-style deconstruction practiced with contemporary finesse…. This book is both a practical teaching manual and an archivable reference work for nondual coaches, therapists, teachers, and students of many stripes. Clarifying the nature of unconditioned presence and presenting a feast of skillful means for facilitating the realization of such presence, this book contains many lively teacher/student dialogues that are at once laser-focused and relationally-attuned: the hallmark of Radiant Mind trainings. This book is a watershed moment in the extraordinary transmission of nondual wisdom from East to West and from mind to mind.

> Ken Bradford, Ph.D.,
> Clinical Psychologist, Adjunct Professor at John F. Kennedy University, author of *The I of the Other*, California.

How wonderful that Peter Fenner is so generously making his masterful nondual training manual available to the public! I highly recommend it to anyone interested in gaining more stability and confidence in nondual awareness and acquiring a language and the sensitivities through which liberating transmission happens naturally and effortlessly.

> Risa Kaparo, Ph.D.,
> author of *Awakening Somatic Intelligence: The Art & Practice of Embodied Mindfulness*, California.

Through his Radiant Mind workshops and books and his Nondual Therapy trainings, Peter Fenner has shared his powerful and effective transmission with thousands of seekers and practitioners. Now, in *Natural Awakening*, he reveals the methods and techniques that have heretofore been available only to training participants—methods that can be applied not only to work with clients or students, but also to one's relationship with friends, loved ones, and above all oneself. I highly recommend this brilliant, original contribution to the teaching and transmission of what cannot be taught.

> Stephan Bodian,
> author of *Meditation for Dummies* and *Beyond Mindfulness*, New Mexico.

It is a rare and precious opportunity, when a teacher like Peter Fenner invites us to step 'through' the teachings, into a deep contemplation of the skills required to transmit nondual wisdom. I hope that teachers, facilitators, mentors and coaches who have an affinity with nondual awareness will make good use of the depth and power of what Peter is offering through this book. This is truly a living wisdom that carries us into uncharted territory and unimaginable blessings.

Shalya Wright,
author of *Everyday Magic*, Victoria, Canada

Like his root teacher, the beloved Lama Yeshe, Peter has a fresh and unusual approach. Through a natural process of deconstruction, underlying assumptions and belief systems that bind us to habitual patterns are revealed. As these belief structures and preferences rise to the surface, the sun of awareness dissolves fixations. As fixations are released, the space of suchness opens, and readers can experience the fresh, open quality of aware presence. *Natural Awakening* shows us how the process of awakening can be facilitated through simultaneously understanding the field from both the ultimate and apparent perspectives. This *Guide* is an invaluable contribution to nondual teachers.

Lama Palden Drolma,
Founder and Director of Sukhasiddhi Foundation, California

Written as a "how to" manual, Peter Fenner's excellent new book brilliantly lays out very practical ways of accessing and integrating nondual awareness. Dr. Fenner shows how simple, narrative conversations are extremely useful in deconstructing the dualistic worldview and leading us, instead, into a direct experience of who we already are. This content-rich book points the readers to a clear and compelling way for "abiding-in-awareness." Highly recommended.

Chuck Hillig,
author of *Enlightenment for Beginners* and *The Way IT Is*, Virginia.

Reading this book was an awakening experience like no other. It opened my eyes and heart through both its incredibly helpful content and also its crystal clear transmission. Anyone supporting others in opening to pure awareness will be enriched and inspired by what Peter presents. My whole being relaxes into a spacious, passionate "Yes!"

Raphael Cushnir,
author of *The One Thing Holding You Back*, Oregon.

I came to Peter Fenner's teaching after years of Japanese Zen monastic training. How refreshing and invigorating! I am so appreciative of his training, scholarship and unique way of making Buddhist nondual wisdom directly accessible to Western hearts and minds. With *Natural Awakening* Peter makes an enormous contribution toward bringing all beings to clarity and equanimity. I am profoundly grateful.

Jan Hodgman,
Soto Zen priest, Focusing Trainer and nondual teacher, Anacortes, Washington.

Acknowledgements

Firstly, I would like to thank my wife Marie Barincou without whose support the entire *Natural Awakening* initiative would have been impossible. She has given me the confidence and inspiration to put everything I know about nondual transmission into words. We've spent thousands of hours in conversation, creating and refining the Natural Awakening Trainings. I'm very pleased that Rashani Réa has written some words about how she sees our creative process, words I couldn't exactly put down myself. Rashani says, "*Natural Awakening* is a co-creation, a natural outpouring of Peter and Marie's personal and spiritual marriage. Marie Barincou is an acutely aware, invisible presence interwoven throughout the many thousands of words on these pages." Without Marie's gifts and commitment *Natural Awakening* wouldn't have happened.

I also thank my teachers for their guidance, support and inspiration, especially those who gave me my initial orientation: Lama Thubten Yeshe, Lama Thubten Zopa Rinpoche, Geshe Thubten Loden, Zasep Tulku Rinpoche, Geshe Ngawang Legden Rinpoche, Geshe Thubten Trinley, Geshe Lhundup Sopa Rinpoche, Chogyal Namkhai Norbu Rinpoche, Sogyal Rinpoche and Traleg Kyabgon Rinpoche. Lama Yeshe in particular pointed me in the direction of "teaching dharma" in ways that were direct and accessible.

Much of this *Guide* was written in the blessing field of Sri Satya Sai Baba at Puttaparthi. It's difficult to describe the support this field provided. For the five years in which the Training and this *Guide* were taking form, I spent about three weeks each year at his *ashram*. I would sit on the verandah in the mandir with my pen and papers working on my latest drafts, adding and augmenting text for an hour or more before his *darshans*, during which, of course, time would seem to stand still as he moved among the thousands in the *mandir*. Then I'd go back my room, enter new text on my Mac and print it out on my portable printer, ready for more writing.

Many people have helped give initial direction to this *Guide*. Pir Elias Amidon, Murshida Rabia Roberts, Margo King, John Steiner and Judith Orloff joined me in a number of focused conversations early on in the process. Elias Amidon probed my mind to discover aspects of my teaching of which I wasn't aware. He has also contributed a very generous Foreword that helps widen the door into these teachings.

Susan Morton sifted through hundreds of pages of workshop transcripts to find illustrative dialogs. Ron and Geri Stewart directed and worked with a team of editors based in Portland who helped with proofreading and final editing. The team included Nancy Burch, Vivian Coles, Kathleen Goldberg, Michael Nagel, Shannon Pernetti, Diane Steinbrecher, Pernilla Siebenfreund and Lars Andersson. Prof. Barry Reed went over the *Guide* very thoroughly checking citations and harmonizing terminology throughout.

My work has also evolved in the context of the growing professional interest in nondual awareness in psychotherapy, teaching and living life. Without this context I wouldn't have had the confidence to go in the direction I have. In particular, I'd like to thank Dr. Jean-Marc Mantel, Dr. Ken Bradford, Dr. John Prendergast, Stephan Bodian and Roshi Sylvia Ostertag. I also thank the stewards of Timeless Wisdom, Prof. Ron Purser and Stanley Arcieri for their long time support.

I also thank Ginny Jordan and the Advised Fund for RSF Social Finance, Melissa Stuart, the Steiner-King Foundation, Karl Beer, Drs. Mariusz and Aleksandra Wirga, and Dr. Tom Rotmann for their generous support of the Natural Awakening initiative and me. I especially thank Ron and Geri Stewart for their tireless and unbelievably gratuitous help in so many ways that I can't begin to list them.

Finally I thank Sumeru and John Negru. I don't know of any other publisher who would grant me the freedom offered by John. I think his secret mantra is, "Whatever you want!" I hope it serves him really well with this volume. I'm sure that my decision to publish this *Guide* and John's willingness to accept it is a confluence of auspiciousness.

Peter Fenner, Ph.D.
April 2015

Foreword

An old Sufi story tells of a land that was bordered on one side by an immense wall, a wall so high no one had ever seen what was on the other side. People had tried to scale it, of course, but their ladders were too short. So finally they just accepted the wall as a feature of the landscape.

One day, as the story goes, a man who was particularly curious came up with a plan to see over the wall. He gathered a great crowd of people and had the strongest ones get on all fours on the ground next to the wall, then the next folks balanced on them on all fours, and up and up until an immense pyramid of people was built that reached nearly to the top of the wall. Finally, the smallest and lightest person climbed up on everyone's backs, pulled himself up to the top of the wall, and looked. And then he jumped over!

The pyramid of people collapsed. Everyone groaned. But not to be defeated, a few days later they returned and formed another pyramid. This time they made the littlest person promise, even if she wanted to jump over, she would first shout down to them what was on the other side. She promised, and then climbed up on everyone's backs. When she finally pulled herself up to the top of the wall and looked, her eyes went wide and quick as a flash, she jumped over! The pyramid collapsed again. Everyone was bummed.

Ultimately, they made another pyramid, but this time they tied a rope around the ankle of the littlest person, so if she jumped over they could pull her back. And so the climb was made again, and getting to the top, the little woman looked, and she jumped over! But this time they pulled her back. Once on the ground, everyone crowded around her.

"Well," they asked, "what did you see?" But the woman was unable to speak. She was mute.

If the littlest woman who saw over the wall *could* speak, she might have sat us all down and said something like what you will find in this book. Not a description of what's on the other side, but *a way to see for ourselves—and to help others see for themselves.*

Of course, the story is just a story, and like all stories it's based on duality—especially the idea that there is a wall dividing our everyday world from "the truth," the nondual nature of all being. That distinction may be how we experience things, but the idea that there is another place, not here, where the nondual truth will be revealed, is exactly what keeps us bound to seeking and to ignorance. When those climbers finally did see over the wall, they saw this. In fact, I imagine they saw exactly what the rest of us see on this side of the wall, except for….

Here again, words can't say. Why? Because, as Peter Fenner tells us so skillfully in this precious guidebook, what's "on the other side" is not a thing. "Since it's not a thing," Peter writes, "it means it's impossible to find. The very process of looking for it is the act of missing it. The sure-fire way to miss the nondual is to look for it."

This puts you and me in a bewildering situation. We've picked up this *Guide* presumably to find out what this "natural awakening" is all about, and to learn how to help others find it. But now we hear it's impossible to find! Then what is this book about?

The bewilderment we feel is a clue. I think here of a prayer uttered by the Prophet Mohammad: *"Oh Lord, increase my bewilderment concerning Thee!"* In Buddhism this bewilderment is called *not knowing*, or *unknowing*. It's not the same as a lack of knowledge, something you could amend by learning. It's more like being present without needing to assert anything about what is present. Unknowing is a kind of precursor to, or even essence of, natural awakening—but again, if awakening occurs, one's unknowing doesn't get filled in. In this sense, "awakening" isn't anything either. When one "awakens" nothing happens. Nothing occurs!

Be forewarned—this book is full of these kinds of statements—subtle turns of thought that either frustrate or push us over the edge of our reasonableness. This is Peter's genius: he uses the *via negativa*—the way of negation—with such grace that we don't know it's happening until we're already launched off into the space beyond intellect.

He then codifies these "launches" with phrases like: *there's nothing to do because nothing is wrong or missing; nondual transmission is contentless; unconditioned awareness is unproduced; it's nothing; it's not nothing; it's not an experience; there's nothing you have to do to be complete; nothing is hidden; nothing is happening; there's no inside and no outside; we can't say if this "is" or "isn't"; there's nothing to understand, nothing to know, nothing to think about; there is nothing to integrate; there are no obstacles,* and so on. These are delivered, not as hypothetical possibilities, but as "the way things are."

I encourage you, while working with the material in this book, to allow these launches to do their work. When you hear yourself saying (as I have), "Wait a minute, Peter, that's too categorical! There *are* obstacles to awakening, otherwise why did you feel the need to write all these words?" consider that your mind is putting up resistance. It's not necessary that his writing and dialogs accurately match all dimensions of your experience—let them dislodge your certainty and increase your bewilderment!

This apophatic approach is central to the method of nondual transmission Peter offers us in these pages. It is combined—especially when he's working face-to-face with an individual or a class—with a minimalist style that is almost uncanny. Peter's capacity to listen deeply and respond perfectly is unparalleled in my experience with spiritual teachers. As if by magic he is able to point out the tangled assumptions that are opaque to us, and without any judgment or arrogance reveal the way to greater ease and realization. His style is simple yet profound, and lovingly sensitive. If you wish some help in freeing yourself and others from suffering – in any realm of life, or help in realizing the clear, joyous nature of our original being, this *Guide* and Peter's work can be trusted.

It may seem contradictory that a guide like this, packed with skills and tips and references to the quintessence of mystical traditions, would repeatedly deconstruct its methods into "an absence of a point of reference"—yet that's the heart of the matter. All authentic nondual teaching comes from this place, from this absence of a point of reference. It could be called complete trust, without anything in which we place our trust. It could also be called effortlessness. I remember hearing Peter remark once that the nondual teaching he does now is without stress, especially as compared to the university teaching he did earlier in his career, which took exacting preparation. Even when he faces a large audience unfamiliar with him and nondual teachings, he confessed he doesn't do much preparation. "No," he said, "I usually think of the first two or three sentences to say. That's plenty. The rest takes care of itself."

Of course, Peter comes to these moments with a vast amount of Buddhist training, and his analytical work in Madhyamika philosophical psychology gives him unique skills in deconstructing our assumptions about who we are and what is so. But he never burdens us with these ontological subtleties. His approach is direct and experiential. And there is a sense of easy welcoming on each page—a welcome into the wonder of recognizing the present moment for what it is.

What makes this book such a precious resource: it is so uniquely generous. After a lifetime of study, contemplation, and teaching, Peter offers us a precise choreography of the moves he makes as he guides people into recognizing the open and radiant nature of being. He doesn't hide anything, or try to franchise his "system." In this *Guide*, he gives his life's work away.

It's probably a truism to say we are living in a time of spiritual revolution. Especially in the West, we are witnessing old forms of dogma and religious control over the human spiritual journey yield to the desire for direct experience of awakening. The notion that enlightenment is something reserved for buddhas, gurus and saints, and can only be achieved after lifetimes of practice, is vanishing amidst the recognition that natural awakening is our birthright, and is already present in this moment. Peter Fenner's work is at the forefront of this revolution. We can be grateful that he was willing to climb down from the top of the wall and give us, in this *Guide*, the clues for how to see for ourselves.

Pir Elias Amidon
Sufi Way
www.sufiway.org

Using this Guide

This *Guide* was prepared to accompany a ten-month Natural Awakening Training I offer to therapists, coaches, facilitators, spiritual and dharma teachers who wish to bring nondual awareness into their work in an elegant and respectful way. I have offered it seven times in Europe and the USA since 2007.

The Training came into being as a result of people asking me how they could develop a similar set of skills to those used in delivering a nine-month Radiant Mind Course. Radiant Mind was created in 2002 for the general public. It has been offered every year since then. The major resources for the Radiant Mind Course have been published by Sounds True in 2007 as a book titled *Radiant Mind: Awakening Unconditioned Awareness* and a set of audio resources titled *Radiant Mind: Teachings and Practices to Awaken Unconditioned Awareness*. Details are at: www.radiantmind.net

The Radiant Mind Course has grown beyond my expectations. The practices and nondual perspective developed in the Course have become a form of spiritual orientation and practice for many people. People often repeat the Course, sometimes several times. A high percentage of people who engage with Radiant Mind are mental health professionals. It also appeals to meditation teachers and spiritual teachers. With this level of professional experience it was very natural for people to ask me, "How do you do what you do?" At the beginning I'd reply, "Look at me carefully, and if you want to know what I'm doing, or why I'm doing what I'm doing, just ask me."

People want to learn how to move a group into a space of referencelessness that is beyond conceptual knowledge. They ask how to bring people through states of serenity and into contentless awareness. They are also keen to learn the ins and outs of deconstructive dialog and how to use paradoxes in revealing nondual awareness. Students want to know how to say "I don't know what 'This' is!" with confidence and authenticity to an audience in a way that empowers everyone to explore the nondual state, and doesn't make them, as a presenter, look foolish.

This input from course participants had the effect of opening up a new dimension *within* Radiant Mind Courses. At the same time that I'd reveal the nondual space, I'd weave in explanations about what I'm doing. For example, I'd explain how I'm deconstructing a core belief, giving people "nothing" to think about, using micro gestures to stay connected and communicate a relaxed atmosphere.

The most effective way to learn is through real-time demonstration and personal experimentation. When people are acquiring a new skill or distinction, it is much more powerful when we directly show people what we're talking about rather than discuss it as a theoretical concept. With a relevant experience immediately at hand, people can see and feel what we are doing. Thus, in many of my dialogs, the process of revealing the nondual is braided with a description of what I'm doing, as I'm doing it.

At a certain point I decided to keep Radiant Mind as a course for the public and develop a new training that has the specific intention of teaching people how to share nondual awareness. I used Radiant Mind as a structural model for the new Training.

This new dimension has been wonderful for me. I'm a keen observer of how I teach and coach. In Natural Awakening I've been inspired to bring clarity and lucidity to what I do, and to make everything transparent. I am an educator at heart. The process of opening into new territory myself means I'm always a beginner. There's very little that I can take for granted. I need to know what I'm doing, or at least have an interpretation about it, especially as I head in the direction of "not knowing and doing nothing."

The work I do has had an element of mystery to it. People are often intrigued to know if this work is skills-based or a function of some insights I might have acquired. They would like to know how a lot is achieved in shifting people's state of consciousness with very minimal interventions. I explain that I'm doing "nothing at all," and that it's all skills-based. It is the union of wisdom and method. To that extent this *Guide* is a little like a surgical manual. It's intended to take the mystery out of what I do, and make it transparent and fully accessible.

Until now this *Guide* has been in restricted circulation within Natural Awakening Trainings. I now wish to make it available to all who can benefit from it. Nearly everyone who has participated in a Training asks if they can share the *Guide* with colleagues, family, friends or students. I also receive many requests for it. While the structure of the Training keeps evolving, this *Guide* is now sufficiently stable and polished so that it's ready for wider distribution.

I'm also encouraged to publish it because many teachers and masters are excellent awakeners but have little interest in showing others what's behind the *jnana* yoga of mind-to-mind transmission. Their capacity for awakening others is embedded within their being and awakening happens just by staying in their field, and following their guidance, rather than through specific explanations and custom-made learning opportunities.

This *Guide* opens up a comprehensive set of distinctions and sensibilities that are needed in nondual transmission. These are the same natural skills that Zen and Sufi masters, Dzogchen and Mahamudra lamas and Advaita yogis use in direct transmission even when these aren't evident to the masters themselves. Whenever a master introduces a student to the nature of awareness, an event is happening that at least runs parallel to the processes described in this *Guide*. If something similar to what is described here isn't happening, there is no contentless transmission. Ideas and concepts about the nature of reality or awareness might be moving in the space, but not the awakening that can't be found.

In a Training, this *Guide* is used as part of a comprehensive set of structures that includes workshops, teleconference calls, small group explorations, support groups, a nondual coaching lab, individual coaching calls, and other written materials. Together these provide a highly focused context for practicing the skills of nondual transmission. The experiential components of the Training are informed by the distinctions and practices that are described in Part One. Details of the Training can be found at: www.nondualtraining.com

As an interim step between this *Guide* and a fully-fledged Training I now offer Natural Awakening Study Groups. The Study Groups are for people who have read this *Guide* and wish to dig deeper into the meaning and application of themes and skills that are covered in Part One. There is a limit of 12 people for each Study Group. We come together every two weeks for a one and a half hour session using a teleconferencing interface. Each session will open with a roughly ten minute introduction by a different participant. We will then all join together exploring the deeper elements of the *Guide*. Details of the Study Groups can be found at: www.nondualtraining.com Recently I've also begun using the *Guide* in conjunction with one-on-one coaching. Details can be found at: www.peterfenner.com

This *Guide* will also benefit people outside of a formal training or personal supervision. Some people gulp down my teachings with minimal face-to-face contact and begin to implement aspects of this approach into their groups and with clients, very quickly. When the experiential background is in place, the distinctions and movements I introduce can make immediate sense and bring a new openness, vitality and energy to the working space.

The *Guide* is also an effective tool for debriefing yourself after you have run a workshop, *satsang*, or had a nondual coaching session with a client. Very often there's a lead-time between working on the spot—exploring new ways of sharing nondualism—and understanding exactly what you and others are doing. This *Guide* will fill in the gaps. It will show you how and where your transmission of nondual awareness becomes diluted. It will help you to identify new movements and possibilities in your work as you move beyond what you already know. If you're a practitioner it's a good idea to have the *Guide* at hand—in your office or lounge room—wherever you spend your "reading time." It will become a valued companion as you deepen your capacity for sharing nondual awareness.

If you aren't yet facilitating nondual work, or using nonduality in a professional context this *Guide* can still greatly accelerate your learning. It will empower you to receive the maximum value and benefit from teachings in which you participate. It will help you discern different ways and styles in which teachers evoke nondual awareness with their students. You'll be able to observe different teachers and say, "She is using 'pure listening' at the moment," "He is dissolving the boundary between speech and silence, or movement and stillness," "She is showing how the unconditioned and conditioned are inseparable," "He's just segued into an unfindability inquiry into the self, using himself as the subject."

However you use this *Guide*, it's important to know that the most powerful way to take it in is by exposing yourself to as much experiential work as possible. The best way to learn is to find yourself as the focus of people's attention with nothing more to offer than "being no one, going nowhere" and discovering on the spot how this interfaces with people's needs and expectations. Even before people enroll in a Natural Awakening Training, I ask them to schedule a nondual event about one month after the first workshop. Though they may not have the confidence to facilitate an event, I know that after the first workshop, and with the support of others, they'll have sufficient resources to guide a small group under a theme like "natural meditation" or "discovering effortless being."

Part One digs deeply into the core competencies needed for effective nondual transmission. It is based on the process I've developed over many years of sharing nondual awareness in workshops, public events and in individual coaching.

It details some subtleties that I don't believe are covered elsewhere.

I suggest you begin by reading Part One at least once quite quickly. On the first reading just take in the movements and dimensions of this work. Don't try to understand everything. Some sections will make immediate sense. Others won't. Some sentences and paragraphs aren't designed to make "sense" anyway. On the first reading you might even skip some sections. You may wish to flick through it and go wherever your interests take you.

As you gain more fluency in nondual transmission you'll find that the distinctions in the *Guide* become potent and alive. Sections that may make little sense on first reading will become rich in meaning and opportunities. In a few months time you'll be able to see things that were previously invisible to you. You'll glance through the Table of Contents and everything will make some sense to you. You'll understand the inner dynamics of nondual transmission. You'll be empowered to discover your own ways of offering the ultimate medicine of nonduality to yourself, clients, students and friends.

Part Two of the *Guide* isn't a formal part of a Natural Awakening Training.

The first Appendix is an analysis of the Indo-Tibetan and Asian nondual traditions that inform the Radiant Mind style of nondual transmission. A lot of connections are made between traditions such as Dzogchen, Mahamudra, Madhyamika, Zen, and Advaita and Radiant Mind. It shows how a very contemporary expression of the Perfect Wisdom (*prajnaparamita*) tradition is linked to different streams of nondual practice. I have prepared this in part to acknowledge the timeless lineage of nondual transmission. This material can also give people confidence that a training that has a totally contemporary feel has a lineage connection with traditions that have been developed, tested, used and adapted by hundreds of thousand of masters over the centuries.

The preparation of this Appendix was inspired by a very fun conversation I had with a long time student Jean-Luc Schneider after a Radiant Mind evening in Geneva. We both took notes during our conversation. The conversation inspired Jean-Luc to prepare his Masters thesis at the Université de Lausanne as an exploration of the "Sources bouddhiques de la transmission de la non dualité chez Peter Fenner et son cours Radiant Mind." (2008) I prepared the Appendix in this volume.

The other Appendices include three selections from traditional nondual resources that have inspired me over many years.

Appendix Two contains the famous *Heart of Liberating Wisdom Sutra*. This is the most succinct statement of nonduality that can be found in Mahayana Buddhism. It is profound and uncompromising in its presentation of nondual realization.

Appendix Three is the famous *Verses on the Realized Mind* by Sosan Zenji, the Third Patriarch of Zen. It summarizes many of the themes that frame Radiant Mind and the Natural Awakening Training.

Appendix Four gives you a sample of Dzogchen nonduality. It is drawn from a text by Longchenpa. I recommend that you read the extract from Longchenpa. This is optional reading.

PART ONE

Distinctions and Practices
of Nondual Transmission

1

Introduction: the Radiant Mind model

In this *Guide* I am using the style of nondual transmission that I offer through *Radiant Mind* as a model for how the transmission can occur in individual therapy and coaching, and in a group setting. I invite you to join me in the space of nondual transmission as you read this *Guide*. It builds on many of the distinctions, themes, and forms of practice and non-practice that are developed in detail in *Radiant Mind*. (Sounds True, 2007)

This *Guide* details the specific skills I use in supporting people in accessing and integrating nondual awareness. In this work I mainly use the terms coaching and facilitating. I describe how facilitation can work both in one-on-one sessions and in groups.

I have woven dialogs into the text at many points in order to bring it alive and show how nondual inquiry can unfold around many different themes. I personally receive a great deal more from reading dialogs than by reading or listening to teachings. Dialogs can show me new ways in which nondual transmission can happen on the spot.

Terminology

I use the term nondual awareness quite frequently in this *Guide* because it's a more widely used term than unconditioned awareness or radiant mind. Here is how I use different terms.

Natural awakening refers to the state of abiding as awareness and recognizing that this is our natural state whenever there is no effort or endeavor to be somewhere else. We are naturally awake in that consciousness is spacious, unconstrained, and unstructured. Nothing happens when we naturally awaken; everything unfolds, just as it does, in this very moment. Natural awakening isn't an event in time. We don't wake up from anything, or into something else. Natural awakening is the awakening that can't be found as a transformation or change of state. We can't find "natural awakening" since there is nothing to see. In this *Guide*, abiding in awareness, resting in nonduality, radiant mind, natural awakening, and other terms such as "This," no-mind, and centerlessness are all referring to the same basic state.

Radiant mind is the state where the conditioned and unconditioned co-arise. It points to the integration of unconditioned awareness in daily life.

Unconditioned awareness points to pure awareness that has no structure and isn't individual. At one level it is completely different from conditioned experience. It is also indistinguishable from conditioned experience because it isn't a thing. It's the only state that is completely open, unstructured, and without content, which is why it's sometimes called "contentless wisdom."

Conditioned body-mind points to experience as it comes to us as thoughts, feelings, and perceptions.

Nondual awareness is sometimes used in the same way I use unconditioned awareness. At other times it is interchangeable with radiant mind. I often see the term nondual awareness used in this way by other teachers as well. The nondual state refers to "This" which includes everything and "This" as the formless, timeless dimension of existence.

There's no limit to the ways in which the nondual can be transmitted. It's possible for some people to deliver the contentless transmission most effectively without speaking a word. Others do it through a high-energy performance that comes close to theatre.

I have my own style of nondual work. It is obviously shaped and limited by my perceptions, beliefs, energy, preferences, and history of spiritual work. Still, I think that by describing how things happen through me, it will help you to discern and discover your own way of sharing nondual transmission. Even if your form of transmission is very different from mine, you'll be conscious of how it is happening. You'll know what you are doing. You'll know where you are. And, if you wish, you'll be able to share this with others. It's best to approach the question of how nonduality is shared through the question of "how it happens" rather than "what you do."

Let me come at this from two extremes. This will help you determine how you would like to relate to the challenge of training in nondual transmission. You will probably find that you are situated between two extremes. From one extreme it's possible to become a nondual coach or teacher by doing whatever you need to do, and not do, in order to be in the space where you are no one, but still connected with whoever is with you. There is nothing more to do. From this space there has never been anything to do, no one to give or receive nondual transmission. And of course, as a nondual transmission, the transmission can never be found. It happens through not happening. The only requirement here is to be abiding in the sphere of unconditioned awareness while being in an uncontrived relationship with whoever is in the field.

This state of being will have a transformative effect and has the potential to deliver a contentless mind-to-mind transmission, though this is not what we are looking for or intending, because there is no one needing anything! If you are in this space, and naturally there, wherever you are, you can put this *Guide* aside. There is nothing in it for you. You have everything you need, by virtue of needing nothing. The quality of your realization takes care of everything. I hope to connect with you so I can enjoy the radiance of your spontaneous, all-pervading presence.

A completely opposite way to approach your development is to view this *Guide*, and the supervision and coaching that accompanies it, as a "lexicon and grammar for nondual transmission." We put aside any notion of needing to "be in the space" or needing any direct experience of nondual awareness at all. We forget about the idea of realization or personal awakening entirely. We engage with this work in much the same way that we approach learning a second language. The virtue of this approach is that we don't need any personal experience at all in order to offer the contentless transmission. This is very much my own style. Transmission without realization! Ultimately, it amounts to the same thing as the first approach. This second approach can be useful if the idea that you need to be realized stops you from offering nondual transmission.

This *Guide*, in fact, is quite like a lexicon. It lays out: (1) a lexicon—a vocabulary and set of distinctions; (2) a grammar—the construction of special types of sentences and questions, the use of "I" "we" "you," subjectless conversations, etc.; and (3) the protocols for nondual communication, intonation, pauses, silences, pacing, etc. If you don't feel that you have easy, direct and natural access to the nondual, you can build up your skills, step by step. Ultimately, the result will be indistinguishable from someone who follows the first route. The two of you will meet in the place where there's no one resting anywhere, or owning anything.

These are the two possible ways of relating to this *Guide*. I am sure you'll find a path within these in which you will gain more confidence and stability in nondual awareness and acquire a language and set of sensitivities through which transmission will naturally happen.

Using either of these two approaches you will become effective as a nondual teacher or facilitator and be able to:

1. Rest in nondual awareness within yourself—the space where "nothing is missing" and where there is no one who can suffer or even assert that one is free of suffering. This is the state of primordial or nondual awareness.

2. Be able to transport others into nondual awareness without ignoring, suppressing, or bypassing their moment-by-moment conditioned experience.

3. Have spontaneous access to a variety of ways to ease people into this awareness.

While this *Guide* is a lexicon to help you as a facilitator, its essence and style are a direct expression of unconditioned awareness. It's meant to be an aid for you to enter and remain in the nondual state both while reading this as well as in the actual practice of sharing nondual awareness with others. You may notice that while feeling attuned or entrained in this nondual state your own style of coaching naturally arises.

A contemporary and accessible presentation of timeless wisdom

My own style of nondual work is based on the wisdom contained in nondual traditions such as Prajnaparamita, Zen, Madhyamika, Mahamudra, Dzogchen, and Advaita. It also has a fresh and contemporary flavor. From time to time when I am working I make connections with these traditions, mainly because many people are familiar with them. The connections also show how the state we are exploring and presencing is identical with the same state that well-known masters and sages talk about as self-knowledge, egolessness, pure awareness, or perfect wisdom. Our experience is identical with theirs—and we can know this with absolute certainty because the experience is precise and identifiable.

Nondual awareness transcends all boundaries—time, space, even generations. Historically, it has been spoken about, studied, practiced, and transmitted for thousands of years, with a quiet energy rivaling that expended on the scientific quest in the West. As a result, the separate identities of vast numbers of people have been in the process of dissolution. Whether through Dzogchen, Zen, or other related traditions, people have been loosening their connection with thoughts, beliefs, and specific behaviors to arrive at the same experience, our shared birthright—unconditioned awareness.

It can be useful to acknowledge the continuity of the nondual lineage into the present because it can give people confidence in what can seem pretty far-out—being no one, going nowhere, doing nothing, and often having paid money to do this!

Even so, comparisons are of secondary importance. The central focus is to gain easier and easier access to nondual awareness and learn how to integrate this way of being into the totality of our lives. As coaches we focus on the result—the experience of the unconditioned. Our ideal is to do nothing more and nothing less than what is needed to fully awaken into this moment.

A contentless transmission

One of the most important things to appreciate is that nondual transmission is contentless. It helps, even just intellectually, to remember this. It serves as a correction if we begin to objectify or qualify this space. Pure awareness can't be divided. There is nothing in it. We can't talk about things being inside awareness because there is nothing outside of this.

The Radiant Mind approach

In the *Radiant Mind* approach we focus on cultivating nondual awareness while fully involved with our regular lives of work, relationships, and lifestyle commitments. This doesn't mean we are looking or expecting to be "in the nondual" throughout all these activities. This can happen, but more than likely it means that we are presencing the nondual on a regular basis in the midst of our daily lives, with all their routines and sometimes unpredictable and dramatic events as well.

What is perhaps a more useful focus is the idea that we can transcend events, problems, frictions, and compulsions while still fully connected with our bodies and with life. It's possible to be with our present reality without resistance and effort. This includes giving up any concern for whether we are experiencing reality from unconditioned awareness or a conditioned perspective. Nondual awareness liberates us from any preconceived idea about how reality should be or be experienced. It is the ultimate state of freedom. It's the state of being naturally awake.

2

Presencing unconditioned awareness

Beginning a session

Within a few seconds of beginning a therapy or coaching session or a workshop, you see there is no beginning because nothing is happening. The experience that nothing is happening, and that nothing is needed, can crystallize very quickly. Still, some form of acknowledgement and introduction might be appropriate.

I usually welcome people. I make a conditioned connection by saying something like, "Welcome. It's a pleasure to share this time with you, exploring the experience of real fulfillment. The work we're doing unfolds in a contemplative dialog. I don't have a lot to say from my side. The aim is to taste and rest in the state of natural fulfillment." At some point I find myself being silent.

If I'm working by telephone, people often ask, "How do these calls begin?" I reply, "Like this." They might say, "Do you have something you want to do? Can I ask you some questions? How does this happen?" I reply, "We will see how this unfolds as we move along. Many different things can happen. Where would you like us to go?"

In subsequent calls I may just say, "How are things going?" I'm very open ended. I am happy with a "fine." That is a complete response. I am not looking for more. There is no work to be done. I am connecting with an absence of a point of reference within me. I check to see if I feel I am here to do something. I let that dissolve.

Discovering your own process

You can find yourself moving quite quickly into the space where there's nothing you have to do. You are transported through whatever issues might be challenging you and you're quickly established in pure awareness. Even though you're aware that people are probably expecting something from you, there's nothing that you need to do. You're not going anywhere, just being, available, there's no pressure coming from inside or outside, no moving anywhere. It is completely effortless, no pressure at all. Natural koans can begin to move through your mind, acting to confirm and stabilize you in the space where there's "no one being nowhere."

Thoughts can arise such as, "Who is doing this?" "Who is doing what?" And your mind doesn't go anywhere with them. You might think, "Are we moving? No. Are we going anywhere? No. Have we arrived? I can't say that either. Who are we? I don't know." You become used to the presence of these types of thoughts. You find yourself quietly in the space where there's nothing you need to do. Concepts pass through your awareness without producing any disturbance. You are just with this process, then at some point—you don't know *when*—either someone says something and you are off and moving, or you begin to distinguish the unconditioned. You might say something like, "The focus of our work together is to connect with the unconditioned dimension of being. Actually, there's no *work* involved in this because we're already here." You start at the end.

Distinguishing nondual awareness

In the next sections I'd like to layout the way in which I introduce people to nondual awareness, particularly in terms of how I initially differentiate the nondual state from our empirical experience. There are different ways in which I invite people to "leap into" nondual awareness, as it were, to realize that we are naturally awake. Having made that leap, I then dissolve the dualistic construction that the nondual can be different from our everyday experience. If people then reduce the nondual to the flux of their conditioned experience, which often happens, I redistinguish the nondual as a space that is radically different from anything we can possibly "experience." I cycle through a process of collapsing the difference, redistinguishing the nondual, dissolving the difference again, until there is a more consistent presencing of the nondual *within* the context of our embodied, everyday life—our thought-world, feelings, relationships, and activities.

I've arrived at this process by seeing what seems to work best "on the spot" in terms of introducing people to the basic state of nondual awareness, while being open, receptive, and responsive to whatever arises in the inner and outer environments.

I'll explain what's behind the moves as we progress through these sections. I use the process I describe in group facilitation and also in one-one-work, especially when this is clearly focused on the recognition of, and familiarization with, nondual awareness. The process I describe shouldn't be viewed as a roadmap. It shouldn't be viewed as a series of steps that are systematically followed. The actual process is organic, free-form, and dynamic.

Is the nondual an experience, state, or space?

At this point I'd like to say just a few words about my use of the term "nondual awareness." There is some discussion these days about the best term through which to point to the nondual state. What we are looking for is a term that doesn't let us create differentiations. This is why many people object to talking about the nondual experience. There are many different types of experiences, and also in an experience there are objects that are experienced and a seeming experiencer. So experience isn't the ideal term. This leads some people to prefer the phrase "nondual state." But this isn't perfect either because there are different types of states and the nondual state is neither the same as, nor different from other states.

Another possibility is to talk about the "nondual space." This has some merit because at one level we can't differentiate one space from another space. There is nothing in space itself to let us do this. Also, there is a connection with the conditioned. We talk about the workshop space, or the space we are in. In general, in this *Guide* I'll use the term "nondual awareness" because it is in quite common usage. I also use terms like no-mind, centerless awareness, nothing, and nothingness.

You will find when teaching that some people object to the use of terms like "nondual," "awareness," and "nondual awareness" altogether. It is strange. They will come to an event because it is called "nondual." Then they will object to using the word "nondual." They correctly point out that "This" is not "nondual" in contrast to the "dual." They might also point out that "awareness" can't be found or qualified, so we can't see "This" as awareness. All this is true, and this is the precise meaning of these terms. These terms have been used for thousands of years to point to the unfindability of the self, mind, awareness, ultimate reality, and so on.

It doesn't make sense to reject the use of simple code words that have been used effectively for millennia. This misses the critical recognition that there is nothing to reject! The idea that a word—any word—could obscure "nothing" is itself misleading. We should heed Vimalakirti's injunction to rely on the intention of whatever words are used to point to the nondual, and not on the specific words themselves. (Thurman, 1976)

I'll also often use the term "This," without spelling this out further. In fact, "This" is a technical term to refer to the nondual in Tibetan Buddhism. The term "*de nyid*" means "just (*nyid*) this (*de*)." *De nyid* means thisness, not this as something in particular but "This" as "This" no matter who we are or what, or when "This" is happening. When I use the term "nondual awareness," it is like a code word for the basic or primordial state; what is also called "*ka dag*" or alpha purity, or just the "A state." When people are in the know—when they can directly recognize this state—it's sufficient to use "just this." A phrase like "nondual awareness" is no longer necessary.

Entering a different paradigm

I usually begin by presenting nondual awareness as being completely different from the mind that compares, differentiates, and makes contrasts. I say that we will be giving our attention to the nature of awareness itself, in contrast to the "objects of awareness"—thoughts, feelings, and sensations. If we weren't aware we couldn't be aware of our thoughts, my words, or this room. We are exploring "*That* which is aware, not *what* we are aware of." I point out that if we "knew" what awareness was, it would be an "object of our awareness," not awareness itself.

I present "abiding as awareness" as something that is radically different from our usual mode of being in which "we are someone who is engaged with the world." I point to nondual awareness by saying that, unlike our conditioned experience, it can't be known, isn't a thing, etc. Nondual awareness is indivisible and unconstructed, in contrast to conditioned experience which is composed of different elements: the different sense fields, feelings, and thoughts. This is important because we can return to the idea that "our experiences are constructed," built out of different elements, when we begin to deconstruct limiting identifications.

When I begin a presentation I often say something like:

> This evening we are here to explore contentlessness. It's easy to explore content, to get involved in ideas, viewpoints, and opinions. But, my invitation for us this evening is to explore—no, actually to access—a dimension of reality that's been very well known to sages in the East and West, but which is relatively inaccessible in our modern, busy, highly distracting lives. When I say "explore," it's not really an exploration because there is nothing to discover or reveal!

> This dimension of reality has been called: natural awakening, objectless awareness, centerless awareness, the mind-itself, buddha mind, and so on. This state is acausal; it is unproduced. We don't need anything more than what we already have in order to be "here." There is nothing we need to know or do. This is effortless. Nothing could be simpler. Nothing needs to change in order to be here—resting in nondual awareness.

> Our conditioned experience unfolds in time—it is always changing. We can touch, feel, sense, and think about it. Nondual awareness, on the other hand, doesn't have any of these characteristics. It's not a "thing." We can't see it, we can't even think about it because there is nothing to think about. Nondual awareness is completely unrelated to you and me as different embodied minds. It's unrelated to the circumstances of our lives or the condition of our bodies and minds. We are born and we will die. We have gender, age, race, etc. Nondual awareness has none of these. It is ahistorical, transpersonal, and transcultural.

I make this radical departure from our usual way of "being someone in time and space" because (1) people come specifically for the nondual; and (2) nondual awareness is far less accessible to most people than our ordinary, everyday world of effort, struggles, thwarted ambitions, and periodic accomplishments. People have no difficulty accessing their conditioned existence. It confronts us; it assaults us; it seduces us. Also, for people who have little or no idea of what this state is, it can be useful to initially present "This" as something completely different from what we "know." When people are immersed in their conditioned minds, they need to be eased, or ejected, out of their identification with the contents of awareness, in order to recognize the nondual.

1. Distinguishing NONDUAL AWARENESS as DIFFERENT from CONDITIONED EXPERIENCE

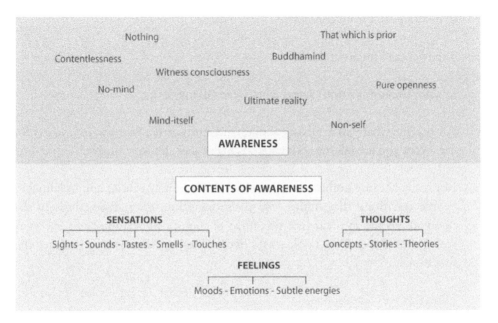

In the language of Buddhist hermeneutics, this presentation of nondual awareness "as different from the contents of awareness" is provisional. It isn't the most refined way of languaging the nondual. When I present it in this way, I'm aware that we are *en route* to a more refined presencing of the nondual. This way of distinguishing the nondual is a skillful process (*upaya*). It isn't the "truth." I know there is further to go. The language of "not this, not that" (*neti neti*) is a pedagogical device that can be used to reveal a dimension of reality that is inaccessible to most people because it is invisible and nondual, i.e., beyond the categories of being and non-being.

The diagram 1, above, shows how I draw a line between awareness and the contents of awareness. It also lists some of the common names used in different traditions to identify the same state that I am calling nondual awareness in this *Guide*.

Here is an example of a dialog with two different participants in which I am clearly differentiating awareness as unconditioned. I am not collapsing the distinction. I'm not showing how awareness is inseparable from the contents of awareness. This comes later.

S: When you say contentlessness I just don't get it.

P: Most of the time we are only connected with the conditioned dimension of experience with everything that's happening—black and white, good and bad, closer and further, etc. But there is also something that's invisible that's happening at the same time. It's not happening, as such, but present as an absence. [In order to distinguish the unconditioned, I move in the opposite direction. I point to this as being nothing. It's not nothing, but at this point I say it's nothing in order to distinguish it from content.]

S: Then we can't say what it is?

P: Exactly, because we don't know what we're talking about.

S: I've no clue what you're talking about. Unconditioned awareness is far away for me. What you are talking about sounds big or vast. It's very elusive.

P: Not really because nothing is hidden. This is absolutely precise and indefinable. People can think that things lose their definition, their distinctness in the nondual. People can fear that this form of inquiry undermines our everyday reality. But this isn't so. Look what's happening here. Everything is intact and functional.

S: I find this very intellectual.

P: This isn't intellectual *at all*. There's absolutely nothing to think about. It's only intellectual because you're still not convinced that there's nothing to understand here. Your mind is still struggling to make sense of this.

S: But those are words….

P: Yes, they are words—we're talking about what's happening, but what's happening isn't an event, or even an experience. At the same time I am talking, nothing is happening at all.

S: But you are still talking, that's why I think there's something to understand!

P: If I'm silent, there's a good chance that you'll still try to work this out. The point is that I'm not talking about anything. You need to listen to this carefully.

There's nothing to see, nothing to do, nothing to think about. This is totally non-intellectual. You're doing the thinking. I'm not. There's nothing to think about. I'm not trying to work this out. I'm talking but it's effortless. I'm not going anywhere.

S: I'm laughing, because my mind is fried! Maybe that's the best thing that can happen! I want to say, "I give up!" At some level I think I understand what you're saying, at some other level I can't.

P: Of course you can't. You cannot understand this. No one will ever understand this because there's nothing to understand. Our "knowing mind" is quite persistent and resilient. Often we have to return to the point of giving up many, many times before we finally, clearly, and cleanly see that there is nothing to understand in the domain of pure awareness.

S: Thank you.

P: Thank you.

The nondual isn't a subtle affective experience or meditational state

I also distinguish nondual awareness in a clear and precise way when people confuse this state with different types of subtle conditioned experiences. For example, people often think that nondual awareness is a state of bliss, or serenity, or love. These experiences can accompany the presencing of the nondual, but they aren't nondual awareness itself. They are conditioned experiences. This is clear because they come and go in the conventional sense. They are refined experiences that arise as epiphenomena when people's reactive responses settle down and the habitual need to understand and interpret slows down. These experiences can be, in fact often are, confused with the nondual.

H.H. Dudjum Jigdral Yeshe Dorje (1904-1987) of the Nyingma school of Tibetan Buddhism is clear about the potential distraction that such a confusion can cause when he writes:

> Now while you are on the path, it will happen that this [*rig pa*—pure awareness] will become mixed with some form of the three temporary experiences—bliss, clarity, and no thought—so when that does happen rest without a whisker of the hope and fear that believes in and grasps at these as special attainments and just that will cut the possibility of the experience turning into a sidetrack. (Duff, 2008)

Purity

A significant focus in group facilitation is to ensure that people receive nondual awareness cleanly and purely. This need is compounded these days because the terms nonduality and nondual awareness are being used quite loosely. They are often used to refer to states that still have some content and structure to them. If there is any association between feeling peaceful, clear, or accepting, and nonduality, this isn't nondual awareness.

There is often a lot of scope to purify an experience so it really becomes nondual, and stays that way. A lot of the work in nondual transmission is "cleaning work." People can enter the nondual, but over time it can become sullied. People begin to identify with the pleasant feelings, sensations, and authenticity that naturally enter the nondual field. Many people have a strong need to attribute some basic qualities to nondual awareness, for example, that it is a state of profound intimacy, unconditional love, sourceless bliss, or imperturbable serenity.

To assess the purity of a state of nondual awareness, we look for the existence of structures within the state. The structures I'm referring to are ideas, beliefs, feelings, interpretations, and reference points. An ordinary, conditioned state is densely structured. With increasing familiarity with nondual awareness, we also experience more lightly structured states of awareness. Structures still exist, but there is an overall sense of more immediacy and less interpretation. The structures become more and more transparent.

It's as if there is a spectrum of states that have a progressively lighter structure along the way to a clean presencing of nondual awareness. The states that we experience can become increasingly pure or structure-free. Ultimately in the state of nondual or centerless awareness there is no structure; so it cannot be described as being positive or negative, ordinary or sublime, useful or useless, as nothing or something. Unlike conditioned states of mind, nondual awareness cannot be lost or gained, because there is nothing to arise or disappear.

Foundations, bridges, and resting places

When people enter a nondual workshop space they quite quickly feel that something different is happening. As a facilitator I have nothing to communicate from my side. My job is simply to clear away all the obstructions (viewpoints, ideas, fears, unmet expectations, etc.) as efficiently and effortlessly as possible. There are no themes, topics, or any subject matter I wish to share. This becomes obvious quite quickly. Sometimes I ease people through the transition that's happening by saying:

> We are entering a different paradigm with this work. The main way it's different from our normal paradigm is that there's nothing to understand and nothing you need to be doing. I'm not asking anything from you. There is no pressure here at all. There is no need for you to be here. We aren't going anywhere. I'm not looking for something to be happening. "This" isn't *a* happening. A need brought you here. But now that you're here you don't need that need. In fact, we are exploring what it's like to not need anything: to be free of the need to learn, understand, gain resources, and so on. We're discovering how to be totally complete with things exactly as they are.

If this is too much I may go back a little bit and simply present our time together as an opportunity to give ourselves a break from trying to change things, fix things up, even if we only do this for a few minutes. For a few minutes we give ourselves permission to accomplish nothing! When I make this offer, many people will say, "Wow, what a relief. There's no pressure. That feels really great." After a few minutes this can even mature into great bliss.

I create a foundation for inquiry by bringing people into the present moment and slowing down their thinking by giving them nothing to think about. This creates an atmosphere of ease and tranquility. This is a foundation upon which it's possible to inquire into the reality of "This" as awareness and not be able to find anything that lies behind the term. Nondual awareness is revealed through the unfindability form of inquiry that is integral to Advaita (Katz, 2007; Maharshi, 1988, 1989) and Mahayana. (Nagarjuna, 2005; Chandrakirti, 2005)

If people still can't connect with this radical presentation of the nondual, we can always go back and talk about it as a state of effortless being, total equanimity, a space that's free of attachment and aversion, and which connects us with ourselves in a totally natural and uncontrived way. We can, in fact, use the epiphenomena that arise, such as feelings of deep peace, acceptance, love, and connectness as resting places *en route* to presencing nondual awareness.

Starting at the end: working at the result level

Another way I help people to leap into the unconditioned dimension is by explaining that we will be working at the "result level." This means that the result (abiding as awareness) is the path. In other words, we begin with the baseline position that nothing is wrong or missing. Everything is complete just as it is. Everyone is complete. There are no problems, nothing to work out, no work to be done. In the midst of everything that's happening, "nothing is happening at the same time."

I am quite up front in presenting this possibility. Sometimes I'll start a workshop by saying, "Well, let's just start at the end. Let's just skip straight ahead. Let's not waste time. Our objective in being here is to arrive at the end of the path, to find what we are looking for in terms of discovering deep contentment, beyond which there is nowhere further to go." I introduce this possibility in a light way. It's a suggestion, but I'm absolutely serious about it at the same time. I don't want to waste people's time. If I'm being asked to think, I'm looking for traction in terms of how to take people beyond the mind.

The suggestion that we can begin a workshop at the place we might hope to be at the end, without needing to do any intermediate work, immediately throws people into inquiry. Some people will protest internally, or out loud, "But I'm here to learn how to get this. There is work to be done. It can't be that simple!" Others will be enticed by the idea, but genuinely feel incomplete. People start to play with the idea that "nothing is wrong or missing."

We can see how this applies right now. You might be reading this *Guide* hoping to gain some insights or additional resources for your work as a coach, therapist, or facilitator. It's possible for me to be writing this thinking that I have some wisdom that could help you, that I need to explain my process clearly, and so on. Yet, if we connect with primordial awareness in this moment, that is all that's needed, now and at any time in the future. If we are "here" we don't need anything more, and this is what is communicated to those around us—friends, clients, partners, and colleagues. "This" becomes the fuel, the essence, of your work as a facilitator or therapist.

If you are "here" I don't need to write anything more. You have all the resources you could possibly need in terms of sharing nondual awareness with others. Nondual awareness will come through you naturally and automatically. You won't be able to stop it! You will activate this recognition in others through the way you listen without judgment, through the quality of your silence, through the way you don't condition the space, through the precision of your questions, and love that is shared because you don't need anything for yourself. (Fenner, 2003, 2006, 2007)

By introducing the possibility that we can be "here" in the ultimate way, without needing to do any psychological processing or make any corrections or additions to our intellectual understanding of the path and goal, we set a benchmark, as it were. The benchmark we establish doesn't preclude the processing of emotions or deepening our understanding of who we are. But, it lets us see how easily we fall into the habit of thinking we need to do more work before we can truly rest and abide in our natural state. With this benchmark in place we can easily see how we habitually create work for ourselves. When someone says, "Yes, that sounds great, but first I need to…." they are re-creating a path. They are effectively saying that something needs to happen *before* they can be complete. Once we've shown people this pattern, we can continue to point it out, each time it occurs. This is how we "take the result as the path."

Undoing the path

Another way I introduce the idea of working at the result level is by pointing out that for as long as we are "on the path" we can't be at the destination. So the work we will be doing consists of dissolving the path. In a sense we are always on a path, moving (forward or backward), resting for a while, or just waiting for something to happen. When we're on a path we are sometimes entertained, having fun, feeling a sense of accomplishment because we are making progress. But often we feel there is a gap between where we are and where we'd like to be. In the spiritual arena we are on an explicit path. Often it is well laid out with stages or levels. People enter nondual work because they are on a path.

Working at the result level involves undoing the path. It consists of identifying and taking away the reference points on which a path is constructed in someone's mind. When there is no path, there is no goal, just pure awareness. Nondual inquiry dismantles the path, and keeps dismantling it whenever it begins to reconstruct through the habit of believing that things could be different from what they are. Sometimes the path begins to be reconstructed through the simple thought, "Now what?" We notice such moves and take them away. "There is no what. There is just this."

We are talking about "This"!

Often I initiate inquiry through an exploration of "This." I dispense with terms like "nondual awareness" about which people can have different ideas. I begin by saying, "What we are sharing together is 'this." This is particularly effective in phone work because there is no shared "This" at the visual level. If we don't elaborate on what "This" is, or say, "'This,' right now, in this second," the "This" must be something different than our physical environment. It's not clear what "This" is referring to, and that is the intention. We've made a break within the stream of conditioned experience and we can use this lack of clarity to distinguish the unconditioned.

The powerful thing about inquiring into "This" is that it gives us a lot of freedom in how we move. We can use the word "This" to point to this as "contentless awareness," or as the undifferentiable co-arising of contentlessness and everything that is arising in the moment.

For example, in relationship to this moment right now, when I say I am talking about "This," I'm not talking about what you are reading right now. I am not talking about your awareness of your computer screen, or printed words on a piece of paper in front of you. When I say I'm talking about "This," I'm pointing to awareness itself which has no content or location. We can't even say "This" is here, because we don't know what it is that we would be saying is here, or not here. We can't say that "This" is or is not, because we don't know what it is that we would be saying exists or does not exist.

The very fact that we can't say what it is that we are talking about means that we are talking about the nondual. If we *knew* what we were talking about, it wouldn't be the nondual. It would be something we could know or not know. By the way, the language I am using now is definitive, because there is nothing to misinterpret; there is nothing to get right or wrong.

Paradox and nonduality

You will notice that in order to talk about "This" we have been compelled to move beyond the language of negation and into the structure of paradoxes. (Fenner, 2007) The paradox right now is that the words that I am writing and that you are reading are unrelated to nondual awareness. They are just symbolic images that have a semantic reference appearing on a screen or paper. Yet, these words allow us to be right here, presencing the nondual as a state that is totally inexpressible because it has no characteristics. In fact, we can't even say that "This" has no characteristics because we don't know what it is that we are characterizing in this way!

At this point unstructured, nondual awareness ceases to be something different from our ordinary, everyday consciousness, because we simply don't know what "it" is that we are saying is different (or the same for that matter).

The nondual is a totally transcending state, but at the same time it isn't rarified, disembodied, or in anyway disconnected from the rich and complex worlds in which we live. This becomes palpably clear when we are in this state: "it" is neither the same as the dualistic mind, nor in any way different from it.

Collapsing the distinction

To summarize, then, my approach is to distinguish the unconditioned as being radically different and keep doing this until someone says, "But it can't be different. It's right here." I then bring this realization into the foreground. It cannot be different from this very moment because the unconditioned is not a thing, as illustrated in diagram 2 below. It's inseparable and indistinguishable from the conditioned experience. In Buddhism this is called co-emergent wisdom (*sahaja-jnana*).

I then move between these two, at times differentiating the unconditioned from the conditioned, and at other times collapsing the distinction, explaining that the distinction or identification of the two is only made by the thinking, dualistic mind. When there is an over-identification with the conditioned—with thoughts and feelings—we re-distinguish the unconditioned. When the unconditioned is reified as something that is intrinsically different from our moment-by-moment, embodied experience, I dissolve the possibility that they can be different.

2. The INSEPARABLE UNION of
UNCONDITIONED AWARENESS and CONDITIONED EXPERIENCE

AWARENESS

No-mind

Nothing   That which is prior

Contentlessness

Witness consciousness

Non-self

Ultimate reality   Pure openness

Buddhamind

Mind-itself

**Just "this"
Universal Matrix
Co-emergent wisdom**

Sensations   Thoughts

Sights - Sounds - Tastes - Smells - Touches   Concepts - Stories - Theories

Feelings

Moods - Emotions - Subtle energies

CONTENTS OF AWARENESS

The progressive presencing of co-emergent wisdom

The diagram 3 below shows how this presencing of co-emergent wisdom can occur in time. The horizontal straight line is a time axis moving from left to right. It also represents the point where someone is resting in nondual awareness at the same time that we are thinking, perceiving, communicating, etc. In this respect it is like the previous diagram. The positions and angles of incline and decline of the stepped line shows how people can move from presencing the nondual in a way in which they are relatively disengaged with the complexities of life, toward a presencing in which the unconditioned and conditioned experience co-arise.

The notes below are like a time-line summary of the process I have been describing above.

A.   This initial upward incline indicates how we move from a place where we are identified with conditioned experience—our feelings, fears, aspirations, beliefs, perceptions, and preferences—through to a clear recognition of nondual awareness as something that is pristine and unstructured. In order to produce a clear recognition of that which hasn't yet been seen, or which has been lost sight of, the nondual is distinguished as being contentless, a non-event, a clearing, without a center or periphery. It is an absence (*med pa*).

3. The PROGRESSIVE PRESENCING of CO-EMERGENT WISDOM

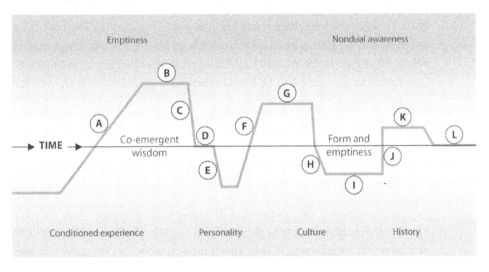

The rate of the incline is significant here. It indicates how quickly and definitively we reveal the nondual as a radically different reality. As a facilitator, if you move too fast you lose people. They get left behind. The space and language in particular becomes too weird. People become confused and disoriented to the point that they'd prefer to be somewhere else. On the other hand, if you aren't willing to leave some people behind, if you feel compelled to make sure that everyone makes it to the end of the journey, you might not even bring one person through to a clear recognition of nondual awareness.

B.   Here we rest or abide in nondual awareness for some time appreciating centerless awareness, with little active involvement in what's happening within and outside of us. The nondual may be being presenced while in a deeply interiorized state—a natural *samadhi* with very little happening in thought and feelings. Whatever is arising liberates by itself (*rang grol*). Thoughts dissolve at the very instant they begin to form. Or, the nondual may be being presenced with eyes and other senses fully open, receiving everyone and everything in the environment, but in a state of total equanimity that's free of preferences and judgments. However, at some point one of three things can happen:

1. People can begin to add qualities to awareness such as bliss, serenity, intimacy, etc. This is not to say that such feelings aren't arising. But people begin to think that awareness is a state of tranquility or interconnectedness. There is a strong impulse to make the "nothing" into something. If this happens we point out that these are conditioned experiences and not awareness itself, as a way of inviting people back into the nondual state.

2. A second possibility is that a thought, memory, feelings, anticipation, etc. arise in awareness and distract someone from continuing to abide in awareness itself. In this case we create space around what's happening. We may invite the person to let things be as they are, without interference or judgment. Or we might engage in an inquiry that dissolves the distraction by seeing that it (the distracting event) can't be found when we look for it using the wisdom mind of nondual inquiry. Or, we can point out that nothing can get in the way of nondual awareness. As a "non-thing" nothing can obstruct it.

3. A third possibility is that people can reify nondual awareness as a reality in its own right. They begin to think that nondual awareness is "nothing," is "contentless," is "unrelated to the personal," etc. We can sense this by listening to the way that people are listening to themselves when they talk about the nondual. People acquire the *via negativa* language of nonduality and begin to listen to their own thinking and words as though they were really saying something when they are talking about the nondual.

C. If and when the nondual becomes reified, I point out that "This" can't be different from everything that's arising because the nondual isn't a "thing" that can be the same or different from anything else. When we say "This" is different, we don't know what it is that we are saying is different, so we can't say that "This" is different from the thoughts, feelings, and appearances that are arising moment-by-moment. This is how I collapse the difference. Usually, the idea that nondual awareness and the dualistic mind are different collapses in an instant, like a deflating balloon. For some time, I may let people think that contentless awareness and the objects of awareness are the same, even though they are neither the same nor different.

D.   Here we rest in the co-arising of emptiness and appearances. If people start to think that there are two things that are actually co-arising, we can point out that "This" goes beyond even notions of co-arising or union (*lhan cig*). Clearly there aren't two different things, so it's impossible to talk about "union" or "inseparability."

E.   While presencing the nondual in the context of being aware of our body and surroundings, at some point a thought, feeling, or sensation arises that pulls us out of nondual awareness into an identification with the conditioned event that arises. Typically people become involved in their thoughts (carried away by a story), caught by a sensation (a sound, an image of a person, etc.), or overtaken by a feeling (a pain, some fear, excitement, and so on). A conditioned event comes into the foreground, reactions of attraction and aversion come into play, until at some point we recall nondual awareness. We think, "Ah yes, wow, I just became engrossed in worrying about my future!"

F.   How we move on at this point depends on how deeply we've become involved with a conditioned event and our familiarity with the primordial state. If we're very familiar with nondual awareness, if we've made the journey many times from being caught up in a fear or worry through to being totally complete without any change in our conditioned circumstances, it might be as simple as thinking, "I've lost my connection to the nondual. But what is it that I've lost. Ah, yes! I remember. It's 'This,' this thing that I can't lose or hold onto. Wow, that is simple. Here I am back in the place where I can't say what it is. How wonderful!" We retrace a journey we've made many times. In fact, often the journey happens automatically. It is like being in a dark basement, in the underground carpark, hitting the elevator button, and presto, within a few seconds we are in the lookout tower, enjoying our lives from a totally different perspective. (This is why the incline back to the nondual is steeper here.)

    If our clients or workshop participants are new to nondual work, they may need some support in the form of unfindability inquiry that lets them dismantle the construction that creates a feeling of lack and contraction. We will help them identify a core construction in their narrative, for example, "I am worried that I won't be able to retain this experience when I'm at home with my family." We will inquire into this construction. We could look for the "I," the "worry," or the "experience that will be lost" and not be able to find any of them. We only need to "see through" one of these concepts for the entire construction to dissolve and allow for a re-presencing of the nondual.

G.   Over time we presence the nondual while retaining a more intimate involvement and connection with the ever-changing flow of conditioned experience. Ever-present awareness begins to pervade our spiritual life, our work, and relationships. Nevertheless, we are still prone to reify awareness, perhaps by creating some theory about how it relates to emotions, relationships, or psychotherapy, or politics. Or, we might feel that the nondual is love or bliss, i.e., something that is conditioned and which can arise and dissipate. So at some point we again see that nondual awareness isn't a conditioned experience, nor is it different from the experiences that are delivered to us through our mind and senses.

H.   Even though we may be quite familiar with nondual awareness and able to easily access this space in *satsang*, on a Dzogchen retreat, or with a nondual therapist, in most people's lives events arise that effectively block access to our primordial state. Perhaps our marriage starts to break apart, our children go off the rails, a parent suddenly needs full-time care, our guru dies, or we become seriously ill. Even for people who are very familiar with the nondual, it's easy to go on a family vacation for two weeks and the nondual takes leave as well!

I.   In these cases it is easy to become engrossed in ourselves for weeks or even months. We either forget about nondual awareness completely, or "know that it's there" but are unable to taste the ease and freedom of nondual awareness even for a few seconds. The journey could be short or long. Perhaps we are identified with a thought for just a few seconds. Or the journey might take several weeks. The challenge in these times is to take the journey we are on. We might think, "I know there is no one making this journey. I know (intellectually) that there is no one who suffers." But still we ache and suffer. If the gateways to the nondual all seem closed, we take on board the first noble truth of the Buddha. Yes, we suffer. If we have needs and preferences then yes, we are bound to suffer. "Clearly, what's happening for me now isn't what I want to be happening. That's the problem. That's why I'm suffering. And there doesn't seem to be anything I can do about it." So, we suffer. We accept the inevitability that we will suffer for as long as we can't accept things as they are.

But we also know that our suffering is a conditioned experience. Our preferences aren't being met at the moment. But everything changes. At some point our suffering will dissolve. We don't know when. But, for sure, it will change. We might suffer more before we suffer less. But the sun will shine in. At some point we will feel better. That is great, but it is also an opportunity to recognize that "feeling better" is still just a conditioned state. We are still in the cycle of pleasure and pain.

J.   Often, all that's needed here is a code word like "centerlessness," or "just this," and instantly we are back here, where nothing is missing and it's impossible for things to be better, because we're in a domain where ideas of better and worse make no sense at all. The sheer vertical movement of this line shows how we can move from a point where we are identified with a conditioned aspect of experience back into full recognition of awareness itself, in an instant. It occurs the moment we recognize that "This" is beyond presence and absence, and hence can never be lost or gained: the moment we see that the gateway to the nondual is always exactly where we are.

K.   Here we are presencing the nondual with an increasing inclusion of conditioned experience.

L.   Here we abide in the nondual, with our senses fully open and actively engaged with the world. We are a clearing—a centerless space—through which our unique life-world moves. Whether we are in deep meditative absorption or actively engaged with the world, we receive everything that arises without any glitches—without any movements of attachment or rejection. All thoughts, feelings, colors, and sensations arise as the play of contentless awareness—like paintings in the sky.

The reliances

Buddhism offers us a useful way to distinguish the paradigm we are working in. It's a framework that points to a different emphasis when we work at the result level—the place where we begin at the end—and only move away from this if students can't directly enter nondual awareness. The great lay Buddhist Vimalakirti describes this paradigm in terms of the four reliances. These are:

1.   Rely on the transmission, and not on the teacher.

2.   Rely on the intention [of the transmission], and not on the words [that are used].

3.   Rely on teachings which are definitive, and not those which can be interpreted.

4.   Rely on nondual wisdom, and not on conceptual knowledge.

1. Rely on the transmission, and not on the teacher

One way we take care of the first reliance in this work is by deconstructing projections that people might have about the level of insight of teachers and coaches. If students or clients project that their teachers have something that they don't have, we invite them to inquire into what this is in a way that they cannot find what it is that they think a teacher may have. We deconstruct the projection that the teacher is resting in a special place. We reveal that the only thing that's unique about their experience is that ultimately they have nothing to share or communicate. This allows students to share a space in which they cannot say that they are in a different space from their teacher(s).

We see this all the time when students talk about a teacher's personality, level of realization, lifestyle preferences, private life, etc. None of this is nondual. Some people want a teacher to be fully realized—abiding in the nondual continually, day and night, without a break. It's great if someone can make a close connection with such a teacher, but it's not necessary. All that's needed is for a teacher to be clearly presencing nonduality when they are offering nondual transmission. Typically, most teachers move in and out of nondual awareness. If they lose it when their children come home grumpy from school, it doesn't invalidate their capacity to offer transmission at other times. Most teachers are like us. They are gradually increasing their capacity to abide in nondual awareness.

What's important is that a teacher knows when they are presencing the nondual and when they aren't. If we are caught up in any identity (being someone)—for example, a nondual teacher or wise mentor—at that time, we can't offer a clear nondual transmission.

2. Rely on the intention of the transmission, and not on the words

The reliances recommend that as much as possible we go directly to the ultimate state, bypassing unnecessary involvement in ideas, concepts, and practices that can be easily misunderstood or misapplied. We rely on transmissions that come from, and lead directly into, the state of nondual awareness. This is sometimes spoken about as "teaching at the level of the result." When we teach at the level of the result, there is no time lag between the transmission and its realization.

There is a tendency that may arise when you consider going directly to the ultimate state. This tendency creates an imagined need for time in order to be prepared to be present. Understanding this as an unnecessary step eliminates the time lag that stops us from being at the level of the result now.

3. Rely on definitive transmissions, and not those which are interpretative

Definitive transmissions point unambiguously to unconditioned awareness. These are gestures, words, questions, etc. that can directly and immediately reveal the unconditioned. Since this approach eliminates the need to sort through all of the explanations about the ultimate, we're only working with that which is definitive—unconditioned awareness. If we try to use the conceptual mind to understand unconditioned awareness, then we become caught up in interpretive discourses, which lead us further from the actual experience of the unconditioned.

Effectively this reliance is saying that it's only when we are offering no content that we can't be misunderstood. So long as we are talking about nothing (not talking about any *thing*) we can be completely confident in what we are saying because there's nothing that can be misinterpreted.

This reliance isn't saying there is no role for provisional guidance or things to do. These may be relevant if people are blocked and can't readily see that the nondual can't be blocked by anything. Sometimes people feel a strong need to do something and can't see that nothing is needed.

Provisional methods are simply transitional steps we create when someone can't instantly see that they are "no one needing nothing."

4. Rely on wisdom, and not on conceptual knowledge

The practices and techniques used in *Radiant Mind* and *Natural Awakening* revolve around unconditioned awareness. This paradoxical space of unconditioned awareness is the source of wisdom. The primary technique is deconstruction, therefore conceptual cognition is eliminated in every moment.

3

Creating the space:
setting the mood, pace, and atmosphere

This chapter will focus mainly on creating the space in which nondual transmission happens. This is more relevant when working with a group because in a one-on-one conversation it's not so difficult to move the direction and energy momentum of a conversation. The area of "space-creation" is an area where individual style is most evident. So please don't use what I am writing here as a model. It is mainly intended to create distinctions.

An anti-frantic atmosphere

By the term "space" I mean the atmosphere, pace, and overall mood of individual and group meetings. I would generally characterize the space that I work in as being tolerant, peaceful, and open. At the processing level it is quite rigorous and precise. At the level of comportment it is loose. The space is also ambiguous. Within this space, people can move through all sorts of experiences. Nothing is specifically cultivated (for example, a koan) and nothing is excluded. That said, I know there are other teachers and facilitators who create very different spaces that are equally effective.

In *Radiant Mind* and *Natural Awakening* the general atmosphere is calm and relaxed, though it's also punctuated by emotional catharsis, high energy exchanges, and outbreaks of laughter and uproarious hilarity. There is no urgency, since we aren't going anywhere, there's nowhere to go. We've always, already arrived. There is always movement and change, and at the same time there's no movement. We are neither still nor moving.

Going nowhere, doing nothing

In a way, the pace of the work is defined by the fact that we are going nowhere and doing nothing. "Doing nothing" means that we're free of all compulsion; there's nothing we need to do or not do. It doesn't mean we are rigid or fixed. We open up the possibility of being present to what is, without needing to move incessantly toward a self-prescribed goal, simply moving fluidly with the changing landscape of emotions and explorations.

In *Radiant Mind* and *Natural Awakening* we show people how to go nowhere and do nothing. We can listen to these phrases in two different ways, and it's important to understand both of them, and how they come together in a way that shapes the directionless direction and transintentional intentionality of nondual work. We move in the direction of going nowhere, of being in the space where we can't say if there is movement or stillness. And we do nothing. What we are doing *is* nothing.

S: When I'm with others, it's harder to stay in pure awareness, so I just want to practice for a few minutes with you. Is that okay?

P: But there's nothing to practice! What we're practicing is no-practice. This is the meditation that's not meditation. It's like the parallel theme—we're practicing not getting into a practice.

S: Yes, that's the place I want to get with you.

P: But you won't get there by looking into the future.

S: I'm just asking for the space to feel what it would be like to do this together.

P: We are, we're doing it now. I'm just pointing out a way in which we can disconnect from sharing effortless being together. There's nothing to get ready for. Nothing is going to happen. What you are talking about is here right now. It's already happened. You're too late! It's here, and it's happening. You can't get into it, and you can't get out of it. It's got nothing to do with nondual awareness. It doesn't matter what you say, what you don't say, or what you do with your body because this is unconditioned space. It doesn't matter what condition you're in, this is always here.

Just feel this. There's a continual stream of awareness happening at the same time that we're with each other. The two experiences are completely different, and they are also undifferentiable. There's no difference between them. We can't separate one from the other, because nondual awareness is not a thing that you can pull apart and extract out of this experience. We can't filter or separate it out, because it has no substance to it at all. It's not a thing.

S: I'm anxious because I don't think I'm getting this.

P: There's nothing to get. That's what I'm saying. You might have to hear this again and again. This isn't a concept. It's nothing. And it's clearly not nothing either, because all of this is happening at the same time.

   There's nothing to understand. We're here. We've arrived. Where? We can't say. But this is it. There's nothing to think about, nothing to work out, nothing to know. Why? Because this is not an object of knowledge. I'm showing you now how this is revealed through words.

S: And you're not showing me anything.

P: Exactly, that's what I'm showing you.

Not knowing

A theme I weave in quite quickly is "not knowing." The needs to know and to do something are the biggest obstacles to abiding in the nondual. They can be like mountains that we drill through, move under, over, or around, until we emerge in the clear space of knowing nothing.

The need to know is endemic in our culture. We need to know everything: exactly what's going on with our body, our net worth, what is inside the smallest known particle, whether there is life on other planets. This is related to our need for security and control. If we know who we are, what we're doing, what's happening around us, what's happening to our loved ones, then we think we have some kind of control on our situation and feel real and safe (until we create something that we don't know).

But, as Alan Watts said, there is "wisdom in insecurity." In many Buddhist traditions the ultimate wisdom is called "not knowing." There are different types of "not knowing," so it's important to clarify what is meant by "not knowing" at the nondual level.

The first type of not knowing is the not knowing that happens at the conditioned level. Actually, there are two types of not knowing at this level—the level of cognition and perceptual experience. There are things that are knowable that we know we don't know. There are things that are knowable that we don't yet know that we don't know. For example, we may not know a foreign language, and we don't (yet) know about living beings on other planets. But, these things are knowable—in time and with the right equipment, effort, etc. There are also things that will be known, but which in a profound sense can never be known, for example, the future and death. We can speculate about the future but never have certainty. There is always an element of not knowing. We know other people die, even though we can't know for certain when this will happen. Our own death is interesting because we may never really know it (in the sense of experiencing it) because we won't exist when it happens!

The second type of not knowing is the not knowing that is unconditioned awareness. This is not knowing because there is nothing to know. What is known is not knowing, since here there is no object of awareness. This is the sort of not knowing that a rhetorical question or koan can stimulate. At the unconditioned level, we don't need to know anything because there's "nothing" to know! That is, there's no "thing," no object, to know. In unconditioned awareness we still retain all the knowledge that we have available to us from the conditioned mind, so there's nothing to fear either. In a sense we lose our mind but nothing disappears.

As facilitators, we can point out these two types of not knowing to help people let go of the idea that there is something they need to know, or look for, to find the nondual state of awareness. If in unconditioned awareness there's nothing to know, then there's nothing to learn to get there. The state is unknowable, and yet it is readily accessible to us, so we don't need to be concerned about "knowing" it.

Often people find it quite unbelievable that there's something that they can't know. The conditioned mind refuses to give up. It is tenacious and wants to know what "no-mind" means, how we can acquire it, and how we'll know when we have it! People will say, "I get that it's a state of not knowing, but I still don't get it. I understand what you're saying, but it still eludes me. How do I find this 'not knowing?' The answer, of course, is by not knowing.

Subhuti, a disciple of the Buddha is very clear:

> Dear friends, you cannot understand because there is absolutely nothing finite to understand. You are not lacking in refinement of intellect. There is simply nothing separate or substantial in *Prajnaparamita* to which the intellect can be applied, because perfect wisdom does not present any graspable or thinkable doctrine and offers no describable method of contemplation. (Hixon, 1993: 65)

No one has ever known the unknowable, because it simply can't be an object of knowledge. No matter how much mental effort or philosophical skill we apply to the task, we can never understand or interpret the experience of unstructured awareness.

Spiritual transformation is different from spiritual knowledge

Another point we can make here is that the work we are involved in is transformational: we are transforming consciousness. This is completely different from acquiring new knowledge or gaining insights.

Typically, when we have an experience that is new and unfamiliar, we try to understand it and categorize it, so we can feel secure that we will know how to deal with a similar experience should it happen again. On the path of spiritual transformation—in particular on the nondual path—it's not necessary for us to understand everything that is happening along the way. If the process of transformation is happening quickly, the mind often can't make sense of what's occurring. Things are changing too fast for us to invent a story or meaning behind the process. This can even give rise to periods of temporary insanity. We can't make sense of what's happening. We think, "I don't know where I am. I've never been here before. How long will this go on for?" These types of "thoughts" are all signs of rapid transformation. After the event, we might try to extract some meaning and understanding, but often life moves on and we never really know what happened "then."

The best way to deal with the uncertainty that comes with spiritual transformation is to trust the process. The process of transformation doesn't need to be understood. There is no work to be done. All we need to do is show up, and be constantly available to whatever is happening. We discover a new way of being: a way of being from birth to death in which life flows through us with less friction and tension.

Demonstrating not knowing

One of our functions as facilitators and coaches is that we model not knowing. We don't do this intentionally. Nor do we indulge in "not knowing" as a way of covering up, or sliding over, our lack of understanding of something that can be known. We need to acknowledge the gap in our "knowledge" when this is real and appropriate.

As facilitators we demonstrate the possibility of resting in contentless awareness while remaining fully functional and effective. We continually model this possibility by giving ourselves permission to not know what is happening, or what we should do. For example, we can ask, "I'm just wondering, what is this? What are we doing now?" A student can observe that we don't know, yet we are unperturbed and peaceful at the same time.

This kind of inquiry models a way of relating to all events as they occur in the moment. Rather than pushing the panic button when we fail to understand why something is happening or how we can control it, we can just see it for what it is, without needing to know. Contentlessness is revealed to be a completely valid experience in which we remain fully functional and effective— in which our thoughts and behavior are clear, coherent, and precise.

In this state there is no need to know, and also no object of knowing. When we ask, "What is This?" there is no "This"—there isn't anything—which is why it is sometimes termed "no thing" or "nothing." We can't know because there's nothing to know. That is, what there is to know is nothing, and what we know is nothing.

Not knowing in this way doesn't preclude seeking relative knowledge when we need it. For example, we may experience ourselves as being nowhere and knowing nothing, yet on a relative level we may need to ask directions because we don't know how to find the house of a friend. Not knowing and knowing are not contradictory.

The need to create meaning

The need to construct meaning from even the smallest event or utterance is instinctive and impulsive. As many people have observed, we are meaning-making machines. We are wired to make connections between things, to weave elaborate stories in our minds, and communicate these to others as realities. The world and our lives are narratives that are constantly being written and re-worked.

Most therapies and spiritual systems collude with our need to create meaning from our experiences. It's easy to listen and then give feedback through the filters of understanding, clarifications, and elaboration. When we lead people in nondual inquiry, it's possible for people to create meaning, but it's also possible for them to just be with what is happening without having to do anything with it. They don't need to work with "what is," to interpret it or explain it. They can just become familiar with "what is." At times, people can feel uncertain about this, preferring an answer, and we can just listen to them without rescuing them with a suitable explanation. Indirectly, we're encouraging them to sit with their uncertainty. It's a perfect opportunity to access unconditioned awareness.

S: I'm listening to everything you are saying, and I have a lot of questions.

P: You're listening very actively.

S: Yes, very actively.

P: I'm wondering what's behind your questions.

S: I want to learn more! All these questions are spinning around in my mind.

P: I can see that.

[Silence]

S: I want to understand.

P: Yes.

S: I'm starting to feel uncomfortable because you're not answering my questions.

P: So far you've only told me that you have lots of questions.

S: I feel I am doing something wrong.

P: How?

S: I don't know.

P: It's natural to feel uncomfortable when we can't work out what's happening.

S: I don't like it. I'm being honest. I cannot stop myself wanting to know. I need to know.

P: You need to know what?

S: Why I exist.

P: Why do you need to know that?

S: Because I don't have the answer.

P: But if you need to ask the question simply because you don't have an answer, you will be asking questions for the rest of your life. A question of that type can be a source of unending frustration. You can never come up with a definite answer to the question "Why do I exist?" You can never achieve closure on that type of question. That is why people ask that same question, millennia after millennia, without getting any closer to an answer that would stop the question. It is the type of question that is designed to stimulate our thinking.

I'm still not clear why you need to know why you exist. From one point of view there is nothing to even think about. You are a happening, and you will continue to happen until you stop happening. And if you're no longer happening you won't know that that's happened.

S: But I just feel I need to know more and more.

P: What do you need to know right now?

[Silence]

S: I need to know what is happening right now. I'm starting to feel quite lost.

P: What do you think is happening?

S: I'm not sure. This feels very strange. What is happening?

P: We are in a conversation in which you are trying to work out what is happening.

S: You must know what is happening.

P: I don't. And I don't need to.

S: You mean we are both lost.

P: Well, no. I'm not lost. I'm quite familiar with this space.

S: Where are we?

P: We are in a space where we can't say where we are.

S: I still feel there is something I need to know, but I don't know what it is. And this is really frustrating.

P: Do you have any idea where you can begin to look for an answer?

S: I don't even know if there is an answer. As I said, I don't even know what I'm looking for. I'm just feeling stuck.

P: Stuck in what?

S: I don't know. I'm just stuck. What is happening?

P: You think there is something you need to know, but you haven't got any idea what it is.

S: Right. So what can I do? I don't even know what to do. I don't even know if there is anything I need to do.

P: Do we need to do anything more with this at the moment?

S: I don't know.

P: Are you okay where you are?

S: I guess so.

P: Are you feeling comfortable or uncomfortable?

S: I really can't say.

P: Are you okay not being able to say exactly what you are feeling?

[Long silence]

S: Yes, I am. I came here this evening with a lot of questions. I don't know what has happened. I have the feeling of being influenced by a very extraordinary energy. I don't have any answers, at least the type of answers I was expecting. But nor do I have any questions. Thank you.

Nondual transmission in one image

The following diagram is very useful. It captures key principles in the *Natural Awakening* style of transmission. It's an easy image to recall. The essence of it applies to all nondual transmission.

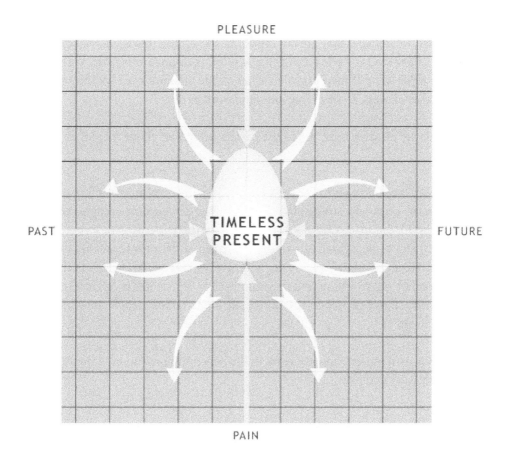

If people are identified with a conditioned experience, it means they are "situated" somewhere in this diagram. One axis is time: past, future and present. The other is the pleasure-pain continuum. It's obvious where people are located in terms of these dimensions. Usually it's clear within two or three sentences of someone's sharing. There is nothing right or wrong about being anywhere on this diagram. It's just an easy way to see where people are. It opens up the possibility of building bridges to the unconditioned (the centerless center).

If someone is sharing a positive breakthrough that's happened to them, they are in the top left-hand quadrant. If someone fears the result of a medical test, they are in the bottom right-hand quadrant. If someone is feeling peaceful and relaxed, they are somewhere on the upper half of the vertical axis. If someone is struggling with physical pain, they are primarily on the lower axis. As we move away from the center, pleasure and pain increase. If someone is thinking about a future event with no significant emotional reaction, they are on the right-hand part of the horizontal axis, etc.

In time and on the pleasure-pain continuum

At the center we can't say whether what we are experiencing is pleasurable or painful. There is no frame of reference. There is neither pleasure nor absence of pleasure: no suffering nor freedom from suffering. Nothing is happening, so it doesn't feel like the presence or absence of anything.

When people share, we notice if they are talking about something that is enjoyable, comfortable, pleasurable, or whether their experience is difficult, painful, or uncomfortable. We listen for how they qualify their experience. If their experience lies on the pleasure-pain continuum, they aren't resting in nondual awareness, so there may be some work to do.

Similarly, if people are in time, referring to the past or future, we move them into this moment right now.

In nondual work we build bridges to the centerless center. The center isn't in the middle. It isn't anywhere because the center doesn't displace anything. The centerpoint occupies no space so we can't say where it is. It's the space where we are right now. There seems to be a center to our field of awareness. We seem to be located at a point in the center. In a sense we are, but if we look, there is no center. We aren't anywhere. We are here, everywhere, and nowhere at the same time. The arrows that radiate out from the center symbolize how the center is centerless and includes everything. When we move people to the center, we aren't taking people anywhere. We aren't looking for movement.

In the next sections we'll explore how we work in the here and now and how we move to a space that transcends pleasure and pain.

Working in the here and now

In *Radiant Mind* and *Natural Awakening* the focus is on the quality of what is being experienced in this moment. We explain that we can't get our hands on the past, and the future doesn't exist. This is the only place we can be. What's relevant is how we are in this moment. We are learning how to recondition ourselves so that we suffer less. The way to do this is to suffer less whenever we have the opportunity. By suffering less in this moment, the next moment is conditioned to less suffering.

So the operative question is: "Is anything missing in this moment?" We look at how to be complete in this moment rather than looking for a strategy or particular resource to use in specific situations in the future.

If a student starts to move into the future, wondering about how they are going to integrate the nondual space into their life generally, or how they are going to handle a specific situation using nondual resources, I either bring it back to "closing the gap" in this moment, or I move into the mode of talking about general resources that can help in many situations. Examples of this include: expanding our capacity to experience pleasure and pain, not making problems out of problems, and working to be complete in the here and now. I don't mix these two together—connecting with the here and now, and offering general resources—because this can get very messy.

In workshops I usually bring it back to the here and now because this is relevant for everyone and there is nothing to misinterpret because we are talking about "being here in the sense of being nowhere." I am more inclined to work "in time," at a pragmatic level, in an individual session where I can tailor what I am saying to the specific circumstances of a student.

I sometimes begin talking about general resources and then return to the "now." I begin "in time" because it can feel more relevant. Going straight to the here and now may produce a disconnection for a student. They can think, "That's okay now, but I'm not going to be able to do that when X is happening." So I talk about things that may happen, opening up a small palette of possibilities. Then, having spoken of general resources, I will say, "But of course the most valuable thing for us to do is to connect with this moment, because right now, if we stay 'here,' then we will be complete." So the best thing to practice is "being here," which we don't have to do because it's just happening.

If I move directly into the here and now, when I see that a student is "in time," meaning functioning in the past and future, and attempting to sort out the best way to deal with the future, I bring their attention to this, saying, "In nondual work we approach this differently. We don't work so much in the 'temporal-causal paradigm,' as this is the paradigm in which we produce something in the future." I remind them that we are not operating causally, rather we are being in the moment without friction and without incompletion. The term "causal" means that what I am doing now is guided by or determined by the intention to produce a particular outcome or consequences in the future. For example, I might want to have a family because I think I have something to offer and it will be rewarding. Or, I might want to take a course to gain more insights or realizations. Rather than join the students' paradigms, we invite them to explore a different possibility.

Listening to the tensing: past, present, and future

The way to determine where students are in time is simply to listen to the verb tenses they are using. If a participant says something like, "I hope I can learn how to release my feelings more easily," I immediately pick up on hope and the fact that this is something to happen in the future. The speaker is located in time. I think, "Okay, we are in time. The focus is on the future. The relevant feeling is hope." These things register immediately. If someone says, "I'm frightened about how I'm going to deal with X," I immediately see that we are not in the type of conversation that's talking about what's happening now. We are in time. If I respond to it in this frame of reference, I'll be in time, too.

Beyond pleasure and discomfort

Nondual awareness isn't a feeling state. Feelings, like thoughts and sense-data, are objects of awareness, not awareness itself. A full range of sensations can be present within a nondual field, but the field or space itself has no structure. When we are naturally awake there is no fixation on content. As the *Heart Sutra* says, in the space of "perfect wisdom, there is no suffering or absence of suffering."

If a student is talking about feeling good, excited, worried, frustrated, etc., they aren't presencing nondual awareness. They are involved with a feeling state. There is absolutely nothing wrong with this. This is life. But from a nondual perspective it means there is room for movement. There are many, many ways of accessing the nondual. We will look at these in later chapters.

If you refer back to the diagram, you'll notice a highlighted semicircle around the top half of the center point. This is to indicate that there is a domain of positive experiences, experiences of contentment, deep relaxation, pleasure, and bliss that can support entry into nondual awareness. If people are located in this region, I usually let things be, or I gently point out that this isn't nondual awareness, rather they are holding onto a conditioned state which will invariably change.

You will also notice that there's a small area in the "egg" beneath the white horizontal line. This area represents mild degrees of discomfort. In many cases I find that low-level discomfort is best worked with by just "letting it be." The types of discomfort that arise from muscular tension, normal daily concerns, feelings of mild anxiety come and go all the time. If we give them a lot of attention, they can increase in intensity. If we normalize such experiences and create space for them to be, they usually dissolve quite quickly. Sometimes people will tell me in a workshop that they have some tension in their shoulder and they would like a nondual way of removing it. I recommend that they stand, stretch, and do some simple exercises to relieve the tension!

Here is a dialog showing how a feeling of mild anxiety self-liberates when there is no resistance.

S: I'm feeling uncomfortable. I'm not sure it's good for me to be here.

P: Is the feeling mild or intense?

S: It's more than mild but not super intense.

P: I understand.

S: Is there something I can do to make it go away?

P: Another possibility is to let it be there: not to resist it. You could try that. It's normal for different sensations to arise, particularly in this work which doesn't support many of our familiar ways of seeing things. You can say to yourself, "Okay, I'm feeling uncomfortable and disoriented. That's okay. Even if I'm in this space for the next two hours, that's still okay." How does that sound?

S: I feel more spacious just taking that in.

[Three minutes later, after a conversation with another student, I return to S.]

P: How are you feeling now?

S: Fine. I was completely involved in what you were just saying.

Positive experiences

When people are exploring nondual work, two opposite things can happen. People can reject positive experiences because they are conditioned, or (more commonly) they can begin to identify positive experiences of bliss, tranquility, and openness with nondual awareness itself. We are aware of both possibilities. In nondual work, it can be valuable for people to know how to hold positive experiences: they can be healing and rewarding in their own right, but they are transient, and not the ultimate experience we seek. Positive experiences can disappear in any moment. In contrast, we can't lose nondual awareness. "We" don't have it as an experience.

Bliss

It's natural for nondual work to produce positive, even blissful experiences. They arise as a by-product of the fact that our thoughts "thin out," and we experience the present moment untainted by future preferences and past experiences. This results in deep serenity, bliss, and joy. People can move into the deepest state of meditative bliss and equilibrium that they have ever tasted. There is no pressure, nothing to get right or wrong, so people move into beautiful contemplative spaces.

These types of blissful states are profoundly healing for both the mind and the soul. They can repair the damage done to our nervous system from pain and trauma. Some people have had few, if any, experiences of bliss in their lifetimes. For whatever reason, whether imposed or by unconscious choice, some people are more familiar with deprivation. Why deprive anyone of the experience of sensate bliss?

In nondual work, we allow people to rest in the healing experience of sensate bliss for as long as it is present, while fully aware that at some point, this conditioned bliss will pass. Once it has, we resume our work in gently moving people through to unconditioned awareness.

The healing power of sensate bliss

The bliss we have just been talking about has a feeling tone to it. We can soak in it, feel, savor, and enjoy it. We can also want it to continue, and resist moving beyond it. In nondual work we can also enter a state of unconditioned bliss. This is the bliss that arises when bliss and emptiness arise together within the unconditioned field.

This is the indivisible union of bliss and emptiness referred to as *sukha-shunyata*. This is a state of supernal bliss that goes beyond the experience of somatic pleasure and the removal of pain. It is the bliss that arises when we allow things to be exactly as they are. When we surrender the desire for anything to be different from how it is, when we stop resisting, this is the unconditional bliss that is associated with unconditioned awareness. This is the bliss that cannot be altered and cannot be lost. It doesn't have a location attached to it. We can't say where it comes from. It is as though it saturates the entire field. It isn't a function of our nervous system being stimulated in a particular way. It doesn't have a feeling tone associated with it. We can't say what it is. It is sourceless and identityless.

Letting things be: noninterference

When faced with a situation or problem, one possible action—or non-action—is not to interfere with whatever is happening. We don't become involved. We allow things to be as they are and keep seeing what happens.

How is noninterference useful? When we resist what is happening, we suffer. Instead, when we give up the struggle against what is happening, we're immediately free and complete. We've liberated ourselves from the prison of our own ideals. We've just stopped interfering with our experience. We're doing nothing—simply letting our experience be, exactly as it is.

Noninterference is a defining theme of nondual approaches like Dzogchen and Taoism. Dzogchen offers the way of letting things be as they are, since this is how they are anyway. It's sort of crazy to want things to be different. Dzogchen closes the gap by leaving things as they are.

It's easy to assume that when something is wrong, we need to "do" something about it: we may need to do some clearing, or deep processing, and simply talk things through with someone! Nondual inquiry doesn't assume that we are complete or incomplete. It's a respectful offering, when you think about it, to allow people to be exactly as they are without imposing deficiency on them. Longchenpa, the great Dzogchen yogi says:

> Don't condition your mind by [trying] to suppress your experience, apply an antidote, or mechanically transform it, but let your mind fall naturally into whatever [condition you find it]. This is the incontrovertible essence of what is ultimately meaningful. (2015)

When we allow space around people's emotions and problems, just by letting things be or "doing nothing," we allow people to experience confusion or ambiguity. By allowing this ambiguity, we open up the opportunity for people to let their beliefs and emotions dissolve spontaneously. In Dzogchen, this is called "natural release" or "auto-liberation."

As facilitators of nondual work, one of our primary roles within the setting is to attune to whether or not people are complete. Rather than watching like a hawk, we're naturally and serenely alert to the question, "Is there anything that seems to be missing?" When "nothing is missing," noninterference is often our natural response. Perhaps surprisingly, when "something is missing," noninterference is also a valid response.

There are times when we can become aware that "something is missing"—someone seems incomplete—because we sense an expectation that we should be intervening or providing an explanation. At times, our response will be to "do something." One of the many ways we can address the problem is to offer noninterference as a concept or theory and explain how people can use it to release their resistance to how things are.

By offering noninterference as a concept, we make people aware that it is always a valid option for them to just allow things to be as they are. A time when it might seem useful to do this could be when someone raises a problem and we decide to "do something"—offer guidance. Here, we can also remind people that the practice of noninterference is all-inclusive; that is, it includes all situations, thoughts, emotions, and it includes all states of consciousness. For instance, when people show concern that they are immersed in conditioned awareness, that is a time when we can point out that they could just let that be. They don't have to resist the conditioned state. At this moment, they can just let that be how it is.

Noninterference also includes not resisting the times when someone is expressing very strong emotions. We don't need people to be happy or not suffering. Nor do we need people to be perfect or enlightened. Someone could be heavily tied up within their identities and we would still be aware that everyone is complete, just as they are. There is no other way anyone could be right at this moment. Why fight it?

Longchenpa writes:

> One doesn't discard [some experiences] and cultivate [others]. [Whether one's experiences] are dynamic or stable, one should let them go wherever they want to go.… When the mind is diffused or dynamic, one isn't discouraged; when it's calm and stable, one desists from wanting [to continue in that state]. (1974)

At other times when we're aware that someone is incomplete, we can find ourselves not needing to do anything. We're letting things be as they are. We have the wisdom to trust that we can simply provide people with the opportunity to put space around their problems, a space that can allow the natural release of these problems.

The important point here is that, although we're aware that the natural release of limiting beliefs and emotions is what can happen when we allow things to be as they are, this is not our intention. When noninterference arises organically, we have no goal. We're neither "applying" nor "practicing" noninterference. It's not an action that we consciously choose to "do." We don't "do" it in any idealistic or formulaic way that presupposes that it is going to dissolve someone's problem. It may not, and we don't have any concern about that. It's just our natural response—sometimes it can seem that nothing needs to be done.

At times like this, to announce that noninterference is what we're "doing" is incorrect and would undermine the "non-action," because people then try to work out our motive, rather than explore their own uncertainty with the situation. To clarify this further, it can be useful to offer the theory of noninterference at times when we've decided to "do something"—that is, provide some explanation—but when we're taking the track of "doing nothing," it's best not to reveal that that's what we're "doing."

In the following dialog, I'm working with someone who has a very negative story around the functioning of her mind. Even here I'm inviting her to let things happen.

S: I'm getting really angry sitting here. I have to share this with you. Other people seem to be getting what you are doing, but it isn't touching me. My problem is that I'm plagued by parasitic thoughts. They just keep turning around in my head. I can't stop them. They are with me day and night. They never give me a break.

P: Is this happening now?

S: Yes.

P: Do you mind sharing with me what is happening?

S: I'm just thinking about my work, what happened in the office today. I can't get rid of these thoughts.

P: Are these what you call "parasitic thoughts?"

S: Yes.

P: That's a very heavy judgment about your thoughts.

S: Well, they are parasitic. They eat away at me. They stop me from being here. Everyone else seems to be peaceful and able to hear what you're saying, but I can't get rid of these trivial thoughts about what's been happening at work.

P: Well, instead of struggling to stop them, can you just let them happen?

S: Of course. I can't stop them anyway.

P: Give yourself permission to think them.

[Silence]

P: Are you thinking those thoughts?

S: Yes.

P: Okay. Just let yourself think them, let them be present for however long they continue. Can you do that?

S: Of course.

P: Can you tell me when they stop? There's no hurry.

S: Well, I'm not sure why you've asked me to do this.

P: You seem to be thinking about something different now.

S: I don't understand.

P: You're no longer thinking about work. Instead you're wondering why I've asked you to give free reign to your thinking.

S: Yes. I'm wondering what you're doing.

P: Before we look at what we're doing, I'd just like to check whether there are any more thoughts about work that need to be expressed. Can you think about that some more? Can you reactivate the images of your office and what was happening today at work?

S: I can't.

P: Come on. You must be able to. You've been at work all day. You haven't had time to adjust to being here.

S: But I can't think about it anymore.

P: I'm patient. Perhaps we just need to wait a little longer.

[Silence]

P: Yes?

S: I can't.

P: That's interesting. Only a couple of minutes have passed since we began talking together, and the thoughts that were burdening you are no longer present. In fact, you can't reconstruct them even when I invite you to!

S: I don't understand this. What am I meant to be doing then?

P: Obviously, right now we are meant to be doing this.

S: But I'm not doing anything!

P: Then there's nothing for you to do.

S: That's impossible. I'm a super-active woman.

P: Really? Prove it to me!

S: I can't. I can't find anything to do.

[Silence]

S: So what are we doing? What is this?

P: Yes, those questions seem to arise at this point. What are we doing? What is this?

S: Yes, exactly. What is this?

P: In some ways, we can let our attention become focused on this question. Whatever thoughts arise, we can let them ride on this question. The question is there because we can't work out what this is. Usually we can say what is happening, even if we acknowledge that it is our interpretation, but right now we aren't able to do that. Nothing seems to be happening upon which to hang an interpretation. What would we be interpreting? That's the quandary. This is happening but we can't say what it is.

Cultivating a homing instinct

The more we rest in unconditioned awareness, the more familiar we become with it and the more readily we can move back toward it. We don't necessarily "know" how to get there; we just home in on it instinctively. The more often and deeply we experience the state, the more natural it is to us. It's a new way of being that we've added to our repertoire. We've tried it on, it seems an easy way of being and, spontaneously, we find ourselves "there" again, wherever that is.

The more familiar we become with unconditioned awareness, the less time we find ourselves having for all the minor irritations and distractions that previously consumed our time and energy. We reprioritize our interests, giving more attention to the experiences of love, freedom, and contentment, and less attention to unnecessary, energy-sapping problems.

Not conditioning the future

In dialogs it's possible for people to take an aspect of their conditioning—a thought or belief that is arising for them in the present or that stems from the past—as the truth and to then allow that to predict or condition the future. For example, someone might say, "Finding love is difficult," as if that will always be the case.

As facilitators, we can be mindful of what can happen when we collude with what people say. If we were to agree, "Yes, finding love is difficult," without any proviso, then we give this construction additional support. We help make it a stable concept that has meaning into the future. If we disagree, "No, I think that finding love can be quite easy," then we're simply casting a different kind of projection onto the future. Then if people struggle to find love in the future, they can't understand why and question their teacher. Or they disagree, "No, finding love is difficult," and then engage in an argument to support their belief. From a nondual perspective, we engage from a place where there is neither agreement nor disagreement.

Facilitators and spiritual teachers have an added responsibility in this regard because of the authority that's invested in them by their students. If we collude with people's beliefs that change is always difficult, we impede their enthusiasm for growth and development. On the other hand, if we suggest that change is easy, we set people up to become disillusioned and despondent when the going gets hard.

Not conditioning the next moment

When we're talking about not conditioning the future in this work, we can talk about it at two levels. What I've just been describing is not conditioning the future at the macro level: the wider future. We can also be aware of how we can condition the future at the micro level: the next moment.

When you're reading this *Guide* for the first time you can't know what the next sentence is going to say. (I don't know what it's going to be. Well now I do. But now I don't.) When we're working with the nondual, we don't know whether someone is about to speak or not and, if they do, we can't predict what they are going to say. If we're truly allowing the experience to unfold in an unconditioned way, we don't even know whether we are going to say something in the next moment. If we're talking in one moment, we're not sure if we're going to finish our sentence or stop mid-sentence. The experience is totally fluid. Whether there will be silence or speech in the next moment is unknown and we're completely unconcerned.

At a wider perspective, we similarly have no idea about how anyone's spiritual development will proceed. We don't expect people to follow the same path, and we don't consider someone more advanced because they have had more exposure to this work. In any given moment, someone relatively new to nonduality has exactly the same opportunity to experience unconditioned awareness as someone who has experienced it before. We see this happen all the time. Suddenly, someone wakes up, gets it for the very first time (with no previous spiritual training), and the long-time meditator sitting next to them struggles inside with a powerful conversation about how difficult it is to open into nondual awareness.

Preferring neither speech nor silence: giving equal value to both

If we're not conditioning the next moment, we have no preference for either speech or silence. We find there is no difference between nothing happening verbally or having verbal content. Not knowing, not conditioning the next moment, means not knowing what will happen next in sharing through language or sharing silently.

When people are together in visual contact with each other and not meditating together, it's easy for people to feel some pressure to communicate verbally or to share content. Based on the *Radiant Mind* and *Natural Awakening* style of nondual transmission, there can be more silence in a group setting than one would expect in most groups. A person's implicit assumption is that we do quite a bit of silence here; however, silence can be a happening or a doing. Doing silence is as distractive as over-talking. The nondual has no content, and if we're doing silence, the very doing separates us from uncontrived silence.

If we're caught up in our ideas, contentlessness cannot come through. That's how people begin to preference silence, rather than seeing that silence simply happens because you're deconstructing people's capacity and need to think about things. Clean, natural deconstruction gives people nothing to think about. It's not like you're trying to do silence. In the space of nondual awareness nothing is happening, not even silence.

The impulse to communicate comes when people are not resting in nondual awareness. The space of nondual awareness often invites a simple recognition with people smiling at each other. We share very gentle, simple ways of acknowledging each other's presence. But there is no impulse, no energy to connect through stories about who we are, and no need for artificial silence.

When working one-on-one with a client, it can feel quite different from being with a group. There can be less content and less talking, and you may feel uncomfortable with the silence. You may wonder what your client is feeling. You may hope it's okay for them. You may become uncomfortable, wondering about your client's comfort. You may have a tendency to break the silence by saying, "How is it going for you?" because the silence starts to feel unusual, intense, or a little bit weird. When a silence arises, we are fully aware of each other, we're not talking, and this is just what happens.

There is a discipline here to neither create a silence or to prolong one. People can identify this kind of work with an experience of silence and try to create it. When this artificial silence is happening, people can believe that mind-to-mind transmission is happening and that silence enhances this transmission, as when Buddha held up the flower. A preference for silence creates this misunderstanding and an attempt to prolong it. In the nondual we hold no preference. We are not trying to shorten or prolong anything that is happening. We allow whatever is there to be there for however long it lasts. When we move out of silence into communication, it's uneventful, and it's totally natural. People don't feel a sudden relief, as with an artificial silence where they're glad to be talking again.

Silence can also move into a more interiorized experience of deep meditation without it being pushed in that direction. Silence sometimes arises as a shared-group experience. We can call that public silence as contrasted with private silence, which is an individual phenomenon happening within an individual, either in groups or alone. Public silence can occur because we're very open to the setting, to the environment, or to the sharing. Sometimes public silence evolves into private silence where interiorized meditation is deeply experienced. In *Radiant Mind* and *Natural Awakening* work, due to the resonance of the field, all individuals within the group may slip effortlessly into a smooth, deep meditation with no struggle, no concern about the time, and no distractions. When this happens you can really feel it and see it on people's faces. In that situation there is the freedom to stop at any time or to continue in deep meditation.

Natural contemplation: effortless meditation

Natural contemplation is the state of finding ourselves in a clear and serene state of pure being, without doing anything—without any need for meditating. In this state the aim of meditation is realized without needing to meditate. We find that we are complete, with nothing to get and nowhere else to go, without being still, quiet, or immobile. This is "natural contemplation." This is the meditation that is sometimes referred to as non-meditation. We are naturally awake without any need for a meditational intervention. It's totally unstructured and uncontrived. There is no particular time of day that we "do" natural contemplation and no particular way that we decide to do it. From time to time, we just find that we are resting in the serenity of unconditioned awareness, while we're doing whatever we're doing within our conditioned experience. Whether we're walking somewhere or doing the dishes or playing with our children, we can find ourselves in natural contemplation, just appreciating the experience exactly as it is without needing anything to be different.

Attachment to suffering: not making problems out of problems

Buddhism and other nondual traditions link human suffering to the presence of, and attachment to, preferences. Whenever our experience falls outside the refined typology of our preferences, we experience some level of discomfort. At the same time, we are also aware that people suffer—there's no escaping this—and so we know that having a problem doesn't have to be a problem! In unconditioned awareness, we accept our experience exactly as it is. It doesn't have to be problem-free. Struggling to be free of problems only compounds problems. It also blocks access to unconditioned awareness, where there is no struggle. Unconditioned awareness never arises through struggling to achieve it.

Something else we can point out is that, unless we're fully enlightened—abiding continuously in nondual awareness—problems will continue to arise and we will continue to suffer. It might be hard to believe, but we're actually attached to suffering. If we weren't, we wouldn't continue to contribute to our own suffering by creating problems. By attached, I mean that we are stuck to our problems. We can't get away from them. They are part of who we are.

The creation of problems is habitual. Regardless of where we are on our path, we create problems because "the struggle" gives us something to do, something to work on. At some level we are at home and comfortable having problems. The construction of problems carries through to the spiritual arena. People struggle with questions such as: "Am I on the right path?" "Do I need a different teacher, or teaching?" And we create problems about problems. "I shouldn't have this problem. It's going to stop me from experiencing unconditioned awareness." We create problems when there aren't any, wondering what will happen if our fulfillment continues forever! "What will happen if I no longer have problems? What happens then?"

If nothing is arising in the space, there is absolutely nothing that we need to do, or contribute. When movement occurs we notice it. We are aware and understanding of how problems arise in the space. From my point of view, it's not a problem if there's a little discomfort. It's a clearing. If some people become frustrated because there's too much talking, this is natural. They may even try to communicate that "this isn't working for them" by closing their eyes and going elsewhere in their minds. Again, this isn't a problem. Conversely, when it becomes quiet and still, with minimal external input, some people naturally find this uncomfortable. It is so easy to fall into the mode of "waiting for things to change." Given that we aren't doing anything, we become particularly aware of how we can create problems out of nothing: experiences of boredom, agitation, blame and projection, frustration and anger. Sometimes we may draw attention to this, but overall there's just an awareness of the ebb and flow of feelings that inevitably arise, and of the different experiences that are always present within a group. If we are open to nondual awareness, it's so easy to create problems along the way. It's automatic and natural.

Also, quite often in the nondual space, people can enter states of deep, deep pain, such as when they are grieving, without even knowing why this is happening, and this isn't a problem. In fact, it would be doing them a disservice to try to relieve this. Often, as the effortlessness of nondual being seeps in, people see how much they have struggled in vain to arrive at this very place where nothing is wrong, and nothing needs to be different. It's not uncommon for people to shed quiet tears of sadness or sobs of deep grief for the pain that they have suffered in struggling to have had a different life.

Is that a problem?

In order to get some direction on how to be with someone, I often ask, "Is that a problem?" If the answer is "Yes, it is a problem," there may or may not be something to do. If the response is "No problem," and it seems it is just sharing understanding and interpretation, I acknowledge that this is how it is in this moment. The question "Is that a problem?" simply orients us, shows us what to engage with here. It opens the view to either allow the problem to be or work with it in order to see through the problem. Our intention is to find clarity as to whether there is a problem or not. We are not here to share viewpoints and ideas, but rather to be present for the cultivation of human fulfillment. If someone responds that what's happening for them is problematic, we listen differently to the sharing than if it is shared more casually.

There are at least three ways of working with this:

1. We can do nothing. We don't engage with the problem as something we have to eliminate. We create space around the problem and let it dissolve in its own time and way.

2. We can introduce the idea of not making a problem out of problems. We reframe a problem to suggest that it is normal. It's normal for humans to create problems. We have this tendency. It isn't surprising that we make problems out of things. We might say to ourselves, "This is what I do. I'm conditioned to do this." As humans we have a biochemical brain. I don't have to take the extra step that I often take

that says, "This shouldn't be happening to me. I'm in a problem. I'm caught in it. I can't see a way out of it. Perhaps I can remind myself that it will run its course, next moment, day, week, or year. This thought or feeling will run through me. I don't have to be too dramatic. I can stay the course without indulging, without energizing this habit. It is a natural tendency of my mind."

3. We can see through the problem. We acknowledge that a participant feels there is a problem and we say, "Okay, let's look at that together." You know the moment you say, "Let's look at that," you've begun an unfindability inquiry. You have a lot of options available in terms of how you can work with problems. You will be receiving guidance from your student or client in terms of whether the problem is mental, emotional, or physical. This will intersect with your ability to inquire into the location, structure, and reality of whatever is problematic. Openings like these can be helpful:

- "Where exactly is the problem?"
- "Is it happening now?"
- "What is happening in you, that you'd prefer wasn't there?"

From these and other questions, you'll find what you can offer.

Re-labeling "this feels uncomfortable" as "this feels different"

One very useful tool when working with people in a direct nondual or deconstructive way is to reframe some of the experiences that can arise as a function of moving into new spaces, as "feeling different" rather than "feeling uncomfortable." It is natural in transformational work for people to enter a space they haven't been in before. This can be a function of the dissolving of normal reference points, and it also happens when we begin to offer nondual transmission in different environments. The process we are in can feel strange, different, unusual, and potentially unsettling. It is easy to interpret unusual spaces as being uncomfortable. If we aren't feeling great or elated, but strange, it's very easy simply to say that "we are uncomfortable." Conversations are happening that we can't comprehend. We aren't even sure who is feeling whatever is happening to us.

In nondual work, we don't gloss over these types of feelings. We can acknowledge that "this is different," and offer people the opportunity to stay just with the experience that "this is different," or "this feels different," rather than labeling what is happening as being uncomfortable, unsettling, or disturbing.

Not denying our conditioned existence

Just as we can make a new problem out of the idea that we shouldn't have problems, we can also make a wider problem out of being in a conditioned state. When we can see that we're attached to something or that we're resisting something, we can become irritated about that because we think we're not doing what we should be doing. Unconditioned awareness has become the new ideal and so we resist the conditioned state.

The polarization of these new concepts—conditioned awareness and unconditioned awareness—is natural. It's our conditioned state to sort new ideas into what is wanted and not wanted. But nondual work is exactly that: it is nondual. There are no poles. Nothing is unwanted. Nothing is wanted either. So if we're drifting in and out of our conditioning, that's just what's happening. We don't deny our conditioned existence. We allow ourselves and others to move fluidly between the conditioned and unconditioned experience, because if that's "what is" at the present time, then how could we possibly have that be different?

As teachers and facilitators, whenever we see people irritated or frustrated with themselves for being embedded in their conditioning, we simply acknowledge that they are making their conditioned state into a problem. We gently remind them that nondual awareness includes all experiences, including conditioned states. We don't reject our natural condition, our natural functioning. For example, we don't add a commentary that we shouldn't have preferences. If we do add that commentary, we accept that too.

> S: You said it's normal for people to want others to have a good opinion of them.
>
> P: Yes, I think that is pretty normal. Many people have that desire.
>
> S: It's a habit?
>
> P: It's part of our conditioned way of functioning. We want other people to approve of us, to like us, love us, create opportunities for us.
>
> S: Doesn't that create a problem?
>
> P: Yes. It does. But that's who we are. That's what we're doing.
>
> S: Even though it limits us.
>
> P: Yes. Right now we can see through the idea of being limited. There are no limits right now, limits in the sense that we feel trapped. We are limited by gravity, the needs of our body and mind. Those limits are here, but they don't in any way stop us being free right now just to be in nondual awareness. In fact, our body and mind are providing the conditions that are needed to presence the nondual.
>
> In a way there are two aspects to our work. We come home to who we are. We accept that we have likes and dislikes and operate out of preferences. And we accept that this compels us to suffer. Okay, that's how it is right now in my

life. Not a problem. Then we can relax around the fact that we will suffer. We're not surprised. It's inevitable. But right now we don't need anything. We have everything that's needed just to be here, totally relaxed, totally open, going nowhere, just communing as awareness.

Then we say, "Okay, so these are my starting conditions. This is who I am. This is where I'm beginning. This is what I'm working with. I'm not in denial of that. I'm not wishing it was different. This is where I am." And then when I relax into that, I can begin to let go of that preoccupation I have about getting it right, not getting it right, how I'm going to perform, how I'm going to function. Then I can get down to the work that's possible in this moment, which is going beyond our preoccupation with ourselves, connecting with unconditioned mind, no-mind—the experience that has nothing to do with us as an individual.

In order to do that, we have to just be comfortable with who we are, how we're wired up. We acknowledge that we make a mess of it from time to time, and we continue to create suffering for ourselves and others, because we're attached to our identities. We don't know how to do it differently, and in a significant way, this is more attractive at this point than the alternative is, which is not having problems. So in some way, we've got exactly what we want.

Denial and being real

If we explore our resistance or problems carefully, we'll see that we're in denial for every moment we've lost our connection with unconditioned awareness. In fact, if we aren't resting in the unconditioned state, we're either resisting or holding onto "whatever's happening for us." This might sound extreme, but if we're identified with our conditioned existence, we live in the construction that there's a right or a better place to be. By doing so, we're denying what is—the reality of our conditioned experience. At the same time, we're denying the reality of unconditioned awareness itself. Essentially, everyone participates in this denial. No one has ever won the battle against "what is." And no one ever will. Yet we spend a good part of our lives denying our conditioned existence.

The conscious cultivation of a more expanded and inclusive relationship to life, which I call "broadening the river of life," has a vital place in nondual work. The experience of the unconditioned state arises as a function of our capacity to let go of preferences, including the need to be happy or content. In the nondual approach, we can expand our capacity to enjoy pleasure and endure pain, while also discovering a space that transcends both. We learn to live gracefully with our habits and weaknesses, and accept our tendency to create problems, without being seduced by the illusion that we can leapfrog over our karmic conditioning.

The way to cut through the denial of our conditions and conditioning is by being real. We acknowledge a student's belief or construction and ask them to be truthful about whether or not that belief is real. For instance, if a student says, "I can't handle my pain anymore," we can say something like, "Yes, but the interesting thing is that you are handling it. You're here right now. And yes, while it is very painful, you are coping." Then slowly and gently it may even be possible to bring them through to an experience in this moment where there is no pain, and it's impossible for them to reconstruct that pain that was so intense just minutes before.

Another way that we can get real is just to point out when people are resisting an experience during a session. For example, if someone says they feel uncomfortable in the space, we can acknowledge, "Yes, this is a different space to be sharing with other people, and 'this' can feel unusual. But does 'unusual' need to feel uncomfortable?"

Or if someone is fighting a problem, trying to let it go by themselves, we can ask them if they need to be fighting the problem. We might acknowledge this and say, "So you're having a problem. Okay." Then we may ask, "Is the problem still there?" If they answer "Yes," we might reply, "Okay, so it's still there," showing them how there's nothing wrong with this. We simply allow what is there to exist as it is—no denial, no struggle—and be with them while they adjust to that. Being real by necessity accommodates the full range of human experiences, from the most shocking and disgusting to the most sublime and ecstatic.

We cut through the fantasy that something is wrong when we suffer. We accept the basic structure and patterning of our experience, our life circumstances, not in a defeatist way but with dignity and grace, because we know that "welcoming what is" is the gateway to unconditioned awareness.

First of all, we accept the truth of suffering, which is, of course, the first of the Buddha's four noble truths. We can say, "Yes, I've got a problem, and I'll work with it in a mature and responsible way." In fact, it's unrealistic to say that it shouldn't be happening. A more responsible answer would be "Yes, I have a problem, now what can I do about it?" or "Do I even need to do anything about it?"

In a nondual setting, getting real can take many forms. For example, it may involve saying quite simply that the difficulty a participant is experiencing isn't unusual. We explain that "This is what happens." As people begin to accept their circumstance, they relax and lighten up. Then we can say, "Do you notice that suffering isn't there anymore, and there's a new sense of lightness and relaxation? Interesting, isn't it?" This can be an especially appropriate statement when the student is starting to reconstruct the problem, and to remind them of the fact that they're having a common human experience, such as loss, illness, or pain, which everyone else also experiences.

Another approach to getting real involves interacting within a client's constructive conversation in order to create a larger frame of reference. This approach can be particularly useful when you sense that a client is not ready to deconstruct the story completely. For example, when someone says, "I think I'll be happy when I find someone who loves me," we could say something like, "Well, it's possible that you may not meet someone who will give you the love that you're seeking.

Most people aren't completely fulfilled in terms of the love they receive. In fact, judging by the rest of the community, I think you would be a unique person if you were able to achieve such love."

We're inviting students to the possibility that what they want might not happen in a way that meets their needs in full. Then we might ask, "So how is that? Can you see yourself living your life in that way?" When the student sits with the possibility for a moment without resistance, they might say, "Yes, I can." Then, we can move the conversation into the present by saying, "It's not happening now. You haven't fulfilled your wish. So what's it like for you?" Gradually, through your being unperturbed and the energy of the conversation, the student might begin to recognize that it's possible to be whole and complete without achieving the particular circumstance they had predicated as necessary for their happiness. In other words, we're pointing them in the direction of unconditioned awareness and validating the quality of that experience.

Living without resistance

A lot of our pain is caused by our denial of the physicality of our embodied existence. Moreover, the nondual perspective can add to people's confusion about the nature of conditioned existence. When the unconditioned is, it isn't. And when it isn't, it is. But in the domain of forms, feelings, and thoughts, when something is present, it's present. When it's absent, it's absent. This is what it means to have a physical body and live in the material world. The world of matter functions in very specific and precise ways. Relative to thoughts and feelings, our physical bodies are highly conditioned. If someone dies or leaves a relationship, it means that they will not be around for us to enjoy their physical presence and company. There's no question about it. If we lose half our investments, it means that we won't be able to go on the vacations we'd dreamt about, or give our children the education we'd planned. So in accepting our conditioning, we accept what it really means to be living in a body that's conditioned by the past and present, and by other people and our physical environment.

At any moment, immense amounts of energy are tied up resisting the reality of the situation in which people find themselves. Imagine the magnitude of energy that would be creatively released and contributed toward the betterment of the world, if we live as a space—or clearing—which no longer resists the realities of our conditioning and the condition of the world.

4

Nondual relationship:
the union of wisdom and intimacy

Intimacy

Central to this style of nondual transmission is the experience of intimacy, since we are in the closest possible relationship with other human beings. We are sharing centerlessness with whoever enters our field of awareness. We are in a relationship in which we are defenseless, inclusive, and uncontrived. There's no boundary between us and the world, no possibility for avoidance, force, persuasion, pretence, or seduction.

The overriding experience is one of being in relationship with another person—an open and interpenetrating relationship in which we're continually touched by other people's experience, by their feelings of fear, anxiety, anger, agitation, excitement, depression, joy, powerlessness, passion, loneliness, celebration, abandonment, courage, and so on. The content of what is being communicated—whether a concern about health, a relationship, work, or spirituality—is secondary. The primary experience is one of being in relationship with the individual we are working with. There is complete connection with the person we are working with because at the level of awareness there are no boundaries or divisions.

In a sense everything is ours, except that there is no findable experiencer. If someone is angry, we receive this. It enters the dimensionless clearing that we are. If someone tells us that they're feeling sad, we know what they're talking about. We know the heaviness in their heart, how it's impossible to smile, how the muscles and flesh on their face have lost their vitality and suppleness, how they may have lost a purpose for living.

Nondual wisdom

Yet, at the same time that we receive without resistance or judgment, we rest in the place where there is no receiver. And weirdly, at first, we see the suffering of others, yet can't see anyone who is suffering. If there is no one who is suffering, then how do we talk about suffering at all? It is weird; there is suffering, we all know what that is, what it feels like, how we try to avoid it. Yet, if there is no sufferer who can be found, whatever it is that we call suffering, it isn't the experience we have when "we" are suffering.

We need to look at this a little bit further in order to get the real nondual perspective on suffering and how this relates to unconditioned intimacy.

From the nondual perspective, the suffering we encounter in ourselves and others is neither real nor unreal. To think, or see, that suffering is an illusion is only half the picture. This is an important distinction. The *Heart Sutra*, for example, is very precise in saying that in the awakened state there is no suffering and no freedom from suffering. The bodhisattva players in this *Sutra* were very careful and precise with their words because they wanted to be true to the nondual experience, and they also wanted to make sure that people didn't misinterpret the state of nondual emptiness.

So yes, from within the state of nondual awareness there's no suffering. That's clear. We just need to look at it. But that's not to say that suffering is an illusion—there's just no suffering. If nondual awareness depended on the presence or absence of anything, it wouldn't be unconditioned. If it depended on the absence of pain and discomfort, it would be a conditioned state; it could only happen if unpleasant things weren't happening. Nondual awareness is beyond suffering and the absence of suffering. It is completely unrelated to either. We can check this out right now. We can ask, "Is there any suffering in this state?" No, clearly there isn't. We can't find any suffering, not the slightest disturbance. Does this mean that I am free of suffering? No, here, I am not free of anything. Nothing is happening, so nothing has dropped out of the picture. I can't say that there is no suffering, because I don't know what that is. When we say that there is no suffering, we can't say what it is that isn't happening. It's impossible.

This is why the Mahayana always says that when we are naturally awake there is no absence of suffering. From the nondual point of view, if we are trying to avoid suffering we are pushing in the wrong direction—we're going away from unconditioned awareness. We are seeking a state that's free of suffering, so we're not directly opening into the unconditioned. From the nondual state there is no avoidance of suffering. This is what allows for unbelievable intimacy—unconditioned intimacy. There is no longer any urge to seek happiness through others, or avoid their pain. Equally, we aren't pushed away by other people's overwhelming joy, or attracted to their suffering!

So, nondual awareness doesn't tell us that suffering is an illusion. The bodhi mind doesn't stop the perception of suffering. We can't extract that from this state. Within the nondual sphere suffering is neither real nor unreal. Of course, it may be that our own or other people's suffering needs to reduce in intensity in order to see this. That's a judgment call that as practitioners and teachers we continually make.

A being who is abiding in the nondual doesn't help in a dualistic fashion, since there is no one helping anyone. When crystallized identities enter a nondual field of awareness and begin to interact with someone who is embodying that state, suffering can't be sustained. It dissolves into a space where there is neither suffering nor its absence, or at least the suffering is ameliorated. Nondual awareness creates a transformational field or vortex that gently or abruptly, but irrevocably, moves people toward radiant awareness.

The bodhi mind totally receives all that is. Everything comes through in a completely unfiltered and undistorted form because it is unbounded—it doesn't have any psychological and emotional barriers around it. It is totally defenseless; anything and everything can enter into it. And boundariless awareness isn't captivated or seduced by the idea of a state that's free of suffering. It's impossible to find a state that's free of suffering. We can't find any suffering in this moment. If we try to find what we labeled as suffering that happened in the past, we can't find that either. We can find the circumstances, the events, but no suffering. And similarly, when we are abiding as pure awareness, it's clear that we will never suffer in the future. We will think we might, but from this space it will be unreal. Likewise, of course, we won't be able to say that this thing called suffering has dropped out of the picture and isn't happening.

And at the same time, and in the same way, and at the same level, the bodhi mind sees that there are no *samsaras* (no states of suffering). They know that nothing can be found—*samsara* (suffering) and *nirvana* (its absence) are always hidden. This is what the bodhi mind brings to the world. In nondual Mahayana this is spoken about as the inseparable union of compassion (the profound insight that freedom from suffering can't be found) and wisdom (the deep and irrevocable insight that there is no suffering). This is the paradoxical state that bodhisattvas play in for eternity. This is the name of the game. Nondual awareness never finishes. It doesn't come into being, and it doesn't stop. There is no finish, no end to the game, because "nothing" is happening.

Some people try to find an intellectual resolution to this paradox by saying that suffering happens at the relative or conditioned level, and that freedom from suffering is the absolute or nondual state. But this completely misses the profundity of the nondual state. There are no two realities. This is neither one indivisible, homogenous thing, nor is it divisible. We can't say what this is. This is why, at this point, we can't say if we are suffering or free from suffering.

I am going on with this at some length because when it comes to the question of suffering, it's very easy to "think" about suffering in a dualistic way. That's natural since our lifelong enterprise has been to escape suffering, and most paths collude with this need and hope.

So how do we get inside this? We don't have to do anything. This is what's happening now.

What we call suffering is like a perturbation in the field or expanse of awareness. This perturbation is known and experienced as suffering by a crystallized identity, a person who has particular needs and preferences. So it's completely consistent for identities (like me) to crystallize within the expanse of awareness and for us to suffer in the myriad of ways that we do—through illness, fear, madness, death, etc. And at the same time, the bodhi mind sees that none of this is happening. There's no illness, no fear, no such thing as madness, and no death! Nondual awareness brings to this perturbation (that someone's suffering) the reflexive awareness that suffering is nowhere to be found, and that freedom from suffering equally can't be found. This is brought forth by the way the bodhi mind brings the vision of nothingness to everything that's experienced.

From within the bodhi mind, we are like a clearing—a centerless space—through which a universe moves. I am me, not because there is a unique me somewhere in here, but because the space I am reveals a unique and distinctive universe. Even though it seems I'm at the center of this, I'm not in here, and there is no center. This means that everyone who enters into the clearing that I am is as intimately related to me as my thoughts and bodily feelings. There's no difference. In the nondual state there is no inside or outside. There is no me in here who exists separate from everything else. It's impossible to locate where I stop and you begin. It's not just impossible to do this, there is no point where I stop and you begin. There's just this, which is everything. This is real intimacy. From within the nondual space we don't invite anything into our life. Everything is already here. We don't push anything away, and we don't hold onto anything. Of course, this doesn't mean that the structure of our relationships takes the same form with everyone. Of course it does not. The people with whom we live, work, and practice have a central role in our lives. Nonetheless, there is nothing artificial or contrived about our relationships.

In the nondual realm intimacy isn't a particular set of feelings, such as feeling really close or connected to someone, or feeling deeply committed or concerned about someone else's well-being. Nondual intimacy doesn't carve out a particular relationship with one or a few other people. Nondual intimacy is all encompassing and all embracing. Nothing is excluded. Everything in our known universe is touched with equal sensitivity and love. It's the experience of total interpenetration of our being to the point where the no one who we are expands to include everything.

Pure listening

The union of wisdom and intimacy begins with pure listening, which is about receiving what is being communicated exactly as it is, like a clear mirror. We listen without introducing any interference whatsoever. To do this, we listen from unconditioned awareness, where we are complete with everything that is being communicated. We don't need anything or anyone to be different.

In everyday communication, we are usually restricted to two types of listening: positive and negative listening.

Positive listening is a listening that is interested, attentive, and often empathetic. This type of listening validates what is being communicated and encourages the speaker to continue building their story.

Negative listening is a listening that is disinterested, distracted, or judgmental. This type of listening invalidates or negates what is being communicated, causing the speaker to defend or retract the story.

Pure listening doesn't validate or invalidate what is being said, nor does it encourage or subvert the communication. When we use pure listening to receive what's being communicated, we are neither interested nor disinterested in what the person is saying. We're not being particularly attentive to what the person is saying, nor are we unattentive. We're simply undistracted from the flow of what's happening, receiving it exactly as it comes.

In pure listening, neither the speaker nor the listener is treated as special. We don't have anything invested in the speaker. Nor does the listener experience any special interest in, or have any preference for, what is being said. For this reason, the listener has no concern for whether the communication continues or ends. The person talking could stop mid-sentence and the listener would remain unperturbed. Everything is complete as it is.

You may well ask, if in pure listening we're not giving the listener special importance, and if we're not listening with empathy, then how are we expressing compassion and staying connected within this interaction? From unconditioned awareness, we are able to remain completely present to the person who is sharing with us, taking in everything they are feeling and expressing as part of our own experience. If they are suffering, we are suffering. Our connection is profound, such that we experience what the other person is experiencing the moment they experience it.

From this shared space, the speaker has no doubt of the quality of the listening. Just as they experience that we are fully present in the space we share, they also receive the experience that we are unperturbed by what they are expressing. This is the union of love and wisdom. It's love without pity or sympathy, which only collude with and compound people's problems. In pure listening from unconditioned awareness, we express love in the form of presence and connection, while also transmitting the wisdom that everything is complete as it is. We know that the pain that the other person is experiencing from conditioned awareness isn't actually what it seems to be. It isn't real. In the nondual space, even the most intense pain cannot be identified. The speaker receives this wisdom, both verbally and non-verbally, from the way we respond (without reaction, judgment, or preference).

Pure listening creates a unique clearing where people's problems can simply evaporate into nothing. From unconditioned awareness, we can identify with another person's experience of their problem and then let it dissolve into our own sense of no-identity. Instead of interpreting their problem, projecting meaning onto it, and reconstructing it, we neither add nor subtract energy from their story. The speaker knows they are being heard, can feel the connection, but has nowhere to go with the story. It loses energy and significance. It dissolves out. The present space is now clear and fresh.

What's important to point out here is that although the dissolution of another person's problems is what can happen when we use pure listening, this isn't our goal. If we're holding a goal to dissolve the other person's problem, then we're not sharing the nondual state: we are creating an interference because we are "in time" ourselves, anticipating or hoping for a particular outcome. Rather, we surrender any need for the other person to be expressing anything other than what they are expressing. There is no work to be done. We just share our space within unconditioned awareness without any concern for whether the person's problem dissolves or not.

Energetic resonance

The Dzogchen tradition has a special term for the way that nondual awareness percolates through the field and gently awakens others to their natural state. They talk about the energetic resonance (*thugs rje*) of a master, such that when we enter the field of someone who is deeply abiding as boundless awareness, there is a type of energy transference or induction that invites us to enter this very same space.

When we are abiding in the nondual, we naturally share this state with others. No effort is required. It's like two bells resonating together. We don't even need to speak. By sharing space with others when we're in unconditioned awareness, we give them the chance to energetically entrain or attune to this space themselves.

Inviting people into our own state of serene completion is one of the greatest gifts we can give others. Particularly when people are upset or agitated, it can be surprising to stay totally connected without buying into the emotions that they are experiencing. Instead, we're fully composed and complete. There's no rescuing energy, no disapproval or attempt to correct what's happening. Because we remain connected with them through their disturbance, they become curious. They might think, "Wow. What's going on for this person? Why isn't this person trying to sort me out?" This leads the other person to explore what's really going on. By modeling our experience that there is actually no problem, we silently share our own serenity and lead them to enquire into this experience. They try it on, see how it feels.

Like pure listening, the effectiveness of this entrainment relies on the purity of our unconditioned experience. Regardless of how disturbed another person may be, our experience is uncompromised. This may mean that there is a creative dissonance between ourselves and the other people with whom we are in relationship. This dissonance invites the others to "step up" to meet us where we are at, which is unconditioned awareness. They may not make it all the way to unconditioned awareness on this occasion, but that's fine. It can happen in steps. The dissonance is useful and, at the same time, we need to watch that we keep other people with us, that it's not an unreachable stretch for them. If the dissonance is too great, they might perceive us as aloof and so we break rapport.

No separation: one consciousness

In the field of pure awareness there are no selves. There is no boundary between ourselves and others, no point where we stop and others begin. There's just a seamless field of awareness within which events arise.

As teacher or facilitators, we are not objectifying our students in any way. This creates intimacy. The communication has a real sense of moment-to-moment connection. Yet at the same time, we don't become lost in the story or the feelings that may arise due to this intimacy. Instead, we remain fully present in nondual awareness. Being fully present implies letting things be as they are. This space of nondual awareness brings us into the moment. In this moment there can never be a problem, as there is no time in the moment for a problem to occur.

In the sense of time, we are intimate and hearing clearly how the other person is experiencing their problem or challenge and how that exists for them in their mindstream. And at the same time, we're fully presencing nondual awareness, which is outside of time. We're resting in the eternal now in which there are no problems. Our intimacy allows the other person easier access to the nondual space. The fact that intimacy and full presence occur simultaneously allows us to move back and forth effortlessly between them. There's an intimate dance between two people, neither of whom can find themselves or the other. It can be delightful.

S: Do you see any benefit in dissolving all of the relative structures into unconditioned awareness?

P: No, none at all.

S: Here, right here, we have the distinctions of subject and object—me and you. This in itself is perfect and complete. But it seems we can also take this further and dissolve the boundaries of self and other, me and you, subject and object.

P: The boundary was never there. We are here and not here as well. If you want, this is the coincident of the absolute and the relative. You're there. I'm here. You can't be here because I am here. But if I try and find where I am, I'm nowhere. I can't find myself. And if you try to find yourself, you can't find yourself. Nor is there any barrier or division between you and me. But you're there, not me!

S: It's a phenomenological distinction, an experiential distinction, of me being here and you being there. How do we dissolve that?

P: Again, we don't need to. It's not there.

S: The phenomenological boundary can be dissolved.

P: Where is the boundary?

S: I guess the boundary is in the contact between me and you.

P: Where is the plane of contact?

S: It's in our relationship with each other.

P: But where am I and where are you?

S: This person [points to himself]. And that person [points to Peter].

P: Again. Where are you? Where am I?

S: You're sitting in that chair. And I'm sitting in this chair.

P: But where is the "I" that experiences you? And where is the "I" that experiences me?

S: I don't know where you are. But you are still there and I am here.

P: Yes, exactly.

Relating to people as streams of consciousness

From one point of view, a person is a beginningless and endless stream of consciousness. As a nondual facilitator, I find it useful to relate with people as a stream of consciousness. The transmission is then a question of introducing nondual awareness into a stream of consciousness. A stream of consciousness has all sorts of patterning within it. An infinite number of things can happen within a stream of consciousness, including traumas.

Relating with people as a stream of consciousness helps us in four ways:

1. We don't become so tied up with personal dramas as they are occurring.

2. It helps to cut through the idea that we know the inner workings and inner dynamics of the person we're in relationship with. It corrects the tendency to get involved at a level of personality, without denying the complexity of what is happening at

the conditioned level. There is no denial of the complexity between thoughts and feelings and experiences.

3. When you are viewing someone as a stream of consciousness, it's much like canoeing down a river. Anything can happen on the river from one moment to the next. Relating with a person as a stream of consciousness allows us the freedom and the time to introduce them to nondual awareness. Freedom because we don't view the other as fixed, and time because each moment is a new opportunity. Even if we can only introduce a flicker of consciousness itself, over time we can learn to support that awareness in a more stable way.

4. When you are viewing someone as a stream of consciousness, you are seeing the contents of awareness just as contents and nothing more, because there is no fixed person involved. Everything that is happening within this flow is the contents of consciousness, so you're not seeing a person within it. The person is the totality of the contents of that consciousness. This is a gracious way to see people because we view them as a totality of events that are happening, not in a fixed and permanent way, but rather as ever-changing streams. Our panoramic awareness gives everyone the freedom to change.

A dialog:

S: As nondual therapists, do we address the ego *per se*?

P: There is no ego, so we're not looking for it, or relating to it. We are relating with someone who exists with all his or her patterns and preferences, and who can't be found at the same time. In a way there is a two-channel communication. There's a simultaneous process of identification and disidentification.

Nondual wisdom sees through the reality of the client and what he or she is experiencing. But at the same time, there's a total identification, recognition, and appreciation of everything that is happening for the client, at least as far as we can receive this and take it in. There's a deep connection and this is the manifestation of love. As therapists, we bring all our capacities to this relationship: the emotional, cognitive, and nondual. We weave a connection with our clients that transports them into a state of consciousness that lies beyond the cycle of pleasure and pain.

We're continually intersecting with mindstreams. I'm joining your experience right now. Our streams of awareness are mixing and merging. The most beautiful contribution we can make to someone else's mindstream is to support that mindstream in reaching a place where there is no suffering and no possibility for suffering. Through a process of authentic communication and natural resonance, we raise a client's awareness to a space where it's impossible to have a problem.

It's a beautiful moment when we can bring someone to the point where they're no longer able to suffer. If we invite them to try to suffer and to reconstitute the problem, it's impossible to recreate it because we're inhabiting a different state of consciousness. All our faculties and abilities are functional; yet it's impossible to suffer. If someone were to say, "Look! I'll give you $10,000 if you can convince me you can suffer," we'd have to decline the offer.

S: Could you say we are bearing witness to the basic goodness of others, seeing their authentic nature, even if they haven't found it right now?

P: Yes. We're connecting with the potential for others to realize buddha nature in this very moment. We know they're going to make the journey into this state. We don't know when or if they're going to make it with us. That's not the point. It's not our business or responsibility to know. We know they will make that journey, and they may complete it in the next instant. This is everyone's potential, and that's all that's required for us to be here, withholding nothing and giving everything.

Listening to, and engaging with, non-verbal conversations

Silent conversations pervade our interactions with other people. They can saturate the interpersonal field. As coaches and facilitators in nondual work, we can become aware of the many different types of "listening." There's the listening we have about ourselves, to our own thoughts and stories about who we think we are and what we're doing. Then there's the listening to our inner conversation that we have about what others think of us. For example, we might be monitoring whether or not what we are saying or transmitting is being understood or accepted. Another type of listening is the listening that we think others are having about what they think we are thinking about them!

In these silent conversations, perceptions occur and constructions are built, story upon story. In the conditioned state, we are deeply engrossed in these hidden conversations. In nondual work, our awareness of these conversations is heightened. Within our communication, we listen for thoughts and constructions, whether they are our own or those of the people we are working with.

Suspension

From time to time, perhaps two or three times in a session, an experience arises in the room generally, often more intensely for the person I am interacting with, that I call "suspension." I just note here that many of the movements in the style of nondual transmission I'm describing in this

Guide happened before I had concepts to identify them (i.e., distinctions) or even before I was aware of them. The distinction of "suspension" or "being suspended" is a good example of this. I became aware of it when someone asked me what was happening after a particular interchange with a course participant. I looked at what she was referring to and thought, "Okay, that's what I would call suspension."

Suspension happens when someone asks a question, expecting a response, and nothing happens. The question stays suspended in the air, as it were, and a gap is created because for a few moments, perhaps a minute, the mind doesn't know where to go or what to do. This isn't a contrived or intentional action. It arises naturally. It isn't used as a technique or a tool. We simply see this phenomenon happening. There's nothing more to do with it. Suspension happens because a facilitator and participant are in different states of consciousness. When we are facilitating nondual work, there's often very little material available with which to construct responses to questions. Questions land in no-mind. We don't have any raw thought material available to fashion into an explanation or interpretation. We'd have to shift gears into a more conditioned state of cognition, and this would be quite unnatural. We hear the question but nothing emerges from our side, and it creates a phenomenon that leaves the person who asked the question feeling a bit suspended, as if in space, thinking, "What happened there? What's going on?"

Moments of suspension can take away people's reference points. They create an opportunity for people to enter our uncluttered mind. Because there's a natural care and respect in this work, "not responding" isn't interpreted as being abrupt, rude, or dismissive. Also, there's a natural closure to these moments of "being suspended" because we either say something, or the question evaporates into thin air without needing to be answered.

Sometimes I'll say, "There's nothing coming up for me in relationship to that question at the moment. I think something will probably come up; I can't guarantee it. I think something more needs to happen, and then I may have a response." Very often after 10 or 30 minutes, something will have happened in the room—in the here and now—that lets me respond using what is actually manifesting right now, rather than needing to go into the mind and memory in order to find a response.

Suspension occurs because we're not answering a question within the same frame of reference in which the question was asked. Sometimes I find it helpful to explain the distinction between "making a report" and "asking a question." If someone is simply reporting what's happening, we can just listen. We don't need to respond. We don't have to add anything to what they've said by offering something from our own experience, giving some feedback, or asking a question. Often people just want to move through the mental elaboration and complexity that can happen in their minds and conversations. Talking out loud helps this movement.

Allowing silence to emerge in an uncontrived manner

I often find myself with nothing to say and nothing to do. This silence emerges naturally because there's very little interpretation happening. Inner stillness is reflected as outer silence. Part of what allows the silence to be there is a rich sense of being connected with people. There's a depth of the communication happening within the silence. It's possible to be in natural silent communion with people, some with their eyes open, others with their eyes closed, for 20 or 30 minutes, just appreciating the space that we are sharing individually and together.

People know that they can stop being silent at any time. We aren't being silent for a predetermined amount of time. This allows the silence to be natural, comfortable, effortless, and potentially very deep, because nothing is being forced. There's no pressure. This is natural meditation: deep meditation without meditating. Even if I have my eyes closed, people know they can still talk to me; they do. They can ask questions, or share their experience, because in the nondual space nothing can be interrupted or disturbed.

Playing at the edges of silence

Silent conversations make a powerful contribution to our nondual work. In psychology, it's often thought to be more useful to vocalize our silent thoughts and work with them in open dialog. There is an obvious and vital role for dialog in nondual inquiry. However, silent conversations can be a powerful way of invoking a form of deconstruction in which many people are dissolving different structures, or points of reference, at the same time. In the nondual space, we don't need to rush into verbal exchange. We don't need to keep the dialog going. Remember, we aren't conditioning the space, meaning we're not pushing it in the direction of speech or silence.

As facilitators of this work, there is always the option of letting participants play out their silent conversations, giving them the opportunity to dissolve their own fixations. Let's look at a quite dynamic silent conversation that opens into nondual awareness.

Within a quiet period shared between you and a participant, you might begin to sense that a participant looks poised to say something, but is unsure about whether to talk, or perhaps what to say. Here you are already playing at the edges of the silence. Together, you are in the ambiguous place of not knowing what is going to happen next. You might be thinking, "It seems like he wants to say something, but he doesn't know what to say." You might be contemplating whether or not there is anything to contribute to what's happening. You might be wondering, "Is there anything I need to do right now other than just being here. He clearly looks like he's ready to say something. I can see I'm not encouraging him, but I'm certainly not suppressing his need either." You are dancing together in a place where talking may or may not happen. Neither of you know. This is quite intimate, and often becomes light and playful.

At the same time, your participant is in his own silent conversation. He may be thinking, "She [you—the facilitator] sees me. She seems to know I have a question. I wonder why she's not asking me what I'm thinking or what's happening for me. She seems okay with it being just like this. This is odd. Perhaps, I don't need to ask my question. If I ask, I wonder what she will say? She'll probably say, 'What's happening for you right now?' I don't know what I'd say. I'm confused. This is different. I don't know whether to talk or not. I'm not sure if what I wanted to share is important or not. Perhaps it isn't. Now I can't even remember what it was that I wanted to say. This is really weird. I don't know what's going on. But it feels okay. Yes, really okay. It's beautiful in some way, to be in this close communication without saying anything."

Often, these exchanges end in an exchange of smiles and laughter—and we don't even know what we are laughing about—which makes it all the more ridiculous and wonderful!

As we can see, there are two types of silent conversations: conversations we have with ourselves, and conversations we have with others in which we speculate about, or anticipate, how they might respond to what we could say or do. You might think, "What's the value in just thinking what we are thinking, as opposed to verbalizing what we are thinking? Surely in the context of spiritual work, the more a teacher knows what I'm thinking the better!"

The power of silent conversations rests in the fact that people can play through in detail what might happen *if* they say something, without saying a word. In a group setting, multiple conversations occur simultaneously. Of course, these are not the same conversations that would play out if they were spoken. If people have some experience of deconstructive inquiry in their verbal conversations with a teacher, they can continue to deconstruct their beliefs in the imaginary conversations that happen in their mind. It's valuable for people to experience how their constructions can dissolve without any overt intervention by a teacher. It gives people an experience of autonomy and independence.

When people aren't given the same level of content or type of feedback that they normally receive in a conversation, they may begin to wonder what to speak about, or if there's anything to speak about at all. They become engaged in silent conversations with themselves that can take them all the way through to unconditioned awareness.

In the same way that participants engage in silent conversation within themselves and with facilitators, facilitators also participate in silent conversations with participants. Many conversations are happening at the same time, as you scan the room and take people in where they are. These are conversations in which you speculate about where a participant is, what's happening for them, whether there is anything you need to do. Within the silence you might be thinking, "I could ask him if he can enhance what he's experiencing in this moment. Will that just give him something to think about, or will it take him beyond his thoughts? I can't tell. I don't think there's anything to say at the moment. Obviously there's not, because I'm not saying anything."

The value in letting conversations unfold silently is that they allow us to dance in a set of open-ended possibilities without prematurely conditioning the space by asking a question, or making an observation that's simply a reflection of our own insecurity. On the other hand, this needs to be balanced with an awareness of the fact that we can also protect ourselves from other people's judgments and perceptions by keeping our mouths closed. In nondual inquiry we're often dancing at the confluence of the conditioned and the unconditioned, sensing the influence of our energy field in activating and releasing fixations.

This is a way of connecting with people at the transition point where someone moves from being silent to speaking. Here we are playing with "not knowing" around the themes of "Am I going to talk first, or are you going the say something?" "Are you going to talk or not?" "Is anyone going to talk?" We are also playing with that dimension of the nondual space in which we neither encourage nor discourage sharing. This play can go on for several minutes.

Adjusting to silence

In Java, Indonesia, there are mystical communities who spend time silently together after evening mealtime. They aren't meditating, nor are they relaxing or snoozing. They're sitting attentively together in shared silence, just being with each other appreciating existence. They may be smiling, gazing at each other, or staring into space. They are completely at ease with sharing the silence.

For most of us in the West, we don't have a model for collective silence. To many, sitting in a space of alert silence with others could seem a radical idea. We've never had the opportunity to get comfortable in or be empowered by shared silence. Sure, we might have shared a long distance car ride with someone, finally exhausting all topics of conversation and settling into a tired and unconsciously agreed silence. A justification for silence is necessary for us to feel comfortable. There's also a central activity (driving) and a goal (to get to our destination) that distracts us from any concern about the silence. But nondual silence is very different. It's the silence that arises because there is nothing we need to be sharing. We are sharing in nondual awareness, and this is absolutely all that needs to happen.

Participants who are new to nondual work may need time to adjust to the abundance of silence that arises in this work. Some people are more likely to relate to the setting for nondual work as a place of discussion. In this mindset, they might feel the need to continue the flow of conversation to feel comfortable. Likewise, people who are new to facilitating nondual work might be more familiar with using discussion in their other work, allowing few, if any, silent intervals. So there can be a similar adjustment period for new facilitators too.

For people new to this work, silence can exacerbate their feelings and fixations. If they feel that they are not permitted to speak or that what they are contributing is not being properly recognized, they may sit in a heavy state, creating all sorts of meaning about the space and the facilitator. This type of silence can be oppressive. As facilitators, we are sensitive to all types of silence. This is the type of silence that might prompt us to reconnect with the participant, either verbally or with a non-verbal glance or smile.

For people who have practiced meditation in the past, they can obtain comfort in the nondual setting when they tell themselves that it is about "meditation." But there is a difference. In nondual work, there is no requirement to be either speaking or not speaking. Silence arises, whether as a result of meditation or simply because people are sitting quietly and don't happen to be speaking at that moment. Silence arises. That's just what seems to happen.

Communicating in deep silence

People who are familiar with nondual teachings often tend to associate this work with deep silence. Some people, in fact, tend to identify nondual work with an unusual level and depth of silence. Although dialog also arises, the setting and the facilitator's minimal input allows unusual depths of silence to arise naturally within the shared space. As facilitators, all we're doing is allowing people to rest in the present moment. We provide little, if any, content. For much of the time, there seems very little for us to do or say, very little for people to build on, to create meaning. In time, they run out of things to try to understand. If they raise something from the past or the future, they can see that the facilitator doesn't seem to give these thoughts much weight, so they're left with the present space.

People then have the opportunity to play with this space. They can fight it or they can be with "what is." Sometimes there may be periods of boredom and tiredness. Perhaps after a break period, the space can seem completely different. Suddenly, there's a profound depth to the space. Participants can look at each other within the space with wonder and love. They're neither bored, nor highly stimulated. They're just sitting in alert presence, with great appreciation for the space. In retreats, this type of blissful consciousness can continue for hours. It's not the experience of unconditioned awareness, however, because there's enjoyment, which makes it a positive experience; whereas unconditioned awareness is neither positive nor negative.

Many forms of nondual teaching produce periods of natural silence, and it's important we understand the function and potency of this experience. In a retreat setting people can spend hours resting in subtle states of bliss-consciousness. In one-on-one sessions people can spend many minutes in deep aesthetic appreciation, as their thoughts dissolve into unconditioned awareness.

In nondual work, silence is equally as potent as dialog in terms of its capacity to enhance or diminish the experience of unconditioned awareness. The creation of meaning is just one possibility, but we aren't compelled to make everything meaningful. It's also possible to just be with "what is" without needing to understand it or make it significant. Resting in unconditioned awareness gives us less to think about because it is ultimately unrelated to our thinking, and the experience is more easily entered when our minds are relatively quiet and serene. When someone just listens to us, without adding to, or taking away from what we're thinking or saying, we aren't sure what to think about or even whether we need to think about anything at all! In the midst of this ambiguity, we can sink into a state of deep, refreshing silence.

These periods of silence can test the depth of the nondual experience because they challenge our need for structure. When we rest in unconditioned awareness, it's sometimes impossible to generate the type of conversations that are expected of us. We find that we don't need to respond, and yet in the absence of a verbal reply, everything is communicated and taken care of. We don't contrive to produce an experience of resting in silence. It arises naturally in this work.

Not all experiences of silence decondition our minds. Silence often does the opposite: it can exacerbate and amplify people's fixations. If people feel uncomfortable, silence can intensify feelings, especially if students feel that the opportunities for communicating are being curtailed or suppressed. Or, perhaps they're feeling comfortable, sitting quietly, and then at a certain point they become uncomfortable. This happens all the time. In this instance, if the silence continues, it becomes oppressive rather than liberating. It can send people into an even stronger identification with their discomfort.

Working creatively with silence

It is clear that silence is important in this work because it can either move people toward unconditioned awareness or, if people are uncomfortable with the silence, it can move them away from this state. For this reason, it is important that we—as facilitators—know how to relate to, work with, and "be with" silence. In particular, we need to distinguish between the naturally arising silence and the times when we, ourselves, are "doing silence." Imposed silence is constraining and counterproductive to the nondual space. When we are abiding as nondual awareness, there is no preference for either talking or not talking.

Because the experience of silence can move people toward or away from unconditioned awareness, an important dimension of nondual inquiry lies in "knowing how to be with silence." In order to "be with" silence, we need to understand silence. When we understand silence, we're able to take ourselves and others into deeper states of natural contemplation. When we don't understand silence, or if we're at all uncomfortable with the silence that emerges in this work, the periods of silence can devolve into something analogous to "doing silence" rather than "being silence."

Sometimes "nothing" happens in the periods of silence. This is wonderful! At other times the silences are rich with communication, which is also wonderful! But, silence only happens with the depth and naturalness that it does through an awareness of the silent conversations that may be happening. In order to work creatively with silence, we need to be sensitive to the different types, or nuances, of silence. For example, there's the silence of confusion in which people don't talk because they don't know what to say. There's an impulse to communicate, but people aren't sure what they want or need to say. By contrast, there's the silence that results when people are withholding, either through fear of the consequences of communicating, or through embarrassment. The sweetest silence is the one that emanates from nondual awareness—when there's nothing to do and nothing to say. We can sense when someone is resting in "what is" because there's no need to communicate anything.

Of course, sometimes the experience of "silent sharing" moves into a more private experience in which our eyes may close and we're no longer in obvious contact with those around us. If our experience moves naturally in this direction, we go with the flow, without anticipation or expectation.

Our capacity to work silently is limited by our attachment to talking and not talking. It's obvious that if we're attached to our own or someone else's talking, we predispose ourselves to interrupt the experience of silence, either by saying something ourselves, or by encouraging others to speak. But an attachment to not talking, to not sharing or communicating, also disturbs the experience of deep silence. If we're attached to the experience of meditative silence, or interior stillness, we're still exercising a preference. If, in any moment, we'd prefer the experience of silence to continue, or stop, this acts to condition the next moment and flattens the potency of the silence to accommodate everything: more silence or renewed speaking. If we're bored, or waiting for someone to speak, or hoping that no one will interrupt the silence, we're conditioning the space. Attempting to control the occurrence or duration of these periods of silence—to "do silence," as it were—is counterproductive. The nondual experience neither discourages nor encourages, speech or silence.

Discerning different qualities of silence: sensing if people are in deep meditation or protecting their beliefs

It isn't difficult to read the quality of the stillness within a person. The contrast between being in deep meditation and having a question on the tip of one's tongue, but holding back from verbalizing it through fear of being inappropriate, is clear. Though in both cases the person is silent. People also suppress the energy for expressing themselves because they fear that I know that nondual inquiry has the capacity to dissolve fixed positions and strong opinions. People can keep things to themselves because they sense that important beliefs and experiences can be equalized in the sphere of nondual awareness.

If I sense that someone is feeling nervous about talking, or they're silent because they're protecting something, then I stay in rich communication with them in the silence. I neither encourage nor discourage communication, but give them the message that we're here in relationship, so that they're not feeling isolated. I do this with a look, glancing their way, making simple eye contact. I'm continually "in touch" with people, looking backward and forward across the room.

Often people in the room are in very different places; some are exquisitely content, with bliss written all over their face and a smile on their lips. At the same time, other people may be confused, bored, or angry. The challenge is to be available and supportive to those who are struggling, in ways that don't undercut those who are drinking from the river of nondual awareness.

When people are struggling, it's often sufficient to communicate non-verbally that we know what's happening for them. The main thing that we're communicating is that we are not unaware. And yet, we are not compelled to do anything with their discomfort. They are simply aware that I acknowledge that there's something challenging them at the moment. If you can meet their gaze, then often that's all that's needed.

Sometimes, however, people are in real protest mode. They have their eyes closed and are frowning, and there's not a lot to do except to let them do that without judgment. We recognize and understand that the work is different and challenging, particularly because we're working at the result level. Therefore it's absolutely natural for people to be reacting in many different ways, including getting frustrated, anxious, fearful, and angry. All of these reactions are totally natural responses, because what's happening may be quite different from people's expectations and preferences. They are not getting answers or strategies about how to make their life better. There are no promises for anything. It's a leap into presencing the nondual—seeing the completeness of the present moment.

From time to time, if I feel like it's becoming a pressure cooker for someone, that it's no longer constructive, or they're experiencing a very strong reaction, and they feel they're not allowed to speak, then I will say, "How is it going for you?" or "What's happening for you at the moment?" We can detect this pressure mainly from people's facial expressions, which feel really heavy.

Reading the depth and stability of interiorized presence in people's foreheads

We can feel when people have moved into an interiorized space, presencing pure awareness, by the energy in their foreheads. When we take people in, we can see the stability of their inner centeredness and presencing by observing the area about one-and-a-half inches just above and between their eyes. We don't look for this. We just see it. There is an obvious visual difference between someone with his or her eyes closed but still engaged in thought and images, and someone who is in a state of deep, inner stillness. We see the difference. It is obvious and clear.

When there is a ground swell of interiorized presencing in the room, then I might follow suit and enter into that state in which we're presencing the nondual with very few relativities arising—very little thinking, or where thinking just dissolves on the spot. This is the self-liberation of thoughts. Thoughts are sparse, feelings are simple sensations, and the heart is at peace. It's not a concentrated state. It's not *samadhi*. People can instantly arise from this state without needing time to adjust. There's no feeling of losing something when we reconnect with the outside world. No going back and thinking, "That was great. I wish I could have stayed there longer." People move into "eyes open and talking mode" without any sense of discontinuity because there is a clear awareness that "This" neither endures nor ceases.

Serenity—thinning out our thoughts

In traditional teachings, serenity practice is likened to allowing the clouds to disperse so that we can see the sun. In this metaphor, the clouds are our thoughts and the sun is unconditioned awareness. The best way to gain access to unconditioned awareness is via a serene state in which the density of our thinking is low. In nondual inquiry, the process we use to do this is what I like to refer to as "thinning out the thoughts." That is, we slow down our thinking and allow spaces and silences, gently clearing the way to unconditioned consciousness. We cultivate serenity in two stages: first, by giving people "nothing to think about," then by allowing people to "be with nothing."

Nothing to think about

For thoughts to be generated, we need to provide content and give them some importance. The nondual setting does the opposite: it doesn't feed our minds with content, and it doesn't give our thoughts any weight. Without content and weight, our thought generation and story-building has no traction. It's like a fire that is running low on kindling. Eventually it dies out. If we jump in, supporting the story with interpretations and further analysis, we add fuel to the fire, reigniting the issues as if they are real.

Just as people can need time to adjust to silence, so they can need time to adjust to a reduction in content. In response to no content, people can become bored, sleepy, or agitated. Some people may find it challenging to stay conscious when they have little or nothing to entertain them. It can be challenging to remain aware and awake in the absence of any cognitive stimulation.

If we remove content too suddenly, it's as though the ground has shifted from underneath them. They can become fearful about what is happening. Some may find the experience frightening or threatening. Therefore, as facilitators we need to be sensitive to this, only gradually reducing our input. Just as fasting can be easier if we gradually eat less and less over a period of time, "thinning out the thoughts" by reducing conceptual input can gradually prepare our minds for thinking about nothing.

For example, we might commence a session with a minimal introduction and gently monitor the space, allowing content to arise as a way of bringing coherence and connection within the field. The key is that we're not colluding or sympathizing with people's stories: we're not doing anything to support or help build such structures. Some questions, such as "Can we do more of this?" or "What would be happening now if we weren't doing what we're doing?" can help to reduce the density of people's interpretations.

For the facilitator, it's a skillful balance between providing just enough cognitive input, while at the same time providing a space that can invite people to experience serenity. Remember, thoughts can still exist. We don't have to remove every cloud to see the sun.

Serenity is cultivated not only in our private contemplative practice, but also in the workshops, and other group and one-on-one settings. In nondual work, the practice of slowing down the mind and thinning out thoughts often happens in the transactional relationship between teacher and student. We need to calibrate the level of cognitive input we provide as we skillfully introduce people to inner peace. There is no need to eliminate thoughts completely and no need to understand what is happening in the present moment.

Being with nothing

The second way we can allow people to thin out their thoughts is by giving them an opportunity to "be with nothing." In this work, we create an environment within which people are invited to be with nothing for minutes and then hours. From our side there is nothing to think or know. This creates a gradient that invites people into not knowing and effortless being. By simply being with people, for an extended period, doing nothing, we automatically invite them into unconditioned awareness. The lack of positive and negative feedback provided in a workshop produces a creative ambiguity which challenges fixed ways of seeing and interpreting things. The ambiguity of the space, the lack of clear markers about what we are doing, and the absence of anything we could or should be learning, supports the natural deconstruction and dissolution of fixations.

Nothing is hidden: you don't need to go looking

A major structure that keeps people on the path is the belief that things are hidden from our experience. This occurs in two ways: we feel that things are hidden from us at the conditioned level and that unconditioned awareness is also hidden. At the conditioned level, we can feel that we need to discover our shadow, latent impulses, unconscious motives, etc. before we can really know the nondual. This keeps us involved with psychological work. We find ourselves looking into our past, our own and other people's real intentions, and our dreams. We do this in order to discover some information, guidance, directions, or experience that we feel is missing. For as long as we feel that something is hidden, then we're on a path and not in the state of fulfillment; therefore, we are not feeling complete.

We can forget that there is no such thing as fully knowing the nondual. There are no graduations. Certainly it can be more fully embodied, but we never need to know more than that which is here right now, or in every moment, to presence the nondual. When we need to know, there is a gap between now and a more ideal state.

When we are naturally awake, nothing is missing. Nothing more (or less) is happening than what is happening. In this work, we can trust that we will see whatever we need to see or know because nothing is ever hidden.

When we're functioning dualistically, it's easy to feel that "Fulfillment isn't happening now," or "This isn't it," or "It's somewhere else, and (hopefully) it will happen but it's not happening yet." Within a causal framework, we think that various things have to be put in place: "I have to become less fixated," or "I have to do this and that," or "Conditions have to be right in order to presence nondual awareness." We might also think, "It's here, but I can't see it; it's hidden from me," or "I'm still under the influence of dualistic thinking, attached to my thoughts, still caught by the illusion of a personal self. Something is here but I'm not getting it. I can't see it. I need to see through something. I need to change my state of consciousness. I'm not getting it because I'm not in the right place within myself."

The idea that nothing is hidden collapses the belief that something more is happening in this moment than what is being received. In nondual coaching we invite people to connect with what is, because we know that nothing is hidden. There is nothing behind this experience, nothing within it or outside of it. This is it, nothing more is happening.

Some nondual systems even collude with this dualistic way of thinking. There is the world of thought-perceptions, and people can think that the ultimate reality is hidden behind this. People can think that the world of appearances in some way obscures a direct appreciation of ultimate reality. This way of thinking sets people up to see conditioned phenomena as problematic, as obscuring the fact that we are naturally aware. This creates a weird impulse to "see through the world of appearance," and "to see through our thinking."

We may believe that unconditioned awareness is constant and unchanging, while everything around us is constantly changing. People can infer that because the unconditioned is contentless and without structure, our connection with shapes and colors, sounds and tastes, feelings and thoughts, contradict nondual awareness. People can think that they have to see the unchanging in some way. The paradigm of conditioned sensory experience is transferred onto the unconditioned. Instead of just knowing that there is nothing to see, that it can't be here, we still try to look for it, which is an impossibility. Because it's not a thing, it means it's impossible to find. The very process of looking for it is the act of missing it. The sure-fire way to miss the nondual is to look for it.

This way of thinking makes the nondual mysterious and difficult to fathom. People feel that something needs to change. They need to see that the world of thought-perceptions is somehow unreal. People can think they need to see things as though they are in a dream. The texts say that, but how to do it?

As coaches, we see the dualistic tendency to separate thought-perceptions from nondual awareness in a way that makes it inaccessible. We work to clarify that nondual awareness doesn't require any change at all. Nothing needs to change. There's nothing to see through because there is nothing to see. Things don't become transparent or opaque. Within the world of thought-perceptions there's multiplicity and each thing is distinct. There is no blurring (unless it is blurry) and everything is highly differentiated, exactly as it is, and at the same time nothing is happening.

When people are sharing, we listen for how they are involved in this construction of trying to look behind their experience for something else that's not obvious. As a facilitator, it's just a matter of tuning into the energy of the student to see if they are looking for something as though it's hidden or lost: using their mind, using their thoughts, trying to understand the non-conceptual, trying to understand the no-mind from mind. When someone says they're not getting this, we feel and see where they are looking. Sometimes it's referred to in more visual terms and happens as a more visual, or seeing process. They may be asking, "Where is it?"

To say the nondual is hidden is like saying, "I've lost something. I have NO idea what it is that I've lost, but I can't find it." This is absurd and frustrating. When we present the nondual as formless we clarify that it can't be seen or known because there is nothing there. We clearly say it's not located anywhere. No one has ever found it because it doesn't exist. It's not a thing.

S: I hear what you are saying about how looking stops me from seeing—from being with this. It's like I think it's somewhere.

P: Yes. And now?

S: I can't get through this barrier of looking: it's not here; it's somewhere else.

P: No, it's not here.

S: It's not here? I thought that's what your were saying: that it's already here; we don't have to go looking.

P: No. It's not here. It's not there. It's nowhere. It's invisible. It's clearer than glass. This is why it's sometimes called the "open secret."

S: It's wherever I'm looking.

P: In a way, yes. But it has nothing to do with what you are seeing.

S: I get it…. That's very relaxing.

P: Hmm. It is.

Distinguishing between a report and a request

Often when people are sharing their experience, they are just giving you a readout of what's happening to them, like a weather report. "It's a bit stormy in here." If we don't recognize that it's just a report, it's easy to jump in and think we need to do something. If it's just a report, we listen and perhaps acknowledge it (thanks for sharing, etc.), but don't need to do anything with it. We don't make a problem out of nothing, or when there isn't one. This again is a feature of working at the result level. If we aren't sure, we can ask for clarification. "I'm not sure if you are telling me that something is wrong at the moment?"

Sometimes, a request to fulfill a need is made strongly and we may ask ourselves, "How much need is here?" Someone may need something from us that will come up later in a workshop, such as pure listening, natural release, or a specific koan, etc. It's important to consider these things.

In *Radiant Mind* work, we offer a training in needing less—how to be complete without our needs being fulfilled—and to find fulfillment and completion through connection with the nondual. While always appreciating the structure and the energy of need in your student, you are working out how much of that need you are required to fulfill in order to move into desirelessness. That's what you're working with. You might ask yourself, "Can I do something?" or "I sense a strong need here, and to what extent do I respond to that?"

Realizing it is serving their cultivation of the nondual state, to remain consistent in the exploration of desirelessness, we balance working with their need and not acquiescing to their need. You're not saying *no* or depriving them; rather you are listening to the need and assessing how to skillfully honor their need as a natural doorway into the nondual state. Being mindful of the obstacles of "needing to know" and "needing to do" can help keep you and your student from getting pulled into their needs.

We find a natural doorway without giving someone 100 percent of what they want, since this just conditions the need to want more. We give people an aspect of what they want, continuing to create the gateless gate, always being on the path, opening into nondual awareness from wherever we are. Essentially, we encourage nondual awareness *wherever* people are, rather than conditioning the idea that something more is needed before we can be complete.

When to use "I," "you," and "we"

In the process of sharing the nondual state with others, you need to be sensitive to your use of the pronouns "I," "you," and "we" because they can imply inclusion and exclusion.

If you say "we" and the person you are talking to doesn't feel that they are anywhere near the state you're describing, your use of the pronoun "we" will only confirm that you are on different planets. Instead of being an invitation to join you, your speaking will alienate them. They'll begin to think, "Well, that's fine for you but I'm nowhere near that state. I don't know what you are talking about."

If someone is close to the experience, then you can begin talking in terms of "we" or "you." It can help nudge your student closer. When you are both clearly sharing the space, you will be talking in terms of "we." You could say, "Though actually neither of us is here, that's what we are sharing." You'll be dancing in the paradoxes together.

You can find yourself alternating between "I" and "we" and "you" in concert with where your student is, vis-à-vis, sharing the space of nondual awareness with you.

The nondual use of "I" and "you"

The use of personal pronouns can reify the experience that we are someone. We need to acknowledge and have a way of distinguishing between different streams of being (embodied minds). The words "I," "you," "we," "Susan," etc. identify different sembodied minds. There is nothing intrinsically wrong with the words. They simply validate speaking at the conditioned level.

Some people feel that the use of "I" and "you" can solidify the sense of a subject, someone, a findable "I," and a findable "you." Some people try to develop a nondual language that begins to avoid the use of "I" and "you." This feels artificial to me. For me, the use of "I" and "you" doesn't seem to be a real problem. I notice that I use them continually: "I'm doing this" and "I'm doing that." I don't find other pronouns like he, she, we, and us, etc. to be particularly problematic either. We have to have some starting point, to work out where bodies will be in time and location, as in saying, "Hey, will you be here tomorrow?" "I" and "you" let us do things, but it doesn't mean we can find a subject. Nor does it signal a disconnection from nondual awareness. Nothing is lost, there is nothing to return to, nothing needs to change in order to presence nondual awareness, and nothing needs to change in the way we use "I" and "you." So my main point here is that we need to use "I" and "you" because they are central ingredients in living at the conditioned level, and essential for coordination and action.

At the same time, we cannot find the "I" and the "you." They are completely unproblematic as long as we remember that there is no experiencer, and the attempt to find one is futile. In the presence of that insight it is easy. The terms "I" and "you" are problematic if they are showing up for someone as an obstacle to resting in nondual awareness.

Distinction between being and having an identity

Let's correct an assumption that some people in nondual practices seem to hold that there is a problem in having an identity. One might think it's a problem having a body, history, memories, age, and other qualities that constitute being an individual. Being an individual means having a unique identity.

In the type of nondualism we explore in *Radiant Mind* and *Natural Awakening*, there is nothing intrinsically problematic about having an identity, so long as we realize that there is no one who's having an identity. Even though there is no one who has an identity, there is an identity nonetheless. So there is no necessity at all to try to be no one and try to not have an identity. I'm not sure what it would mean to not have an identity, as it just reinforces the identity of being no one, a someone being no one, which reinforces the someone! And the point is that the nondual space allows for all possibilities, allows for all identities. It allows for the identity of Peter Fenner, for example, to change over time without that being problematic. It allows the identity we call Peter Fenner to acquire new experiences or possible futures without that idea disturbing nondual awareness. To feel we have to be no one to presence the nondual at the level of body, feelings, and thoughts, places a condition on the nondual experience.

S: I feel quite emotional about this. I've been resisting being a teacher for many years, and the resistance has been coming up again this morning. I feel that teaching is an escape. We're all sitting here going into "nothing matters." I don't want to let go of my thoughts or my feelings. I don't want to let go of my body. This feels wonderful, but I also feel I am betraying my incarnation.

P: How?

S: You keep deconstructing that I am my body and that I have a mind. This disconnects me from my experience as an embodied person.

P: Is that happening now?

S: Yes. I'm not fully connected with my body.

P: How would things be different if you were fully connected?

S: Well, I'd feel like I had a body, that I *was* my body.

P: When you walk outside this room at the end of a session, does it feel like you are walking out of the room?

S: Yes, of course.

P: Can you please stand up for a minute?

[S Stands up]

P: Did you stand up?

S: Yes.

P: So, I'm not sure what the problem is about not being fully embodied.

S: But you're also teaching that there is no self.

P: I'm not teaching. We are looking together to see what is here, and what's not here. We're exploring who you are. And it seems that what we discover is that you have a body, but at the same time we can't find who has it, who owns or inhabits your body. That's completely paradoxical. But, it seems that's how it is.

S: I feel trapped.

P: In what?

S: I'm trying to find a way out of that conclusion.

P: Why?

S: It makes me feel uncomfortable.

P: Where?

S: In my chest, everywhere in my body.

P: In your body?

S: Yes.

P: This question might frustrate you, but who has your body?

S: Here we go again. I don't know.

P: So both seem to be happening: strong sensations in your body, and the experience of not having a center—not being able to find who is having those feelings.

S: Yes, I'd say that's right.

P: How does that feel?

S: Interesting…. Different.

P: Has your body disappeared in any way?

S: No. I'm feeling a lot of energy.

P: Are you still aware of the shape of your body? You can see your legs and arms and hands.

S: Of course.

P: You are all here?

S: Yes, but it's weird. I feel an incredible amount of energy.

P: Are you comfortable with that?

S: Yes. It's great.

5

Continuous presence:
releasing glitches in the flow

In the process of sharing nondual transmission, it's easy to get sidetracked from time to time, to become involved in the content of our own or other people's experience in a way that we lose connection with the unconditioned. This chapter identifies some of the glitches that can arise and shows how to move through them and reconnect with the nondual. Of course the quickest way through all of this is to see that a glitch is just a construction. Something happens and we think or feel that we've lost a connection to the nondual and have thereby diminished our capacity to function, for the moment, as a nondual coach or facilitator. We forget that the nondual isn't something we can lose or gain—it doesn't function like that.

Creating glitches

In offering nondual transmission, it's natural that we will create glitches or incompletions from time to time. We know we are in a glitch if our identity kicks in and we become involved with ourselves. We lose connection with the space, with the people or person we are with, and start to think about how we are appearing, or we distract ourselves from ourselves by giving an outwardly focused attention to other people, ideas, and concepts.

There are two ways in which we create glitches or incompletions. Either we don't do what needs to be done, or we do what doesn't need to be done. We find out a few seconds later that we've been loose or tight with our words or expression. We know we are in a glitch because we are in time. We are thinking about what's happening, or hoping someone will say something, or looking forward to the end of a session or an interaction.

If an incompletion is created while you are working, you retrace your steps and address it immediately so you can move on without any residues. For example, if you see that someone has misunderstood you, or you just don't know how someone has heard you, it's easy to ask, "How did you hear what I just said? Can you please play it back to me?" You sense that if you glide over this opportunity, that in five minutes you might still be thinking, "I should have asked him what he made of what I said." We are all familiar with saying something, while facilitating a group or in a coaching call, and immediately thinking, "That wasn't necessary." Because there is a lot of space in this type of work, we begin to sense in advance if this is likely to happen. Over time we find that the phenomenon of doing things that don't directly support the presencing of nondual awareness occurs less and less frequently.

Working with your own identities

In authentic nondual work our personality stays out of the way because there's nothing for us to take credit for, since nothing is happening. We're not doing anything so there's no one to take credit for anything. At the same time, you're fully responsive to whatever is happening in your field of awareness, since everything is happening within you as it occurs in others.

Ideally, if you are facilitating nondual work, you'll find yourself naturally relaxed, open, and fluid. At the same time you are solid and grounded. It's also natural in a workshop environment, especially when there's a lot of attention focused on you, that you can become involved in yourself. The same thing can happen if you're coaching someone who you find particularly intimidating. You might start to feel uncomfortable, exposed, raw, nervous, or inadequate. You might start to think, "They must be able to see I'm nervous, that I don't know how to move. They must know I'm feeling unsettled and wanting this to shift." Conversely, it's also natural to become involved in a positive public identity. We might feel quite accomplished, proud of the way we are managing the space, even responsible for how well things are unfolding.

It is great that these identities emerge because they give us real opportunities to move through identities that we are embarrassed by or proud of. They show us the place we are trying to protect and conceal, and the personal attributes that we are happy to "have on display." If we can identify it, it might drop away immediately. You will work through it anyway, simply by staying with it and letting your attachment to this identity dissolve. You really have no choice since you're in an exposed position.

You might think, "How did I end up here? I haven't got it together. I'm not like this or that person. I shouldn't be up here in front of these people parading like I am enlightened." And then you see that "This" has nothing to do with enlightenment. "This" isn't about enlightenment. "This" isn't about anything. Enlightenment is the type of constructed projection we are working with.

Here are some ways to work with these crystallized identities:

1. Accept the feelings and thoughts.

2. Do some internal work. Ask yourself, "Who is feeling uncomfortable?" etc.

3. Know that your experience will change.

What you'll find is that you continually grow with this work as you find yourself presenting nonduality in new environments, in different cultures and language communities, with different sets of expectations, larger numbers of people, and unexpected events (for example, people walking out, behaving strangely, etc.). The discomfort will move through your system and you'll return to a state of natural, uncontrived ease and grace.

The unconditioned neither changes nor stays the same. We can't say that it changes because there is nothing to change. Some people conclude that it remains the same, but we can't say this either because there is nothing to remain the same. The conditioned is always changing and this brings different flavors and challenges to our presencing of the nondual.

Deconstructing yourself: working with your own conditioned identities that can arise in nondual facilitation

Sometimes when we are facilitating nondual transmission, "things go wrong." We start to construct that things should be different. We start feeling uncomfortable, and we'd like things to shift. We think, "This isn't working," and we'd like things to move on. We start looking toward the end of an interaction, wondering how to negotiate our way through the space.

The source of our discomfort could be obvious. For example, a lot of negative judgments might be coming at us from the group. We might be feeling incompetent, overwhelmed by the sheer amount of energy in the room, not knowing how or what to do with it. This invites some work on our "selves."

First, we recognize "This" is what's happening, and there's nothing in this very moment that we can do. That moment has gone; we lost the opportunity! And this moment has gone as well. There is "just this," and just like every moment, it is taking care of itself. Second, we can begin to do some inquiry about "who" feels threatened by the people, the energy, or the dynamic. We connect with the space that's inside, and begin to see that there's no difference between the inside and the outside. If the energy feels hostile, this is just a label. What's happening gives us another opportunity to see our preferences and to let go of what we would prefer. Everything, no matter what it is, is an expression of the play of appearances in awareness.

Sometimes, if it's a threatening energy, as in someone criticizing how I'm doing things, how I'm facilitating a workshop, then I watch any predisposition to defend myself. Instantly we see that we can't defend ourselves, because there's no one to defend. There's no one at home to be threatened. Were we to move in the direction of self-preservation, this would solidify the space and duality of self and other, which in turn could lead us to justify what we're doing, explain our actions, or begin to collude with people's desires and preferences. So we receive whatever's being offered. We let it come in and move through.

People can only be criticizing the form, so we return to the essence of the transmission, which is selfless and centerless. We can totally trust our manifestation and how this interfaces with other people. We can respond by saying, "I hear what you're saying. You're directing it to me, and now I'm wondering 'who' it is that you're talking to. If I try to find who is listening to what you're saying, I can't find who's listening. I can repeat what you're saying, but I can't find who is hearing it." In this way, we move the conversation into contentless awareness.

Or we can say, "What exactly is it about what I am doing now that's problematic? Is it happening now?" We bring the inquiry into the here and now. We can add, "If I do something that you find problematic, will you please bring it to my attention, and we can look at it together?"

If someone doesn't like the form the work is taking, it's an opportunity to look at attraction and aversion. We can also observe the habit of becoming preoccupied with forms.

If someone has a strong opinion about something, I will often just leave it. I'll make a judgment call and determine—is this going to be workable, or is this something that they're really going to get offensive and aggressive about if I begin to challenge it through an unfindability type of inquiry? At some other point in time, next year, ten years, or another lifetime, then they might come back to it and loosen the grip on that opinion.

The trap in facilitating is to think, "Ah, that was a great session. It worked really well." As soon as you do that, the contrast to that thought exists. Then sooner or later a session will come along in which you'll think, "What happened there? I don't want to go back there again!" Stay open in a way that allows all sorts of manifestations to occur, and do not be involved in people's opinions and preferences. When the trap does arise, then there's work to do, to totally open up and see that everything happening is an expression of awareness and consciousness itself.

Ability to experience the nondual in reactive situations

If people seem to be attacking you by questioning your skills, competence or relevance, or rejecting what you are saying, these attacks give you opportunities to discover images of yourself that you are attached to. The very fact that you feel attacked, invalidated, or challenged in any way means that you are identified with a particular image of yourself.

Feeling irrelevant to the process at times

There are times when you are (notionally) facilitating nondual work when you'll feel irrelevant to the process. The energy of a person or group may move in a direction that seems tangential to the transformation of consciousness in the direction of nonduality. You may feel that the energy has become fragmented and superficial through excessive intellectualization or caught in a subterranean stream of deep emotions that block easy access to the unconditioned.

When this occurs, just be with what is occurring until the moment when you become actively involved in the process again. Just notice your own reactions and thoughts during this time, knowing that the moment will return in two minutes, or 30 minutes, in which you will be relevant again. The instant you are called on, there you are, free of all history, in the moment, working with complete naturalness and a sense of total continuity.

Not getting lost in personal experience

It is easy to agree with your student about an experience they are having. This may fix the experience into a construct that holds both of you. Your personal experience may not support transporting them into the nondual.

At first, through wanting to establish rapport, there can be a pull to want to be in relationship with a student. We may find ourselves saying, "The same things have happened for me," or "I've been there too," or "I understand what is happening for you, as the same thing is familiar to me." When we respond in this way, we're not fully in service of the nondual. When we're in the role of being an agent for nondual transmission, we don't need to tell people that we know what is happening for them because we've been there. When we speak from the nondual, we don't enter a structural relationship based on the conditioned mind. When it's possible to be present in the nondual, that's what happens.

We're not there to be in a personal relationship with the person with whom we are working. There is a radical intimacy that is naturally available, but no one is in relationship with anyone. A different dynamic is happening. There are no defenses and nothing to conceal or demonstrate.

When the nondual is new to us, it can feel artificial; it can feel impersonal and unnatural. Sometimes there can be a sense of loss and the feeling, "If I wasn't doing this, in the role of a facilitator, I'd be having a different conversation." Part of what's happening is the loss of a personal story. In a workshop or coaching call, we are in service of the nondual. Outside of that in other settings, there are opportunities to share about difficulties and challenges with someone else.

Complete in the unconditioned

When we're working with the nondual approach—or in any other context for that matter—how do we know when an action that we take is complete? We know because, following our action, we experience no residual feeling about that experience. We don't worry about what happened, thinking we could, or should, have done something differently. There's nothing further to do, so we can move onto the next moment and allow each moment to be fresh and unique.

We don't feel that there's anything lacking in our action or experience, nor do we feel particularly excited or pleased with ourselves. Following an event, such as a workshop or nondual session, that's it! Now we are here, not there! Another way of saying this is that the "event" was "uneventful." Some conversation has happened, some explanations, nondual inquiry, natural contemplation, and deep sharing. All this has arisen and been processed with authenticity and naturalness. Nothing was omitted, and nothing has been added that was unnecessary.

When whatever arises is dealt with presently and cleanly, there is nothing left to do. If we notice after a nondual session that we don't feel any need to dwell on or debrief what happened, this is a marker that we've operated naturally and authentically from no-mind. There's nothing to review. We can move on and be present to the next person, situation, or moment we encounter.

Every moment that's disconnected from unconditioned awareness, however, is incomplete, because it allows us to get involved in the workings of the conditioned mind, which processes, analyzes, and compares. It's the conditioned mind that thinks we can do things better, that finds some people to be a nuisance or annoying, that creates experiences of pride and arrogance. It's the conditioned mind that says, "I hope the next session will be smoother than the last. I didn't feel authentic. I wish so-and-so wasn't in the course; he's totally in his head."

The unconditioned state is the only state that's truly complete because in this state attachment and aversion no longer function. We're not operating out of our past experiences and conclusions about people or situations. As the great psychoanalyst, Wilfred Bion has said, we work without memory or desire.

Our responses are based on what is occurring, rather than what we know how to do, or would like to be happening. Indeed, we have no concern for the future. We're not trying to control what is going to happen, nor in any rush to react. We're content to be with what is, allowing space around that, and then looking for what seems to be our natural response. When we can tune into natural action through buddha mind, we are secure in the knowledge that there is no other way that we can possibly be other than how we are in this and every moment. So we have no regrets. We are complete in the here and now.

S: This morning, when you began talking, I went into this space of complete fulfillment. Everything that you described in the sense of nothing being missing. It was absolutely blissful. I love that—the peace and fullness in that, with nothing special going on. I thought, "This is unconditioned awareness."

But as the day has gone on, I'm not feeling that at all. I'm feeling more and more anxious. It's become clear to me that I don't know what this is. I don't understand everything you're talking about. This makes me feel really anxious, even my need to ask this question. I'm confused. I don't feel complete. I just needed to say that out loud.

P: This moment—it's incomplete?

S: It doesn't feel complete.

P: What's happening that makes it incomplete?

S: I don't know; the anxiety. I feel like yelling out, "I'm incomplete!"

P: You can do that. What's stopping you? Let's scream that out. Just let it happen, if it's there to come out. Be incomplete. Be fully incomplete. Be totally complete in being incomplete. Can you do that?

S: That's so wonderful. Somehow you have said it for me. I don't feel incomplete anymore.

P: Next time it's your turn.

[Laughter]

Ways to achieve completion

When we are coaching and facilitating, we can achieve completion in the moment by:

- Accessing unconditioned awareness, where we see that there is no one who is complete or incomplete.
- Dealing with any messes or incompletions that have resulted from our past actions, as we face these consequences in the present moment.
- Tuning into the future consequences of our present actions and making adjustments to these actions as we take them.
- Exploring desirelessness, where we have no need for anything to be different from how it is.
- Shifting our negative moods, which cast a shadow over the present moment and prevent us from feeling complete.
- Designing our conversations so that we remain complete in the present moment.

Ways to reduce slippage

I use the term "slippage" to identify those times when the dance of silence and inquiry loses traction in terms of its capacity to ease us into abiding as awareness. We slip when the presencing of awareness devolves into a preoccupation with beliefs, feelings, and sensations. You might say, "But in the nondual there is no movement; we can't go forward or backward because there's no medium in which to move." This is so. Slippage happens at a relative level when we are on the journey from being someone to becoming a centerless clearing. On this journey, sometimes our wheels are spinning; we think our ideas and explorations are constructive, but in reality we are running on the spot, or even getting deeper into positions, opinions, and experience. Slippage is like pedaling a bike and going nowhere because we're just sharing viewpoints and consolidating thoughts.

It's easy and natural for people to engage with nonduality at a discursive level if they've invested decades in practice and exploring ideas. It's also easy to be distracted from the nondual entirely and become engrossed in conversations about teachers, metaphysics, psychology, and personal experience.

When we're free of bias or agenda, we can easily discern the energy and directionality of a conversation about inquiry, feelings, freedom, choice, the self, practice, etc. Within a minute or two we know if we are going *into* or *beyond* the mind. We can see the potential convolutions in a conversation. If we can agree or disagree with what is being said, there is scope for elaboration. Slippage happens if we indulge, or even subtly encourage, these conversations.

This type of collusion can be detected by the tone of our voice. Our voice comes from a different place in our throat if we are speaking to the immediacy of what's happening, in contrast to what we think we know. I can't say exactly what the difference is, but you can hear it. The first is fresh and self-evidently relevant. The second is stale or recycled. When we are speaking from this moment, our words (right now) aren't conditioning the next sentence, or what we'll be saying in one minute. We don't have a topic or theme that we are pursuing. We might be saying something we've said many times before, but it is still fresh because it's pertinent to what is happening here right now. When our words are conditioned by what we know or where we think we're going, it's like replaying a recording of something we've said before. A reverberation occurs—an echo in our ears—from previous times we've said a similar thing.

It can happen that you're halfway into a sentence and you realize, "These are just my thoughts about such and such. This is a construction. This is not where it's at." The only teaching that can be relied on is contentless transmission because it's the only transmission that can't be misinterpreted. It doesn't have any content.

Slippage also happens when we collude with people's need for advice. Giving advice is a weak way to support people because it's pointing to the future. I'm not saying there's no room for advice. It's just weaker than the ultimate resource of awareness in the here and now. Ninety-five percent of the time we give people advice, they are not going to use it. So it's really a waste of time giving it! It can even be counter-productive because people can beat themselves up for not using it.

One useful response is to say, "I do have my own thoughts about that, but I feel that the most valuable thing for us to do is to continue to gain familiarity with nondual awareness because it is the ultimate medicine and solution that we are looking for. The most valuable way to prepare for the future—any future—is to abide as awareness. The best thing to do is simply become more and more familiar with 'This,' this state, this moment, here right now, in which there's no suffering, and suffering isn't even possible." We simply declare that something more profound is possible, and that it's happening right now.

Up until now we've been talking about how slippage happens in conversations that become discursive or constructive. Another way we can create slippage is by discouraging sharing and communication. If we think that the intellect or constructive mind is an obstacle on the path to presencing pure awareness, we distort the working space. We throw people back onto themselves and unwittingly encourage people to silently process whatever is happening for them. The working space can lose its edge and devolve into a form of private meditation that amounts to little more than following the machinations of the mind.

Correcting the oscillation between polarized beliefs: gently moving people into "positionlessness"

It is useful to recognize that people usually don't move from having a strong position about things like choice, personal identity, and the role of practice, through to viewlessness in one movement. In the process of dissolving viewpoints, people often move from one extreme to another. This happens because people are looking for some grounding, some reference points, even if this means adopting an opposite way of thinking than they'd previously had.

We see this in the case of believing we have a choice and then moving to the position that there is no choice.

When we inquire into what's behind the idea of choice, we can't find anything. At the end of an inquiry, it's easy for people who believe in choice to suddenly flip and think that there is no choice. They move from one position to another. People do this because it's more comfortable knowing how things are, even if they're different, or opposite, from how they thought about things beforehand. This isn't the intended outcome of an unfindability inquiry. This form of inquiry is intended to see through every viewpoint or belief. We don't arrive at a conclusion or end-point.

When people flip to an opposite position, I often let them be with that for a while because it's a correction that's happening. They've over-corrected. But, that's okay. It balances things. There's still energy in the initial belief, so resting in the opposite belief for a while balances the energy. Then, at some point—if the initial belief hasn't reconstituted—we can begin to dismantle that new position and bring them to the free ground of "positionlessness."

People often move to an opposite position when they use the Advaita form of self-inquiry. We begin with the feeling that we exist. Inquiry reveals that we can't find ourselves. That's it. But it is easy for the mind to conclude that there is no self. When we dismantle the self, that's all that's happening. We simply cannot *find* a self. That doesn't mean "there is *no* self." This is not designed to lead to a conceptual conclusion that "I don't exist," when previously we thought that "I do exist." We can look into that concept, too. "Who is it that does not exist?" We find that we can't say "who" it is who is not there. We can't say that we don't exist. We neither exist, nor don't exist.

The oscillation process is a continual correction. As people move too far, we continue to bring them back. In this work we're exploring being free and open, not limiting our experience by overlaying conceptual restrictions on what we think is possible and not possible.

When I say, "We move people out of their positions," this doesn't mean that we find some middle ground. There is no middle. The middle is an extreme. It's the extreme of *not* being extreme. In the same way, having "no position" is also an extreme position if we think about this as not having a position. Positionlessness is beyond having and *not* having positions.

Mind empty: nothing to say

Often you'll find that it's impossible to say anything. Nothing comes along. You haven't been silenced. It's just that in the absence of an explicit need, there is nothing to do. At times you might even wish that something would grip you, that a good idea would come along, that your thoughts might crystallize into a theme, that you might see something that you could comment on, or that someone would say or do something so that you could respond!

Working in eternity

The work we do in *Radiant Mind* and *Natural Awakening* consists of continually and gently moving people out of polarized positions, such as thinking that reality is like this or that, that there is a doer or there isn't a doer, that there is something to practice or nothing to practice.

It's important not to look for a conclusion to that process of continual correction. It will only produce frustration. From the bodhisattva point of view this never stops; we have no expectation that this process of settlement, movement, and correction will stop or continue forever. It doesn't matter. It's not the point.

Sometimes it feels like shifting someone away from one position into another, even though this isn't the final intention. The intention, in a way, is to be nowhere and everywhere simultaneously. We can move someone from one position to another. When that becomes reified it's time to move them away from that position.

Handling conversations that are easy to get caught up in

There is a set of conversations that it's easy to get caught up in, in the sense that you find yourself having a belief and voicing it, or even defending it. These can include claims that we are free, that there is no choice, that there is or isn't a self, and that there is or isn't a doer. Depending on one's education, culture, and history of spiritual practice, it's easy to find a personal belief system being invoked, and for you to end up "saying something." It is also easy to get caught in the dualistic structure of truth and illusions, buying into the need to see through the veils of illusion, overcome our ignorance, etc. Or a participant may question if deconstructive inquiry is a form of spiritual bypass. Often a question about love in unconditioned awareness arises.

These questions can cause problems because it's easy to become involved with them at an intellectual level. We have probably thought about these same questions quite a bit ourselves, so it's easy as a coach to begin to draw on our own personal ideas rather than see through the constructions that are being offered by a student.

Nondual inquiry as a form of spiritual bypass!

It's important to move slowly with this. It is impossible to avoid anything when presencing the nondual, but I feel that people need to discover this for themselves. We can explain that the unconditioned isn't capable of destroying or suppressing anything. If anything, it makes us more vulnerable. We have no defenses, but this isn't a problem because there's no one to protect. I suggest people move slowly and see what happens.

I've explained in detail how, in order to purify, deepen, and extend the experience of nondual awareness, we need to take care of our lives at every level: the material, social, emotional, and spiritual. Please don't mistake what I'm saying here about always giving priority to unconditioned awareness as an example of what some teachers and facilitators are calling "spiritual bypassing" or "bypassing the relative."

When some teachers use the term "spiritual bypassing," they're talking about the way that people with a particular predisposition can engage with the nondual perspective in a way that disconnects them from their emotions, relationships, and social responsibilities. This can happen if people understand the ultimate level of being only through the language that can be used to reveal it, rather than as a direct experience. Since the ultimate level is often spoken about as a state of egolessness that transcends all moral imperatives and goes beyond choice and decision, some nondual traditions talk about relative reality as being illusory.

If people are relating to the ultimate only through a discourse of nonduality, they're only seeing part of the picture, the part that's framed in negations. If they don't have the direct experience of unconditioned awareness, they can infer that there's no finite self, no choice, etc. and that they're relieved of the need to take care of themselves and others at the relative or conditioned level.

The possibility of bypassing the relative is compounded by the fact that some nondual traditions include yogic practices designed to propel people into disidentified states—different types of *samadhis*—in which people aren't even aware of the phenomenal world. These states have nothing to do with unconditioned awareness, emptiness, or *shunyata*, as this is understood and experienced in Buddhism.

We really need to be clear about this. This is why it's very important to work with an experienced teacher. It's unfortunate that some facilitators are using the phrase "hanging out in emptiness" to refer to practitioners who seem to be disconnected from the world. Emptiness or *shunyata* has a very precise meaning in Buddhism that's unrelated to how people are using it in this phrase. I prefer to translate *shunyata* as "openness" rather than emptiness in order to avoid the misunderstanding that it's a state that's separate from the world. As I've explained, the experience of unconditioned awareness automatically reveals the intricacies of our conditioned existence.

It's also important to see that when we're presencing unconditioned awareness, it's impossible to avoid anything. Unconditioned awareness doesn't have the capacity to suppress anything. It's a structureless state. It doesn't have any energy in it. It's not an escape route. It's a state in which we're fully present to everything that's arising. The experience of unconditioned awareness dissolves the barrier between ourselves and others. We become more responsive and responsible to other people because they're no different from us.

This is intellectual and abstract!

Nondual transmission isn't abstract because there's simply nothing to know. The unconditioned isn't some rarefied metaphysical or spiritual reality. It isn't subtle or difficult to understand. All that's required is to clearly see that there's nothing to know. The abstractions and intellectualizations come from people's own minds. A nondual coach or teacher has nothing to say, nothing to describe, because nothing is happening. People need to arrive at the point where they can see, starkly and clearly, that "This" is impossible to know.

I still haven't discovered the best way to show people that nondual awareness isn't abstract, that the intellectualizing is just the working of their own minds. The working of the mind, especially the need to know, becomes more obvious when the space is cleared of all concepts and directionality. In a way I am being seduced by the thought that "I haven't discovered something!" I think there is something to discover, when the unrelenting truth, in relationship to the unconditioned or nondual, is that there is "nothing to get."

When confronted by this reality, the mind can become overactive in its attempts to get "This," to understand it, in any way at all, intellectually, experientially, or as a concept. Anything would do! It's our own minds that make this process intellectual. It's a pure and clear reflection of our minds and can function when there is simply nothing to know. This has nothing to do with the "subject matter"—nondual awareness. It is simply the wheels of the mind, spinning in the sand, getting nowhere.

Is there love in unconditioned awareness?

As the state of being naturally awake begins to take root, some people fear that it may threaten their experience and expression of love. They arrive at an assessment that there is no love in the unconditioned. The type of love that seems to be at stake covers the full spectrum, from physical intimacy, the love and care we have for our family and closest friends, through to the concern we have and the active contribution we may make to local and global communities.

Normally when people talk about "love" they're talking about a conditioned experience. In the unconditioned space we can't find love; we can't find anything. But this doesn't mean that love disappears at the level of living in the world and being in relationship.

In general, nondual work produces a maturation of love and enhances the authenticity of our relationships. For example, if people have a tendency to be withholding for fear of being hurt by relationships, their fear can dissolve. This allows people to share more deeply and naturally because, at the most essential level, they know that there's nothing to protect. Intimacy becomes more available and accessible.

On the other hand, if people's expression of love and style of caring is built on a need to be valued and appreciated—to be making a palpable difference to other people, the community, and the world—this need will slowly dissolve. This will change the shape of their caring. People who are driven by a moralistic imperative to help others may begin to feel a genuine equality in all relationships. The tendency for help to be delivered in obsequious, imposing, or even invasive ways matures into genuinely respectful ways of helping that enhance people's capacity for growth and natural self-reliance.

From a conditioned perspective everything is threatened by the unconditioned. The unconditioned empties conditioned phenomena of any intrinsic value or meaning. This is true of spiritual experiences and feelings of anger, jealousy, fear, and love. Spiritual experiences, for example, are rendered worthless in the sphere of nondual awareness because we are already in a space that can't be enhanced or improved upon. If someone tells us about anything that happened—including a satori experience—this has nothing to do with pure awareness. Whatever happened in the event has become "experientialized."

Within the sphere of nondual awareness we're no longer tied up in our own identity. In a sense we enter other people's realities. Other people's experience becomes our own experience to the extent that we can receive it. We can sense the way people are thinking and feeling. Two mindstreams merge in a flow of consciousness that has no boundary or division.

When we are not preoccupied with our own existence, our own emotions or fantasies, we receive more. There is less interference, and a deeper and more subtle appreciation of other people's experience emerges.

Radical intimacy

In this work I prefer to talk about "intimacy" rather than "love." This gives us a fresh opportunity to invent what we mean by the word "love." Rather than saying a lot about love and be accused of debasing a concept, intimacy can be approached more openly. The word intimacy works better than the word compassion, because compassion is typically understood in a dualistic and hierarchical way. We can give something to someone, something that they need. Compassion can be expressed by seeing what another needs and working to fulfill that need. Intimacy allows us to be with people without any defences and free of any self-serving agenda of being a "helper" or kind and sensitive person. Intimacy gives us the opportunity to enter a situation openly in whatever shape it takes. There is no element or energy from our side wanting to gain anything because we are already fulfilled.

Within unconditioned awareness, we take care of others in the same way we take care of ourselves because we find no difference between ourselves and others. We get a feel for this in teaching, and participating in conference calls. When someone brings something into the field, we don't feel it's "their" issue or problem. It's entered into the field to be fully responded to and authentically so. It's a partial penetration into other people's realities. Other people's thoughts and feelings aren't arising with the immediacy and with the clarity with which we experience our own thoughts and feelings. It's more like a shadowing, more opaque, yet our own experience is qualitatively the same. We may think, "Something's going on and I don't understand what is happening." We can be experiencing ourselves in an identical way, yet we don't know exactly the sequence of their thoughts or how to exactly sense their body language.

From within nondual awareness we are just a clearing—a centerless space—through which a universe moves. I am me, not because there is a unique me somewhere in here, but because the space I am reveals a unique and distinctive universe. Even though it seems I'm at the center of this, I'm not in here, and there is no center. This means that everyone who enters into the clearing that I am is as intimately related to me as my thoughts and bodily feelings. There's no difference.

In the nondual state there is no inside or outside. There is no me in here who exists separate from everything else. It's impossible to locate where I stop and you begin. There is no point where I stop and you begin. There's just this, which is everything. This is real intimacy. From within the nondual experience we don't invite, or exclude, anything. There's no one home who is capable of doing this!

Everything is already here. We don't push anything away, and we don't hold onto anything. Of course, this doesn't mean that the structure of our relationships takes the same form with everyone. The people with whom we live, work, and practice have a central role in our lives. Nonetheless, there is nothing artificial or contrived about our relationships.

In the nondual realm, intimacy isn't a particular set of feelings, such as feeling really close or connected to someone, or feeling deeply committed or concerned about someone else's wellbeing. Nondual intimacy doesn't carve out a particular relationship with one, or a few other people. Nondual intimacy is all encompassing and all embracing. Nothing is excluded. Everything in our known universe is touched with equal sensitivity and compassion. It's the experience of total interpenetration of our being to the point where the no one who we are expands to include everything.

Working with the question of love in the here and now

I find that the best way to work with the concern about whether there is love in the nondual is to work with this in the here and now—in terms of what is happening in the workshop space or conversation we are having in this very moment with the person who has raised the concern.

We can begin this by saying something like, "Let's see what's happening now. Let's use what's happening here as our model. Your question is arising as a function of our work together so let's look at this experience. We're in the field of nondual awareness now—we're presencing our natural state—so this is the best place for us to find an answer to your question."

We bring the question directly into this moment by asking, "Is love missing right now, in our interaction, in the space we are sharing, in this room?" Normally people will answer "No." I've never heard anyone say "Yes." If they do, then we can look into that. "What's missing? What's happening that wouldn't be happening, if there was love here right now?" We can then move with that inquiry. Generally people won't be able to identify anything. If they did identify something we would look at it. For example, perhaps they might say, "If there was love here I'd be feeling it in my heart. There would be a warm and open feeling in my heart. And that's not happening." Then we can ask, "Is that the only way that love can manifest?" They will probably say no, and we can join them in a gentle, respectful conversation that takes us into the space of intimacy with no boundaries or defenses.

At the conclusion of this type of inquiry I often say, "If at any point you feel there is no love, please say so. Please bring it to my awareness." Then we can look at it again.

How will this change me—will I be happier?

Questions that frequently, and naturally, arise in any type of transformational work are: "How will this change me?" "Will I be more effective?" "Will I suffer less?" People would like to hear that their lives will be richer, more harmonious, and that they will be better able to deal with challenging situations. It's tempting for people to infer that such change will happen. People in transformational programs regularly offer personal accounts about how they feel more peace and openness through engaging in nondual work. They report how their relationships and communications improve, and their fears and anxieties decrease. People validate their participation in this way. New participants are comforted and reassured by such reports. Promotional materials often imply such things as: "You will discover a space where there is more intimacy, openness, and less struggle, etc."

However, as soon as people are fully engaged with nonduality, we can't promise anything. There are two reasons for this. First, the focus of our work is on nondual awareness. If we give attention to change at the conditioned level, this throws us into time and causality. This attention doesn't create an entry point into nondual awareness. In fact, it distracts us from the unbounded panorama of pure awareness.

We can't know how the infusion of nondual awareness within a mindstream will influence someone's evolutionary path. Even here, in saying that nondual awareness influences how we think, feel, and perceive, I am telling a story. I am moving away from the language of the unconditioned where there's nothing to say, nothing to describe, where the nondual can't influence anything because it isn't a force or power or energy. It is nothing. I acknowledge that I am no longer talking from the nondual. I'm aware that what I am about to say can easily raise as many questions as it seems to answer. I preempt this by saying, "I'll give you my thoughts on this, but it will be quite brief because this is just the way that I try to make sense of things."

Wonderful things *do* happen when we engage in nondual work. People experience super-deep, super-smooth, and totally effortless sessions of natural meditation. They are able to feel totally complete, even blissful, in the midst of illness, irresolution, or environmental threats. My approach is to acknowledge these "side effects," but not dwell on them. They don't become a focus of the work. In fact, these types of effects arise more consistently and comprehensively when we don't give them any attention.

People often attribute these changes to the work they are doing. It can be tempting to agree with them and to interpret positive change to the work they are doing. I listen to these reports with pure listening. I don't reject them or accept them. I'll say that's great, but I don't make a link between the nondual program and the positive changes that are happening.

It's a trap to attribute such changes to spending more time in nondual awareness. We then begin to assess the effectiveness of nondual work in terms of changes that are happening at the conditioned level. But the unconditioned isn't ongoingly revealed and presenced when we are anticipating and tracking changes at the conditioned level. When we anticipate and track changes, we are no longer engaged in nondual transmission.

The second reason I don't make promises that people's lives will improve is that I don't know what will happen for someone, tomorrow, next week, or next year. While I'm sure that nondual awareness only serves people positively, it's impossible to know what's going to happen in a person's life. We can't know what those challenges will be. Someone's life may move from being peaceful and easy to becoming demanding and stressful overnight. This happens all the time. Everyday thousands of people are losing their jobs, needing to sell their home, welcoming a newborn child into their family, and dealing with the news of a terminal illness. The stresses involved in some of these experiences can last for months or years. Engaging in nonduality doesn't provide insurance against relationship problems, financial loss, illness, or death.

All we can confidently say is that the more time we spend in nondual awareness, the better we will be able to handle life's challenges, no matter what they are. Once we've experienced unconditioned awareness, this healing experience percolates through the layers of our conditioning. There is a natural and effortless process, which is different for each complex being, and it happens in its own time. At times, this de-conditioning can happen quickly, and then we might regress and find ourselves confronting something that has been deeply held within our conditioning. At other times, de-conditioning happens slowly and steadily. The entire process may take more than a lifetime. We might never reside permanently in unconditioned awareness. We have no concern for this. We can simply let the process happen in its own way.

Does nondual awareness influence the conditioned?

There is another question that often follows from the previous one. I think that people are trying to approach the same question from a less direct angle. People ask about the nature of the relationship between the unconditioned and conditioned dimensions, in particular how unconditioned awareness influences the flow of conditioned experiences. Does it change the way we think, feel, see, or hear things?

I don't have anything to say about this. This can be quite dissatisfying for people, but my mind can't go there; I can't theorize about this. As soon as I hear "nondual awareness," my mind as it were, sources this state, and I can't say that it does or doesn't influence my embodied-mind experience because I don't know what unconditioned awareness is. If I begin to say something about this, I very quickly feel that I am deceiving people. If we move into the conditioned mind, there's no limit to what we can say about the connection between the unconditioned and conditioned. But even though we are using words like "unconditioned" or "nondual," if we are talking about a connection or relationship, we are no longer referencing the unconditioned.

I use this question of "What is the relationship between the two domains?" as an opportunity to continue to reveal not knowing and not needing to know. I see the differential, between what people want to hear and nondual awareness, as an opportunity to clearly reveal nonduality as a state that is neither the same as the flow of conditioned experience nor different from it.

As soon as we begin to source nondual awareness, we can't say that our actions of body, speech, and mind are influenced by the unconditioned because we see that the unconditioned doesn't influence things. And similarly, we can't say our actions influence the unconditioned because it isn't influenced or conditioned by anything. So the question stops there.

From the conditioned point of view we can say a great deal about how our state of mind supports or hinders the presencing of nondual awareness. The *Radiant Mind* book has a lot to say about this. We can talk about conducive conditions, creating bridges, desirelessness, etc. because here we are talking from within a domain where there are causes and effects.

In summary, we are left with an eternal paradox, the type that inevitably emerges at the boundary between thought and no-mind. From the place of viewpoints and interpretations, the flow of conditioned experience is influenced by the presencing of nondual awareness. But from the unconditioned perspective there is nothing that can influence the flow. This is effectively the same paradox that is summed up in the Zen saying that observes, "In the sphere of no-mind, everything changes and nothing changes."

What about choice?

For many people it's important to believe that they have choice. If people are offered a perspective that challenges the idea that they are free agents, many people will offer a quick and robust defense of their freedom to choose. We now have a language for it. People use the word "choice point" to identify a moment in the flow when personal choice, or volition, can be exercised.

If we inquire into the concept of "choice," we can't find anything—a phenomenon, an action or mental event—to which it refers. What we mean by "choice" is that we, at least sometimes, have the capacity to follow (choose between) one action rather than another. At a certain point, two different actions are possible and we choose to follow one. This is the language of choosing. But we can never *show* that we could have done something different from what we have done. We can *say* that we could have done something different. We think like this all the time. "What I should have done is…." But, we can't prove that we could have done something different in any meaningful way.

At this point a few people might say, "Well look, I can choose to walk out of this room." In order to show there is a genuine choice, they would have to show, if they walked out of the room, that they could have stayed in the room. The only way to show they could have stayed in the room was to stay in the room and not walk out.

The only real proof would be *to have done what we didn't do.* In which case we couldn't have done what we did do. So, still we have no demonstration that we can choose.

At this point it's easy to conclude that there is no choice, that it's a fiction. In other words, we slide to an opposite position. "Ah, there is no choice. There's just choiceless awareness. No doer, nothing behind our actions. There's just a conditioned flow of phenomena that's inseparable from awareness." We are still looking for a way to make sense of this. "There is no choice" has now become a point of view.

If this happens, we look into it. We inquire into the idea that there's "no choice." What are we saying *isn't* possible because there's no choice? What *can't* happen?

    S: What can't happen is that we can't do something different from what we have done.

P: How can you prove that's not possible? Can you demonstrate to me that you can't be somewhere else in this moment?

S: How do I show you that I can't be somewhere else? I'm doing it now by being here.

P: Yes, I agree you are here. But that doesn't show me that you couldn't have been somewhere else as a result of choosing to be there.

S: I can't prove that I can't be somewhere else because I can't make a choice to be here. I am just here. No choice is involved.

P: What *can't* you do?

S: I can't choose to be somewhere else. I can't think that I could have chosen to do something that would have landed me somewhere else.

P: But you just thought that!

S: What?

P: You just thought what you said you couldn't think.

S: Well yes. I can think that. But I can't do it.

P: Do what?

S: Prove that it's impossible to do something, in my mind, for example, that would have me, like, move in a different direction and have me experiencing something different in this moment from what I'm experiencing right now.

P: What type of mental event are you talking about?

S: Well, it's the moment where things are not fixed. We're at a choice point. It's like a tipping point. We could do, or not do something. We could say, "Yes" or "No." Both are possible and we decide to say, "Yes."

P: So choosing happens when we decide.

S: Yes. The mind gives a sort of directionality to thought. It can be subtle or strong, and this moves thinking in a certain direction. It's like giving an intention or impulse to a particular thought. Sometimes there is a process of vacillation before the decision occurs.

P: And you are saying that everything you have just described doesn't happen?

S: No, it happens. All that thinking happens. But it doesn't mean that what I think happens, actually happens.

P: Is what you're describing completely unrelated to reality? Is there a complete disconnection?

S: No.

P: Which part of what you described doesn't happen?

S: The part about giving energy to a particular thought.

P: That doesn't happen?

S: No.

P: It isn't possible?

S: No.

P: Does anything happen?

S: Where?

P: In the place where it doesn't happen. I'm still trying to find what it is that can't happen.

S: I am completely lost. I can't think about this anymore.

Perhaps you can't see yourself doing an inquiry in "what does happen," and show that if we can't identify what's not happening, then we can't say that it doesn't happen, because there is no *it*. A simpler way to dismantle choosing and not choosing, is to show that thinking that we choose or don't choose, doesn't mean these are happening. I can think, "I am choosing to be here, or "I'm not choosing to be here." In either case, it's not possible to say that you've made a choice either way. Is it possible for you to think you've made a choice and not have made a choice and be wrong? Can you think, "I choose to be here," right now? Can you do that? Now can you think, "I didn't choose to be here." Can you think that? So what you think isn't necessarily true.

Illusion and reality

People often bring a construction to nondual teachings based on their histories as spiritual seekers. This construction surfaces in the belief that what we're experiencing now is somehow deceptive, and that in order to be free we need to "see things as they really are."

It's easy to assume that we suffer because we don't see things accurately. Spiritual and psychological work supports this interpretation. The knowledge (*jnana*) path is explicitly framed as a project of discovering the truly real, in contrast to that which is only apparently real. In order to rest in nondual awareness, we must be able to see things as they are, rather than seeing them through the filter of our dualistic mind!

People can tie themselves in knots trying to work out what's real and unreal. We think, "Ah, something must be happening, but I'm distorting it. I need to cut through my delusions and then I'll know what's real." This is how we create a path, and find it very difficult to arrive at a point where what is, is! We live in a confused and muddy arena in which we try to work out what is real and unreal without having any grounds for making such discriminations.

But, contrary to a lot of teachings, trying to discern whether an experience is real or unreal doesn't provide an entry point into nondual awareness. Rather, it does the opposite. We keep ourselves busy trying to "see through the illusory nature of the ego" or "discern the real through the distortions of reactive emotions." The project of trying to cut through delusions and uncover the hidden truth or the "really real" produces a lot of confusion and frustration. We enter nondual awareness not by thinking, and not by effort and struggle, but by seeing that "This" is all that is, and that we can't say if this *is* or *isn't* real.

In nondual awareness there is no substantive distinction between illusion and reality. There just "is what is." What is here, is here. What isn't, isn't. It's that simple. A consciousness resting in nonduality doesn't go any further. There's nowhere further to go. There's no need to say that "This" is real or unreal.

The key to dismantling the belief that it's possible to say that what we are experiencing is "really there," or somehow "there but not really there," is to show that it's impossible to distinguish between these two. We can think and talk about how our experience might be real or fabricated, but immediate experience never delivers this information to us. Also, when we look carefully at the meaning of the terms "real" and "illusory," we see that they don't say anything!

Facilitators and coaches can have some difficulties dismantling the "illusion versus reality" construction because, often times, they've spent time processing this question themselves and the residues of this construction can easily reactivate in their own mindstream.

What's needed is an inquiry that dismantles the dualism between illusion and reality. This inquiry clarifies what it means to say that something is real or unreal. If we say that what we're experiencing is real, it means that it's not unreal. In saying "This" is real we are making a contrast. We're saying that it's not unreal. So we need to know what "This" would be like if it were unreal, or illusory in some way, in order to say that it's real. We need to know *how* our experience would be different. But this isn't possible.

If we can say what "This" would be like if it was illusory, then it's no longer illusory because we know it's not real. Things are only illusory if we *don't* know they are illusory. If we *know* that an "illusion" is an illusion, it is no longer an illusion. We are no longer capable of being deceived by it. We no longer think that something that's not real is real.

Things are only illusory when we *don't* know that they are unreal. That's what it means for something to be an illusion; it seems to be real but it's not. We can't see that it's not real. We take its reality for granted. But, this is what it means for something to be real. So if something is a genuine illusion, this means it is real. Things aren't real per se. They're real only because we can't see, conceive, or imagine that they're unreal.

If a student is involved in a construction about needing to cut through the veils of ignorance, we can begin by bringing the inquiry into the here and now. "I hear what you're saying. Let's bring this into the here and now. Let's look at what's happening now. This will keep us out of our metaphysical minds."

Then we ask a student to show us how they can say that what they are experiencing isn't *really* there, or how they *can't* experience something that *is* there to be experienced. "Within your field of awareness, as it's being received right now, which parts are being received accurately as they are, and which aspects are being distorted in some way? Which part(s) are real, and which are being superimposed on reality?"

People can be quite resistant to this particular inquiry because it destroys an important foundation for the spiritual endeavor. Without the project of "cutting through illusions," people can feel that their opportunities for spiritual freedom are being undermined. Of course, the opposite is the case. It's impossible to be free if we need anything, including needing to know if "This" or any experience is real or fabricated.

I can't see what's really there!

The following conversation with a coach will give you some ideas about how to work with a student's belief that his or her perception of reality is somehow distorted. In this case, we are looking at the idea that a specific attribute within the field of awareness is being misperceived.

> S: What happens is that the ideas I have about something stop me from seeing it accurately. For example, you are there but I don't see you properly because of my projections. My projections add stuff that isn't there. And there are other things I just don't see. So I think things about you that aren't real.

P: Which parts of what you are seeing or thinking about are unreal?

S: Well, I think you are very patient, but I'm not sure. It could just be my projection.

P: Is that what you are thinking?

S: Yes.

P: So there's no distortion then.

S: What do you mean?

P: You accurately experienced what you were thinking.

S: Yes.

P: What about how you are seeing me. Are there bits in your perception, some colors, additional hair, that aren't there? Some extra fingers, maybe! Are you changing what I'm wearing? I've got an Australian accent. Are you putting it through some type of filter so it comes out differently?

S: Of course not. You know that's not what I mean.

P: Is that what you just thought?

S: Yes.

P: Did you miss some thoughts that were there, or think some that weren't actually happening? Or did you distort what you were thinking? Did you think your thoughts differently from how they were actually occurring?

S: I don't think so. How would I know? But that's not what I mean. You're playing with me.

P: What's the game?

S: You know what I mean, but you're going in a different direction.

P: What do you mean?

S: Going back to my example, I think you're patient, but I really don't know. I've only seen you in public. I don't know what you are like when you're at your home. My thoughts shape my perception.

P: Yes. I imagine that if you spent a day with me at home, your ideas about me would change. But I still can't see that you're *not* experiencing something that's happening. Can you point to something that you think is happening now that you're not experiencing, but which is here right now, available for you to experience? This might be happening in your thoughts, visually, or in your body?

S: How could I know?

P: I don't know.

S: I don't see how I could experience something if it's not happening in my field of awareness. So where does this leave us?

P: Here.

[Silence]

P: Shall we look at the other side of this?

S: Okay.

P: I'm wondering if you are experiencing something now that's not really happening.

S: Well, I'm imagining having this same conversation with my partner at home this evening. And that's not really happening. I'm here with you now.

P: Were the images and thoughts about being at home actually happening, or was something different going on.

S: No, they were there.

P: So far, you haven't shown me something that wasn't happening, but which you experienced nevertheless.

S: I'm not sure I can.

P: Would you like some time to find an example?

S: I can't see how I can. But I'm still sure that sometimes my perception is distorted.

P: I understand. So when this happens next, please tell me and we can look at it again.

The creative function of ambiguity and the conversion of confusion into objectless awareness

The style of nondual transmission I'm using as a model in this *Guide* is characterized by quite a high level of ambiguity. By ambiguity I mean that sense of not being able to see things clearly and crisply. For as long as people are trying to "work this out," there's an element of ambiguity in the space. The space can become ambiguous within minutes of a workshop or session beginning. People begin to wonder, "What's happening here?" "What is this?" "Is there a right way or wrong way of being here in this space?" "Is there something I am meant to be doing?" It's ambiguous because there are no clear guidelines. I don't tell people what they will be doing. I don't give many reference points in terms of what people should or shouldn't be doing. I don't introduce things for people to think about. I don't offer much in terms of concrete methods or procedures. People are looking at us for some readout on what the ground rules are. Here, there's no formal meditation. It's not a dharma discourse. The format only becomes obvious as we move into it.

I might begin by saying, "The focus of our work is contentless transmission. This means that there is no topic, as such, that we are investigating. We are learning how to be here in an extremely simple way, in which everything is complete and we are fulfilled in every moment." And I might leave it at that. This already creates ambiguity and potential confusion.

S: How are we going to do that?

P: The way that we're doing it now.

S: I don't understand.

P: Yes, that's possible. This may include not knowing.

S: I still don't understand.

P: Exactly. That can happen. It's happening now.

S: What's happening? I don't get it.

P: There is nothing to understand. There is just this.

S: What?

P: This.

S: You mean being here.

P: Yes, being here. But I am wondering where "here" is.

S: Here is here, in this room.

P: Yes, I'm wondering where this room is.

S: It's in Paris.

P: And where is that?

S: In France, on earth.

P: Where is that?

S: In the universe.

P: Where is that?

S: Can't say.

P: Is it here or there?

S: I can't say. There's no there, because that's part of this, too. So really there's not even here.

[Silence]

The ambiguity is creative because it gives rise to natural koans. It stimulates the emergence of exactly the type of questions that seed effective nondual inquiry.

The level of confusion that's created is essentially a function of how much mental energy is being deployed in trying to work out what's happening. From a facilitator's side, there's no one doing nothing. Questions may begin to arise: "How is this helping me?" "Is this helping me?" "Is this *meant* to be helping me?" "How can I use this?" "I don't even know what this is." While intellectual processing occurs in the form of inquiry, fundamentally the work is an invitation to move to a different level of consciousness in which there's nothing that we need to know.

Again, I find that the best way to convert confusion into objectless awareness is by being up-front early on and clarifying the end result. Often I'll begin by saying, "What we're exploring here is contentlessness. There's nothing to understand, nothing to know, nothing to think about. You cannot understand this because this is not an object of knowledge." It requires a certain authority to put your cards on the table in this way. But it's possible. You can also do the same thing, more as a mutual exploration, by saying, "According to nondual traditions…." The phrase "according to" transfers the authority to whatever source you mention. Your function, then, is to keep the exploration on track.

In the following dialog, you'll see that things opened up very quickly at a certain point. This can often happen, without any warning, because things are happening at a mind-to-mind level, at the same time that we are sharing words. Things shift unexpectedly. It's as though there are two processes. We have the verbal content that is moving at a certain pace and in a certain direction. At times this can be a little slow and laborious. Sometimes when people are in the public eye they don't like to give away too much too soon! There is also a mind-to-mind, a being-to-being communication, that's happening between a therapist or facilitator and a client.

This liminal channel of communication can be ahead of the spoken conversation, in terms of producing a shift in state of consciousness. Suddenly a breakthrough happens that's relatively disconnected from the conversation that's happening. Often we can feel the vortex we are creating, but we can't see how or why things suddenly open up. There's no need or point to going back and trying to work it out. I figure that if I need to know something, I will. Not only can we not say what's happened, but there's no interest in doing so. All that's happening is what's happening now.

S: Well, I still feel there is something I need to know, but I don't know what it is. And this is really frustrating.

P: Do you have any idea where you can begin to look for an answer?

S: I don't even know if there is an answer. As I said, I don't even know what I'm looking for. I'm just feeling stuck.

P: Stuck in what?

S: I don't know. I'm just stuck. What's happening?

P: You think there is something you need to know, but you haven't got any idea what it is.

S: Right. So what can I do? I don't even know what to do. I don't even know if there's anything I need to do.

[Silence]

P: Do we need to do anything more with this at the moment?

S: I don't know.

P: Are you okay where you are?

S: I guess so.

P: Are you feeling comfortable or uncomfortable?

S: I really can't say.

P: Are you okay not being able to say exactly what you are feeling?

S: Yes, I am.

[Silence]

S: I came here this evening with a lot of questions. I don't know what has happened. I have the feeling of being influenced by a very extraordinary energy. I don't have any answers, at least the type of answers I was expecting. But nor do I have any questions. Thank you.

Here is a dialog that illustrates confusion in the student, and a movement toward openness.

S: I'm feeling confused.

P: Is the confusion happening in your body or your mind?

S: It's in my mind. A little bit in my body, too, because I'm feeling uncomfortable.

P: About what?

S: About how self-inquiry actually works. How does this form of inquiry take us beyond the mind?

P: You're wondering what the connection is between nondual inquiry and nondual awareness.

S: Yes.

P: So that sounds quite clear for me. You don't sound confused. You're saying that you don't understand something. Do you know that you don't understand that?

S: Yes.

P: So you're clear about that? You're not confused about that?

S: No. But I'm not sure if I can understand it. That's what I'm confused about. Should I be trying to understand how it works? I'm not clear. You see, I'm confused.

P: You're not clear about whether you should understand that or not.

S: Yes.

P: I'm trying to find some confusion. And it sounds as though you're quite clear that you don't have an answer. I'm still looking for your confusion.

S: What's coming up for me now is the frustration of not having the answer to that question.

P: Okay, wonderful. You have a question and you're feeling frustrated. I imagine that the frustration is there not just because you don't have an answer but because you need an answer, and you don't have it.

S: Yes, exactly.

P: What type of an answer are you looking for?

S: Hmmm…. One that has me actually experiencing the connection.

P: The connection between what and what?

S: Between self-inquiry and the nondual state.

P: And at the moment there doesn't seem to be a connection?

S: There doesn't seem to be a connection.

P: What is "self-inquiry?"

S: Well, the best example is asking the question "Who am I?"

P: Okay, so you ask the question, "Who am I?" and what happens?

S: I don't know.

P: Okay. You ask "Who am I?" and that's what happens.

S: Yes, but I don't know what happened.

P: Yes, exactly, that's what happens.

[Silence]

P: How are you feeling at the moment?

S: Ummm…a little like I've been found out.

P: That you've been found out? By who?

S: By you.

P: What have I found out?

[Long pause]

S: I don't know.

P: So, what do you think? Is there a connection between inquiry and nondual awareness?

S: Clearly. It's happening. I can see it.

P: What's the nature of the connection?

S: I can't say.

P: Are you confused?

S: I don't know. But it's not a problem.

This is all unreal!

Sometimes people say that *everything* that's being experienced is an illusion. The whole phenomenal world is like a dream. The following dialog shows how I worked with this construction.

S: None of this is really real. It's all an illusion. At some point I'll wake up and see that this is all unreal.

P: How will you know when that happens?

S: Well, it will be like waking from a dream. Suddenly, I'll see that all this isn't real.

P: Can you tell me what will change? What will be different?

S: I don't know. But when it happens I'll know it. I'll know that I'm seeing reality as it really is.

P: But I thought that's how it appears to you now. It seems to be real.

S: Yes, but then it won't just seem to be real. It will be real.

P: But, I thought you said you'll be seeing this as an illusion.

S: Yes, I'll know it's an illusion.

P: Then it won't be an illusion, will it?

S: I don't understand.

P: It will be a real illusion. You'll know it's not real so there won't be any deception. You'll know exactly what this is.

S: Yes, but what will it be then? Will it be an illusion or will it be reality?

P: It won't be an illusion because you know it's not real. And it won't be real because you know it's an illusion.

S: What happened then?

P: When?

S: Just then.

P: I don't know.

S: What are you doing? I don't know what to think now. What is this?

P: What do you mean "This"?

S: What's happening now?

P: Just this, it's simple.

S: Is this real?

P: I can't say. What do you think?

S: I have no idea.

P: Is it important?

S: It doesn't seem to make any difference.

What happened in this dialog is that we connected with immediate experience and saw that there's never a foundation for saying that what's being experienced is real or illusory.

What can I do when I lose nondual awareness?

This is the type of question where we can take on the questioner's assumption that "nondual awareness can be lost." Nondual awareness cannot be lost because it's not a "thing." We can't find it and identify it, so how could we lose it? This is a point where nondual transmission can happen and be stabilized: by staying true to the realities of this state. If we are abiding in awareness it's impossible to get caught up in the "concerned conceptualizations" of others. We keep coming from the nondual. There is total congruity between what we are saying and the nondual because we are simply describing what is "so" for us in this moment. In another moment it could be different. We could be asking the very same question, "Is there something I can do to reconnect with awareness?" But, in this moment we are speaking directly from awareness itself. We are channeling this state, in a way.

Certainly it's easy to think we can lose the state of nondual awareness. It happens dozens or thousands of times to nondual practitioners. We enter the state, and at some point, it seems it's no longer there. It's easy to move back into the conditioned mind because there are so many triggers in our lives—our children, our partners, other family members, colleagues, the stock market, or particular situations.

The best approach is not to become preoccupied with losing the unconditioned state of awareness. We *will* think that we've lost it. There's no doubt about that. Okay. So be it. No big deal. And it's also possible for us to think the "second thought," "What is it that I think I've lost?" and immediately see that there is nothing to lose.

The most immediate way to re-enter unconditioned awareness is to remember that there is nothing to lose. We simply begin at the end again. This brings us straight back to unconditioned awareness. If this doesn't work, we can read a pithy instruction, listen to a teaching, use anything that shows us that "This" can't be gained, as things we can own or even have, and so it's nothing that can go away. It isn't anywhere. It doesn't act in the way that conditioned experiences come and go.

I don't have the time

One of the most common sentiments that people voice when sharing the nondual is that "This (the nondual) is great, but my life is so busy. I just don't have the time to do nothing, as we are here. I've got the meals to prepare, my email, phone calls with family and friends, making a living! All I really want is to spend my life being here, but I have all these other commitments that

I can't walk away from. No way. What can I do? How can I respond to the demands of life and still cultivate the connection to nondual awareness?"

I respond to this plea in different ways. First, I will point out that the 'doing nothing' that's happening in a workshop or coaching session can't be compared with inactivity. I may say, "It's true that in a contemplatively-based workshop we aren't playing a sport, surfing the internet, engrossed in a movie, negotiating airport security, or visiting our parents, but the 'nothing' we are doing—that's happening here—is ultimately unrelated to being still, or inaction. At the very least we can see how, right now, it's possible to be doing 'nothing'—abiding in awareness—and talking, listening, making notes, standing up, sitting down, and moving around. I also know that you can re-enter this when you are having lunch (or dinner) with people from this group in an hour or so, if you choose. All that is needed is for someone to say, 'Okay, now we are well fed. Our stomachs are happy. What else is possible in this moment? The unconditioned, where is it? Where is what? Ah, here it is. We are back where we were in the last session. How wonderful!'"

It's true that, as beginners, it's easier for us to enter awareness when the environment is simple, stable, and undemanding. But, it's also important not to make a correlation and think that "This"—being here—is just doing nothing. We aren't doing nothing in the way we typically use that phrase. We aren't sitting around aimlessly, watching things go by. We are resting in a pristine state of being: a state where we could rest, fully aware, without a flicker of boredom or distress, for eternity. This is completely different from "hanging around, letting time pass by, doing nothing, until something comes along."

Another more robust way in which I respond is to say, "I hear you. Your life is engaged and busy. But is it true that you really want to spend more time resting in awareness? I think that, if we really wanted to spend more time 'here,' somehow we'd figure out how to do it. The Buddha worked it out—how to be permanently free—as have hundreds of thousands of other sages. What's clear is that there is a fundamental change in priorities. For the Buddha, the priority wasn't having a roof over his head, or knowing where his next meal was coming from. Something completely different was going on. So different that he didn't need a roof over his head, money in his pocket, or fallible human company. It's easy to say, 'Ah, but he could renounce all those things because he was enlightened.' But this is a cop out. For the Buddha, the only thing was abiding in liberating awareness, needing nothing, rejecting nothing, and letting his life unfold with no concern or pre-occupation about tomorrow, or the next minute. His power and influence as the founder of a new religion came precisely from his capacity to encounter everything that came his way: scorching heat, drenching rain, an empty stomach, ridicule, adoration, assassination attempts, numerous smear campaigns, without any of these producing the slightest mental or emotional disturbance. Such was the power of his unconditioned love and nondual wisdom."

If the same priority was alive in us, we wouldn't be who we are. It's very simple; we'd be a completely different person, someone so different from who we are, we couldn't even recognize ourselves. We would see a clone of our body, but the speech, functioning, gait, comportment, lifestyle, network of friends and colleagues, and career (if we could still call it that) would be completely different—like someone from a different planet. For a start, we wouldn't be saying, "I don't have enough time to rest in awareness. My life is too busy. I have too many other commitments." I'm not criticizing you here. I'm in the same place. I plan for my future comfort. I think I'd have more time for the nondual if I didn't have to process immigration applications every second year, if I didn't need to manage the business aspects of Timeless Wisdom, if I was younger and more vital, etc.

There is nothing to be gained in thinking, "I don't have enough time for this work." We rest in awareness for as long as we can. If we could do more of "This" we would. I have no doubt about this.

I invite people to be honest and realistic about how they are with this. Complaining about your time being limited and committed, and wishing it were otherwise—that there wasn't so much to do, there weren't so many responsibilities—merely fosters conflict. No one ever entered (or re-entered) this state by thinking, "I wish I could do more of this." Unless, of course, in thinking like this we see that there is no "This" to want more of! No one has ever entered buddha mind wishing that their life was different. In this work we embrace what is, aware of our deepest longings and our present choices, acknowledging where we are with love and understanding.

The *Bhagavad-Gita* speaks about the practice of desireless action (*nishkama-karma*). When time is available, we sense that there's nothing we need to do, and so we do exactly that. We find a quiet place and abide in unconditioned awareness. In the rush of getting things done we may forget the possibility of being "here," but not entirely. Unconditioned awareness is always there, silently in the background, needing and expecting nothing but somehow drawing us into it. Knowing that the ever-present possibility can shine through at any moment, we grow in our capacity to find the time for abiding. We remember how sweet, peaceful, spacious, and free this space is, and we receive it as the sourceless gift of the universe. We find a few minutes each day, and each week, to rest in nondual awareness, and we plan ahead for a retreat so we can dwell more deeply and uninterruptedly in timeless presence.

How can I maintain this state?

Questions that often emerge in nondual work are: "This is great. How do I keep this going? How can I maintain this when I'm at home and at work?"

Here we just need to point out what's happening. At a certain point within the nondual state someone connects with a good feeling. They start to think that they are onto something good with the nondual state: it works, just being here, effortlessly, no pressure or friction, and so they want to know how to keep this going. What happens, though, is that as soon as someone wants to keep "this state" going, it's no longer the unconditioned. The unconditioned doesn't come into being or go out of being. We can't stop it or maintain it. It's not like that. Whatever it is that we think we want to keep going, it's not the unconditioned. So we point out that it is totally futile trying to maintain this state, because there is nothing to maintain.

Integrating the nondual: how do I apply this in daily life?

Questions inevitably arise about how to integrate this work into daily life. How do we apply the nondual in specific situations, such as communication breakdowns in relationships or at work? I always work with this in the same way. I bring this into the here and now and essentially offer two options.

The first option is to deal with the question in terms of the frame of reference in which the question is asked. In order to do this we would need to shift gears, and we can point this out to people. Instead of resting in the nondual, or somewhere in the vicinity of this, we will need to move into a different state of consciousness. We might say, "In order to respond to your question, I'll need to move out of where I am at the moment, and into a state of consciousness in which we speculate about a possible future situation that may or may not happen. Then I will need to apply myself to your question and try to come up with something that might be useful to you."

As a second option we can point out how everything we do conditions the mind, and if we move into the causal-temporal paradigm, we will be conditioning ourselves to do this even more. We will be conditioning ourselves to relate to life in terms of thinking about the future, preparing ourselves for potential problems, looking for obstacles, and seeking solutions. Life will be a series of problems and solutions, successes and disappointments, obstacles and breakthroughs.

People would like to keep the state of the unconditioned going, and they'd like to use the nondual to work with challenging situations in their life, such as problems in relationships, health issues, etc. They want to work out a strategy or come up with a plan of action, something they can do in the future, which they feel will make them better able to cope in the situation. Questions arise: "What can I do?" "How do I best approach this issue?" "What tools do I need?"

In the second option, there's no work to do. There is nothing to integrate. The integration happens automatically. The best work for us to do, now and for the future, is to abide in the nondual space whenever this is possible. This creates a predisposition to continue in this state, and to re-access it more easily in the future. This supports us being totally complete in this moment. We're not thinking about the future, and it's not showing up in the field of awareness in a way that is problematic.

When people ask how to apply *Radiant Mind* or nondual work in their daily life, I often say, "We don't need to worry about how to apply this, because right now we can see that there is nothing to integrate, nothing to apply. The integration is happening just by being here. In terms of integration there is nothing better to be doing in this moment, than just being in the way that we are being." We invite people into this second way of being—being present in this moment, rather than wondering how to bring this into future experiences.

> S: I have the impression that the experience of the unconditioned state has three components: sensations, emptiness, and clarity.

P: Perhaps. What is it that has these three qualities?

S: Our experience of the unconditioned state.

P: Which is what?

S: The experience cannot be described, but it can be colored by the fact that we haven't integrated all the aspects of our life experience.

P: What do you mean by colored?

S: The unconditioned state from a relative point of view.

P: I'm not sure what you are saying. Can you say it differently?

S: From an ultimate point of view we can't talk about this. No speech is possible. But we need to integrate this into our entire life, all our activities.

P: Why?

S: To become better human beings.

P: Okay. And right now, is there anything we need to do?

S: Yes, we need to integrate this so that it's more available and accessible in the future.

P: How do we do that?

S: That's what I am asking you.

P: It doesn't feel to me as though there is anything that needs to be integrated. No integration is needed. It's all being done. What isn't integrated with this, right now?

S: The past and the future at least.

P: If the past and future were integrated into this right now, what would be different?

S: For example, last night I was not aware of being asleep, so I didn't integrate my sleep into unconditioned awareness.

P: What does that mean? I don't see how you conclude that if you are presencing nondual awareness right now, that this means you should or would be aware when you are in deep sleep. Does this mean you would be aware of all the experiences that happened to you as an infant, including when you were in deep sleep in your mother's tummy?

S: Well, not all the way back, but I imagine that if I realize nondual awareness then I will be aware when I am dreaming and sleeping. Nondual awareness penetrates everything, right?

P: You seem to be talking about awareness as something. I understand that you'd like to be in this space 24/7. I see that you want to do something so that might happen. If that's your objective, is there anything more that you can do right now?

S: I can be more aware.

P: How?

S: Well, I'm going to let this experience infuse everything I'm thinking and feeling.

P: What is going to infuse your experience?

S: This.

P: And, is that not happening?

S: There are some things that aren't being infused by awareness.

P: For example?

S: At the moment the unconditioned is in my mind. I'm aware of it in my mind. It isn't in my body.

P: How can awareness be *in* your body?

S: I don't know. It means I'd be aware of my body.

P: And you're not?

S: I am.

P: So what's missing?

S: I'd be aware of what's happening inside my body, because my awareness would go into every cell.

P: How would it do that? What is it that would get inside every cell?

S: I don't know.

P: The way we integrate the unconditioned and the conditioned is just by being here. There's nothing more to do. We can't integrate the unconditioned into the conditioned because it's not a thing. Here we are, thinking, feeling, talking, aware of the past, anticipating the future, remembering that we slept last night. All of this is happening within the sphere of awareness. Here we are beyond integration because there aren't two different things that need to be fused or brought together.

The best preparation for the future is always to rest in pure awareness

The people you work with in sharing the nondual will (hopefully) feel that unconditioned awareness is a wonderful state to be able to access. They will recognize that it is the ultimate state, if this is pointed out to them when they are resting with clarity. However, even with this recognition the tendency to focus on the presumed needs of the future is quite unrelenting. The supernal quality of this moment is easily displaced by the concerns of tomorrow, next year, and beyond. The relevance of resting in awareness, now and for the future, may not be apparent. And so the inevitable question, spoken aloud or silently thought, is something like, "How will doing this—resting in awareness—bring me what I want in my life?" "How will 'This' contribute to my career, my family, relationships, health, and economic security?" "Wouldn't I be better off spending my time and resources in getting my act together, working on my problems, building my career skills, doing good works?"

It can be a stretch to see how resting, totally content, in our natural state is directly related to the happiness we seek in the long term. It's easier, often compelling, to believe that the best thing to be doing in any given moment is managing our investments, taking in a movie with our beloved, playing football with our children, or reading this *Guide*. It's easy to be caught up in time and causality, thinking, "I need to take care of my [you name it] in order to have the leisure to contemplate the nondual." "I need to do X so that I can have Y."

What's missing in this way of thinking is that we have no problem at all being drawn into the complexities and demands of life. We talk as though we had a real choice—that we could spend more time resting in the simplicity of the moment—but that the reality of our lives gets in the way. If it weren't for the fact that we have to make sure our children have a good education and save for our retirement, we'd be sitting merrily in our meditation hut, riding the bliss-waves of nondual awareness. Whereas the truth is that we're addicted to our varied and various projects.

They have such a grip on us that we're sucked back into them even when we have free time and space to allow our busy minds to merge in centerless awareness.

We rationalize that in order to be fulfilled we are better off giving attention to advancing our career, finding or nurturing a meaningful relationship, spicing up our wardrobe, taking care of our appearance, and so on. We forget that at their very best more money, supportive relationships, and a pleasing appearance only give us very temporary and unreliable versions of fulfillment. We forget that the only way to be genuinely and reliably fulfilled is by needing nothing. This is why it's so easy to become embroiled in the never-ending pursuit of chasing after extremely transient sources of happiness and fulfillment.

In stark contrast to our habitual way of functioning, when we are abiding in the nondual it is clear that the best thing we can ever be doing, now and for the future, is to be "here"—abiding in awareness. This sounds radical. It is radical. It can sound ridiculous, naïve, even dangerous to suggest that there is never anything better to do than rest in awareness. "Surely if we are physically ill it is better to see a doctor and follow her advice, perhaps take some medicine!"

We need to be resting in awareness in order to say that "This" is the only game in town, because then—at that time—it is true. It's self-evident when we are resting in awareness that nothing can compare to this. This is priceless. "Being in this moment," in the ultimate way, delivers everything we can possibly want, because we don't need anything.

If we aren't resting in awareness and we begin to talk like this, we'll most likely be pulled into telling people how they should live their lives in order to rest "here" longer. You'll sense the difference. You'll be talking theoretically about awareness. If you are in the zone, you're compelled to share what I've just been saying. What you're saying is no longer personal. Your words and sentences are directly connected to the nondual. The only practice is to be "here"—where nothing is practiced—whenever this is possible.

There is a wonderful case in the *Book of Serenity* (Case 94) that goes like this:

> Once upon a time, when Dongshan was ill, a monk asked him,
> "You are ill, teacher, but is there anyone who doesn't get ill?"
> Dongshan said, "There is."
> The monk said, "Does the one who doesn't get ill look after you?"
> Dongshan said, "No, I look after him."
> The monk said, "How is it when you look after him?"
> Dongshan said, "I see that there is no illness." (Cleary, 1998)

What does this mean? It means that we take care of the conditioned dimensions of our existence in the *most perfect way possible*, by taking care of the unconditioned. If a conditioned event—an illness, a soured relationship, etc.—is really displacing the possibility of resting in the nondual, we take care of these conditions, not as ends in themselves but solely to support our connection to, or with, our natural state. We see a doctor, take medicine, have an operation, see a therapist with our spouse, change the risk profile of our investments, replenish our energy, in order to abide more consistently in awareness. We lean into the conditions that support resting as awareness, rather than get carried away by the minutiae of our lives. Our primary intention is to track awareness, instead of following the movements of the stock market or planning our next vacation. The only way to bring the nondual into our life is by being here, recognizing that "This" doesn't conflict with anything, and that everything in our life is taken care of, just by being here.

The significant thing to realize is that everything we do that's underscored by attachment and aversion conditions our experience further. If we're in a flow state of being kind and compassionate, we condition these intentions and sensitivities within us. If we're often in an internal battle, angry, or withdrawn from life, we're conditioning ourselves to do more of these. If we embrace the practice of "just sitting," it becomes a natural, comfortable, even pleasurable experience, and we're establishing the conditions to continue this activity in the future. The more time we spend abiding in awareness, the easier it is to return to our natural state whenever the internal and external conditions support this movement. At some point this movement becomes irrevocable. Like the force of gravity, we come back "here," just as we are now, even in the midst of our busy lives when other things can seem so important.

The more we rest in awareness, and experience the gifts of being in this space, the more it becomes an important, essential, ingredient in our lives. We automatically return "here," even when we think we've lost the connection. In fact, thinking that we've lost the connection becomes the easiest way back here, because we instantly see that there is nothing we can have lost! This is how we develop and deepen buddha nature. This is the path to full awakening. As Anyen Rinpoche says, the moments of buddhahood become longer and more frequent. (2009) We discover that drinking the ultimate medicine is always the most rewarding possibility. It is clear that when we are "here," nothing can beat this. We don't need more security, more distractions, or a younger body. Even the idea of more pleasure doesn't make sense because our minds are incapable of creating a fantasy-image of what that would look like. Whatever we could create, it would be shallow, fleeting, and trivial compared to the fusion of the totality of our being with unconditioned awareness.

One of the wonderful things that happens as we abide more frequently in nondual awareness is that we can access this state even in the midst of intense and difficult challenges. Even though nondual awareness isn't a conditioning agent, the presencing of awareness within a mindstream creates a predisposition to re-enter this state in the future. We might be in the middle of a big upset with our partner or children, or dealing with a work or health issue, seemingly lost in the inner or outer conflict, and then the simple act of remembering dissolves the reactivity without any residual animosity, recrimination, or self-doubt.

The path consists of becoming more and more familiar with less and less suffering. When we gain familiarity with nondual awareness, we move from being totally wrapped up in our identity—consumed by our emotions and needs in one moment—to being open and spacious in the next. We develop the capacity to directly experience how emotional reactions and overwhelming experiences can self-liberate in an instant without effort, leaving us empowered to meet challenging situations from a space of love and openness.

There is no bypassing happening here. We're not suppressing intense feelings, or avoiding the fallout from an emotional outburst, or relinquishing something that's important to us. I'm talking about the extraordinary possibility of being free to be open, undefended, and fully present in the moment.

I'm writing this not by way of telling you how to respond when someone says, "But surely there are times when we need to forget about this, and just do the dishes, or the shopping?" My intention is to show you that it's possible to speak definitively about the nondual, even when we know and acknowledge that we have limited access to this space. People hesitate to talk like this, knowing they are no different from the people they are teaching. We get distracted in exactly the same way as our clients or students, but this doesn't stop us from saying, with full awareness, that "being here is the best preparation for everything: for falling in love, having a family, getting ill, and dying."

I share in this way. Naturally some people would prefer to receive teaching and transmission from someone who rests permanently in this state. But that's not the case. They have me with them; that is how it is! When I say that the rays of awareness shine in periodically, people sometimes try to convince me otherwise! They tell me that I'm mistaken. "'This' is always here, you just don't realize it. You can feel frustrated and still be resting in awareness." People are very kind. But this is a little absurd. I reply that there are times when it's totally clear to me that I'm suffering, even though as I've said, and will say again, it's impossible to find what we call suffering in this moment, in the past, or in an anticipated future, when we are resting in awareness. I know that it's possible to retrace the steps back to full awareness, but that completely escapes me a lot of the time. The seeming inconsistency between what we say and how we live our lives doesn't stop us from saying, with absolute certainty, that "being here is always the ultimate place to be."

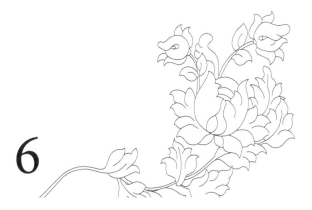

6

Mastering ways to stabilize presence: some skillful means

In this chapter we will focus on the more proactive ways of nondual transmission. We will give quite a lot of attention to different ways of dismantling people's constructions. The themes will include:

- Identifying fixations and fixed frames of reference.
- Using different forms of deconstructive inquiry.
- Detecting the state of consciousness people are coming from.
- Talking about nothing.
- Dancing in nondual dialog.

Observing fixations

Some people coming into this work might have previously read or heard about the Buddhist noble truths and are already aware that fixations—the desire to have things be other than how they are—are the source of suffering or *dukkha*. In the conditioned state of awareness, we're regularly fixated because we're viewing our experience in a dualistic way, imposing our preferences on reality. We believe something is either right or wrong, too big or too small, busy or calm, or we prefer her, not him. Our work could be too tedious or too general, too rushed or too slow, or simply not getting us where we think we need to be, and we feel dissatisfied or incomplete.

As coaches and facilitators, we don't assume people know what fixations are, nor are we compelled to give an up-front definition, because definitions keep the mind busy assessing, refining, redefining, etc. I find that the best way to discuss anything is to have an example in front of me to point to, to look at and examine. Fixations are continually arising; there's no shortage of them. So we just begin to gently observe them as they arise. For example, if someone needs a definition of fixation, we have a fixation then and there—the need to define it!

In this work, we heighten our capacity to see fixations by creating an environment that's relatively free of overt structure and direction. There are no assumptions about how people should be. There is no right or wrong way of being in the space. There is nothing that can't happen, and nothing that's being encouraged. In this way, whatever's being expressed by participants is a function of their internal dynamic.

As this kind of space isn't biased toward the preferences of one particular personality type, it can be just as effective for people who prefer structure, conceptualization, or discussion, as well as those who don't. For example, at any point in time there could be talking or silence. Some people will notice their preference for talking over silence, while others will recognize the reverse. Some people will agree with what is being said, while others will recognize an opposite preference. As a "nondual" or inclusive space, it is totally open.

To the extent that we're fixated, we introduce a bias or distortion into our experience of ourselves and of the world. Even if we believe that we don't get trapped in these extreme categories, we're immediately caught in the dualistic category of being inside or outside of them. Rather than seeing things as they are, we view the world through the filter of our opinions and preferences. We're constantly trying to avoid what we don't like and obtain or prolong what we do like.

Fixations also manifest in our bodies and nervous systems as contraction, tension, movements, gestures, postures, and other bodily phenomena. In response to the mind's fixations on certain experiences, the body becomes fixated as energy gets stuck and concentrated in certain parts of the body. Such fixations may cause stiffness or limited mobility, discomfort, and even intense pain.

Observing our fixations is as simple as seeing what's in front of us. Once we know how to recognize them, fixations become apparent just as effortlessly as the sights and sounds that present themselves to us in everyday life.

In general, there are two ways to stimulate the observation and transcendence of our fixations. One way is to impose a rigorous level of structure and consistency upon one's physical activity. In this way, fixation reveals itself as the ego attempts to affirm its own uniqueness and independence against a background of sameness and interdependence that's imposed from outside. Zen

Buddhism and other traditions based on a monastic model tend to choose this way for stimulating and working with ego fixations.

An alternative way to observe fixations is to remove all structure and meaning. In this way, there's no reason for doing or not doing what we're doing, nor any way of determining whether we're on or off track in terms of our spiritual aspirations. Habitual fixations reveal themselves as we search for grounding and reference where there isn't any, create our own systems of meaning in order to have a purpose, and track our performance and progress.

I find the second method to be particularly effective for disclosing and dissolving obvious and subtle forms of spiritual and psychological fixation. As I practice it, nondual work occurs in a space that is created by the progressive removal of specific and generic structures and assumptions, which in turn allows people to see how their experience is constructed. For example, there are no practices or conversations in this work that specifically allow people to conclude that a workshop or retreat has or hasn't a purpose. Such a space brings people's constructions of meaning, purpose, and outcome into high profile because it doesn't collude with these constructions. As a result, participants and students get to discover what they, and they alone, make out of the space.

In addition, because the space neither validates nor invalidates a student's constructions, it isn't skewed toward any particular personality profile. For example, it's biased neither toward encouraging conceptualization and suppressing emotions, nor toward encouraging emotion and suppressing conceptualization. This environment allows participants to experience the structure and behavior of their personality without distortion. Consequently, everything that's created within the environment is an accurate reflection of what occurs away from that environment. The belief that "something is missing or wrong" emerges in the same way that it does in other situations in life.

As I've already suggested, the initial practice is to observe how our thoughts, feelings, perceptions, and actions reveal our basic responses in terms of liking or not liking what's happening to us. We begin by observing whether we're attracted or averse to what we're experiencing as our experience changes and evolves. For example, thoughts that signal attraction include: "I like this," "I want this to continue," or "I want more of this." Thoughts that signal aversion include: "This is unpleasant," "I wish this would stop," or "I wish I was doing something else." In this way, we become attuned to the signals that indicate we're in a reactive position.

Spiritual fixations

Many people who come to nondual teachings, *satsangs*, etc. are familiar with nonduality and have ideas about it. The fact that people know this stuff, and perhaps have had awakening experiences, or have sat with genuinely realized masters, doesn't mean that they have no reference points. They may be in a non-referential state when they are with you, in which case they are making a beautiful contribution to you and the group. But often, even experienced people will offer you their ideas and beliefs about nondualism, rather than give you direct transmission. So quite a lot of the time, you may find yourself working with their spiritual fixations.

People can become particularly fixated about the path they have chosen, defending this path or a particular teacher, holding their choice up as something that is admirable, or generally getting excited that they are on the "right path." Participants might feel that when it comes to their daily routine, they aren't polarized to the same extremes as they have been at other times. If we're wondering whether we're fixated or not, whether we're in conditioned or unconditioned awareness, or whether we're on the path to enlightenment or not, then we're still in the experience that we need to be somewhere other than where we are now—we're still fixated.

In talking about spiritual fixations, it is helpful to remember that people may need to hold some sense of faith in the spiritual process that is occurring for them. It keeps people engaged and provides them with an overall sense of security that is especially helpful when they are faced with the uncertainties that can arise in a spiritual setting.

Fixated about fixations

The other distinction that's worth making when talking about fixations is that it's possible to become fixated about whether or not we are fixated. Once people have heard about fixations, they want to rise above them. Fixations and preferences get packaged up—along with beliefs, emotions, and the conditioned state—as "bad," or as "no go zones." We mentally rap ourselves over the knuckles when we see ourselves fixated. Fixations become a new obstacle to unconditioned awareness.

Teachers can have a particular tendency to become fixated about fixations, because they're trained to observe them. It's possible to go on autopilot, attempting to find fixations that may or may not even exist. We can look for hidden fixations, and those that have not yet shown themselves but threaten to in the future if not unearthed, rather than allowing fixations to arise in their own time. In nondual work, we let ourselves become aware of fixations as they arise, rather than actively searching for them. We also notice our own tendency to get preoccupied with fixations. We neither give in to our desire to find fixations nor resist this desire.

The good news is that we can't be fixated about nonduality because it's contentless; there's nothing to hold onto, or think about. But if we have an idea about what "it" is, then we can become fixated: about getting it and not getting it, getting it and losing it, prolonging it, etc. It's wise to assume that our transmission will have material in it that people can lock onto and make into something. This is why I find it useful to create an egalitarian space in which people are invited to offer their own observations about how I may be conditioning the space.

Lenses through which to observe fixations

Nondual awareness is often spoken about as being positionless. What does that mean? At an energetic level, it means not being oriented toward our experience in a biased way. At the conceptual level, it means not having a position or viewpoint in relationship to beliefs and not having a reified interpretation about what is arising in the field of awareness. It means that we aren't limited by the dualistic structure of thought. We're not confined by labels such as good or bad, attractive or unattractive, stupid or intelligent.

In nondual transmission we see how our own and other people's experience is very often biased, giving emphasis or preference to one pole of a dualistic structure. An awareness of the basic dualistic structures through which we engage life provides us with different lenses through which we can discern more subtle expressions of the basic tendencies of attraction and repulsion. The following sets of lenses will help you to discern the ways in which we miss the undistorted field of pure awareness by becoming involved in, and oriented to, reality in a biased way. I recommend that you sensitize yourself to these biases so that you can begin to track them whenever they are happening. I invite you to notice how you:

- Agree or disagree with what others are saying or doing (more often silently).
- Resist or submit to what is happening.
- Try to help or hinder your own and others' course in life.
- Seek to bring attention to yourself, or divert attention away from who you are, or what you're doing.
- Try to please people, or alienate them.
- Dramatize or trivialize your own or others' experience.
- Attack and defend, or give in, when threatened or challenged.
- Try to contract or expand your field of influence.
- Are inclined to expose yourself to perceived threats, or how you try to shield yourself from internal or external dangers.
- Try to make things easier, or more difficult, for yourself and others.
- Feel pride or shame about thoughts, appearance, personal history, emotions, accomplishments, etc.
- Express interest or disinterest in others' thoughts, conversations, lifestyles.
- Validate or invalidate your own and others' beliefs.
- Attempt to intensify or dilute your experience.

It may seem peculiar to view these tendencies as biases, reactions, or fixations, since many appear to be healthy and normal, even constructive and necessary to get by in life. How could it not be a good thing to be helpful, or feel self-protective in the face of challenges, or stand up for our beliefs? What we're looking at here are personal and consensual biases that limit our capacity to be with "what is" exactly as it is.

In the nondual space we live in a domain that's beyond disinterest and interest; we neither favor things that are easy, nor seek out those that are challenging. The nondual space lets whatever is arising be there, just as it is. It does not seek to change, fix, or categorize anything. It doesn't assess if something is appropriate or not, right or wrong, good or bad, serving us or not. When we are swayed by these biases, we interrupt the effortless flow of our natural primordial state. Any effort to shift or extend the present moment dilutes the quality of the state of pure presence.

The great thing about the lenses I have listed is that they make it very easy to detect energetic distortions and conceptual biases. It's possible to get tremendous value, just by being guided by any one of the pairs. In Tibetan Buddhism, for example, many practitioners are guided, in an extremely powerful way, just by one set of lenses. They move through life without rejecting anything or trying to put anything in place (*dgag sgrub med*). You could say they are wide open, and traceless. They don't produce any interference patterns. The wonderful thing about this phrase is that it has a very wide semantic range. The two words "*dgag*" and "*sgrub*" are extremely rich in meaning. As a pair they can mean:

- Neither suppressing nor encouraging.
- Neither disapproving nor approving.
- Neither negating nor affirming.
- Neither stopping nor producing.

In other words, we cease making things wrong, for example, when we lose 25 percent of our investments, or our partner is diagnosed with leukemia, or we can't find our keys. Nor do we try to ramp it up when things are going well. We don't try to perpetuate positive experiences. We don't get down on ourselves when things go wrong. Nor do we give ourselves credit when things are great and wonderful.

When we understand the above phrase in this way, and begin to make it the primary modus operandi for our life, the results are formidable. In fact, if you think about it, the idea of not trying to stop anything that happens, nor trying to produce any result or outcome from our actions, is terrifying. So clearly, it is a very powerful principle.

If we were to live this principle at the deepest level, all notions of control, agency, domination, and victimization would be abandoned. These beliefs would be replaced by an unfabricated and irreversible trust in each and every manifestation that's delivered to us through the sphere of unconditioned awareness that defines our life. We would trust the capacity for awareness itself to automatically liberate and release every thought, feeling, and sensation into the infinite sphere of reality (*dharmadhatu*).

Even though we're not yet able to commit the totality of our lives to the principle of living beyond our preferences, we can certainly realize this state from time to time. In the same way that people overestimate their capacities, for example, "If it weren't for my children, parents, or cat, I'd leave everything and spend my time in solitude resting in awareness," we also underestimate what is possible. People often think that only highly realized masters can access a space that is not influenced by our preferences.

It isn't difficult to abide in such a space, at least from time to time, in which we can receive all sorts of information and sharing without judgment or appraisal. We're doing it regularly and reliably in nondual teaching events. We can be there right now. We are discovering how to open into the vastness that receives everything just as it is. This may not be easy with strong physical sensations, but it is quite easy to manifest this principle with ideas and beliefs, and this is a good start.

Sometimes people think that when they abide in nondual awareness more constantly, their lives will be roughly the same, but with much less suffering. This is a hope. We would still like to have the friends we have, stay in the same relationships. Perhaps our work might change and become more rewarding. Our financial situation could change, but certainly it wouldn't worry us any more. This is a strange way to think. The nondual is a radically different space through which a person can live her or his life. Very few people can do it. We can enter this space from time to time, but only when the conditions are supportive.

Still, it's very useful to have a sense of the vast magnificence of entering reality to such an extent that we no longer exist as a tiny person who struggles against major odds to accomplish very meager results, such as getting a degree, passing through one or two marriages, making a trip to Sikkim, etc.

I recommend that you spend one week tuning into the way you agree and disagree with all the ideas, and expressions of values and lifestyles, that enter your awareness. I invite you to discover how everything is equalized in nondual awareness.

Bodily awareness

The way we hold our bodies, and how and where we move, and are moved in them may reveal fixations that are manifesting in our nervous systems. Besides shaping the way we move in the world, fixations also express themselves in our posture, gestures, movements, contractions, and in the ways we act to protect ourselves from, or expose ourselves to, other people and the environment. We may not be aware of our preferences, but they are extremely powerful nonetheless. They draw us into certain situations, and hold us there, and they repel us from other situations.

As a nondual facilitator or therapist, our ability to observe and read the outer manifestation of people's needs and preferences, is clearly vital if we are to help release people from the grip of their defenses and pretenses, independently of how they are wanting to appear. There is nothing spectacular or psychic about sensing moods and feelings of sadness, embarrassment, boredom, defiance, anger, fear, excitement, pride, and so on. All that's needed to be an accurate instrument is to inhabit a ground in which we are neither preoccupied with our own experience, nor manifesting excessive interest in the "other" as a way of avoiding being with ourselves. When we are empty inside, we see more on the outside. We can also tune in to the flow of subtle energies in our own physicality, as this is perturbated by the moods and emotions of those around us. With this sensitivity, our own body becomes a high-powered tool for entering the experience of others, as though from the inside.

This mode of full-body sensing can help us perceive the authenticity and meta-messaging of those with whom we are sharing nondual awareness. Consciously or unconsciously, there is often a disconnection between what someone is saying with their words and the messages from their body and energy. For example, a fluency with nondual teachings could lead us to conclude that someone is resting in awareness. They are "saying all the right things," but their facial expression, tone of voice, or hand or body movements may indicate otherwise. Someone may say, "I'm fine." But the subtle markers tell a different story. The very way that they say, "I'm fine," may show that something else is happening inside, for example, some distress or worry. This is not a game of catching people out. Rather, we see that someone is concealing their condition and that this involves some type of disconnection. It could even be that someone's outer "coolness and collectedness" might be masking their joy and excitement. We are called to meet people as we receive them, and at times this also means that we talk *directly* to the person behind the surface expression.

Not only can we discern the moods and masking when we are physically with others, we can also distinguish nuances in their communication, including nuances in the silences that arise in workshops and phone conversations. Within these silences it's easy to detect important differences. Someone may be silent because they don't know what to say; we can sense from their energy that there's something more but they don't yet know what it is. Or, people can be silent because something's being withheld; or they may feel aloof. People can be silent because they fear a particular response if they express themselves. They may be worried about looking stupid, or feeling embarrassed. The silence that's easiest to detect is that which arises when people are simply resting in what is, in the moments when there is nothing to do or say. This is easy to sense because there's absolutely no pressure, or even suggestion, that we need to be doing something from our side. Our capacity for attunement deepens, to the point where working by telephone is as effective as meeting people face-to-face.

One of the most wonderful things that happens in nondual work is that when we, as facilitators, coaches, and therapists, are in intimate contact and resting in no-mind-itself, we have no judgments about others. This can give people permission to sink into deeply held spaces, sometimes of pain and grief. People can trust that we won't meddle or interfere with a delicate and private journey they are making through their past.

I don't point people in the direction of these experiences. I never suggest that someone "tunes into what's happening inside." Rather, our own awareness that everyone is an extremely complex and mysterious gestalt of thoughts, images, memories, and sensations lets us receive people in a very deep and touching way. Our mere presence allows people to release profound losses, traumatic memories, indiscretions and infidelities, feelings of vengeance toward others, and so on, without us doing anything except staying connected in the sphere of all-inclusive awareness itself.

In order to deepen people's awareness of more subtle dimensions of their embodiment, and allow our awareness to permeate more deeply into the core of their being, we notice the physical manifestations of moods, emotions, and preoccupying thoughts. We are equally aware of what people are saying and their mood of serenity, agitation, fear, boredom, harmony, simmering anger, embarrassment, resentment, resignation, pride, hopelessness, excitement, anticipation, etc. We sense something of the physical sensations they may be experiencing, such as heat, cold, nervousness, tremors, excitation, lethargy, vacuity in the chest area, tension in the abdomen, neck and shoulders, weakness, exhaustion, discomfort, and so on. We know that images and memories will often accompany these sensations.

As facilitators we're also aware of what we're transmitting from ourselves. Whether we are conscious or unconscious of the process, people are continually assessing the congruence between what we share verbally and our body language. This isn't to say their assessment is always accurate, but they are making them, nonetheless. It's human nature to do so. For example, we continually assess people's sincerity. In doing so, we look for congruence between what people say and what they are thinking. In part, we assess people's motives and intentions on the basis of how they communicate non-verbally. Likewise, when we are sharing nondual awareness, people are assessing whether we are in the space that we are talking about. "Is this real for her?" "Is this the space he is in right now?" If there is a dissonance, people will sense it. They may not be able to conceptualize the dissonance, but they'll feel that "something is off." People may think, "I can't put my finger on it, but his words seem fake in some way." "He's concerned with his image." "He is trying to convince me." "He's pulling rank." "He is hiding behind his teachers." "She's trying to add authority to what she's saying by sharing her own path."

The nondual only arises when we are in the space of pure awareness ourselves, or close to it. If we are close to it, the intention of a group will often draw us into the mutual presencing of the nondual. If we are caught in our own reactivity to what's happening, it's best to own this. We can use it as a teaching tool. Rather than try to be "above" the manifestations of our human conditioning, we acknowledge what's happening. If the grip of our preferences doesn't easily release, we can always say, "Wow. Something is going on for me here. I'm feeling a bit uncomfortable right now. I don't know what's going on. This is new to me. When I say that, I'm wondering who this is happening to." We talk ourselves through the self-identification, releasing this through inquiry, and lead those who are with us into this open space as well.

In our work as facilitators, coaches, or therapists, it's important that we're aware of what's arising in our bodies, and what that may be communicating to our students and clients. A yawn may point to disinterest or boredom; leaning forward signals interest and implicitly encourages more of what's being said. These and other bodily signs can be read by clients as either discouraging or energizing their communications. If we're genuinely accessing pure presence, we're neither interested nor disinterested in what's happening, and our non-verbal expressions will reflect this.

Fixations do not require "fixing"

Ultimately fixations don't require fixing. It's sufficient to simply observe and acknowledge their presence. We don't even need to suggest that people do things differently. The mere recognition of our reactions is often sufficient to release us from their influence. As mentioned earlier, with the growth of this awareness uncalculated corrections occur. Feelings of attraction no longer magnetically grip our bodies, and feelings of aversion no longer repel us. We find there is less energy directed to reactions and fixations, and problems naturally dissolve.

Actually, if we inquire into the nature of fixations, we find that they don't have any substantial existence. Fixations are not things, they're just another way of describing the feeling that something is missing from our experience right now. When we can't find any fixations anywhere, our fixations dissolve, and we realize that there is actually no clouding or distortion occurring and nothing to be clouded or distorted. Everything is just as it is.

There are no obstacles!

In the same way that people can become fixated about being fixated, we are conditioned to create obstacles in the way of abiding as awareness. The way I work with "obstacles" is to look for them in a way that they disappear. We work in the here and now, with whatever "obstacle" is manifesting in this moment. We look for the actual obstacle, what it is, where it is, and what it is obstructing. We do this much more in the spirit of a scientific investigation, than a philosophical inquiry. We look for the obstacle, rather than think about it. In this process we are embarking on an "unfindability investigation." We are looking for something that seems to be clear and obvious, but we are looking with the eye of wisdom or prajna, which sees through constructions, which sees that an "obstacle" is a label. If we try to find what it is labelling, what it's actually pointing to, we can't find it.

If we look at the concept of an obstacle more carefully, we can see that, in relationship to unconditioned awareness, there are no obstacles. Why? Because unconditioned awareness isn't the type of thing that can be obstructed. Sometimes I make an analogy between the arising of obstacles and putting our hand in front of our face. If we put our hand in front of our face, it obscures whatever is behind it. We can't see whatever is there because our hand is in the way. Our hand, in this case, is an obstacle to the experience of the shapes and colors that lie behind it. But if there's nothing behind our hand, no forms of any kind, our hand doesn't obscure anything. Our hand is there, but it isn't an obstruction. Unconditioned awareness has no structure. It doesn't have a shape, color, or any content. So nothing can obstruct it. Nothing can get in between us and the experience of unconditioned awareness. When we look closely, we can see that the idea of obstacles is just an idea. It's a concept, a label we attach to whatever we think gets in the way of freedom and fulfillment.

In fact, the idea of "obstacles to unconditioned awareness" is another obstacle! But, we don't have to worry because, as we have just discussed, this is simply a concept. What are we doing here right now? We are dancing in a paradox of unconditioned awareness!

You might ask, "How do we get from there to here—from the idea and experience of obstacles, to seeing that there are no obstacles, to realizing unconditioned awareness?" We get there—which is here—by seeing that there is nowhere to travel. We've already arrived. There's nowhere else to go. There is only ever the here and now.

Introducing the idea of constructions

In *Radiant Mind* and *Natural Awakening*, we re-introduce the idea that experiences are constructions. Buddhism says our empirical experiences are compounded or constructed. When we view our experiences as constructions, it gives us a handle on them. It lets us deconstruct or dismantle them and release the energy from attraction and aversion. We are no longer captivated by the construction and can see through it, thus releasing us from a limiting view of reality. If we can see how an experience is put together, we can take it apart.

Take anxiety, for example. When you are engrossed in the idea that you're feeling anxious because you're in a new relationship, you might think, "I feel uncomfortable; is this the right or wrong thing to be doing?" Your experience becomes narrow and crystallized around this. Energy is being tied up in this construction, in being anxious. If we can dismantle the core construction to find/not find the "me" that is anxious, and see the "me" feeling anxious as a construction, we can dismantle it. As we notice no clear person is available to feel anxious, the feeling and its texture begins to dissolve. More is available in the experiential field. Energy is released with the removal of aversion because normally anxiety is something we want to be rid of and try to push away. In addition, there is a release of worrying about the future, and a release of the energy involved. You may have the sense, "I'm no longer involved in myself. I'm no longer tied up with what is happening with me. I'm free and am no longer stuck in a pattern, a complex or reactive response."

Often I'll engage in a conversation that begins like this, "Okay, you say that's what you are experiencing. I acknowledge that. But for a moment let's view it as a construction, as something that's assembled. What I hear you saying is that right now you are confused and wondering what is happening here. Can we look at that as a construction?" If the student says yes, we can begin to look at "What is it to be confused?" "What or where is *here*?" and perhaps even "Who are you?"

Recognizing the soft spot in a construction

In the previous section I introduced the concept of "constructions." I suggested a shift in our frame of reference that lets us see the constructed nature of experience. When people are sharing their experience, we see it as an interpretation of reality. This shift—from taking things as being given to us, to seeing how experience is composed or built out of different concepts, stories, and ideas—lets us dismantle the constructions that cause us to feel limited and trapped.

The "soft spot" is the easiest way to enter into a construction. It's the place where there is going to be least resistance. The soft spot is the most indefensible element in a construction. I don't go looking for the soft spot. I go there naturally because this work is effortless. This recognition is acquired in time and through experience. As a person is sharing, I hear that it's a construction and begin to feel for the most ambiguous and vague words that they use to describe their experience.

When describing the nondual, some people will have a metaphysical concept. We look for something in their words that will be difficult to find. If someone is offering something that's already vague, then we move in the direction of dismantling the construction by looking for words that are difficult to define, words that will start to slip through their hands as soon as they try to define them and say what they are.

In general, we are looking for the most amorphous concept in a construction as the focus of our unfindability inquiry. I am looking for something that will be difficult to find, if we really look for it. Ideas like awakening, freedom, self as experiencer, are very vacuous. Feelings like fear, anger, jealousy, and anxiety aren't as empty, but they are more vaporous than physical sensations like headaches or indigestion.

The following dialog shows how to find the soft spot in a construction. I'll add a commentary as we move through this inquiry so you can see the considerations that are playing in my mind. They need to be processed rapidly. This is an unconscious competency. No special gift is needed to see the distinctions that guide my input in these dialogs. It's simply a matter of having the distinctions pointed out and understanding them. Once we've seen these structures many times in different configurations, we can't help but see them. The moment someone shares an experience (offers us a construction) a range of ways of working opens up, like a spreading fan.

This dialog looks into a metaphysical construction. These are the easiest to see through.

> S: For me the word that comes closest to describing this is "luminosity."

[Note here that the participant isn't saying, "I experience this as luminosity." If I was to focus on the "I" that thinks or experiences the luminosity, I would be ignoring the substance of the belief that this is luminous. So I wouldn't do that. If the student has said, "My experience is that this is luminosity," then his experience is more central to the claim. I still wouldn't inquire into the "I" because I want to pick up on a belief that seems important to him. The easiest element to work with is "This." But I will work with the idea of luminosity as well. It will still be quite effortless.]

> P: This is luminous?

[I'm just getting confirmation that this is what we are looking at.]

> S: Yes.

P: When you say "This," what are you talking about?

[I'm getting more clarification. I'm just checking that "This" is meant to be the unconditioned.]

S: Awareness.

P: Okay.

[I could leave this inquiry here, with a simple "first range" positive qualification (see pages 173-175). I'm not agreeing with this. I didn't say "Yes." "Okay" isn't as strong. It's more like, "I hear you."]

S: Yes, it's like, this is filled with light. This is light.

[He is answering himself in order to elaborate a little more.]

P: And what about at night, when the sun is down and the lights are off?

S: Well, the same thing. Not exactly, but yes, even if it's pitch black, this is still luminous. It's like the light of consciousness.

P: What is that?

S: It's the capacity for consciousness to witness everything.

P: Where is the light in that?

S: Well, it's not light like the light from the sun or from electric lights. It's the fact that everything is visible. It's all light.

P: And at night?

S: Well, we can hear and taste and feel. It's all that.

P: Where is the luminosity in that?

S: I said, it's not light like light. It's not a physical phenomenon. Consciousness is luminous because it sees all.

P: That sounds like a definition. I'm trying to see what you are talking about.

S: You can't because it's not a thing. This is not visible. You can't feel it, or think about it.

[Things switch here for the student. He's suddenly in the groove. He's taking over from me. This is great. I can probably just sit back and watch him have the joy of channeling the nondual. This is far better than me directing the dialog. He has the direct experience of speaking from the unconditioned.]

P: What are we talking about again?

S: This.

P: Just checking....

S: Luminous is just another word. It doesn't mean anything. I could just as well have said awareness, mind, this. It's all the same thing.

Here is another dialog. I'm including it to point out the components of the construction.

I'm also adding it here because it shows how a dialog can sometimes fail to bring someone through to "not knowing." At a certain point the dialog loses traction. This dialog doesn't move through to unfindability. This happens. If I've been in a dialog for three or four minutes and I sense it could drag on for several more minutes, I'll bring it to closure.

S: I feel that I need to meditate more in order to "wake up."

[Here we have the concepts of "I," "meditation," and "waking up." In my mind now I've got three things—there's "you" as a possible thing to inquire into. There's the phenomenon of "meditation" which is already pretty loose. I know that "meditation" is not a tightly defined concept. We can say that everything that we're doing is meditation because we're aware, and awareness is meditation. The phrase "waking up" is again very loose, particularly if we're relating it to nondual liberation. I've narrowed it down to these three possible entry points, but I haven't decided which one to go for and to move with yet, so I invite the participant to tell me a little bit more about how this will work. It'll help me clarify how I'll move into an inquiry.]

P: Can you tell me a little bit more about that? How will it work that you will wake up through meditation? Can you describe the actual process to me?

S: If I sit and be still and put my awareness on just being, then I can experience more of the nondual.

[Now I've been given yet another construction. Things are very rich here. What I'm going to do is to give attention to the idea of "being" because I know this will be very hard to pin down. What I'm picking up on here is the belief that if you give attention to "being," then that's how it will work. This is the potential soft spot. The concept I am working with is the idea or feeling of being. It may change, but that's where I'll begin. You can see the possibilities have already changed from the first construction. This is what happens. Inquiry or dialog isn't like a philosophy tutorial discussion in which you can ask someone to define their terms and commit themselves to those definitions. This is free-form inquiry. It requires more skill because you need to go with the flow, while being precise and deft in channeling and transforming the conversation into an unfindability inquiry. I'm sensing that it will be difficult to keep the construction "You can give attention to being" intact under investigation. So I'll work with that. It could morph into something else, but this is a good place to begin.

You might think, "Is all this going on in the few seconds it takes for someone to say a simple sentence. Your mind, Peter, seems very busy!" Not really. It's no different than experiencing this extremely complex set of visual sensations that's present in our visual field if we lift our eyes from this page for a moment. Effortlessly we are distinguishing (and we can instantly name) different colors, shapes, surface textures, lots of different objects, etc. Similarly, we can cultivate our listening to effortlessly "hear" everything I am describing. We look and see in a different way, through a different set of lenses. Just as a thief sees homes and banks (well nowadays, online transaction systems) in terms of how they can steal the contents, we hear people's constructions through the lens of how we can get inside them and undo them.]

P: From what you're saying, "being" is separate from you. There's a "you" who gives attention to "being."

S: Yes.

P: When you're giving attention to "being," what are you giving attention to? What is this thing called "being" that you give attention to?

S: "Being" is being aware of the present moment.

P: "Being" is just being with this moment, for example?

S: Yes.

P: And if you're not being aware of the present moment, how is that? Can you, right now, not be aware of this moment?

S: That's hard.

[The only way any concept has meaning is through a contrast with what it is not. If the student is saying anything here in using the word "being" or "being aware," there must be something that stands in contrast to it. Being must butt up against something. The most obvious contrast is "not being aware." So, I'll ask what that's like: how it is to "not be aware." I'm saying this like it's a natural question to ask. If I shared everything that's going on in the background here it would be weird and counterproductive. It would sound as though I was being very strategic, which I am, but it's effortless. I couldn't do it differently and nothing personal is invested in the process.]

P: Perhaps if we do it together it might be easier!

[I sense an opportunity to lighten things up here.]

S: Do you mean, not be present to this moment?

P: Yes.

S: How?

P: I don't know. I thought you were implying we can "not be present to the moment."

S: Well, I'm not sure about that right now. It may not be possible. But I think at other times it is possible.

[He is being a little vague and slippery with these responses. It comes through in words like "not sure," "may not" and "I think." Also, the student is moving away from the here and now by talking about how things might be at other times. One way to protect our beliefs is to clothe them in "maybes" and hypotheses. This inquiry will lose traction without more precision and clarity, but this needs to be done without pushing things. Otherwise I could get a reaction that would retard or derail the inquiry. Remember, this is not discursive. I am looking to undermine the capacity for thought to capture "This."]

P: When we aren't present to the present moment, what's happening?

[I will go along with the hypothesis, and reframe it in the present time: "What is happening?"]

S: Well, it happens when I am distracted.

P: What happens when you are distracted?

S: My mind wanders off into stories about the past and future.

P: Where do those stories happen?

S: In my thoughts.

P: Are those thoughts happening as you're aware of them?

[Notice how I am keeping this in the present tense even though this is still not being completely referenced in the here and now by the student. The present tense keeps nudging us into this moment.]

S: Of course.

P: So you are present to what's happening!

S: Yes. But it means I'm not aware of things, like what's immediately in front of me.

P: What aren't you aware of right now that's available for you to witness?

[We are now squarely in the here and now.]

S: I'm not sure.

[Again, he is moving into diffusion.]

P: I'll give you time to think about it.

[I'm going to challenge the student here by giving him time to get clear.]

[Silence]

S: What am I meant to be doing?

P: You are seeing if there is something that you can experience right now which you are not experiencing.

S: Ah, yes.

[I am going to pull out of this now. He isn't serious in this. He is playing a bit dumb. I sense he could slide around here for a long time. I'm losing traction. I'll soon be wasting people's time. I'll try to complete this dialog in a smooth, even invisible, way that doesn't invalidate anyone or anything.]

P: [Silence]

[I stay connected with the student, but just start connecting with other people, slowly giving more attention to the group as a way of transitioning out of this dialog into whatever happens next.]

I will give you another example of finding the soft spot in a construction that's dealing with everyday experience rather than a spiritual belief. Here the construction involves a feeling.

S: My problem is that I'm continually worried about my mother. She is old and living by herself. I'm always concerned that she's going to fall over and injure herself and be unable to get to the phone. She could die because no one would know.

[I could work with the claim that the worry is continuous, but this would be working at the relative level. The worry is not continuous. But if we move in this direction, we would have to concede that it's happening some of the time. So it's best to look for something that will dissolve the problem entirely. Okay, so what are the components of this experience that can be "seen through?" Strictly speaking, every component can be seen through, in the sense that ultimately we can't find anything behind any concept. The concepts in this experience that point beyond themselves to awareness itself are: me (I), worry, mother, the problem, concern, living, falling over, to be injured, phone, to die, to know. We could inquire into the reality of any of these. I could work with the "I" but this can become a bit repetitive: playing the same card all the time. Also, some people reject this direction on the grounds that it bypasses feelings. We could "see through" the student's mother, but this would be very weird. It's counterintuitive and would involve opening up a dialog that in all likelihood would produce a lot of resistance. There's a constellation of feelings around worry and concern, so I'll go with this. Also, the feeling will be accessible in the here and now.]

P: Are you feeling worried at the moment?

S: Yes, it's pretty continuous.

P: Where do you feel it?

S: In my stomach.

P: How big is it?

S: It's about three inches across.

P: Does it have an edge to it so it stops suddenly, or does it gradually get less intense?

S: Hmm. It stops suddenly. It's very dense and then it just stops.

P: What's on the other side of it?

S: Hmm. Nothing. I can't say. There's nothing there.

[What I'm doing here is making a close connection between the feeling and nothing. It's not nothing. We can't say what is there.]

P: Is the feeling, the worry, moving, perhaps like churning; is it rigid?

S: It's solid, like it's stuck there.

P: What keeps it in place?

[Often a disconnection happens between the raw feeling and an image that the mind superimposes on the feeling. Here I'm aligning myself with the presumed physicality of the feeling. If I use physical images, then often at some point the feeling won't fit this model and it will be very difficult to locate the feeling. You might be saying at this point, "There's nothing nondual in what you are doing." You are encouraging the construction of a form in space, rather than deconstructing it. This process is guided by "seeing through" and "unfindability."]

S: I can't say. I don't know.

[Again, I am bringing the feeling into contact with "not knowing."]

[Silence]

P: How's the feeling at the moment?

[I'm keeping this objective by saying, "How is the feeling?" rather than "How are you feeling?" which could go anywhere.]

S: It's not as strong.

P: Let's just stay with it for a little while and see how it evolves.

[Silence]

P: How is it going?

145

S: It's gone. I can't feel anything.

P: And your mother?

[I'm bringing it full circle here. I wouldn't do this with a metaphysical construction. It's not necessary to retrace the origins of the dialog. If the construction involves a short-lived feeling or emotion, I'd also just leave things as they are at the completion of an inquiry. It's easy for things to return if you give them attention. Here we are talking about a feeling that has been persisting for some time. So I return to it, to at least acknowledge that it's not continuous and that there's a state of consciousness in which her thoughts about her mother don't arise, or if they do they aren't problematic.]

S: It's okay. There are things I can do. And I'll do them. Right now there's nothing to do. I'm fine. I really am.

[A quite profound shift has happened here for this student. It's a mixture of accessing the nondual and seeing some practical actions she can take. We don't need to talk about this. She's probably been thinking about different possibilities around caring for her mother for several months, but dismissed them, probably through attachment to the worry. Now that she is more clear of the worry, some practical actions, that are easily achievable, are presenting themselves.]

Thinking something is true doesn't make it true

At some point, usually quite early on, it's important to simply declare that just because we think something is true, doesn't make it true. Think of examples within your own life. Usually there's not much dispute about this. Once this point is made we can return to it, again and again.

Nondual inquiry: deconstructive conversations

A unique feature of nondual work is the use of conversations that directly reveal unconditioned awareness. These conversations dismantle the structures of our conditioning and introduce us to the experience of contentless awareness. They are the life-blood of the nondual traditions of spirituality and nondual work. They penetrate the seeming reality of our reactive feelings and emotions in a way that dissolves their existence. They are rarely encountered in daily discourse. Most of the conversations we engage in are constructive. They unfold as a commentary on our experience. We interpret what's happening in the moment. We produce histories to explain what has happened, and project into the future, anticipating what will happen. One thought follows the next as we elaborate, modify, develop, rework, add detail, change direction, validate, invalidate, approve, disapprove, and so on.

Deconstructive conversations move in the opposite direction to most of our usual conversations. They reverse the process of elaboration and complexity. They locate the "core distinctions" upon which a conversation rests. They then show that the core distinctions don't refer to anything. This might sound mysterious at the moment, but it will become clear soon.

The most powerful technology for deconstructing fixations was developed in the 2nd century by Nagarjuna, Buddhism's greatest philosopher and founder of the Madhyamika system. Some say he is India's greatest philosopher. The Madhyamika system offers a very comprehensive set of deconstructive tools that are used by yogi-philosophers in their private meditation and transformational debates with fellow philosophers. The Madhyamika method for dissolving limiting constructions is called deconstructive analysis (*prasanga-vichara*) or unfindability analysis. This type of inquiry lies at the heart of Mahayana insight meditation (*vipashyana*). It is designed to break apart an interpretation of an experience and so let a person have direct experience of reality.

The nondual form of Hinduism called Advaita uses a similar form of inquiry within the practice of wisdom or *jnana* yoga. *Jnana* yoga leads to a disidentification with the conversations that structure our personal identity and experience of the world. These traditional methods are forms of cognitive surgery. They presuppose a level of concentration and thought-control that exceeds the capacity of most people. This makes them relatively inaccessible to most of us.

In nondual inquiry, suffering and limitation are deconstructed in conversations, rather than through meditative or debating routines. Sometimes the conversations are slow and contemplative. At other times they move in a highly dynamic way in which a facilitator may puncture a veritable torrent of ideas and opinions about the unconditioned.

The final experience is the same—that our problems simply can't be found. But it's delivered with an informality that's consistent with the repartee of therapeutic conversations. The conversations may have an air of casualness about them, but they're also highly precise. They can unfold gently or as a dynamic and fast-paced exchange of questions and responses that deconstruct a nest of ever-more subtle assumptions and fixations.

Feeling the difference between constructive and deconstructive conversations

Nondual inquiry dissolves or deconstructs the mental structures that shape our emotions and give us a fixed point of view. I use a variety of terms to describe a similar process. I use nondual inquiry, deconstructive inquiry, deconstructive dialog, deconstructive contemplation, unfindability inquiry, and "seeing through." While these terms all describe a similar process, there are different nuances and emphases in these terms. The nuances generally follow the different meanings that these terms have in traditional nondual literature.

For example, in terms of how I use these terms, "nondual inquiry" describes a quite proactive and penetrating form of inquiry that usually happens in dialog. It can also be stimulated by reading and audio input. It can also happen as an individual inquiry. "Deconstructive inquiry" is much the same. I use the term to signify a process of digging into complex constructions in order to dismantle them. "Deconstructive contemplation" identifies how deconstruction happens in a contemplative space that includes silence. Here deconstruction is stimulated by an induction field that gently dissolves constructions without any visible intervention. When the field is strong, deconstruction happens automatically. People find they are no longer able to sustain their constructions. Thinking self-liberates and we rest in nondual awareness, without any reference points. "Unfindability inquiry" states the intention of all nondual inquiry, which is to *look,* without being able to find what we are looking for. "Seeing through" sits behind all forms of nondual inquiry, from the dynamic to the contemplative. "Seeing through" is the vision which sees constructions, for example, the construction of suffering, *and at the same time* sees right through them. I discuss this later.

In order to engage in nondual dialog, or create an induction field that influences a group, it's essential to be able to easily see, and quickly feel, the difference between conversations that are constructive—that maintain or add to the fabric and density of a point of view—and conversations that dismantle constructions by dissolving or transcending them.

There are two components to this recognition. The first is recognizing the trajectory of the conversation that someone is sharing with you. The second component is being aware of the influence of every contribution you make, in terms of whether it provides fuel for more construction work, or whether your input—verbal, non-verbal, and silent—takes energy out of the project of creating meaning and understanding.

Generally speaking, when people share, they are constructing. People listen to their thoughts as though they are describing something that is true and real. When people vocalize their constructions, this often gives them added validity. Sometimes, especially in the context of nondual work, you can feel that through their sharing, people move through a construction into abiding as awareness. This can happen without any input from your side. In this work, you develop a natural and acute awareness of the way in which people's thinking and sharing adds to the validity and tightness in their understanding, *or* moves them beyond the mind—beyond being identified as someone experiencing something.

From your own side, you are aware of how you can get caught up in someone's construction, by hearing that it is true, reasonable, or even just plausible. Or, alternatively, how you add energy to a construction by judging that it is wrong, naive, or unimportant. Here you create resistance through your rejection of someone's experience. This type of collusion or rejection often happens within seconds of someone's sharing. After just one or two sentences, it's easy to find oneself agreeing or disagreeing with someone's understanding. The moment they say "I," we think there is someone there. The minute they say, "…feeling stressed…" we think, "Ah, that's really happening."

In order to help you feel the difference between constructive and deconstructive conversations, I'll give you examples of both. They all begin at the same starting point, with the question "What is this?" They then move in different directions. I've added notes to help you see what's happening.

Constructive conversations

Example one

A: What is this?

B: This is awareness knowing itself. We are aware of everything that's happening and we know it.

[There is already a dualism in this interpretation. There is a "we" knowing "awareness." It is easy for casual dualisms to become solid and seemingly real.]

A: Yes, we see things differently, but the awareness is the same because awareness is empty. It is just awareness, and so there is no difference between your awareness and my awareness.

[This interpretation buys into the idea that sameness applies to awareness. But sameness is saying something; "same" means "not different," so duality is still at play. Also, there is still a "you" and "me" in the picture.]

B: But sometimes we lose that awareness.

[By using the word "that" rather than "this," this state starts to become objectified or removed from "this—here, right now." Also, we are now in the dualism of "loss and gain."]

A: Yes. But actually it is ever-present.

[Attribution of a quality.]

B: As a field of infinite potentiality.

[More qualities.]

A: Right, it's that sense of vibrancy. The way that everything is here, pulsating with energy. Everything is interconnected in the field. I was reading something about the quantum field recently and they were saying the same thing. There is a field that's in between, like matter and nothing. It's the same as "form" and "emptiness."

[A lot of construction is happening here. This could easily go on for several minutes. You can feel how the conversation is now in the realm of descriptive metaphysics. You can also feel how it has moved away from the pure presencing of "this."]

Example two

A: What is this?

B: This is this. That's all that can be said.

A: Yes, we can't talk about it because it's not an object.

[Agreement is being expressed, so it means there is something that's being agreed about. This can be the seed for objectification.]

B: It includes everything that is.

A: Nothing is excluded.

B: It includes everything that's happening now, at least everything we're aware of.

[Talking is starting to happen. We now have the possibility of things happening that we aren't aware of.]

A: For example, I'm feeling really hassled at work right now, and it includes that.

[We are now quickly moving into the content of awareness. It only takes a few more steps from here to have completely lost connection with "This" as contentlessness.]

B: Yes, how could it be excluded, because it's happening?

[There is only a tenuous connection with the unconditioned at the moment.]

A: I'm not sure about that?

[Phrases like "not sure," "I think," etc. show that we are clearly in the domain of sharing points of view, finding agreement, having different understandings, etc.]

B: There is nothing inconsistent about being angry and still presencing the nondual. I get angry but there's always awareness. Anger is just a form of energy. The nondual doesn't stop you from getting angry. The nondual can't stop whatever is happening from happening. It's just our conditioning that makes anger negative.

[The second sentence refers to "personal experience." You can hear how this is coming from the mind. It is being delivered as a preferred belief system. There is no longer any connection with "This" as centerless awareness.]

A: That's not my experience. When I get angry it means I have become a victim of my preferences. I lose the connection with the nondual and get completely tied up in content.

[This contribution to the conversation also references "personal experience." We clearly have different constructions that are playing out here. We have "people" with different identities (e.g., being a victim of emotions) who have feelings and preferences, etc. Time is also being constructed by saying, "When …." In this context "when" is obviously referring to the past. Again, this conversation could go on for several minutes, either reaching some level of agreement, or with the participants coming to the conclusion that they have different experiences of the nondual!]

Deconstructive or unfindability conversations

Example one

[In this conversation the deconstruction is being driven in a quite direct way by A. It also displays a more logical way of dismantling a position or viewpoint.]

A: What is this?

B: This is nothing and everything. It's contentless, indivisible awareness arising as inseparable from the intersection of an infinite number of viewpoints, or at least as many viewpoints as there are conscious beings.

[This is what is often called the "both and" mode of interpreting "this." But it still involves a dualism. Two seemingly different things are said to be inseparable. This is a construction and as such it can be deconstructed.]

A: When you say that the infinity of different viewpoints are inseparable from indivisible, contentless awareness, are they the same or different? Is contentless awareness identical with the world of contents and appearance, or are they different?

[This question has clear deconstructive potential because it drives B into saying that they are either the same or different.]

B: They are both. They are the same, but also different.

A: I don't understand that. How does that work? I'd like to understand what you mean by saying that awareness and appearances are inseparable. Are you saying that the totality of awareness is identical with the totality of appearances? Or that some part of awareness is identical with appearance, but some other appearance, or aspects of appearance, are different?

[This is another question being guided by knowing that we cannot say how, where, or why awareness and its contents are the same or different. It is pushing B to clarify her thinking.]

B: It's the totality. Infinite awareness is identical with the multiplicity of phenomena. There is no difference between them.

A: So the world that's full of different shapes, colors, tastes, sounds, feelings, and different thought forms is contentless, without any structure or divisions at all?

[Again A is trying to drive B into contradicting herself. This is a more logically driven unfindability inquiry.]

[Silence]

B: Hum. Yes, that's what it's like. You can't understand it.

[B is declaring this is so, but agrees that it doesn't really make sense.]

A: So you are saying that which has no form, has structure and form?

B: Well yes. But no. That's not what I am saying. I know it sounds crazy but it is like this.

A: So this room and all its various contents are empty space. There are no forms, no divisions; we don't have bodies that are separate and have different parts.

[Again, A is driving the inconsistency of B's position.]

B: No, obviously not. There is a difference between awareness and what we are aware of.

[B is getting confused and backing away from the idea of the identity of awareness and the contents of awareness. She is still looking for some type of stable understanding of how this fits together.]

A: Now you are saying there is a difference.

B: Yes, obviously there is a difference.

A: But you said before they were the same.

B: I give up.

A: What do you mean you "give up?"

B: There is "this." Wouldn't you agree?

A: When you say "This," I don't know what you are referring to.

B: "This."

A: What?

[No ground or reference points are being provided by A because she is "nowhere."]

B: "This." You know what I mean.

A: I'm sorry, I don't. You're not telling me anything.

B: Exactly. That's what this is.

[A big shift happens for B at this point. There's no explanation for this. And no need for an explanation. This often happens. It's like a quantum shift into a different level of consciousness.]

A: I see. You're talking about this.

B: That's what I am trying to tell you.

A: I understand. You're talking about this.

B: Yes. That's great. I get it.

A: You get what?

B: Nothing. There is nothing to get. I get it. That's it. That's brilliant.

A: Brilliant. How is this brilliant? Nothing is happening.

B: That's true. That's what's happening. Nothing is happening. Absolutely nothing.

Example two

[This is a more gentle sharing with equal contributions. It begins with light constructions and then moves into deeper levels of sharing contentless awareness.]

A: What is this?

B: For me, nondual awareness is a feeling like my heart is wide open. It's like the world is just entering into me. It's like I am the world.

A: Are you experiencing that now?

[A is bringing the conversation into the here and now.]

B: Yes. What is happening for you?

[This could invite A to reference a personal experience, but it stays quite open.]

A: I can't find a "me," so in a way things are happening, but they aren't happening to me, or for me.

B: When you say I can't find a me, who is it that can't find a "me?"

A: I can't say.

B: Who can't say that?

A: It's weird—I am saying it, but there's no me in here.

[This is "both-and" language.]

A: Before you said it felt like your heart or chest was wide open. I can't remember the exact words you used.

B: Now there is no boundary—no inside or outside.

A: Is there a feeling or type of visual sensation associated with it?

B: It's a feeling of being totally open and it sort of has a visual dimension to it. It's like the seer (who is seeing) touches everything that's seen.

A: It sounds like you are still describing something, whereas for me, I feel I can't say anything about nondual awareness. It's just this. Ordinary existence, except that there is nothing more to do, no striving, no need to be anywhere else.

B: Yes, it's that too.

[There is still a subtle shaping of the space in these responses by B, though this is dissolving quickly now.]

B: When I say "open," it's not how it is. It's not open in contrast to closed. I don't know what this would be like if it were closed. So I can't really say it's open. This just is.

[B is deconstructing his own constructs.]

A: Yes, in a way we can't even say it "is" because there is nothing that "is." It neither "is" nor "isn't."

[A continues the deconstruction taking this beyond the dualistic notions of existing or not existing.]

The unfindability of unfindability

It's important at this point to also see that we can't find an unfindability inquiry. It's quite common, after all this discussion on nondual inquiry, for people to think that the term "unfindability inquiry" refers to something that exists or happens. People can begin to relate to nondual inquiry as a tool or technique that they need to master in order to offer nondual transmission. People become involved in the "technology" of how it works, both when it's happening, and outside of teachings or sessions, they also forget that unfindability inquiry itself cannot be found. Whenever we look for it, it dissolves in front of our eyes.

Nondual inquiry is and isn't something. It is something, in the way that I have just shown you and the way you discern the distinction between "constructing" and "deconstructing." A deconstruction has been woven consistently into this *Guide*. If you've gone this far with me, you're already using this distinction yourself. However, if we try to find such a thing as deconstruction, or nondual inquiry, or "seeing through," we cannot find anything.

Deconstruction is, itself, a construction. And like every construction, if we try to find what it's really pointing to, we can't find anything. If we try to find the phenomenon of deconstruction, in our looking, the deconstruction deconstructs. Which is exactly what deconstruction is. It's happening, but if we look for it, we can't locate it. We can't find it in the words, sentences, or phrases that we think make up a deconstructive conversation.

We can't find what it is that we cannot find, and we can't find what it is that's allowed us to find that we cannot find what it is that we thought could be found. We cannot find the unfinding.

Nondual inquiry as a specialized conversation

In order to communicate the distinctive structure of nondual inquiry, I've identified a number of different conversations that are relatively unique to the transmission.

Presenting nondual inquiry as a conversation can be useful for two reasons. Firstly, it makes it easier to discern the structure and function of different interactions within nondual transmission. It allows us to describe this form of transformation in a precise way. The second reason for viewing nondual inquiry as a conversation is it aligns with the "conversational nature" of Western group work.

The conversations I'll describe can be used with groups and individuals. The conversations aren't original. The same, or similar, ones are used by other teachers and practitioners. They can also be found in the spiritual texts of Buddhism and Hinduism.

The impulse for inquiry

When people first come across inquiry and deconstruction, they can look for opportunities to use it. From the nondual space there is no need to engage in inquiry. Rather, what happens is that a student or participant sees something that we don't see. For example, they say, "I am just not getting this." We see that for them there is an "I," a "this," and they are not "getting" it. We don't see what they see. Of course, it is easy to not see what others are constructing because we're not inside the construction. Our "not seeing" allows us to validly inquire into what they are talking about. For example, we can ask, "Who doesn't get this?" "What is 'this' that you don't get?" "When you say, 'not getting it,' what exactly is 'not getting it'?"

You can recognize and work with any of the three components of a construction: subject (person), relationship (attachment, understanding, resistance, etc.), and object (thought, feeling, etc.). Rather than elaborate or build on this construction, we can work in the reverse direction. We break it down into its core constructions. When someone says, "I want to feel free," we can inquire into "Who are 'you'?" "What is 'free'?" "Where is 'free'?" and "How do you do 'want freedom'?" We will talk more about this soon.

Types of deconstructive conversations

The fact that I'm distinguishing "different conversations" might give the impression that nondual inquiry can be broken into discrete elements. To some extent it can be reduced in this way, at least for training purposes, though in practice this work is organic, spontaneous, and highly interactive.

In nondual inquiry there's no agenda, as such, beyond the constant openness to introduce a student to unconditioned awareness, to stabilize this space, and allow the student's painful thoughts and feelings to dissolve in the fresh experience of unconditioned awareness. The task is to facilitate this movement, and not interfere with it.

The primary role of the coach is to be aware of the opportunity to drop into this space of effortless being, in which there is nothing more to do and in which we come home to that state of complete fulfillment—the space of nondual awareness.

When I'm working with people, I don't predict what will happen next. I don't know in advance how a session will unfold. I don't know if it will be punctuated by periods of deep, meditative silence, or whether it will consist of a dynamic exchange of questions and answers.

The skills I present throughout this *Guide*, including the different types of deconstructive conversations, rest in the background as an ever-present set of possibilities, any one of which may come into the foreground and guide the interaction.

In any particular session, a number of these types of conversations might come into play, with each one blending fluidly with others. Perhaps the best way to relate to the structure of this way of presenting nondual inquiry is through the example of our first language, or any other language in which we feel at home. Language is highly structured. We only need to make very small mistakes to be speaking ungrammatically. It's highly structured, and even unforgiving in terms of the precision of its rules. But once we know the language, we have a great deal of freedom about how we use it. We can use it to describe feelings, elicit information, create relationships, speculate about the future, and so on.

In order to facilitate nondual work, we need to have some fluency in these conversations. Firstly, I'll just briefly describe them. Some conversations can be categorized in more than one way.

Shifting to a meta-position

One of the simplest ways to see through a problem is to dis-identify from it. This simple approach to working with someone can release them from the hold of their disturbing thoughts and feelings by creating some detachment from, and space around, their difficulties. Although we may not completely deconstruct a problem, by creating a meta-position where we stand outside our stories and interpretations, we have the possibility of seeing through them. We see our problems for what they are. Rather than being trapped inside them—held in the grip of our reactions—we see our problems with some distance and objectivity. A meta-position allows us to shift our perspective and look from a more spacious place at the story we're telling ourselves about our circumstances and predicaments.

A very effective question for producing a shift to a meta-perspective is: "What am I doing right now?" This is an approach we've undoubtedly used many times in our lives. Some people call this "going meta." I am sure you recognize how a change to a wider perspective has helped you on many occasions to be relieved of some obsession or burden over a troubling incident, person, or situation. We may have been worrying or strategizing about something, caught in a disturbing self-created story about what might happen to us or how someone has perceived us, and then, often out of the blue, we see the truth of it. We see there's a false assumption in our thinking, or we recognize that we're making a projection; we see ourselves replaying an old pattern, or we realize that we are making a drama out of something that doesn't really matter. When we do this, we've moved into a meta-position.

One way to call this forth in someone we're working with is to ask, "What would you say you're doing now?" This question usually stops the story and invites the person to look at what they're doing as though they were seeing it from the outside—how someone else might see them—rather than being caught up in it from the inside. We're inviting them to become an observer of the story-creating process, rather than identifying as the story's creator. Often people will spontaneously see for themselves that they may be indulging in self-pity, or complaining, or justifying their rage, or invalidating an accomplishment.

If someone is really struggling to see what's happening for them, we might make a suggestion from our side. "What I see happening is that you are really angry about…." But, it's way more effective if someone can see for themselves what's going on. This way there's no room for dispute, or even partial disagreement.

It's useful to have a dozen or so names for the reactions that typically arise for most people. Some of the most common ones are blaming, complaining, justifying, enduring, commiserating, explaining, seeking sympathy, and stroking. When we see ourselves "doing" these, this immediately produces some release and freedom.

Doing this over time gives people a tool with which they can observe for themselves the intentions and the pattern of their communications. They become their own teacher and are able to draw on their own wisdom. They're able to create some distance from what they've said or done and see through it. If not, they can be assisted by a question, such as, "Can you see that what you're doing is constructing a problem?"

In this process of guiding someone into a meta-position, it is important that nondual coaches be aware of their own reactions, judgments, and expectations. We are called to listen with openness, compassion, and a healthy detachment. We receive the content with an ear to the overall function of the story. If we choose to focus on the content, we track the structure of the story and seek its "soft spot" in order to dismantle the story through unfindability inquiry. If we bring our awareness to the feelings and possible intentions behind the construct, we can then invite the person to a meta-perspective through which the pattern beneath the behavior can be observed.

If we are skilled in deconstruction, we can afford to become involved in the internal structure of a problem in order to facilitate its deconstruction, because we know we won't get caught up in unnecessary detail. We won't be sidetracked. The core construction will stay in the foreground. The story won't trigger a belief or emotional reaction within us that would interfere with cleanly dismantling a construction. Very often a participant or client is best served if we point out that a problem has been constructed, and encourage them to look at this for themselves. Instead of getting directly involved in the problem itself, the person is invited to explore what's been presented from a larger perspective.

When we ask someone, "What would you say you're doing now?" the person may respond, "I'm talking (or thinking) about this event (or relationship)," or "Isn't it obvious?" or "Actually, I can't say." We can then explore with them what they're "doing" through that particular response, rather than what they are "saying." We shift the language from the story to the action or behavior, and the primary feeling that's arising. "I'm sad." "I'm furious." "I'm really worried." With this type of meta-processing it's also possible to see how we are attached to our problems: how we enjoy feeling angry or incensed, and how we indulge in feelings of hurt, guilt, and self-pity.

The point in seeing things from a meta-perspective in the context of nondual inquiry is to get at the core problem itself. We go beyond the story and see exactly what it is in the moment that we are indulging or resisting. The specific details are secondary to the core problem itself. We seem to be able to generate very similar problems again and again, from the infinite matrix of memories, circumstances, and interactions that constitute our lives. What's significant is the habit of using our minds, emotions, and energy to construct problems at all.

Natural koans

Koan practice is usually associated with Zen Buddhism. Koans are questions or puzzles that cannot be solved—at least conceptually. In Zen, koan practice has been formalized and institutionalized. The entire koan system of Rinzai Zen is a form of contemplative inquiry that deconstructs the conceptual mind in order to reveal unstructured awareness—an experience that in Zen is called "no-mind." But koans are actually timeless. Koans arise naturally in our minds when our experience of the conditioned state expands to include unconditioned awareness.

The silence that occurs in this work is often filled with natural koans. As people move into a less familiar way of being, they begin to wonder what's happening and what they should be doing. When our familiar points of reference dissolve, questions arise such as: "What is this?" "Where am I?" "Am I moving forward or backward?" "Am I moving at all?" "Is there something special I should be doing?" "Who am I?" These questions are all koans because each one of them is a key that can unlock the conceptual mind, and take us into the unknown. By letting one's thoughts ride on the question, all sense of having a fixed position or frame of reference can dissolve.

In nondual inquiry, we use naturally arising koans as tools for deconstructing our habitual ways of thinking. The silences that punctuate the nondual space often give birth to a gentle cascade of natural koans. By letting our thoughts ride on these koan-type questions, fixed ideas about who we are, and what we are doing, can dissolve into the infinite expanse of unconditioned awareness. We surf the koans through the deepest layers of our consciousness into the unstructured mind.

In our journey from a structured (knowing) to an unstructured (not knowing) state of consciousness, fixations reveal themselves as natural koans. Natural koans are questions that can't be solved with the analytical mind and whose resolution opens us up to the experience of nondual presence. In nondual work, we provide a space for natural koans to arise.

Questions that arise for you during meditation are your koans. They may be questions or declarations like:

- Why am I doing this?
- Is there any point in this?
- Who is doing this?
- This is a waste of time.
- I am bored.

A common feature in all of these questions is that they refer to "This," the experience that's happening, or "I," the person who is meditating. Often we don't go on to ask the next question, "What is this?" or "Who am I?" We assume that we know what we're thinking about in the first set of questions. These two questions, "What is this?" and "Who am I?" are at the heart of many forms of deconstructive inquiry.

"Who am I?"

The Hindu form of nondual inquiry is based on the question "Who am I?" This question aims at connecting people with the "witness consciousness." In a setting of nondual inquiry, it may be preferable to ask a question such as, "Who is experiencing this (problem, feeling, etc.) right now?" This question is more immediate. It keeps us in the experience we're having in the present moment. What we're asking is, "Is there an experiencer separate from the experience?" Or, saying it slightly differently, "It's clear this experience is happening, but *who* is actually experiencing it?" It is worth experimenting with different versions of the core question. Sometimes it is easier to work with questions such as: "Who is receiving this experience?" "Where exactly are you?" "Where is this question being received?"

The following dialog is a classical, straightforward self-inquiry that follows the question of who is feeling, who is thinking, etc.?

S: There's a sensation arising, and again I use the word "I" because I don't know what other word to use. There's something that senses that sensation.

P: So who's using the word "I?"

S: This constellation of a person, the one who thinks she's someone.

P: Who's that?

S: The one that is sitting here.

P: Who's sitting here?

S: There's more sitting here than the person I call myself. But that person is the one that uses the word "I."

P: Okay. So who thought that? There's a train of thinking, that you just presented, that just happened. Who thought that? Who's the thinker? Where is the thinker of that?

S: I can't locate it.

P: Who can't locate it?

S: This person I'm calling "I." There are words that come up, and I don't know if they mean anything for me right now.

P: So who thinks that what's happening now might not mean anything?

S: I'm searching for an answer.

P: Who is searching for an answer?

S: It's a thought or an identification that's attached to thinking there's an answer.

P: Okay. Who is thinking that? Who's thinking what you're thinking now?

S: What's arising in me now is a sense that I want to just be quiet.

P: I appreciate that. Who wants to be quiet?

S: The one who's standing on the edge.

P: Who feels that they're at an edge?

S: This thing I call "me."

P: Who says, "me?" Who says the word "me?"

[Silence]

S: I don't know.

"What is this?"

The main koan of Korean Zen is the question: "What is this?" In nondual work, this is a wonderful koan that's easily introduced into the space once there is sufficient dis-identification with the immediate conditioned reality of sense impressions, feelings, and thoughts.

I prefer the question "What is this?" over "Who am I?" The question "Who am I?" is more introspective. It tends to point us inward. Some people on the spiritual path can become confused by the question "Who am I?" It can disconnect them from their problems rather than deconstruct them. The question "What is this?" doesn't point us in any direction whatsoever, because "This" includes everything inside and outside of ourselves. We don't know where to look! And that is what the question is designed to achieve.

When and how to pose these questions

With skill, these questions can be consciously introduced into the practice of nondual inquiry. However, the same questions that can be used to release us from our thinking can also embed us further in our thoughts. Generally, someone needs to be in a fairly refined, unstructured state of mind before we invite them to contemplate these koan-type questions. If they're introduced prematurely, the effect can be counterproductive. If we ask these questions too early, when people are in a thick interpretation, the questions will only invite elaboration. The questions will lock into people's belief systems and lead them to construct responses. They'll produce more thinking rather than a dis-identification with thoughts. If the questions are well-timed, they lead directly into an unmediated experience of the present moment. The questions are asked without any suggestion that they should be thought about or contemplated. They aren't designed to be answered!

Making the unconditioned into something

A question that can arise naturally for people when they first experience unconditioned awareness is: "What is this?" If this question needs to be answered, the presencing of the unconditioned can quickly devolve into a conditioned state. The habit-energy of the knowing mind tries to understand "This," and in the process the "nothing" becomes "something." When this begins to happen we can point out that from the conditioned state there is a need to understand and label "This," to put it into a category. People like to leave an experience knowing what has happened for them. We also feel it will be easier to re-enter an experience if we know what it was.

When the question "What is This?" is asked in reference to nondual awareness, an appropriate answer is that it isn't anything—it's nothing. We invite people to look around. We see that everything is here; everything is functioning perfectly and coherently. At the same time, we sense the immutable vastness of the unconditioned—the infinite reality-sphere that neither changes nor stays the same. For some, it can be difficult, even frightening, to meet the words "nothing," "no thing," "vastness," or "absence." These words conjure up images of a void, or groundless, empty space. Or these words communicate something that sounds utterly boring, uninspiring, uninteresting, or even a threat to the fulfillment of our perceived needs and objectives.

Even so, I find that "no thing" is an extremely potent word for pointing to the unconditioned dimension of "This," especially when we further qualify that we can't even say this is a "non-thing," because we don't know what it is that we would be negating. At this point it's very difficult to think more about "This," since whatever we are thinking about, it isn't "This." This calls forth an "unknowing," within which the nondual clearly manifests.

Removing concepts: tracking and managing the gradient of the non-conceptual transmission

Gradient is the rate at which we move in the work. It relates to slippage. Imagine taking people on a journey up a mountain. If the going is too hard, the rate of change is too quick and too steep, you lose people; they can't keep up with you—that's the idea of the gradient. The primary thing that determines the incline of the gradient is the rate at which you remove content from the space. If you fill the space with content and concepts, things for people to think about, the gradient will be kept low, even flat. If you just come in and do absolutely nothing, don't create any connection with people, don't create any context, but sit in nondual awareness and hope that people are just going to join you there and somehow it will all happen, the gradient will be too steep.

You track people's level of comfort and discomfort. If people are feeling too uncomfortable too much of the time, if they're feeling too disoriented, if they can't cope with ambiguity or the lack of reference points, then it's too steep a gradient. If you bring some context to the space, then people can continue to be there with you and move into the space that includes pure unconditioned awareness.

With a very flat gradient, we accomplish little; we continue to be involved in a conversation in which our habits and opinions are just flowing forth and there's no movement toward accessing or abiding in awareness. As a facilitator, I don't want to waste people's time. But we also acknowledge that if the rate of change or gradient is too steep, you can literally lose people. They will walk out. They can think, "I don't get this. This is just not giving me what I want. I am looking for stuff that will help me with my life, but this is so far out I can't get it. I don't know what's going on here. These people are acting like zombies. He contradicts himself. And there's nothing in this for me." In this case, it has moved too fast.

Experiencing "nothing"

When people experience nondual consciousness or natural awakening for the first time, they often ask, "What is this?" The most accurate response we can give is to say that it's nothing, or that it isn't anything. There's nothing here. Everything is here, but there's also the experience of nothing.

The conditioned state can tend to conceptualize the nondual experience, labeling it as incomprehensible, boring, or too easy or simple. If this occurs, we can just gently note that we have moved out of the structureless state and are now trying to impose a structure on our experience.

Having met with thousands of people who are knowledgeable in the areas of psychology and spirituality, I've found that they tend to begin constructing on the basis of very little evidence or experience.

Some people who are familiar with unconditioned awareness are uncomfortable describing it as "nothing." They feel that people might interpret this nihilistically and find it uninteresting. They are concerned that people will in fact become frightened about the possibility of accessing and becoming familiar with the nondual experience if it is a state of nothing—without any structure or content. Still, I find the term "nothing" useful because it can correct our tendency to construct meaning, thereby obscuring the experience.

En route to experiencing contentlessness, people may find themselves thinking, "This is very strange. I don't know what is going on. I'm not sure what I'm saying. I've never said this before. I'm not sure if this is right or wrong." As they move from the known to the unknown, the experience can be quite ill-defined. People aren't sure how to interpret what's happening around them. Their own experience of themselves changes to the point where they may not know who they are. The routine story they have about themselves doesn't seem to apply.

In fact, the experience of not knowing who we really are can become routine. Through this work we become familiar with experiencing ourselves as someone whose existence is being continuously and freshly revealed as new aspects of our conditioning, *and* as the primordial and constant dimension of unconditioned awareness. Unconditioned awareness provides a clearing within which we can evolve in an unimpeded way. In this process we continually encounter ourselves as a stranger—as someone we've never met before. When we're experiencing nondual awareness, our belief system no longer defines the boundaries of our identity. Even during the intervals between our experiences of unconditioned awareness, our belief system becomes more relaxed.

Experientializing the space of nondual awareness

With the importance we place on experience, it might sound like a positive thing to experientialize the space of nondual awareness. But it's not. Here I am talking about how to recognize the process of making "nothing" into something, thereby losing the connection with the nondual. We know that nondual awareness isn't an experience. It's not a thought. It's not a sensation or feeling. Still people have a tendency to experientialize it, i.e., to make it (the nothing) into something. This is because we normally share *through* our experiences. It's also the way we remember things.

We see this very clearly when people talk about an awakening experience. People will say, "I was on a retreat, and I had an awakening. The self dropped away, everything changed and became luminous." Two things are possible here. They're either describing a change at the conditioned level (which was great) or they're describing an awakening into nondual awareness that they've subsequently experientialized. They're sharing it with us as something that "happened." They're talking in the past tense about an event. If someone is talking about an awakening that happened last year, or ten years ago, *as a significant event*, they're not abiding in awareness. We can't remember nondual awareness because there's nothing to recall! It's easy to think that natural awakening happens at a particular time and place. It does—but it doesn't. It isn't an event.

In nondual awareness nothing happens. There's not even any awakening because there's no medium within which the awakening can occur. There's no before or after. People degrade the nondual space by talking about some of the experiences that may, or often do, accompany that state. And then they confound these with awareness itself.

People might speak of feeling really serene, that everyone is divine in their own unique way, or that everything is totally perfect. In a workshop setting, people can be in a state of pure awareness in which nothing is happening and then, after some time, they want something to be happening, rather than just continue to abide in the "no-thing" that's happening. So people will introduce concepts, like appreciating the love, the intimacy, or the feeling of connection that's happening. They are taking something that's not an experience and making it into one. These are some of the ways in which people experientialize the state.

The moment that "This" is spoken about as something that's happening, as a process or an event, or as anything that involves a feeling, or change in thought, "This"—as contentless awareness—has been experientialized. We no longer have "This."

The experientialization of awareness can also happen when people are reporting a present-time state. For example, they may be talking about something that's happening for them in the moment we are listening to them. They may be telling us that they are awake right now, or abiding as awareness. In this case, we listen to ascertain if this is happening *to them* or *for them*. Is there an "assumed I," a presumed experiencer? If there is, there must be something to experience. If there's nothing to experience, there's no experiencer. So we listen to see if they are revealing the nothing that's happening to no one.

In this space, nothing's happening. It's completely uneventful. If someone is in the fruition state, abiding in awareness at the moment, a so-called awakening experience is irrelevant. It's not even surfacing because we're in a state where there's nowhere further to go, and there's no need to talk about it. It's a non-event. They can see that it didn't in fact happen, in just the same way that nothing's happening now.

This is why the *Heart Sutra* says, "There is no liberation." When we're in the fruition state, abiding in awareness, there is no liberation. This is not a state of liberation. There's no freedom here. There's no "awakening" into this state. This is ordinary mind, our natural condition.

Sometimes when people begin to share experiences of awakening that have happened to them, I warn them. I say, "Look, if you're going to share this with me, I will engage with you in a way that your experience will be deinvested of all the value that you've built into it. I'm going to ask you exactly what happened, and you're not going to be able to tell me. You're not going to be able to find it. Or what you find will just be the pleasant attractive accoutrements that accompany the presencing of pure awareness, not awareness itself. The good news is that our inquiry will lead us straight back into the awakening you are talking about."

Seeing through—thinking about nothing

In Buddhist contemplative psychology the nondual is realized and established through two closely related practices: those of inner peace *(shamatha)* and higher insight *(vipashyana)*. In a traditional setting these practices are quite differentiated. For example, people may specifically do a *shamatha* retreat following a set protocol in timed sessions. Yogis also practice *vipashyana* in a very structured way, as I describe in Appendix One of this *Guide*.

The way I work is much more organic, largely because I work with group dynamics. I also dismantle structures rather than put them in place. Nonetheless, the model for nondual transmission offered in this *Guide* is informed by the distinction between inner peace *(shamatha)* and "seeing through" *(vipashyana)*. "Seeing through" is the way I translate *vispashyana*. These two steps mutually support each other. They aren't strictly distinguishable. In this work we practice serenity for its direct relationship to resting in crystal-clear, lucid awareness. The two practices mutually inform and empower each other.

The logic in creating a foundation of inner peace is that it's easier to engage in nondual inquiry when we are feeling calm and peaceful. When we are experiencing inner peace, we feel that things are fundamentally good and that we can really relax with things as they are. In this space, no energy is being wasted trying to understand what's happening; no effort is being expended hoping or trying to change what's happening. If we want to be somewhere else—physically emotionally, and mentally—we feel trapped to some extent and our focus is on just getting to the end of a session. In this state people aren't fully predisposed to inquire into the reality of the self and other constructions.

So we begin by letting the thoughts and emotions settle down. We enter *shamatha* by giving the mind nothing to think about. I don't get straight into this. If we empty the space of content too quickly, it can stimulate the mind. People become confused, disoriented, and their minds may become more busy. However, I'm surprised at how quickly people can calibrate to having no content offered to them. When there are fewer concepts, beliefs, and viewpoints being thrown into the space, it becomes meditation, even though no one is meditating. Eyes are generally open, people are aware of their environment, they are settled, ready for anything to happen, including nothing. We don't seek to explore any issues in our lives or understand a metaphysical concept of reality. We may enter natural meditation where there is no aim or object of reflection. As this practice unfolds, there is less and less to think about until finally there is nothing to think about.

Then when things come up from within the group, or with a client, we can inquire into the reality behind the concepts and constructions people offer through their questions and sharing. So in a sense, *shamatha* begins by "not having anything to think about." And *vipashyana* is entered through the questions people ask and "seeing through" the reality of concepts like mind, self, awareness, seeing, choice, freedom, absence of freedom, suffering, and the absence of suffering.

Inner peace comes from the side of the client or group as they become progressively more comfortable doing nothing, and having nothing in particular to think about. At the beginning, the *vipashyana* dimension arises in response to the questions being asked by participants. A facilitator or coach takes a participant's question, or their expression of a point of view, and dismantles this by seeing through the concepts. This same process can be called nondual inquiry, or unfindability inquiry. We show that there is nothing here for those concepts to describe. This process, which is often stimulated by nondual inquiry, is called "seeing through." We look for something and we can't find it.

At the beginning, the process is driven by the facilitator or coach. But after a few hours of exposure to this work, people start seeing through their constructions, without needing to be guided by a skilled facilitator. They will deconstruct their interpretations of who they are, what is happening, and what this is, internally, sometimes by playing out a possible conversation with the facilitator in their own mind. The deconstruction that happens in "seeing through" allows us to rest in a pristine state of awareness that is free of all content or reference points.

As the Buddha is quoted in the Mahayana teachings:

> When the universal panorama is clearly seen to manifest without any objective or subjective supports, viewless knowledge awakens spontaneously. Simply by not reviewing any appearing structures, one establishes the true view of what is. This viewless view is what constitutes the buddha nature and acts dynamically as the mother of wisdom, revealing whatever is simply as what it is—empty of substantial self-existence, unchartable and uncharacterizable, calmly quiet and already blissfully awakened. (Hixon, 1993: 124)

With serenity in place, we then move forward, bringing lucidity to what may still be a feeling state, with an invitation to see through to a space of sheer "no-thing-ness." Once people's thinking becomes sufficiently still and quiet, we can move into an inquiry mode. We might begin this inquiry by asking, "What would you say is happening right now?" You notice that I don't ask "What is happening right now?" but "What *would* you say is happening right now?" This is intentional. "What would you say…?" already creates some distance between what is happening and our interpretation of it, i.e., what we might say.

Another way to transition into "seeing through" if the energy is a little too thick, if people are too comfortable and a little lethargic, and no questions are being asked of you, is to invite people to think about "This"—this as nothing.

When we direct the mind back toward that which has no structure, that which isn't a process or event, which isn't a thing, the mind has nothing to think about. The invitation to think about "nothing," to think about that which neither is nor isn't, undermines the very capacity for thinking to occur. "Thinking about nothing" becomes impossible because there is no basis for conceptualization or any other spinning of the mind.

If structures of interpretations about "This" do arise, we can do nothing with the responses. We can hear them as people sharing a report, and let them dissolve without interference. Or, we can dismantle these structures. Some of the common overlays are: "This is the source or creation of all that is." "This is a field of universal or infinite potential." "This is the play of universal or divine consciousness." "This is the awareness of awareness." "This is unconditioned love." These are all constructs that in different ways superimpose "something" on the "no thing." They are saying that it is something rather than something else. Clean nondual inquiry can assist us in seeing through any attempt to understand or interpret "This" by seeing that there is nothing to which these interpretations refer. Whatever concept is used, there is nothing behind it.

So, to summarize, the practice of seeing through all presenting constructs *(vipashyana)* leads us to "having nothing to think about" and thus "thinking about nothing." Because there's no foundation for our thoughts, our thinking naturally slows down, the habit of needing to know weakens, and we rest in a state of inner peace and tranquility. This in turn creates a stable foundation of easy-going, undisturbed inquiry. Now having less mind stuff with which to identify, our capacity to see through conceptual structures deepens. Before long the self-liberation of thoughts and sensations happens spontaneously and automatically. Serenity and "seeing through" are working synergetically and allowing us to rest in effortless, lucid awareness indefinitely!

Speaking from the unconditioned

The most powerful and effective inductions into unconditioned awareness happen when we speak from within the state of no-mind, or natural awakening, itself. While some people feel that the only way to share "This" is through silence, in fact words are extremely powerful when communicated from within this state. When words describe contentlessness with the same precision, immediacy, and obviousness with which we could describe an insect resting in our palm, our words can induce the very same experience in others, since no sense information is needed to get this. I would say that some verbal content is nearly indispensable for most nondual transmissions.

Pure speaking is the oral transmission that arises when we speak spontaneously from unconditioned awareness. When we're speaking from this place, there's no forethought or strategizing; we don't know how or if we'll finish a sentence. We don't have a preconceived image or idea of what we'll be saying. We aren't concerned about the consequences of our words. Nor do we attempt to convince anyone of anything. We are simply present in the here and now, speaking about what is immediately apparent, the timeless, transpersonal, contentless awareness. This is in contrast to ordinary talking or teaching, in which there is content to communicate: where we develop our ideas before and during speaking, and we have an intention that our ideas are accurately received.

As facilitators, therapists, and coaches, it's also important to recognize how sometimes we start out sharing directly from within the state of nondual awareness and we talk ourselves out of it. We overrun the transmission and begin to share our ideas and opinions. Our "understanding" takes us over and we suddenly find we've reified awareness and no longer are speaking from within it. If or when this should happen, it's best, as always, to acknowledge what's showing up in the moment. "I see I'm now talking about the unconditioned," you might say, "and no longer from it." Acknowledging what is and isn't happening in the present is both a useful teaching and also a catalyst for you and your participants to return to this state.

For myself, it's inevitable that when I speak from this space I contradict myself, often in the same sentence. If this is disconcerting, we may explain that we've reached the boundaries of thought and language, and that we're now in the realm of paradox. Our words—all words—are unrelated to "This" since "This" is not a thing or non-thing. When we talk about "This" we are bound to contradict ourselves. We are using concepts and concepts are by definition based on dualist structure. Things are what they are, because they aren't what they aren't. I am me because I'm not you. If there is no concept of an "outside," there's no concept of an "inside."

We may also need to meet student projections that we aren't, or can't be, in the unconditioned state because we're talking and "This" can only arise in silence. This is just another opportunity to say that we aren't talking about anything.

In pure speaking we continuously accommodate and naturally adjust to the listening of the other person by attuning to their receptivity and/or confusion through their body language, statements, or questions. We shape what we say as a natural response in the dance of communication rather than as a script or strategy. What's central here is that there's a bridge between ourselves and others that invites them to be with us, to experience and express their authentic engagement. Thus, we may not need to continue speaking when we sense the other person has fully received our offering. Or we might stop sooner rather than later when we perceive that our words are unnecessary, or aren't landing. In this way we honor what's actually happening instead of clinging to a forceful agenda.

Since we're speaking from "nothing," the content of our communication will also be "nothing." People won't be able to say "what" it is that we are talking about. If they can understand what we are saying, we again say, "I can't know what I'm talking about because there is nothing to know. If I don't know what I am talking about, how do you know what I'm saying?" They may say, "You are talking about awareness." And this is the moment to say, "This has nothing to do with awareness." We do this in the service of revealing unconditioned awareness.

Facilitators who are new to the nondual approach may feel awkward attempting such an unfamiliar conversation. It's like learning a new language. The familiar structures of therapist/client or teacher/student are upended in the state of not knowing. This state, which is also known as the "great equalizer," dissolves all boundaries and differences in role, since here we rest together as absolute equals in being unable to know, say, or even think about what "This" actually is!

While this way of working can be confusing and challenging to our need to be coherent, sound intelligible, make sense, and be wise, at some point we are compelled to contradict ourselves, even in the same sentence. If we stay true to the reality that can't be captured by polarizing concepts, paradoxical locutions will emerge spontaneously.

We aren't alone in this. A survey of nondual literature that spans Greek, Indian, and Chinese cultures instantly reveals that we are simply joining a transcultural lineage in which hundreds of thousands of masters have used paradox and negation when sharing "This."

I find the best way to introduce unconditioned awareness is through free-form dialogs rather than text-based teachings. In free-form transmission, the text that we teach from is the narrative that's being delivered by participants themselves. This ensures that the dialog is relevant, potent, and opportune. Dialog gives us the most direct route into the structures of interpretation that are limiting people's access to the nondual in the moment.

If our talking from the nondual produces some confusion, this is fine. It's to be expected and it's potentially very useful because it's an opening to the unconditioned. We might ask a question such as, "What are we talking about now?" Someone might reply, "I don't know," to which we can respond, "I'm not surprised because I don't know either. In fact, I can't know, because we're not talking about something. Even though we're using familiar words, we don't have any subject matter. There's nothing here to be confused about!"

Contentless conversations—talking about nothing

In order to be able to talk about nothing, we need some fluency in a special type of conversation that can look like other conversations, except that there is no subject matter. These conversations are used to induce an experience of the nondual state. This is the real transmission of unconditioned awareness: the sharing of no content. Zen speaks about this as the mind-to-mind transmission, Dzogchen as "direct introduction" or pointing out instructions.

In these conversations we distinguish that which can't be distinguished. We point to unconditioned awareness by showing that we can't point to it. We weave our subjectless conversation into the thematic conversation of the person with whom we are in communication. We braid our contentless responses with the other person's communication until their mindstream is brought to the experience of unstructured awareness.

Talking about nothing is the ability to string together coherent sentences that have no subject matter. We begin by engaging our student in a conversation most probably about the absolute or ultimate, and then from our side, while staying in a tightly coordinated conversation, we slowly extract the content. In this conversation we are looking to arrive at the point where we can say, "Do you know what we are talking about?" And our student will say, "I don't know." We capture our student's stream of thinking and take it nowhere.

The types of things we say when we are talking about nothing are:

- What I am talking about has nothing to do with what I am saying. It is completely unrelated to these words.
- The only thing we can know is that we don't know what I am talking about.

We are continually undermining the capacity for our talking to be referring to anything.

Two types of nothing

There is the nothing that is an absence, that is displacing, that is emptying. Sometimes we point to this type of nothing as an interim step.

Then there's the nothing that's not nothing, that's not an absence. This is the nothing about which we can't say whether it is something or nothing. People come to see that when we say "nothing," this is shorthand or a code for a state that is neither structured nor unstructured. It is "This" in the sense that this word points everywhere and nowhere at the same time.

Declarations

Declarations have the power to bring things into being or into focus.

There are times when it can be very powerful to just declare that the nondual dimension is a totally different space. You can say, "We are working in a different paradigm." "We come at this differently in this type of work." These types of declarations can shift people's perspective and loosen the grip of conditioned patterns of thinking and expectation. This kind of declaration comes from a confidence with this work. We don't do it by comparing nonduality with anything else. In fact, we can't compare it with anything else; this is part of what makes it radically different from our usual ways of processing experience.

Interrupting

In nondual work, or any work for that matter, the moment we are seen in the role of helping or supporting people in any way, people are prone to present us with problems and ask for our advice about how to deal with them. They look to us for a solution, a new perspective, or a practice. We might help them by saying something like, "I'd like to stop you at this point. I hear what you are saying, but in the paradigm we are exploring, we work with things differently. We're not trying to find solutions to problems. We are working to produce a change in our state of consciousness—a transformation where the problems you are describing do not, and in fact, cannot arise. How do we do that? There are many ways, but one way is to connect with what's happening in this very moment. What is happening in this very minute that's problematic? What you have been talking about are things that happened in the past, or your worries about the future. But those things aren't happening now. The actual events are images in your mind. What's happening right now? How are you feeling right now?"

We move with finesse, gentleness, and invitation. "We are going to move in a different direction, and it might be interesting and different from the direction you are moving in." Rather than grabbing a participant by the hand and going in their direction, you are making a genuine offer to take a look in a new direction.

Rejecting an interpretation

Rejecting an interpretation may happen when people offer constructed understandings of the nondual. If there is content to their understanding, we might reply (even quite emphatically), "No, that isn't what I'm talking about. I'm talking about 'This!' And this has nothing to do with *feeling* connected with the infinite. 'This' isn't a feeling."

This is an important tool that needs to be offered authentically. It's another way of making a correction. We aren't making anyone wrong since they can't be wrong about nothing!

Nuanced inductions

It is important to be able to talk on a continuum that ranges from gently suggesting that it's possible to be complete right now, to *declaring* we are complete in this moment and that "nothing is missing." We only do this if it can be received at least partially. If the person we are talking with rejects our suggestion or declaration, it would be better not to have made it, since it disempowers our speech.

Describing and revealing

It is vital to be able to distinguish between talking about the ultimate, complete perfection, and revealing or presencing it in the here and now as a function of what we say and the way we move between speaking and being silent.

There are two ways to differentiate between describing and revealing. One is by listening to ourselves, to "where" our words and sentences are coming from. Are they coming from our direct present-time experience of the unconditioned, or from our memory, or from teachings we have received or previously given?

The other is by listening to or "taking in" the person(s) with whom we are communicating. We are looking to see a transformation in people's state of consciousness. If people are just listening with their minds, just taking in concepts, and we begin to give them something to think about, we are only describing the state.

The four ways of talking about nondual awareness

There are four ways or ranges in the way people can conceptualize awareness. The ranges guide us to increasingly less reified ways of languaging the nondual space.

An awareness of these modes can help us determine the purity of a person's state of awareness in terms of whether they are resting in pure contentlessness, or a conditioned state of consciousness. It also gives us a graduated way of introducing people to nondual awareness, and helps us guide someone into a totally unconditioned state that's free of all metaphysical or conceptual overlays. These four ways give us a guidance system for nondual transmission. When people are sharing their experience of no-mind, or unconditioned awareness, we're listening to the structures of the language they use.

This framework goes back to the Buddha. It is called the four ranges (*koti*).

The Four Ranges

❶ **The affirming mode:**
The language of affirmation and addition

"This" is.
"This" is the Self, the "I AM", God,
the ultimate, Christ-consciousness,
Pure Being, Source, Oneness.

❷ **The negating mode:**
The language of subtraction

"This" is selflessness.
"This" nothing.
Neti, neti (not this, not this).
"This" is contentless, infinite, unconditioned,
timeless, nondual.

❸ **The both-and mode:**
The both-and mode
embraces and includes opposites

"This" is personal and impersonal
at the same time.
"This" is nothing and everything.
"This" is and is not.

❹ **The neither-nor mode:**
The neither-nor mode excludes possibilities

"This" does not exist, nor does it not exist.
"This" is neither gained nor lost.
"This is neither something nor nothing.
"This" is neither free nor bound.
"This" is neither conditioned nor unconditioned.

1. An affirming mode

In the first range, the unconditioned can be qualified with infinitely diverse qualities. There is nothing to qualify, so there's no limit or restriction on the qualities that can be applied. "This" is commonly spoken about as "the One," unity consciousness, supernal bliss, all-encompassing love, unalloyed peace, etc. Advaita uses the phrase "being, awareness, and bliss." These are positive ways of talking about the ultimate state. The first range lets us qualify the ultimate with infinite designations. As soon as we have just one quality, we can think about what it means. "If this is unconditioned love, what is that? Is it love or loving? Is there a difference between these? What type of love is this? Is it relational? How is it different from the love between lovers, or between a mother and her child, etc.?" Books have been written about this. If we introduce another quality, such as bliss, we can ask if there is any relationship between bliss and love. How does this ultimately work?

2. A negating mode

The second range is the negative range. This is where we say, "This is not a thing. We can't find this. This is contentless and centerless. We cannot find ourselves. There is no self." This is emphasized quite a lot in nondual transmission. This is the "not this, not that (*neti neti*)" language we find in Advaita. We spend time in this range in both *Radiant Mind* and *Natural Awakening*. This way of languaging the nondual helps to correct our strong, ingrained habits of being sure about our own existence, and the existence of an independent world, out there. Negation is easy to make sense of, even if it is counterintuitive. The language goes in. It's not nihilistic. It just balances the habitual "realism" that's hard-wired into our brains.

There is still a lot of scope for thinking in this range because every conceivable attribute can be erased. There is no doer, no seer, no thinker, no speaker, no walker, no eater, no driver, etc.

3. A contradictory mode

This is the "both-and" way of talking that embraces and includes opposites; reality is personal and impersonal at the same time; reality is the nothing which includes everything.

In the third range, we come to a point where "This" both is and is not. It is because it isn't. There's no self, but the no-self is known by me. I can't find myself. It seems that "I am and I am not." This is nothing. But no, it's not nothing. It includes everything. This is nothing and everything, at the same time. There is no boundary between me and you, because there is no me who can be different. But, in some sense, you are there and I am here. There is a difference. We are the same and different.

The popular Dzogchen phrase, "the basic space of phenomena" is a third range description because two opposite (or nearly opposite) things, "space" and "phenomena," are effectively identified. In Tibetan, this is *chos* (phenomena) *gyi* (of) *dbyings* (space or matrix). This is the same as when the *Heart Sutra* says, "form is openness" and "openness is form."

This mode can be useful. It can arise very naturally for people in nondual work. But it still gives our mind something to go home with! There is still room to move. If you feel into the third range, you'll see that the mind can still try to understand this. It may be frustrated in this endeavor, but we can still ask, "What is the relationship between this as nothing and this as everything? Perhaps this is like an invisible field or a matrix of infinite potentiality that allows unique realities to form and dissolve, exactly as they do." Or, in relationship to the self, "This is an incredible mystery.

There is no self. But this is known. There is a knowing, without a knower. But not everyone knows this. In order to know this, you need to know that you don't exist. How is that possible? If there is no self, how come some people know this, and others don't?" The third range still lets the mind roam, even though it's confined within a narrow bandwidth. We can still write a book about God and creation, the ultimate and the relative, or like Sartre's *Being and Nothingness*. The third range doesn't stop the mind, once and for all.

4. A neither/nor mode

In the final stage, people say, "Ah, there's neither a self nor no self. We are neither trapped, nor free. There's no suffering in this space, and also no absence of suffering." The mind can't go anywhere with that. It's nondual. We can't even ask "How?" or "Why?" because there's no reference point at all. The mind simply stops. We can't elaborate on either pole because they mutually negate each other.

If the discourse goes naturally into this mode, it's great. I don't push it into this mode; otherwise, people can just learn the jargon, the phraseology, and end up "talking the talk," thinking they are in the ultimate state when in fact they are telling you something!

My approach is to slowly ease people into the final level where there are no reference points. I'm aware of the language that people are using in terms of these four different ranges. The ranges provide a grid. People's location within a particular range is one factor in determining how I work with them. There are many others as well. Also, I let people rest at different points in these ranges. It's not like I try to move people through them quickly. Sometimes people jump from one to four, or from two to four, or one to three. Sometimes you work with this quite rigorously, dismantling at each level, because there's a reference point that's implicated in every one of them except for the fourth one.

The main thing with these ranges is that as we move through them, they give us less and less to think about.

Coherence and discrepancy in the language used to describe the nondual

The language people use to describe the state they're in can be consistent or inconsistent with the space they are in. Someone can be abiding as nondual awareness and not have a precise language for sharing that space. And if they come to that experience with a lot of affirming concepts, then, they can be sharing it using the language of the oneness of everything, or the unity of everything. It's possible that they could be in nondual awareness. But, they'll be communicating in the only language they know.

We might say, "That's great." We let them rest with that conceptualization for a while. Or we could say, "Interesting, the idea of one. What is that? Can you say this is one, not two, not a multitude?" Then they might say, "It's just one." Then we can deconstruct this as a boundary, a reference point, because one stands in contrast to two. This is still dualistic. They might say, "I can't even say it's one." They have now moved into the negating mode. We can move people through this by asking; "What is this, if it's not one?" Then they might see that they can't even say it's not one, because here we are still saying something. We could ask, "What is the 'it'?" Then they might say, "It's not one and everything is one," thus demonstrating the contradictory mode.

They are moving through the ranges. We help people refine the way they are languaging "just this" by deconstructing points of reference. They may respond, "Wow, I can't even say that! I can't say that it's one or not one."

Identifying three ways of talking about unconditioned awareness

Given that unconditioned awareness represents the gravitational pull of this nondual sharing, it's important when listening to people to be able to discern where they are. The fact that people are using the language of nonduality doesn't necessarily mean that they are in nondual awareness. Here we want to acknowledge that it's possible for someone to say or believe that they are in nondual awareness, and not be in this state. We need to have a way of determining if they are in a state of not having a reference point. They may be "nowhere" or they could be identifying nondual awareness with a particular experience.

The person we are listening to is using the appropriate concepts. For example, "There is no I," or "No inside or outside," or "This is everything and nothing at the same time," or "This is a co-arising of form and emptiness." They're using language that's consistent with descriptions of nondual awareness, consistent with the languages of nonduality. But it's still possible that they are not resting in nondual awareness. We need to be able to identify the source of their languaging. We need to be able to sense where their language comes from.

Generally, when people are talking about nondual awareness there are three possibilities:

- Talking from within the state.
- Referencing a past experience.
- Drawing on teachings they have received.

It's important to know which of these is happening because this guides the nature of our interaction. We're listening to distinguish and identify whether someone is in a nondual state or not. If they are, there's nothing to do. If they aren't, there may be something to do. Here are some guidelines to help you determine where people are.

1. Talking from within the state

When someone is talking from within the nondual state, they know they aren't talking about anything. If we ask them what they are talking about, they'll say, "Nothing," or "I don't know," or something like that. But, you might think, "Perhaps, they have learned that this is the 'right' thing to say." When someone is in the nondual, we notice an automatic process of deconstruction happening. Awareness is continually deconstructing whatever is arising in their mindstream. They may use a concept to signify where they are, but they will quickly and naturally qualify this by saying, "It's not that either."

When someone is naturally awake, we can feel the absence of a reference point, the resting in nothing. It's totally clear that they don't need to say anything; there's absolutely nothing that they need to prove or demonstrate, because there isn't anyone or anything that needs to be heard.

2. Referring to a past experience

In this instance someone is referring to an experience they've had, are recalling, are trying to re-enter, as best they can, and speak about that. They are speaking from within or about the state that has happened. If you sense that they are referring to a memory of an experience they've had, you can quickly clarify this with the question: "Is this happening for you now?" There's no judgment in this. The function of this is to support a person to be in the nondual. That's what they are here for. You can ask, "Is this happening in this moment; are you in this place now?" If they say no, or they are working with a memory they have had, invite them into the present moment by asking, "Can you share what is happening, and what you are aware of now in this moment?"

3. Ideas acquired from teachings

A third possibility is that someone says they are in the nondual because it feels like the state that's described in the teachings or literature. They are referring to concepts they have acquired through their engagement in nondual teachings and Books. It is significant to look at what they are telling you they are familiar with or experiencing in this space. You can work with this in the same way as in possibility 2. If someone is wanting to tell you something, this is a clue that they are in a conditioned state of awareness, because there is no desire, no need to show someone anything while resting in nondual awareness. In nondual awareness we share joyfully and lightly from that space. Watch for earnestness or seriousness, as it may be a clue of conditioned awareness, since in the nondual state you are nowhere, and there is nothing to defend, no one to be. If you sense that they want, or need to tell you something, this indicates that an idea or experience sits behind the nondual.

Checking questions

The experience of natural presence, the unstructured state in which there is no point of reference, can be transmitted and realized with varying degrees of purity. When we engage in nondual inquiry it may be valuable to assess the quality and purity of a person's unconditioned state. "Checking questions" are a means by which we can do this.

While we recognize that there is no such thing as a pure experience of unconditioned space, which we're naming "nothing" here, the challenge for us is to transmit its purest expression, a state free from conceptual interpretations and contexts. Awareness is neither pure nor impure, since there is nothing in it.

We can use checking questions in our work with others as well as with ourselves. One "checking question" we can use is: "Can you enhance the experience that's happening right now?" A person's response can show if she or he is resting in an unstructured state. If the response is "Yes, it could improve," the person is identifying with something that can be enhanced or diminished, something that could be different, or better, in that moment, or in fact any moment. This shows that some conceptual residue is present within the experience of nondual awareness, and that they're relating to some structures rather than structureless awareness itself.

Even when there's a clean experience of "nothing," if this lacks depth and stability, it's easy to create some significance around the experience, or for the structure to reactivate. If we choose to help the person recognize the fully unconditioned state, we may choose to take a further step. We might, for example, work with deconstructing the structures that have arisen. Alternately, we might simply recognize the presence of peace and serenity when most of the concepts have dissolved, and acknowledge and enjoy the shift when the mind is relatively unengaged.

Another question that can give direct feedback on where someone is within the range of conditioned to unconditioned awareness is: "Is there anything we need to do in this moment?" If the response is to say nothing, or to communicate that there isn't anything of any nature to do, we can rest in silence or continue a conversation. If they say, "Yes, there is something we can do," or even, "Yes, we stay where we are," this shows some type of identification, even if it's subtle and easily released.

If the person is open to it, we can work with whatever is arising as an interpretation of the moment and dissolve it with nondual inquiry.

If the person tells us that the experience couldn't be better, in order to check the authenticity of this response we might ask, "Can you hold onto this?" A good indicator that they're resting in unstructured awareness is being met with silence. There's nothing to say, no need to communicate. There is a shared knowingness that this can't be conceptualized.

Here are some other checking questions. They can be helpful in uncovering conceptual residues in the process of moving from the conditioned to the unconditioned. Much of our conditioning naturally seeks answers, progress, results, etc. This is in contrast to the unconditioned, in which there is "nothing," no questions or answers, and certainly not questions that need to be answered.

- What would you say you're doing right now?
- Can this experience be enhanced? If the response is "Yes," What is this that you're wanting to enhance?
- Can you do more of this?
- Can you lose this?

- Is anything missing right now?
- Are you making progress?
- Is there anywhere to go right now?
- Is there anything you need to do right now?
- Is there anything you need to be thinking about?
- Is this pleasurable?
- Where are you now?

We usually offer these questions only when we discern that someone is in a spacious, uncontrived state of being beyond ideas of loss and gain. In initiating this inquiry we should be sensitive to not setting the person up for conceptual constructions. If that happens, the question has produced the opposite to its intended purpose. We also use checking questions to release any structuring of this state that may be arising within our own stream of awareness. For example, when we are resting silently with a group, the question can arise: "Is there anything for me to be doing in the moment?" or "Could we do more of this?" We let these ideas dissolve by themselves, since there is nothing that needs to be done. The idea of doing more of this doesn't make any sense.

Checking questions often become natural koans because they have the capacity to redirect people back to the experience of unconditioned awareness. This can easily happen for those who are familiar with the state of pure awareness.

Dancing in the paradoxes of nonduality

In the West we have a long-standing habit of being very earnest and serious about our psychological and spiritual endeavors. We feel compelled to communicate without any hint of inconsistency or inner contradiction. This habit comes from our Greek philosophical heritage.

If we're "seen to be" saying one thing in one sentence and contradicting ourselves in the next, we fear that people will judge us negatively. They might think we're confused, superficial, irrational, or even a little crazy! People are uncomfortable with paradox.

Paradox and contradiction are inevitable when we enter the space of unconditioned awareness. We welcome paradox because it points to the reality that cannot be captured by our thoughts.

In nondual work, paradoxes arise within our thought stream in two ways. Firstly, when we try to describe the unconditioned state with real accuracy and precision, we are often led to use sentences that contain internal contradictions. The more rigor and clarity we bring to our descriptions, the more we are compelled to use paradoxical formulations.

Secondly, when we speak from *within* an experience of the unconditioned state, about unconditioned awareness, paradoxes can flow forth as a joyful and exuberant expression of mental energy that is usually trapped by the need to appear sane and sensible. An engagement with these paradoxes and absurdities can produce an explosion of hilarity and laughter that shatters the seriousness with which we usually take ourselves and our practices. They also let us experience unconditioned awareness as a highly discerning and dynamic state of consciousness.

If we let go of our need for conceptual consistency, these paradoxical thought-forms can lead us directly into unconditioned awareness. They can act as a springboard, especially for people who are familiar with the nondual state.

So what are some of the paradoxes that emerge when our thoughts encounter the unstructured expanse of pure awareness? One of the most obvious paradoxes is that unconditioned awareness is simultaneously something and nothing. It is because it isn't. And it's the only thing that is because it isn't. Everything else is because it is. When we try to think about it, we think it is something, but we can't say what it is. It is something and it is nothing. If you are confused by this, don't worry. This isn't rational. It doesn't "make sense." If we think it does, we haven't understood it!

What are we doing now? We're playing in two paradoxes of unconditioned awareness: that it's presenced by its absence, and known through being unknown.

Another exquisite paradox is that at the completion of the nondual path we realize that we haven't traveled any distance—no path has been traversed and we haven't attained "anything." But we also realize that if we hadn't believed that there was a path and made the effort we have made, we wouldn't have arrived at the point where we are right now. Even though we now know that our struggle and commitment was all pointless, in the absence of this effort we would still be drifting in the illusion that there actually is somewhere to go and something to achieve. Without doing what we didn't need to do, we wouldn't realize that we didn't need to do it.

Some people label this play as "mind games." In a sense it is, but not in the way that people typically use this phrase. People tend to label this play as a mind game when they become frustrated with their inability to make sense of what's being said. However, if we label this activity as a mind game, we lose an opportunity to keep the experience of the unconditioned alive and vital. So long as we don't overdo this play, it can be a delightful way of experiencing unconditioned awareness manifesting as a dynamic display of thought and interaction.

S: You often contradict yourself.

P: Yes, I do.

S: You say "This" is completely different from everything we know and that nothing changes.

P: Yes. We can't talk about "This," yet we are doing it right now.

S: There's a lot of paradox involved.

P: Totally. There's one paradox after another. When conditioned awareness meets unconditioned awareness it changes the structure of thinking. We reach the limits of thoughts, and if we're still thinking, this comes through in paradoxes. Normally, we can think about things. Things are discrete and we see how one thing relates to another. This lets us sound logical and coherent. We can "make sense" of things. But when we start thinking about nothing, the whole paradigm shifts. We begin to talk "non-sense"—not gabble, but we're no longer talking about something that can be "sensed." We naturally move into paradox and say things like, "It's nothing, but it's not an absence. It's a shift, but actually nothing changes." It's one paradox after another. If we just let our mind ride with the paradoxes, it's a way of entering the space and it's what I call dancing in nondual logic. It's like a dance. It's fun.

S: And it's done lightly.

P: Yes.

S: There's no purpose to it.

P: Yes and no. It's just a dance. It's light and it also opens into nondual awareness because we aren't talking about any thing. It's playful and functional at the same time. It keeps the relationship with nonduality alive, bright and dynamic.

Here are two other examples of playing in paradoxes. In the first one, one of the players is playing at the expense of his partner. This changes half way through.

Example one

A: What is this?

B: Nothing.

A: You're saying that because it's the "right" answer.

B: Okay, it's something.

A: You're not serious.

B: About what?

A: About this.

B: What's this? What am I meant to be serious about?

A: This exercise. You're just playing.

B: Okay. I'll be serious. I'm serious now.

[B has been playing with A up to this point. This can happen, but it can backfire if the listener interprets that they are being played with.]

A: We are exploring the question, "What is this?"

B: Right.

A: So?

B: When you say, "What is this?" I think, "What is what?"

[B has stopped playing games with A.]

A: What do you mean, "What is what?"

B: When you say "This," I think "what."

A: What is this?

B: What is what?

A: I don't know.

[Now they are playing together.]

B: What are we talking about?

A: I don't know.

B: You don't know!

A: No.

B: Are we talking about anything at all?

A: We are talking about whether we are talking about anything.

B: And?

A: Is this nondual awareness?

B: No idea.

A: Does it matter?

B: It doesn't seem to make any difference to anything.

A: Maybe it would help us to know.

B: Do you need help?

A: No. Definitely not.

B: So it doesn't seem to matter.

[Silence]

Example two

A: Are we in the same space?

B: I don't know.

A: What is it that you don't know?

B: I don't know.

A: Then how can you say that you don't know what this is?

B: I can't.

A: Where are we now?

B: Here.

A: Where's that?

B: Well, it's not there.

A: Where would there be?

B: There is no there. There is only here.

A: Then where is here? There's no here either.

B: We're nowhere.

A: That's impossible. How can we be nowhere? Something's going on here.

B: How can "we" be nowhere? Who is nowhere?

A: You and me. No one!

B: What are we talking about?

A: No idea!

B: I have no idea what we are talking about.

A: Neither do I.

[Silence]

Articulate contradictions

In many years of teaching and practicing nonduality I've found that dancing and communicating in paradoxes is the most difficult aspect of this transmission for people to acquire. Somehow we need to make a leap of faith and be willing to articulately contradict ourselves in a totally up front and confident way. If someone says to us that we've just contradicted ourselves, we need to be able to say, "Yes, that's right. I have because that is how it is. There's no other way to accurately describe this state."

At a certain point we betray the experience of the unconditioned if we aren't willing to say that the unconditioned state is because it isn't, that it's totally unrelated to our conditioned existence but indistinguishable from it, that it can't be lost or gained yet it repeatedly arises and disappears.

When our thoughts are born at the point where the conceptual touches the non-conceptual, we are compelled to use paradox, negation, and absurdity.

Dance steps—moving out of the mind into nondual awareness

It often happens in facilitating and coaching that people get stuck in an intellectual groove. It's difficult to shift the conversation from one in which people are offering their own theory about the relationship between the brain and awareness, their experiencing of presence, or asking us how to access unconditioned awareness in the middle of an argument. Here are some simple steps that can help move people out of their minds and into nondual awareness.

Step 1. Describing or revealing. When you find that things are stuck at the level of knowing and understanding, this can be the time to offer a distinction about the difference between *describing* (talking about) the unconditioned, nondual awareness, etc. and *revealing* it. Thinking and talking about nondual awareness is equivalent to talking about the menu or comparing road maps. When the unconditioned is revealed, we presence it; we rest in no-mind, in not knowing. So, for example, you might say, "We've been talking about nondual awareness quite a lot. Let's try accessing this state. Instead of talking about it, let's be there. How does that sound?"

Step 2. So where are you now? If there's agreement, you can ask, "So where are you now? Would you say you are presencing nondual awareness now?"

There are essentially 3 options here: *yes, no,* and *I don't know.* Let's see how we can work with each of them.

Step 3a. I don't know. If someone says they don't know, I usually leave this as it is. We rest together in not knowing until this changes and something emerges. Even if our student's mind is still active, "not knowing" is usually a useful transition experience. It helps people acclimatize to not knowing. After some time they might say, "How would I know?" We can then move with that, saying, "There would be nothing to know." If there's no urgency, it's fairly easy to move into nondual awareness. "What is it that you don't know?"

Not knowing is referenceless. It's a tender place where we gently entrain "not needing to know." If this state of not knowing devolves into an experience of feeling quiet and relaxed, we can gently point out that this is a state that can change. It exists in contrast to something else. We redistinguish nondual awareness as "This," this state—not what we are thinking or feeling, but this state as pure, contentless awareness. We are gently supporting each other in just being here, without being able to say where here is.

If people begin to try to aspire to know what "This" is, we can say that no one has ever known what "This" is because there's nothing to know. Even the Buddha didn't know. This helps people relax into not knowing.

Step 3b. No, this isn't nondual awareness. Another common response from a participant is that, no, they aren't in nondual awareness. They might say, "No, I'm not. I don't know what it is, so I can't say I'm experiencing it." Or they might say, "I'm not feeling restful," or "I'm troubled by something that happened at work today."

A good question to ask here is: "What is it that isn't happening now?" Often, the answer comes, "I don't know." You can then reply, "If you don't know what it is, how can you say it isn't happening now?" They reply, "I can't."

You can pause here for a little while. This can be a very quick induction into not knowing. Often it won't be this simple, but nothing is lost in testing this out. If a student comes back and says, "What's not happening is that I am not feeling peaceful. My thoughts are racing." Then we declare that this state—of nondual awareness—has nothing to do with what we are feeling or the structure of our thoughts. It's completely unrelated to anything that's happening within the flow of our conditioned experience. If we are in this state, people can often leap right in and join us! You'll notice that we don't become involved in the reasons why "it" isn't happening. In one swift move we take people beyond their thoughts into the space of being nowhere.

P: To think we're not in unconditioned awareness is simply a thought; it doesn't mean anything.

S: I'm not in unconditioned awareness. I'm hearing all this talk about it, and I know I'm not in it.

P: Let me ask you a question: "What is unconditioned awareness?"

S: I don't know.

P: So how do you know you're not there?

S: Because of the way you talk about it.

P: Yes, but if you don't know what it is, how do you know you're not there?

S: Okay, I'll let you know how I know.

P: You're hoping that you can work something out, come up with a good reason.

S: I'm not in timelessness. I'm completely in time.

P: Same here. It's just coming on twelve minutes past eleven.

S: I'm in time, but I cannot say that I'm not in time. You can say that.

P: You just said it: "I cannot say that I'm not in time."

S: You're playing against my mind. That's good. How can I shake the strong conviction, or belief, that I'm not in unconditioned awareness?

P: But you're thinking:,"Now I'm not in unconditioned awareness." You're thinking that you're not.

S: Yes, and I can't shake that thought.

P: You don't have to shake it. It's just a thought. You don't have to do anything with it. It doesn't mean anything—"I am or I'm not." What's the difference? One's just got a "not" in it, and it's three letters.

[Long silence]

S: I'm either suffering through the attachment to the thought, or I don't know how to dislodge the belief.

P: But you don't have to relate to this as suffering. You can simply feel this as some build-up of intensity. You could perhaps say it's like flushing something out. So you don't put the label "suffering" on it. Just let something move through. Just let it happen, and don't judge it.

Step 3c. Yes, this is nondual awareness. A final option is that someone says, "Yes, I am in nondual awareness." To this you might ask, "When you say 'This is nondual awareness,' what are you referring to?" Then it's easy. The student says nothing (unable to say what this is), or something as simple as "This." And that's enough. Or, they begin to construct an interpretation. If they begin constructing, you might find a way to see through the constructions.

Final words

Thank you very much joining me in exploring the presencing of nondual awareness in ways that let us share this state easily and naturally with others. Everything I have described in the *Guide* comes directly from my own experience in teaching and sharing. In most cases immersion in the field of guiding and facilitating nondual transmission preceded my awareness of distinctions that can be used to describe the processes I use. In other cases I became aware of a distinction, or set of distinctions, prior to seeing them show up clearly in my work. An example, is the "four ranges." I knew about this from my undergraduate days but it only came to inform my work about 25 years ago.

It is quite possible that your own integration of natural awareness will follow a similar route. I imagine that some of the processes and distinctions I have described will make immediate sense to you. They may already inform your work. I suspect that some of the energetic and conceptual distinctions I make around space creation, the integration of shamatha and vipashyana, deconstruction and talking about nothing may not yet be reflected in your work and personal experience. My recommendation is to experiment as much as you can in sharing awareness with others. There are many ways to do this. It's wonderful if you can create your own groups. Many of my students run regular nondual groups in North America and Europe.

If you already facilitate groups it may be possible to progressively morph your group to include more nondual inquiry and abiding. If you are a therapist or coach it may be possible to bring a group together by selecting clients who already have a predisposition to meditation or the nondual. In your individual sessions with clients you can begin to open up many of the themes in this *Guide*, for example, "working in the here and now," "seeing experience as a construction," allowing more silence to arise, not conditioning the next moment, letting things be as they are, and experimenting with deconstruction and "seeing through." If facilitating this type of work still seems to be a little way down the track for you, *satsangs* and other nondual teachings provide excellent opportunities to share your experience of the nondual and develop a capacity and authority to speak directly from awareness.

If you then return to this *Guide* from time to time, I'm certain that it will make more and more sense and empower you to discover and refine your own ways of sharing the nondual.

PART TWO

Resources

Appendix 1

The lineage of this work

This Appendix details the connections between the work that unfolds in the *Radiant Mind* style of nondual transmission, and a range of nondual traditions. The traditions covered mainly come out of India, China, Tibet, and Japan. I'm confident there is value in reading this even if you only have a peripheral interest in *Radiant Mind*. The Appendix gives you an easy way to mine a range of nondual traditions for methods and perspectives that are most suited for nondual work in psychotherapeutic, coaching, and workshop settings. Your own work may bear little resemblance to *Radiant Mind*, but I'm sure you will find resources in the ancient traditions. I hope that these pages will inspire your work and allow you to feel a deep connection between your own expression of nondualism and the forms it assumed in different cultures and epochs.

Radiant Mind is a contemporary adaptation of Mahayana nondual wisdom. While it is delivered without reference to Buddhist traditions, the methods and framing perspectives can be found in various Mahayana traditions that developed in the first millennium.

This Appendix describes the correspondences between *Radiant Mind* and traditional Mahayana practices and perspectives. Generally I'll describe the traditional structures first and then show how they are used and sometimes adapted in *Radiant Mind*.

When I make these connections, they are correspondences. They serve to show how there are significant parallels in terms of the principles, practices, and the ultimate intention of *Radiant Mind* and those found in various nondual traditions. *Radiant Mind* hasn't come into existence as a result of researching and stitching together various aspects and methods of the nondual traditions mentioned in this Appendix.

This Appendix could leave you with the impression that *Radiant Mind* is a pastiche that's been assembled by surveying nondual traditions, lifting out various methods, and reassembling them in a new package. The opposite is the case. *Radiant Mind* has slowly evolved over a period of twenty-five years. It has come together as a function of personal experience and involvement in many nondual traditions and working directly with people in workshop settings. *Radiant Mind* isn't a conscious creation. It's simply what happens when a facilitator has access to a wide range of possibilities and is working intuitively and on the spot with a person or group in order to find ways to introduce people to nondual awareness and help to stabilize that state.

Radiant Mind is very minimalist. It's simple and flowing, yet deep and subtle. *Radiant Mind* unfolds smoothly and organically. It's often impossible to know what will be happening in the next moment. This Appendix helps to describe the contemplative movements and dialogical interventions that are available to a facilitator at any moment. It shows how important principles drawn from traditions such as Mahamudra and Dzogchen help in creating the atmospheric culture and space of *Radiant Mind*. It also shows how facilitators have access to an extremely rich set of possibilities for introducing people to unconditioned awareness.

People can participate in *Radiant Mind* without even knowing that it has Buddhist origins. It's never labeled by people as a meditation course or dharma teaching. It's neither of these. When they are first exposed to *Radiant Mind*, most people can't say what it is. People who have been involved in a variety of nondual approaches for many years begin to see what's happening. They begin to see the connections that I'm describing in this Appendix. This Appendix essentially serves to show how most of the possibilities that are available to facilitators at any point in time can be found in one or more of Asia's major nondual traditions.

The Four Noble Facts (*arya-satya*) are a classic framework for describing Buddhism. *Radiant Mind* can also be described through this framework.

Four Noble Facts

1. The existence of suffering (*dukkha*). In other words, we suffer and this is the fundamental problem of human existence. Everything we do is in one way or another an attempt to alleviate suffering. Suffering in *Radiant Mind* is understood as the experience of lack, the experience that something is wrong, something is missing, something is happening that shouldn't be happening, or something that should be happening is not happening. The sign that there is an element of suffering is a wish or need for things to stay the same (attachment),

or change (aversion). *Dukkha* is really shorthand for the cycle of pain and pleasure. Since *Radiant Mind* techniques are a bridge out of suffering, they are only relevant when *dukkha* in this sense is occurring.

2. Suffering has a source. The source of suffering lies in our attachment and aversion to what is happening in the present moment. This in turn is a function of having preferences. The structure of our preferences is comprehensively summarized in the eight worldly concerns. (Nagarjuna and Mipham, 1975: 29) We are:

   - Attached to receiving possessions and averse to losing them.
   - Attached to praise and averse to denigration.
   - Attached to having a good reputation and averse to a bad one.
   - Attached to pleasures and averse to pain.

In *Radiant Mind*, the focus is on attachment and aversion. When someone is sharing their experience, the question of whether they are trying to hold onto an experience or push it away is more significant than the structure or content of the experience itself. It's often possible to identify a person's attachment and aversion in terms of these worldly concerns. It's worth noting here that when the Buddha says that the source of suffering is grasping, this includes attachment and aversion. Some people tend to interpret grasping only as attachment (wanting things, experiences, security, knowledge, etc.) and feel that aversion isn't really a problem. But attachment and aversion are equally problematic. They are different sides of the same coin. Aversion is simply being attached to not wanting something.

More fundamentally we oscillate between needing to exist and not exist. We relate to ourselves in terms of the two possibilities of existing or not existing. When we think of ourselves as being a fixed "thing," we then will suffer because we feel our very existence is being threatened. We fear the ever-present possibility of being annihilated. At other times we suffer because we are unable to avoid our existence. We suffer simply because we exist. Existing is painful and we'd prefer not to be.

3. Within a dualistic paradigm there is a cessation of suffering. The cessation of suffering and the cessation of the possibility of suffering occur through the realization of selflessness, that there is no one who suffers. Within a nondual paradigm the fruition of the path is further refined as a state in which there is no suffering or cessation of suffering (*Heart Sutra*). Similarly, it is a state in which there is no self or absence of a self. From within the nondual, there is neither an experience of being trapped or being free.

4. From a dualistic starting point, this liberating realization is accomplished by following a path of practice and insight. There are many paths. *Radiant Mind* integrates approaches mainly from nondual traditions.

The path

Radiant Mind is designed to transmit nondual wisdom (*prajna*) as this is realized and communicated within the Perfect Wisdom (*Prajnaparamita*) tradition. Overall the approach is framed by the Four Reliances and the Three Statements of Garab Dorje.

The *Radiant Mind* path utilizes many techniques and perspectives drawn from different Mahayana nondual wisdom traditions, principally Zen, Madhyamika, Dzogchen, and Mahamudra. Different terms are used within these traditions for the ultimate state. For example, no-mind (*mu shin*), emptiness (*shunyata*), pure awareness, suchness, reality itself, bodhicitta, etc. *Radiant Mind* isn't distracted by historical polemics that create differences between these states. These terms intend to refer to a state that has no structure, a state that is impossible to differentiate from any other state, because it doesn't have any characteristics. Therefore, it is also impossible for these words to be referring to different states!

The techniques and perspectives of *Radiant Mind* are integrated into a holistic framework. A relatively unique feature of the *Radiant Mind* transmission is the way we work at the boundary between:

- Speech and silence.
- Concepts and realization.
- Conditioned and unconditioned.
- Practice and attainment.
- Meditation and relationship.
- Autonomy and intimacy.
- Communal and individual freedom.
- Active and receptive modes of practice.

We work particularly at the interface or junction between these polarizations because the focus of *Radiant Mind* is in realizing nondual awareness beyond the restrictions of a formal meditative practice. *Radiant Mind* is designed to bring nondual awareness into the structure and fabric of our daily lives. In workshops the transmission and inductions happen in a group setting. For example, the silences that arise are never imposed on the group. They emerge naturally because there is nothing to share for some time. Silences can transform gently or suddenly into dynamic exchanges between participants, or between participants and a facilitator. When this happens there is no disruption to the space, because the space isn't being conditioned by the superimposition of structures and routines. The workshops have the flavor of a group entry into nondual awareness that's guided by deconstructive dialogs, which lead into periods of natural, effortless silence that transform again, after an indeterminate amount of time, into more dialog and deconstruction.

Also, a large proportion of the work in *Radiant Mind* happens when people are at home and "out and about." We use communication technologies, such as teleconferencing and video conferencing, so that people can regularly connect with nondual awareness in the midst of daily activities. People come together, sharing the space of being complete, with nowhere to go and nothing to know, while they are at work or at home in the mornings and evenings.

The Four Reliances *(pratisarana)*

Radiant Mind is also framed by the Four Reliances that are mentioned by the famous lay Buddhist Vimalakirti in the thirteenth chapter of his *Vimalakirti Nirdesha*. (See Thurman, 1976) In this famous Mahayana text, Vimalakirti recommends that we rely on:

- The [quality of the] transmission, and not on the person [delivering it].
- The intention [of the transmission], and not on the words or symbols.
- [Transmissions which are] definitive, and not those which are [open to] interpretation.
- Non-conceptual wisdom, and not on conceptual knowledge.

These are fairly self-explanatory. The first point to note is that it's easy for people to believe that they aren't adequately prepared to take these reliances seriously. Many people feel they must forego relying on non-conceptual wisdom and on the definitive transmission of the real liberating insight until they have acquired more knowledge or accomplished more practice. People can feel they aren't ready for "final-stage transmissions." Vimalakirti is recommending that we rely on final-level transmission as much as possible. We only revert to conceptual knowledge when nondual awareness is genuinely inaccessible.

In *Radiant Mind*, we routinely find that many people can presence nondual awareness. It's not such a highly advanced state that we can't even touch it for several decades. People often underestimate their capacities. Nondual awareness can be developed to a highly advanced level, but initial first-hand experience is quite easy to gain.

One way we take care of the first reliance in *Radiant Mind* is by deconstructing projections that people might have about the level of insight of teachers. If *Radiant Mind* students project that their teachers have something that they don't have, we invite them to inquire into what this "something" is. Through this inquiry, they cannot find what it is they think a teacher may have. Teachers deconstruct the projection that they are resting in a special place. Teachers reveal that the only thing that's unique about their experience is that ultimately they have nothing to share or communicate. This allows students to share a space in which they cannot say that they are in a different space from their teacher(s).

Definitive transmissions point unambiguously to unconditioned awareness. These are gestures, words, questions, etc. that can directly and immediately reveal the unconditioned.

In summary, the Four Reliances recommend that as much as possible we go directly to the ultimate state, bypassing unnecessary involvement in ideas, concepts, and practices that can be easily misunderstood or misapplied. We rely on transmissions that come from, and lead directly into, the state of nondual awareness. This is sometimes spoken about as "teaching at the level of the result." When we teach at the level of the result, there is no time lag between the transmission and its realization. Dzogchen and Essence Mahamudra offer such transmissions.

The Three Statements from Garab Dorje

In broad terms, *Radiant Mind* is shaped by the famous summary of Dzogchen formulated by the founder of Dzogchen, Garab Dorje in his *Three Statements that Strike the Essence*. (Reynolds, 1996: 42) Garab Dorje defines Dzogchen as:

- Direct introduction to one's own real nature.
- The clear recognition of this unique state.
- Continuing to abide confidently in this state of freedom.

Following Garab Dorje's model, the focus of *Radiant Mind* is to:

- Introduce people to a space of contentless awareness in which nothing needs to be done and nothing needs to be thought about or understood.
- Help people identify this state when it's present by demonstrating that there is nothing to do or to know, nothing that can be enhanced or degraded. The authenticity of this state is determined by questions that reveal whether consciousness is structured or unstructured.
- Support people in remaining in this state by observing how they move out of it by making it into "something"—anything—that can then be lost and gained. This "making it into something" can occur in a number of ways, for example, by trying to figure out what it is or wondering how to maintain or discover it in future situations.

Different streams of nondual transmission

Radiant Mind draws on aspects of different nondual traditions and brings them together in a seamless, integrated process for the transmission of nondual awareness. I'll describe the particular features of these traditions that relate to *Radiant Mind*. I'll also show how they are used and sometimes reframed in *Radiant Mind*. I'll begin with the Madhyamika.

Madhyamika

Madhyamika means Middle Way. This tradition was brought into existence by the brilliant Buddhist philosopher Nagarjuna in the second century. Nagarjuna is celebrated as Buddhism's, and perhaps India's, greatest philosopher. He is a primary lineage holder in all the major nondual traditions of Buddhism. The Madhyamika places the original Perfect Wisdom (*Prajnaparamita*) traditions in a more intellectual environment. The Madhyamika continues to use the words openness/emptiness and nothingness to refer to the unconditioned dimension.

This tradition is useful in *Radiant Mind* because it creates the possibility of working directly with people's intellectual constructions. We are educated to place a lot of reliance on ideas, theories, and belief systems. We are trained to question, to think about things, and understand reality and ourselves. Many people are proud and confident in their ideas.

Some teachings tend to dismiss our reliance on intellectual knowledge and acquisitions. People with strong minds and well-developed intellects can feel invalidated by nondual teachings. I often hear people judging others as being too intellectual, just tied up in their heads. It's easy to receive such feedback as negative, and this only serves to distance and alienate such people from the nondual transmission.

I've even seen nondual teachers giving this type of feedback. I think this is sometimes a reflection of the fact that such teachers can't keep up with the theories and abstract conceptualization of their students. The going gets too hard—they don't know how to dismantle people's constructions, so they just offer a generalized assessment, saying, "Your mind is getting in the way," hoping to get things back on track, into their comfort zone!

There is a place for saying that nondual awareness has nothing to do with what we think, or believe, or feel. And there is also a place for going inside people's constructions, for meeting them on their own terms, and showing people that what they are talking about can't be found, or that their thinking is fundamentally incoherent.

The Madhyamika shows us how it's possible to engage with other people's belief systems without getting confused, or lost in them, or seduced by people's explanations or arguments. The Madhyamika is a positionless system. It has no theory, concepts, values, or beliefs of its own whatsoever. Its sole function is to reveal the clarity of nondual awareness by dismantling every possible construction that is presented to the deconstructing intellect of the Madhyamika practitioner. Madhyamika practitioners use the mind to transcend the mind.

The Madhyamika offers road maps (or templates) that help guide us in the process of entering and taking apart a system of belief or framework of interpretation. Madhyamikas have also furnished us with dozens of tightly-framed inquiries for showing that ultimately we can't find anything: ourselves, others, a state of liberation, suffering, change, stability, perception, God, or Buddhas. Everything disappears if we really look for it, including the disappearance itself!

The Madhyamika also offers a number of very useful distinctions for tracking the process and pathways through which fixation can be deconstructed.

Interpreting experience as a construction

The idea that our experience is composed of different elements goes back to the original teachings of the Buddha. Our sense experience and cognitive processes are called *samskrta*, which means that they are compounded. Even though our experience is a gestalt that seems to exist and function independently of concepts, beliefs, and interpretation, it is composed of a multitude of elements.

The Mahayana takes this idea further, saying that the mechanism we use to construct or put together our experience is conceptual designation (*prajnapti*). Our experience is constructed in the sense that we make "something" of our experience. It becomes "something" because we put labels or concepts on things and then work out relations between them. When we associate a component of the experiential field with a name, this simultaneously conceals and reveals the thing that is labeled. It reveals something because we know what the name is referring to. It also conceals what is labeled because we can no longer see what is there without the label. Without a label we don't know what a tree is, what type it is, color, etc. We live in a dense field of conceptualization that gives shape, structure, and functionality to our universe. The most fundamental concepts are "self" and "other," or "self" and "world," "past," "now," and "future," "inside" and "outside," "body," "life," etc. Once we have two concepts, this invites the creation of many more since we can ask how they are related. In Mahayana Buddhism this process is called conceptual proliferation: one (which is already two) giving birth to the universe.

In *Radiant Mind* we regularly take what seems to be a pure gestalt and say, "Let's look at that as though it is constructed. I know it feels like an experience—and it is an experience—but let's also look at it from the point of view that it's been constructed or assembled." When we view our experiences as constructions, it gives us a handle on them. It lets us deconstruct or dismantle them. If we can see how an experience is put together, we can take it apart.

Often I'll engage in a conversation that begins like this, "Okay, you say that's what you are experiencing. I acknowledge that. But for a moment let's view it as a construction, as something that's assembled. What I hear you saying is that right now you're confused and wondering what's happening here. Can we look at that as a construction?" If the student says yes, we can begin to look at "What is it to be confused?" "What or where is here?" and perhaps even "Who are you?"

A middle way: the correction of polarized positions

According to all Buddhist traditions, our experience of reality is continually interpreted through dualistic categories of thought. Thinking is dualistic because it is based on making contrasts. In order to have the idea of freedom, we need the concept of being trapped (not free), good depends on bad, inside depends on outside, the idea of self depends on the idea of other (not self), existence on nonexistence, etc.

The correction of polarized positions leads to the discovery of the middle way. It's important to realize that the middle way isn't a point or place that lies between two extremes. The middle way isn't a position. We can't say what it is. If we think that the middle way is a space where we aren't located at an extreme, this reduces the "middle" to another position—another extreme, in fact. The extreme of being in balance or neutral in contrast to being at an extreme. The middle way isn't a place or mode of being where we aren't functioning dualistically. The moment we think like this, we're involved again in another dualism, the dualism that sets duality and nonduality apart.

A lot of the work in *Radiant Mind* consists of continually, gently moving people out of polarized positions, thinking that reality is like this or that, there is a doer or isn't a doer, there is something to practice or nothing to practice.

It's important not to look for a conclusion to this process of continual correction. That will only produce frustration. From the bodhisattva point of view this never stops; we have no expectation that this process of settlement, movement, and correction will stop or continue forever. It doesn't matter. It's not the point.

Sometimes it feels like pulling someone away from one position into another, even though this isn't the final intention. The intention, in a way, is to be nowhere and everywhere equally. We can move someone from one position into another. When that becomes reified, it's time to move them away from that position.

Under-negation and over-negation

This phenomenon of moving between extreme positions is called under-negation and over-negation. These concepts help us see how someone is positioned and how we move in bringing them into positionlessness. Under-negation occurs when we hold that things exist in their own right. This is the baseline position through which we experience ourselves and the world. We exist and the objects we experience are taken to exist from their own side. Our thoughts have a reality of their own, as do feelings and emotions. When people engage in work that questions the reality of our assumptions and foundational perceptions, it's possible to slide to an opposite position. When the reality of a self is questioned, people can conclude that there is no self. This is called over-negation. Too much is negated and people end up denying the reality of a self, the world, causation, etc. The middle way is positionless. It isn't a conclusion.

Seeing through (vipashyana)

The discovery of the middle path is equivalent to realizing nondual awareness, openness, identitylessness, or no-thing-ness. This is accomplished by "seeing through" dualistic fixations. Seeing through leads to the activation of wisdom (*prajna*). Seeing through is a form of contemplation that can be found in all Buddhist traditions. There are different forms of seeing through. In Madhyamika, seeing through is based on a deconstructive form of inquiry (*prasanga-vichara*). It is also called unfindability analysis. This is a form of inquiry that systematically dismantles all points of reference about any subject matter. *Radiant Mind* is informed by, though not tied to, this form of inquiry.

Unfindability inquiry

Unfindability inquiry is a form of logical investigation which shows that nothing can be found to exist (*yod mi rnyed*—see *Madhyamikavatara* 6.160). This form of inquiry is applied to the seeming reality of a personal self and phenomena.

Here I will briefly outline how yogis go about deconstructing a fixed personal reference point using a method called the Diamond Grains Routine. *Radiant Mind* conversations never move with the precision that's possible when yogis are explicitly dismantling a self-concept. Yogis have usually trained for decades in this method. The procedure they use, however, does guide the general direction of some *Radiant Mind* conversations.

The Diamond Grains Routine

Nondual traditions offer many ways to realize the state of unconditioned freedom. Some approaches lift people out of their fixations by gently redirecting the energy that fuels reactive ways of functioning. Other approaches go inside the structure of our conditioning and systematically disassemble attachment and aversion (the sources of suffering) by deconstructing the experience of being a unique, self-existing person.

The deconstructive methods of the Madhyamika are an example of the latter approach. The Madhyamikas developed a super-charged method called the Diamond Grains Routine—so called because, like a diamond-tipped auger, it progressively grinds away the belief in being an autonomous, independent self. The Diamond Grains Routine offers a highly controlled way of cutting through (1) the strong, inborn feeling we have of being "a finite person," of being a "somebody;" and (2) any beliefs we might have acquired that lead us into thinking that "we" are in some way an unconditioned no-body.

We don't use the tightly structured Diamond Grains Routine in *Radiant Mind* because it's incompatible with the gentle, organic flow of *Radiant Mind* work. The Diamond Grains Routine was developed by, and for, career-yogis—masters of meditation who can sit in contemplation for hours at a stretch following highly-regulated patterns of inquiry that dissolve the experience of being a separate self. The same forms of inquiry are used to dismantle destructive impulses, hard-formed beliefs, and dualistic fantasies about the state of liberation.

I will describe this form of deconstructive inquiry in some detail even though we don't use it in the same way in *Radiant Mind*. As I move into the description, I'll also show how it informs the conversational forms of deconstruction that are used in *Radiant Mind*. In general terms, the Madhyamika template sits in the background as a road map. When yogis use it there are no detours. They know exactly what they are doing and where they are going. Deconstructive inquiries in *Radiant Mind* follow more circuitous routes because they arise in spontaneous dialogs. Nonetheless, a knowledge of this template can bring a level of precision and fruition to the more informal unfindability conversations that happen in *Radiant Mind*.

The Diamond Grains Routine proceeds through four steps.

1. Locating what we are looking for

In the first step the meditator determines what is to be negated—or in less technical language, makes a decision about what is going to be investigated. This involves distinguishing an object, such as the self, and then determining that this is the object to be analyzed, and nothing else.

This also happens in *Radiant Mind*. If I feel the possibility of moving into an unfindability inquiry, I ask the person with whom I am conversing, "What is it that you are actually talking about here?" I seek an informal agreement about what it is that we will be looking at.

When Madhyamika yogis deconstruct their own self-existence, they use various techniques in order to connect with the deepest layers of their existence. For example, they might vividly imagine that someone is about to take their life. This immediately produces a very strong experience of "me," of "my entire existence." This becomes the object that is implicated in the contemplation. Once that profile is established, it remains in place throughout the contemplation.

A Madhyamika practitioner makes a firm commitment about the defining characteristics of the object in question and agrees not to reconsider, or renegotiate, this definition once the investigation is under way. Ambiguity dilutes the contemplation. Similarly, if one changes the feeling, thought, or concept that's being analyzed part way into an investigation, one has to go back and reestablish the object under investigation. This disrupts the deconstructive process.

In *Radiant Mind*, it often happens that people will try to renegotiate what it is that they are talking about. When people begin to sense that the thing they say is real is starting to seem less real, they will often say, "Well, that's not what I am actually talking about. What I mean is…." When this happens we know that we either have to reestablish the previous object of investigation, "I thought we were talking about X"—or we need to begin a new unfindability inquiry based on the new experience, concept, feeling, or interpretation that's being offered.

In *Radiant Mind* when we move in the direction of an unfindability inquiry we don't know how far it will proceed. The inquiry might move through to a point where there is no fixation or grasping. Or the inquiry might abort prior to that point. *Radiant Mind* inquiries are gentle, and take the deconstruction of fixed positions, beliefs and attitudes through to a point where students can integrate the dissolution of a story, belief or feeling that previously defined their existence.

2. Two possible ways in which things can exist

The second step is called "ascertaining the pervasion." Here the meditator selects a contrasting relationship through which to analyze the object selected in the first step. The meditator commits her- or himself to a principle which says that two mutually-excluding alternatives exhaust all the ways in which something can exist. In other words, if something exists, then it is either A or not-A. If the object is our mind, for example, it is either physical or non-physical. If it can be shown to be neither physical nor non-physical, then we can't say anything about it because "being physical" and "being non-physical" exhausts all the possible ways in which the mind could exist.

If the meditator is seeking to realize the selflessness of her own identity, she will normally look at the experience of the self in relationship to the contents of experience. The contrasting relationship usually chosen when investigating the reality of our own existence is that we (the self) are either (1) an object of experience; or (2) not an object of experience. There is no third option because these two exhaust all possibilities.

Steps one and two are locked in place in order to reduce any slippage in the contemplation. They are designed to ensure that no residual reference point remains at the completion of a meditation.

The third and fourth steps investigate the coherence of these two options. A self-contradiction is produced for each of these alternatives.

3. We can experience our "self"

The first alternative is that we are an object of our experience. In Buddhism the field of experience is called the *skandha*. In Buddhist psycho-biology the *skandhas* are composed of forms, feelings, perception-thinking, predispositions, and cognition. This option describes what Buddhists call the in-born *(sahaja)* way of experiencing ourselves. We not only think we are our body and mind, we feel this way too. If our physical existence is threatened, we experience this as a threat to our own existence. Essentially, everyone experiences themselves this way, quite independent of their culture and education.

However, the self cannot be an object of our experience. If the self is an object of experience, then there is no one, no self, to experience it. A self that is an object of experience can't be experienced. So we can't say if it exists or doesn't exist.

In *Radiant Mind*, unfindability inquiries often begin at this stage. Certainly the second step, "ascertaining the pervasion," is omitted because it is much too formal. A typical *Radiant Mind* dialog that follows this third step might look like this:

P: It's easy to be aware of the contents of awareness, what we are experiencing, for example, your body, the surroundings, my words, and so on, but who is experiencing these?

S: I am.

P: Can you experience yourself, the "I" that you are speaking about?

S: Yes, it's me.

P: Where are you?

S: Here, in my body.

P: Where in your body?

S: In my brain, throughout my brain.

P: Is that what you think, or is that your direct experience?

S: It's my direct experience. There is a type of energy in my brain. This is where I experience everything. This is where everything comes together.

P: It's an energy.

S: Yes, an alert energy.

P: Can you experience that?

S: Yes.

P: If you can experience that, it's an object of awareness. If you experience it, it can't be you, the experiencer. It's what you are experiencing. Where is the experiencer?

S: Behind my eyes.

P: Can you experience that?

S: Yes.

P: What are you experiencing that with?

S: My brain.

P: Is that what you think?

S: It's my experience.

P: Yes, but we are looking for "who" is experiencing whatever you are experiencing. Let's look at this another way. Where are the sensations that you are experiencing being received? Where are my words landing, for example? Where are you receiving the visual sensation of this room? I'd like you to investigate this more like a scientist, looking for where these sensations are landing, rather than thinking about it.

S: I'm receiving them here. I'm here, for example, and not over there. I'm not where you are.

P: Where am I?

S: Over there, sitting on that chair.

P: This is my body. This is something I can experience. It's not me. Where am I?

S: I don't know. You should know that.

P: I don't. I don't know where I am.

S: That's impossible.

P: I am looking, and I don't know where I am.

S: Who is looking?

P: I don't know. I can't see any looking actually. There's no experience of "looking out from."

S: Yes, but you know what's happening. That's you.

P: Who is me?

S: The knower.

P: Where is the knower?

S: It's your awareness.

P: Where is that? Where is my awareness?

S: In this room.

P: If it's in this room, it's something that could be experienced. Where am I as the experiencer?

S: I don't know. Wherever you think you are.

P: But where I think I am are just thoughts. They aren't the thinker. Where is the thinker?

S: I don't know.

[In this inquiry I shifted the investigation into the unfindability of my self. This can be an easier access into the state of selflessness, especially if we sense that someone is becoming defensive, or simply declaring, again and again, that they exist, without offering evidence. It's less threatening to use oneself. We become a proxy through which another can taste the unfindability of an experiencer.]

4. We can't experience our "self"

The second option is that we are not an object of our experience. This is the opposite of the previous position. However, if we aren't an object of our experience, we similarly can't know that we exist because we can never experience our "selves." We lie outside the field of our experience. So, again, we can't say if such a self exists or doesn't exist.

At this point there is nowhere else for the mind to go. The meditator's mind is left with nowhere to move in terms of being able to say whether there is or isn't a self. The self or "I" doesn't exist, but equally it's not nonexistent either. As I explained, at the beginning of these types of contemplations, yogis implicate their existence in a very powerful way. They put everything on the line—the experience of being a person at a very deep, existential level, and all their beliefs about the existence and nonexistence of a self. They also bring a laser-like concentration to their contemplations. The forward thrust of their contemplations projects their mindstream into a space-like equipoise that's free of all conceptual elaboration and which can last for several hours. If and when a concept of being someone reconstitutes, they gently deconstruct the reference points that are congealing and re-enter the space-like equipoise.

In *Radiant Mind*, the fourth phase of the analysis comes into play when people begin to identify with the idea that there is no self, that they are no one, that there is no doer, no thinker, or experiencer—no "I" as a subject. In Buddhism this is called an acquired concept (*parikalpita*) because it arises as a product of our thinking and philosophical education. People can slide into this way of thinking after seeing that they really can't find a self or experiencer. They think, "The 'I' is just a thought. I can't find the thinker or experiencer, so therefore there is no self." This, however, is still a conclusion. Instead of thinking that we exist, the mind concludes that "we don't exist." It's quite easy for this belief to be further reinforced by exposure to some nondual teachings that talk about there being no self and no doer, without qualifying that these terms are shorthand for a state in which there is no self and no non-self.

If someone arrives at the conclusion that there is no self, this becomes a new object of investigation. We begin to explore the idea(s) that there is no self, no thinker, no doer, etc. The following dialog shows how the notion that there is "no self" can be deconstructed. The dialog communicates the flavor of a fairly robust deconstructive conversation.

S: The "I" has disappeared. In this awareness there is no "me," no "I," no thinker or doer. There is no one here.

P: Is that where you are at the moment?

S: Yes, all identification has dropped away. There's no "I," no "me."

P: Are you saying that you don't exist?

S: Yes. I don't exist.

P: Are you talking to me?

S: No. There is talking, but I am not talking.

P: Who isn't talking?

S: No one is talking. There is talking, but there's no me in here who's talking.

P: When you say that you don't exist, what are you telling me?

S: That there is no "me."

P: You're saying that the "I" which doesn't exist, doesn't exist.

S: Yes.

P: Do you know what it is that doesn't exist?

S: Yes, me.

P: But I thought you said you don't exist. If you don't exist, how do you know you don't exist?

S: There is just awareness being aware of itself. There is no "I."

P: You need to help me with this. I don't know what it is that doesn't exist. If something doesn't exist, I have no idea what you're talking about.

S: The "I" doesn't exist.

P: But I thought you were telling me there is no "I."

S: That's right.

P: When you say you don't exist, I have no idea what doesn't exist. It's like you're telling me that there is something that doesn't exist; I can't tell you what it is, but it doesn't exist. I just don't know what you're talking about.

S: You do know, the sense of "me."

P: But you have just told me there is no "me."

S: Well there isn't, but it can seem to exist.

P: What can seem to exist?

S: "Me," here talking to you, there's an "apparent I."

P: But you told me there is no "I;" that no one is talking to me! Now you seem to be saying there is something.

S: Not really. There's just the illusion of a self. There seems to be an "I," but if we look for it, it disappears.

P: If you look for what?

S: The "I."

P: I thought you were saying it doesn't exist at all.

S: Well, no, it doesn't but it seems to.

P: I don't understand this idea that you seem to exist. What seems to exist?

S: The sense of an "I."

P: Where is it?

S: I don't know.

P: What does it feel like?

S: A sense of solidity in the chest.

P: But that would be an object of experience, so it can't be the "I."

S: That's right. There's no "I;" there's no experiencer.

P: So where's the illusory "I?"

S: That's a trick question.

P: Not at all. You are speaking about an illusory "I." I'm just trying to understand what you are talking about.

S: Well, you can't find it because the illusory self doesn't exist.

P: When you say you don't exist, I'm not getting it. I simply don't know who or what doesn't exist. "Who" aren't you?

S: I don't know. I don't know what's going on now.

P: Who doesn't know?

S: I don't know.

P: Do you exist?

S: I don't know.

P: Do you not exist?

S: I don't know. I can't say.

P: Are you okay with this?

S: I have no idea.

P: Are you okay having no idea?

S: Yes.

The four ranges

The Madhyamika tradition also provides a very useful framework for tracking the movement from being exclusively identified with conditioned reality, in which things exist and don't exist, to include the unconditioned dimension that is free of all ontological projections.

As a framework for dismantling conceptual positions or reference points, the Buddha used a simple guidance system called the four ranges (of discourse). There are four possible ways in which something can be. Something—a person, a feeling, a thought, or a sensation—either (1) is; (2) is not; (3) both is and is not; or (4) neither is nor is not. These exhaust the ways in which things can exist.

The Madhyamika interprets these as a sequentially graduated presentation of the nature of reality. (Chandrakirti, 1979: 181) Chandrakirti writes,

> Even though…there can be no assertive speech nor any discursive thought with respect to it (i.e., ultimate reality), none-the-less this truth can certainly not be known if it is not didactically argued. In bringing this truth to those who need guidance, there must necessarily be recourse at times to a graduated (*anupurvi*) teaching. The four corners represent increasingly more accurate ways of talking about reality.

Radiant Mind tracks the frame of reference in which people are functioning by observing how they talk about reality. The four ranges trace a movement from more to less identification with conditioned experience. The four ranges give directionality to the conversations that happen in *Radiant Mind* work. They locate a speaker's consciousness in terms of being located in: (1) An ordinary state of consciousness in which the "I," suffering, etc. are real; (2) a coarse understanding of nonduality that annihilates the experience of a self, feelings, etc.; (3) a more refined insight that includes conflicting positions; or (4) a final state that is without a reference point. These four modes also help to determine the purity of the experience of nondual awareness.

1.   The affirming mode gives positive qualities to the ultimate state; for example, "it" is one, pure, and complete.

2.   The negating mode identifies the ultimate state as nothing, no-self, contentless, etc. This mode can be useful when first initially revealing the unconditioned. Even though it represents a case of over-negation, it can act as a correction to the normal way of experiencing the world and giving attributes to ultimate reality.

3.   The contradictory mode embraces and includes opposites; reality is personal and impersonal at the same time; reality is the nothing which includes everything. This mode can be useful.

4.   The final mode is the neither/nor mode which leaves the mind with nowhere to go, nothing to think about. If the discourse goes naturally into this mode, it shows that people are resting in nondual awareness.

Radiant Mind doesn't push the conversation into this fourth mode; otherwise, people can just learn the jargon and end up "talking the talk," thinking they are in the ultimate state when in fact they are telling you something!

The union of serenity (*shamatha*) and "seeing through" (*vipashyana*)

In Buddhism the experience of contentless wisdom, or unconditioned mind, is cultivated through the twofold practice of serenity and clear seeing. *Shamatha* means peace, tranquility, or serenity. *Vipashyana* means penetrating insight, clear seeing, or "seeing through." Just as we can see through a window without becoming preoccupied with the specks of dirt on the glass, we can see through the obstacles to unconditioned mind without having to obliterate them. In orthodox Buddhism serenity is cultivated prior to, and parallel with, seeing through. The two practices support each other and ultimately merge in the union of *shamatha* and *vipashyana*.

In *Radiant Mind*, the integration of serenity and seeing through happens very early on. In fact, the two forms of practice aren't rigidly differentiated from each other. The two practices are combined in the one fundamental practice of "having nothing to think about." This slows down the mind, leaving us with no reference points, and opening us into contentless awareness. I'll explain how this works.

Serenity—thinning out thoughts

Seeing through constructions can be difficult if energy is tied up in struggling to escape from the burden of boring or uncomfortable thoughts. If our minds are too active, even inquiry only produces more conceptual proliferation. For this reason, initial access to unconditioned awareness can be enhanced by slowing our thinking down so that people feel more peaceful and serene. People discover a place where there is more composure and less urgency.

The essence of serenity practice is to reduce the density of our thoughts. "Thinning out thoughts" is my way of describing the process of slowing down the thinking process so that conceptualization becomes less dense and less significant. (I'll return to this later when I make some connections between *Radiant Mind* and Dogen's Zen.) Thinning out our thoughts produces an experience of inner peace within which unconditioned awareness is more easily recognized.

In a nondual transmission there is no need to try to stop thoughts completely because the experience of seeing through allows thoughts and feelings to be present without disturbing the state of nondual awareness. When we're resting in pure awareness, our thoughts, no matter how light or dense, are incapable of producing reactive emotions. People just need to arrive at a point where thoughts can move through awareness without producing any disturbance.

Nothing to think about

In nondual work, the practice of slowing down the mind and thinning out thoughts often happens in the transactional relationship between teacher and student. Thinning out the thoughts generally occurs in two stages. First, thoughts can be thinned out by not feeding the interpretative process. This means not digging for problems (in the language of Dzogchen, "letting things be as they are"), not asking for information or understanding, and not giving people things to think about. We stay in communication while gradually reducing the amount of information that's being processed. When we calibrate the rate of reduction of cognitive stimulus correctly, it is quite easy to enter a state of peace and inner settlement.

Seeing through—thinking about nothing

In stage two, when a person's thoughts have slowed down somewhat, we may move their thinking into an inquiry into the nature of unconditioned awareness. When we try to think about nothing—not an idea we have about nothing—but absolute nothing itself, we can quickly enter into the experience of the unconditioned.

If "nothing" is a bit abstract, we can explore "space." We can offer space as an object of contemplation. Space is very effective because, again, how can we think about it? Where is it? What is it? In Buddhism, space is non-compounded. There is nothing in it. Space doesn't give us anything to think about. This is why space is often used as a springboard into nondual awareness.

When we think about nothing, we have fewer and fewer thoughts because our thoughts have no content to attach to and so our capacity for conceptual elaboration is seriously undermined. This is the point where the cultivation of serenity transforms into the practice of "seeing through." The practice of not giving ourselves (or anyone else) anything to think about simply reduces the topics we can use to stimulate our minds. The practice of "thinking about nothing" becomes untenable—in fact impossible—because the practice simply doesn't provide a basis for our conceptualization.

The relationship between the practice of serenity and seeing through should now be clear. The practice of serenity begins by giving us less to think about. In *Radiant Mind*, we develop serenity through contemplations in which there is no object of reflection or contemplation, nor any theme or issue in our lives that we need to explore. As this practice evolves, we have less and less that we need to think about until finally there is nothing to think about. At this point the practice converts into an inquiry into nothing. We might ask, "What is this state that has no structure? Is it a state at all?"

At a certain point "thinking about nothing" transmutes into "having nothing to think about;" the mind is at rest, in its natural state, seeing the co-arising of conditioned structures (thoughts, feelings and sensations) and openness. The techniques of serenity and seeing through continue to support each other in an ever-deepening reciprocity and ultimate fusion. Thinking about nothing becomes untenable because there's no foundation for our thoughts, and this naturally slows our thinking down even further. This in turn gives us less thought material with which to identify, which deepens our ability to see through conceptual structures. Finally there is nowhere further to go. We can't say what we are doing or not doing, or who is doing or not doing this. We rest in the primordial and effortless state of natural meditation.

In summation, *Radiant Mind* is a post-modern form of Mahayana Buddhism that's inspired by the Deconstructive (Prasangika) form of Madhyamika, especially by the precision of their unfindability inquiry. *Radiant Mind* is also in complete alignment with Dzogchen and Mahamudra, especially in terms of how they bypass "the path" and offer direct introductions into pure awareness. I'll return to these connections shortly.

Zen and Radiant Mind

Zen is another Mahayana tradition that is closely connected to *Radiant Mind*. Zen developed in China, but traces its origins to a silent teaching the historical Buddha gave in India. The Buddha held up a flower and just one disciple, Mahakashyapa, received the contentless transmission that lies beyond words.

Zen and "ordinary mind"

Zen is helpful in the way that it normalizes the realization of unconditioned awareness by calling it "ordinary mind" (*heijo shin*). A common obstacle to realizing nondual awareness is to think that it must be totally different from our everyday experience of living in a body, taking care of worldly concerns. It's easy to have very fanciful projections about nondual awareness. Instead of seeing that this is it, people go looking for it elsewhere. "This, right now, in this body, sitting at home surrounded by my family and animals is too ordinary. It's got to be different." People forget and don't realize that nondual awareness is uneventful. Nothing is happening! This is noted in Mahamudra, which also uses the term ordinary mind (*tha mal gyi shes pa*) to refer to the ultimate state.

Even after presencing nondual awareness, people can doubt that this is the state that's realized by the famous saints, sages and yogis because they still have a residual expectation that it must be dramatic, sublime, or out of this world. It could be seen as "out of this world" because it's totally unconditioned, transcultural, and transtemporal. It's not even a biological state. Yet, at the same time, it's totally ordinary. It's inseparable from who we are right now. Nondual awareness is chopping wood, carrying water, getting the kids off to school, and going to the supermarket.

Zen is also aligned with *Radiant Mind* in its confident and upfront use of paradox and self-contradiction in talking about nondual awareness. Both the ordinariness and paradoxical nature of awakening are brought together in a famous Zen episode that's cited as case (koan) 19 in the *Mumonkan*. (*The Gateless Gate*, Trans. Eiichi Shimomissé, 1998)

> Joshu asked Nansen, "What is the way?" Nansen answered, "Your ordinary mind—that's the way." Joshu said, "Can it be grasped?" Nansen replied, "The more you pursue it, the more it slips away." Joshu asked once more, "How can you know it is the way?" Nansen responded, "The way isn't subject to knowing or not knowing. To know is to be deluded. To not know is being blanked out. When you clearly find the way, it's as vast and boundless as infinite space. How can we talk about this in terms of affirmations and negations?" On hearing this, Joshu was awakened.

Not knowing

Zen also serves *Radiant Mind* in the way that it robustly cuts through the habits of trying to understand nondual awareness with its declaration that nondual awareness is a state of not knowing (*fushiki*).

The official history of Chinese Zen (Ch'an) begins with Bodhidharma, a south Indian master who traveled to China in 520 CE. The ruling emperor, Liang Wu Ti, was a patron of Buddhism and keenly interested in Buddhist philosophy. When he heard that Bodhidharma had arrived in the country, he invited him to the court and tried to engage him in discussion. Confident of his spiritual accounting, he asked Bodhidharma how much merit he would have accrued from all the charitable work he had undertaken—the schools and hospitals he had built, the Buddhist texts he had printed for free distribution, the monasteries he had founded, the alms he had given, and so on. "None whatsoever," Bodhidharma replied. This didn't exactly please the Emperor, but he asked a number of other questions, all of which Bodhidharma answered in an equally unsatisfactory and cryptic manner. Finally, the Emperor asked, "What is the first principle of the Dharma?" "Vast emptiness, nothing sacred," said Bodhidharma. "And if this is so, who is it that is speaking to me?" "I do not know," replied Bodhidharma. The Emperor, now completely exasperated, banished Bodhidharma from his kingdom.

Even though nondual traditions clearly and consistently speak about nondual wisdom as nonconceptual, objectless, and beyond the mind, as Westerners we bring to our engagement with these traditions a long-standing habit of believing that realization comes through knowledge. This is the only way we know how to do things; we try to understand, to comprehend, to work things out. In many ways this habit is compounded by the thousands of Books that have been written about openness and other concepts for the unconditioned.

Zen cuts through this habit with one concept, by telling us that nondual awareness is a state of not knowing. And when the question arises, "Okay, but how do I do that?" Zen answers, "By not knowing how to do it!" A koan that exemplifies this is where a student asks the Zen Master, "Which way is the path?" To which the master responds, "Go!"

There are also clear parallels between Zen and *Radiant Mind* in relation to the use of koans and the practice of "just sitting" (*shikan taza*). Working with koans and "just sitting" are central practices in the Rinzai and Soto schools, respectively. A form of koan work and a style of "just sitting" arise within *Radiant Mind*, mainly because they emerge as skillful methods (*upaya*) within a nondual approach to fulfillment.

Zen koans

Koan practice is usually associated with Rinzai Zen. The koan method of practice was institutionalized in China in the twelfth century with Sung masters and was further formalized in Japan in the thirteenth century. The entire koan system of Rinzai Zen is a form of contemplative inquiry that deconstructs the conceptual mind in order to reveal unstructured awareness.

The koan is a kind of puzzle or problem, a conundrum which defies conceptual resolution. A master gives a student a koan with the intention of bringing to the surface a fundamental dilemma that lies within the student's mind and which obscures awakening. Sometimes the koans are dialectical in structure. For example, they might report a terse exchange between a famous master and a student.

A well-known koan of this type comes from an exchange in which a monk asked the ninth-century Chinese Joshu, "Has a dog buddha nature or not?" Joshu answered, "Mu!" In time, this developed into the koan "Show me mu!" The challenge to "Show me mu!" ultimately means "Show me your experiential understanding of the open-endedness of being." Alternatively, a master might deliver the koan to a student by holding up a staff and saying, "This is not a staff. What is it?"

Koans are found in other traditions as well. The famous Tibetan Dzogchen yogi Longchenpa used an interesting koan. He'd ask a student to fetch something for him that was some distance away. When the student was half way there, Longchenpa would yell out, "Stop!" and then do nothing more. That's a koan. When a Mahamudra master asks a student if her or his mind is colored, that's also a koan. When Ramana Maharshi asks, "Who is seeking?" that too is a koan.

Natural koans

Koans are actually timeless. They are the questions that naturally emerge whenever people begin to lose their familiar frame of reference in terms of who and where they are.

In *Radiant Mind*, we often use naturally arising koans as tools for deconstructing reference points. The contemplative space that opens up in *Radiant Mind* gives birth to a gentle cascade of koan questions such as: "What is this?" "Where am I?" "Am I moving forward or backward?" "Am I moving at all?" "Is there something special I should be doing?" "Who am I?" These questions are all koans because each one of them is capable of deconstructing being someone, located somewhere. People surf their way into no-mind by letting their thoughts ride on these koan questions.

The arising of such questions, in an unplanned and informal way during contemplative dialogs and periods of natural silence, differs from koan practice in the Rinzai lineages. In Rinzai, koans are formally introduced to students who can work with them in a concerted way over a long period, even years, until they achieve a significant breakthrough into unconditioned awareness. They then move through a set of koans in a quite systematic way, then revisit earlier ones, in order to deepen and consolidate their realization.

A common feature in all of these questions is that they all refer either to "This"—what's happening, or "I"—the person who's thinking. Often we don't go on to ask the next question—"What is this?" or "Who am I?" We assume that we know what we're thinking about in those first set of questions. These two questions "What is this?" and "Who am I?" are at the heart of many deconstructive dialogs.

"Who am I?"

The Hindu form of nondual (Advaita) inquiry is based on the question "Who am I?" This is called "inquiry into the self" (*atma-vichara*).

In *Radiant Mind*, I often prefer to ask a question such as, "Who is experiencing this (problem, feeling, etc.) right now?" This question is more immediate. It keeps us in the experience we're having in the present moment. What we're asking is: "Is there an experiencer separate from the experience?" Or, saying it slightly differently, "It's clear this experience is happening, but who is actually experiencing it?" Or, "Who is receiving this experience?"

"What is this?"

In Korean Zen, the main koan is the question "What is this?" The first record of this koan occurs in an exchange between the Sixth Zen Patriarch Huineng and a young monk named Huaijang, in which Huineng asked Huaijang, "What is this and where did it come from?" Huaijang couldn't answer. But he took the question away with himself and used it as his sole form of inquiry for several years until he realized what it was pointing to. He then returned to see Huineng who again asked him, "What is this?" Huaijang replied, "To say it is something misses the point, but still it can be cultivated."

In *Radiant Mind*, the question "What is this?" arises in a natural and authentic way. It isn't inserted as a practice. At some point the question is just there and often it is verbalized, "What is this?" In a way we are asking, "Where are we?" We don't know what "This" is and we are seeking to know what "it" is, whatever "it" is that we are seeking to know. At some point we see that "This" isn't anything. There is no it. It does not exist. What does not exist? The "This" that we are now experiencing—that we are always experiencing—in fact, does not exist. It is and it isn't. In fact, it is because it isn't.

The question "What is This?" is powerful because it doesn't point us in any direction whatsoever. "This" potentially includes everything inside and outside, or it could mean nothing! We don't know where to look! The question takes us into "not knowing."

Checking questions

There is another set of questions that arise in *Radiant Mind* that are similar to koan questions, but used slightly differently. I call them "checking questions." Some of these are, in fact, the same as natural koan questions.

Checking questions are used to verify the quality of a person's nondual state. We can direct these questions to ourselves and to others. Normally they only arise when someone is in a quiet, open, and spacious state of being. These questions reveal whether a person is resting in a structured or unstructured state. An example of a checking question is: "Can you enhance this experience?" or "Could this be better?" Contentless awareness is beyond improvement or degradation because there is nothing in the state to enhance or dilute.

If we receive a positive response to the question "Could this be better?"—"Yes, it could"—this shows that the student is (or we are) in a structured experience—there is something happening that could be improved or enhanced. If we discover the presence of residual reference points within the state of unconditioned awareness, we can go one step further, into pure contentlessness, by realizing that there is nowhere further to go!

If a student responds that the experience couldn't be better, he or she may or may not be identifying with some experiential content. We can check this by asking, "Can you hold onto this?" If no response is forthcoming, because the question no longer makes sense—there is no "This"—this may be nondual awareness. We can talk, or not talk; it doesn't make any difference.

Some other checking questions are:

- Is something missing?
- Is there anything we need to be doing right now?
- Is there something we need to be thinking about?
- What are we doing now?
- Can this be enhanced?
- Can we do more of this?
- Could we lose this?
- Is this pleasurable?
- Where are you now?
- Are we making progress?
- Are we moving?
- Are we going anywhere?
- Is there anywhere to go?

In *Radiant Mind*, we take care that these types of exchanges don't become a conditioned set of questions and responses in which a student learns the "right" response—to shut up and be quiet!

When we ask these types of checking questions, we're also sensitive to the fact that they could become a trigger for conceptual construction. If a student begins to think about a checking question, then it has missed its intention.

Just sitting

In *Radiant Mind*, meditation is introduced as making a break with the routine, outcome-oriented activities of life, such as managing finances, processing email, seeking sexual fulfillment, preparing meals, and helping children with their school work. Having stopped and made a break we sit, or lie down, and "do what we are doing." We call this "just sitting" rather than meditation. "Just sitting" is meditation without a reference point, because there is nothing that we are meant to be doing, or not doing. The moment we sit down our practice is fulfilled. There is nothing more we need to do, because we are doing what we are doing. We do this for as long as we do it—either doing nothing or thinking that we're doing something, going nowhere or thinking that we're going somewhere, being no one or thinking that we're someone.

While this form of meditation is extremely open and totally forgiving, internally it is identical with the Soto Zen practice of *shikan taza*. *Shikan taza*, which also means "just sitting" or "simply sitting," was offered by the great thirteenth-century Japanese master Dogen, not as a means to an end, but as the fruition of practice itself. (See *Hakuin, Zazengi*, in K. Nishiyama and J. Stevens (tr.), *Shobogenzo*, Vol. I: 40) *Shikan taza* is being in the place where there is nothing more that needs to be accomplished.

According to Dogen, *shikan taza* occurs within the physically precise posture of zazen, i.e., half or full lotus position, tongue against the roof of the mouth, one hand on of top of the other, thumbs touching, etc. (See his *Fukanzazengi: Guidelines for the Universal Practice of Zazen*.)

The reason we don't ask students to assume a rigid posture and sit for a set period of time is that these "conditional requirements" can conspire with our innate tendency to create meaning and purpose out of nearly everything that we do. *Radiant Mind* addresses our tendency to make a project out of meditation by taking away many of the cues that can signal that we're sitting for a purpose. We could say that *Radiant Mind* is framed by continuous free-form *shikan taza*. When I say "free-form," I mean that it isn't constrained by a special sitting posture.

Non-thinking (*hishiryo*)

Radiant Mind is also guided by Dogen's distinction of "non-thinking." Dogen distinguishes between thinking (*shiryo*), not thinking (*fushiryo*), and non-thinking (*hishiryo*). Non-thinking is "no-mind." Non-thinking is not, not thinking. Dogen describes zazen as "Thinking of not thinking." When asked how to do this, he writes, "By non-thinking."

Here Dogen is harkening back to a well-known story about Yakusan Igen, who lived in eighth-century China. One day after Master Yakusan had finished zazen, a monk asked, "What are you thinking of in the immoveable, mountain-like state of zazen?" Yakusan replied, "I think of not thinking." The monk asked, "How do you think of not thinking?" Yakusan answered, "By non-thinking."

Thinking is the activity of trying to go somewhere with our thoughts. We think in order to understand, solve a problem, and overcome our suffering. Thinking is directional and positional. It keeps us located (positioned) and in time. *Shikan taza* is designed to cut through thinking because we aren't going anywhere! We're not trying to become enlightened or achieve realizations.

In *Radiant Mind*, we regularly point out when people are in time and going somewhere with their thinking, for example, trying to solve a problem, move through their confusion, understand the unconditioned, work out how to integrate nonduality into their lives, meditate to heal past traumas, and so on. When this happens, we invite people to observe how this "way of thinking" creates a gap between where they are and where they would like to be.

Another strategy for "closing the gap" is to not think. If thinking just perpetuates the gap, the solution is to stop thinking. We try to not think. But in order not to think, we have to work out how to do this. In order to move from thinking to not thinking, we have to think about not thinking, in which case we are thinking. Not thinking is still directional and intentional. Thinking never becomes not thinking.

In *Radiant Mind*, we notice how people become frustrated when they can't think their way into the space where nothing is missing. This is the point where thinking becomes burdensome and people seek to calm their minds, dis-identify from thoughts, or find the gaps between thoughts. We change tack and try to get outside the mind completely. Often people explicitly ask how to stop thinking—how to not think. When this happens we invite them to see what's actually happening in trying not to think. We point out that, in asking how to stop thinking, we're asking to be given something that we will think about. People rarely say "Give me an answer that I can't think about!" even though this is the intention of many facilitator responses in *Radiant Mind*.

Dogen was very kind. Instead of confining us to "thinking" and trying "not to think," he throws us right into the middle of this dilemma by advising that we "Think about not thinking." He could equally have advised us to "Not think about thinking."

In *Radiant Mind*, we follow Dogen right into the heart of this dilemma. If we know that we aren't thinking, we are thinking. How else can we say we aren't thinking? If we're not thinking, we don't have a concept of this. There's nothing that we can identify as "not thinking." If we aren't thinking we can't think about not thinking, or anything else for that matter. We can't say that not thinking is not thinking, unless we're thinking. Sometimes people cite their own immediate experience as proof that they aren't thinking. This is easily clarified by asking them if that's what they think! On the other hand, if we are thinking, we can't think about not thinking, because in not thinking there's nothing to think about!

At this point people often say, "Now what? I don't know what to think." This is the point where we may join our students in the possibility of non-thinking. Non-thinking is just being with what is. This is the sense of "just" or "*shikan*" in *shikan taza*. We are simply present to whatever is happening because this is all that's happening. In non-thinking, thoughts are just there—wherever they are—as a natural function of our conditioning. In non-thinking we aren't trying to get anywhere with our thoughts. Hence we can never be frustrated. Thoughts move through without any rejection or grasping. In the language of Dzogchen, thoughts self-liberate on the spot. Dogen describes this as the "pure presencing of things as they are" (*genjokoan*). We are neither in (thinking) nor outside (not thinking) of time. There is no inside or outside and no subject and objects. Yet everything manifests exactly as it does. We can't say what this is, and we don't need to. We can't do this because we don't know what we are doing.

Mahamudra

Mahamudra is a Buddhist nondual tradition that emerged in India around the eighth and ninth centuries. The first Mahamudra master was Saraha, who delivered his transmission through *dohas*—spontaneous songs and poems that directly revealed the state of pure awareness in listeners.

Mahamudra is often translated as the Great Seal. Maha can mean great, transcendent, or universal, and mudra can mean symbol or seal. Here mudra has the sense of "touch" and "expression."

So it means that everything, without exception, is comprehensively embraced (and liberated) within the field of nondual awareness. Mahamudra is another way of saying that contentless awareness (*maha*) is inseparable from the boundless expanse of appearances (*mudra*).

The great names associated with Indian Mahamudra include Shabari, Tilopa, Maitripa, and Naropa. The Mahamudra transmissions entered Tibet between the eleventh and twelfth centuries. In Tibet the transmission moved from Marpa, to Milrepa, and Gampopa (1079–1153) who developed a four links (*yoga*) model of Mahamudra transmission. Mahamudra is practiced within all the so-called New Translations schools of Tibetan Buddhism: Sakya, Kagyu, and Gelug. We are fortunate that this transmission is very vital and alive in the Kagyu school and readily accessible to Westerners.

There are three main traditions of Mahamudra: scriptural (*sutra*) Mahamudra, tantra Mahamudra, and essence Mahamudra. *Radiant Mind* has close parallels with *sutra* and essence Mahamudra. Essence Mahamudra is a transmission that awakens nondual awareness by relying on a bare minimum of simple, yet profound pointing-out instructions. Like Dzogchen, it is oriented to immediate awakening without reliance on fabricated interventions. Essence Mahamudra is found in the original songs of Saraha. Saraha is famous for the introduction of non- (effortful) action (*las med*) and non-meditation (*sgom med*). This lineage was brought to Tibet by Marpa who received transmission from the Indian *siddha* Maitripa. *Sutra* Mahamudra is a form of transmission built on the foundations of serenity and seeing through.

Most contemporary Tibetan Mahamudra masters rely on the systems of transmission that are found in the works of Dagpo Tashi Namgyal (1513–87) and the ninth Karmapa Wangchug Dorje (1555–1603).

A number of connections can be drawn between *Radiant Mind* and Mahamudra. The main parallels and borrowings, which I'll describe in separate sections, are:

- A focus on the nature of awareness (*rang rig*) or consciousness itself (*sems nyid*).
- An accessible form of seeing through.
- The state of non-meditation.

Consciousness itself

In many nondual approaches, the focus is on realizing selflessness. This is the focus of Madhyamika and the Advaita self-inquiry. The focus in Mahamudra is realizing the nature of mind or consciousness itself. There is no difference between the states of openness, identitylessness, pure awareness, consciousness itself, and self-knowledge (*atma-vidya*). However, it is less threatening for some people to inquire into the nature of consciousness rather than their own existence. When they are faced with an inquiry that questions their own existence, some people emphatically declare that they exist. It's unthinkable that they could not exist. A conditioned reaction can be triggered in which they continually declare, like a broken record, "I'm here. I can't say exactly where. But I'm here, in here [perhaps pointing to their chest or head]. That's obvious."

In this case it's very useful to inquire into the nature of consciousness itself as a way of entering identitylessness. There is less identification involved and hence less resistance.

Mahamudra and "seeing through"

Mahamudra offers us a different type of "seeing through" or "unfindability inquiry" that is often more accessible to Westerners. We recall that the Madhyamika approach is guided by a form of logical inquiry that's designed to reveal the open nature of reality by driving us out of the conceptual mind. In our efforts to coherently and consistently establish our own existence (or nonexistence) we are forced to contradict ourselves. Most of the Madhyamika literature is also deeply embedded in the Indian and/or Tibetan philosophical milieu. It can be difficult to extract the transcultural essence of the Madhyamika approach from the complex philosophy systems with which it is often engaged.

Mahamudra and Dzogchen, on the other hand, are readily accessible. They require very little or no reworking to be immediately relevant to modern Westerners. The questions that are used in Mahamudra to reveal pure awareness are clear and simple. And the language is existential and universal.

It's helpful to list the range of questions used in Mahamudra. They offer a set of questions, anyone of which can serve to connect people with awareness itself or consciousness itself; many terms are used for the same state.

The following questions are drawn from an instruction Guide written by Dakpo Tashi Namgyal (2001) titled *Clarifying the Natural State*. I have slightly modified the wording of some questions. I've added the headings that Tashi Namgyal uses in order to show the intention of each set of questions. Tashi Namgyal indicates that some practitioners work through these questions sequentially and others move quite freely between them. [p. 39]

In Gampopa's four links model, the practices of "seeing through" and "pointing-out" are the main focus of the second link, which is called the yoga of simplicity or non-elaboration. The first link is the yoga of one-pointedness. This is where practitioners build a foundation of serenity.

Determining the essence of mind—the ground

The questions that one asks are:

Does our mind have a shape, a color, a location, a support or material substance? [p. 28]

223

These possibilities are investigated one by one. If something comes up we continue looking, more carefully, examining the characteristics of mind to its very depth. [p. 28] For example, if we think our mind has a location, we ask where exactly is it? Where are its boundaries?

We continue with this investigation until we realize the mind as an open clearing (*gsal stong*) that defies any description at all. [p. 29]

Tashi Namgyal notes that when Mahamudra masters are checking the realizations of their students, they need to determine that their students are answering such questions from their direct, immediate experience, and not simply giving the "right answers" that they have no doubt read in texts. [p. 29] He recommends that masters present questions and propositions to students that will confuse them if they aren't speaking from a direct experience of pure awareness.

If a student is responding from her or his direct experience, the responses will converge as a coherent expression of referencelessness, even when a student isn't using standard terminology to communicate the state they're in. Tashi Namgyal also notes that there can be a disparity between the quality of a student's realization and his or her capacity to express it. The fact that someone is very articulate doesn't mean that they have gained realization. And the fact that someone becomes tongue-tied doesn't necessarily mean that they aren't resting in clear openness. [p. 29]

Determining the essence of thoughts and perceptions—the expression

In this phase we investigate inner events that happen within the mind, namely, thoughts and perceptions. When a coarse thought-state such as anger arises, we look and ask: Where is it? Does it have a support? What is its essence (what makes it what it is)? How does it appear? We do the same for subtle thought-states.

Then we examine subtle or coarse perceptions: feelings of joy, sadness, the projections of "friend," "competitor," or "enemy" onto people. We try to see what exactly it is that makes them what they are. The result is that we can't find exactly what it is. We can't find any one characteristic that lets us say that something is what we think it is.

We then narrow this down to investigating individual thoughts and perceptions.

We continue along until we see that thought cannot be identified and that perceptions are an insubstantial impression of unobstructed presence. [p. 31]

Resolving that thoughts are mind [p. 32]

Another set of investigations involves looking at how thoughts evolve and subsist in time. We investigate the formation, subsistence, and dissolution of thoughts by asking questions such as: Here is a thought: What did it come from? Does it subsist or remain? And finally, does it just stop, or does it dissolve over time? We do this for coarse thoughts, such as anger, and subtle thoughts until we see that they are clear openness without any essence or defining characteristic.

Resolving that perceptions are mind [p. 34]

Another set of questions involves looking at the relationship between visual appearances (*gzugs snang*) and the mind-itself. We ask: Are visual sensations different from, or identical to the mind? If they are identical, how does this work? Does the mind become a visual perception? Or does the visual perception become mind? If they are different, are they spatially separate from each other? Can they exist independently of each other?

These investigations lead to seeing that perceptions and the mind are neither the same nor different. With this realization in place the contemplation is extended to include the full range of sensations from all the senses, from the most disgusting to the most beautiful and refined.

Investigating the calm and the moving mind [p. 36]

In order to be able to rest in awareness itself in the midst of all mental activity, we investigate side-by-side experiences of mental stillness and turbulent thoughts. Are these composed of different substances? We continue with this investigation until we see that the calm and the moving mind are identical in being groundless, intangible, and indistinguishable from the open clearing in which they appear.

Resolving that all experience is non-arising [p. 37]

At this point we clearly see that all contents of awareness are unconfined expressions of clear, open awareness itself. Now we can ask: What is the natural state of this awareness? What is it?

When we look for awareness we see clearly that it is unconditioned and has no characteristics. It is naturally awake (*rang sangs*), intrinsically pure (*rang dag*), and automatically liberated (*rang grol*). As such, our real nature can't be improved on, or damaged. [p. 37]

Pointing out events

The "seeing through" methods of Mahamudra are often enhanced and clarified by so-called "pointing out" events given by a master. The process of receiving pointing out instructions from a master can be very formal. Pointing out events can also happen casually, and quite unexpectedly. In a pointing out event a student directly realizes nondual awareness.

In *Radiant Mind*, pointing out instructions arise as natural events in a contemplative dialog. They are woven into the conversations that happen in workshops and individual sessions with students. There's no formality involved. They aren't pre-planned or rehearsed. In a way, facilitators are constantly preparing the ground for giving pointing out instructions and then supporting students to rest in that state once it opens up.

Pointing out innate mind-essence

Here a master points out the pure nature of the mind-itself—the formless, contentless *dharmakaya*. The master then shows that "this state"—the realization of awareness itself—is identical with buddha mind and other names that are used to indicate this ultimate state of evolution, for example, the non-arising *dharmakaya*, our basic natural state, the innate mind, etc. A master shows that "This" is the essential nature of awareness of all conscious beings. [p. 41-42] This is effectively the same as the second of Garab Dorje's points that was mentioned at the beginning of this Appendix, namely, the clear recognition of this unique state.

In *Radiant Mind*, we similarly show how the state of pure awareness, that people can glimpse or rest in for some minutes at a time, is the same as the contentless dimension of buddha mind. It is the state that lies at the end of all spiritual paths and seeking, precisely because we are no longer anywhere. There is no longer a path or goal because there is nowhere further to go. We are beyond all reference points. It's important to point this out because people can access the ultimate state and fail to realize that it's identical to the state that's attained and spoken about by all realized nondual masters.

Pointing out the co-arising of thoughts [p. 43]

Here a master introduces a student to awareness itself while thoughts are arising, and points to the total compatibility of the arising of thoughts and the presencing of awareness itself, and to the fact that thoughts can't be distinguished from the space of clear openness. This is called "seeing the natural face of the co-arising of thoughts" or "thinking dawning as the *dharmakaya*." [p. 44] This is the point where it makes absolutely no difference whether we are thinking or not thinking. We no longer have any bias toward the mind being calm or dynamic.

Pointing out the co-arising of appearances

This is where a master points out that appearances are indistinguishable from the aware and open nature of the mind-itself. Appearances are neither inside nor outside of the mind. They are the very nature of contentless awareness itself. This is called "seeing the natural face of the co-arising of appearances" or "appearances dawning as *dharmakaya*."

In *Radiant Mind*, similar or identical investigations arise in the flow of people's personal engagement with the field that is created in a workshop or personal session with a facilitator. I often introduce these types of inquiries by saying something like, "Here we are 'looking' for what seems to be real and obvious. We're not thinking about the mind or awareness. It's easy to have lots of theories and ideas about these things, especially if we have read about these topics. But we're not doing philosophy at this point. We're more like scientists. We're looking at seeing what is really here. "Where is awareness? Does it have a boundary? Does is stop somewhere, etc.?" These types of inquiry also happen silently in people's private reflection, as a function of the vector toward nondual awareness that's activated within the *Radiant Mind* field.

Mahamudra and the Radiant Mind culture

In the Indian siddha lineages, Mahamudra was transmitted in an organic, free-form, even anarchic way. Most of the siddhas were free-wheeling adepts who had no institutional ties. If a student was able to receive transmission, it happened automatically without forethought, preparation, or delay. The siddhas didn't even think in terms of students or disciples. Every action they performed arose as the spontaneous, uncontrived expression of pure presence, so everything they did had the potential to gently ease, catapult, or even shock people into the same state of effortless being.

In Tibet the Mahamudra lineages became quite formalized and institutionalized, at least on paper. Often practitioners worked their way systematically through a series of contemplations that built on each other, progressively moving them beyond fixed reference points as well as the subtle super-refined states that arose through their practices.

The extraordinary levels of Mahamudra

It would seem that there is nowhere further to go, but Mahamudra now introduces the two extraordinary levels! These are the two final links in Gampopa's four links model. These are the yogas of one taste (*ro gcig*) and non-meditation (*sgom med*).

These two yogas can be understood in a way that we can all relate to in both an ordinary and extraordinary way. This distinction isn't made in the Mahamudra teachings, but it is easily extracted from the way they are spoken about. The ordinary understanding of one taste and non-meditation is directly relevant to *Radiant Mind*. The extraordinary understanding reaches beyond the scope of *Radiant Mind*. It firmly situates Mahamudra within the psycho-cosmology of the Mahayana and the ultimate goal of complete and full awakening called buddhahood. I will describe the extraordinary way in which these final yogas are understood because it shows the limits of *Radiant Mind*.

One taste

One taste is a translation of *ro* (taste) and *gcig* (one). It signifies that within the sphere of nondual awareness, all conditioned experiences are equalized. Every possible event within the field of awareness—from the most sublime and exquisite to the most excruciating and horrifying—is equalized, in the sense that no one experience is preferred over any other one. Phenomena and awareness dissolve into each other so that reactive perturbations within the field of awareness are simply impossible. The full range of experience—from the heights of *nirvana* to the depths of *samsara*—is a play of sense-data in the sphere of formless awareness. Attachment and aversion are comprehensively neutralized. No one is left to prefer any thing.

In *Radiant Mind*, we speak about this process as the deepening of the state of unconditioned awareness. At the beginning we are only able to rest in unconditioned awareness when the prevailing conditions are close to our preferences. While we can truly enter nondual awareness, our capacity to enter the state is still conditioned. We need conducive conditions: a relatively peaceful environment, distance from the daily distractions and pressures of work and family, the support of a facilitator or community, etc. As we progress we're able to expand the conditions. Our preferences gradually become less significant influences. We find that we're able to abide in nondual awareness in situations that would previously have produced a reactive response and thrown us into self-identification.

Even so, the state of one taste, as described in Mahamudra, is clearly beyond the reach of people who participate in *Radiant Mind*. The possibility of remaining spacious and totally equanimous in the face of everything that life brings us—physical pain, illness, emotional anguish, loss of loved ones, our own death, etc.—points to our evolutionary potential, but doesn't live within us as an expectation, or reality.

Mahamudra takes the realization of one taste further by virtue of the fact that the appearing mind (the mind that co-arises with appearances) is paradoxical. It is simultaneously saturated with content and contentless, undifferentiable and infinitely differentiable, in time and outside of time, causal and acausal. Two incompatible paradigms co-exist in total synchrony and harmony! Ultimately we can't say that phenomenal events are discreet or unified—one or many. Yet, at a relative level every seemingly finite event is inseparable from the boundless and timeless expanse of awareness. Thus, "It may seem both as if many single mind-moments occur and as if there is one entire interconnected network of subtle propensities." (Brown, 2006: 365) In this way, pure awareness is intimately connected to the fabric of causes and conditions that shape the structure and evolution of each and every relative reality, throughout time and space. The implication here is that it's possible to effortlessly penetrate and fathom every conditioned event that has and will happen in limitless space for all crystallized identities through the structure of this very moment of our conditioned experience.

This links Mahamudra directly to the Mahayana idea that the scope of an embodied consciousness can expand beyond the limits of the physical senses and brain capacity to include deeper and more comprehensive knowledge of the complexities of people's inner and outer realities, the relationship between these, and their individual and collective evolution through time.

According to the Mahayana, individual consciousness is clouded or veiled by cognitive coverings. Unlike emotional obscurations, these are invisible. However, when they're removed, cognition expands giving Mahayana masters direct access to the psychic processes of sentient beings. In Mahayana there is no limit to this process of consciousness expansion and expression. The process of expansion leads to the state of buddhahood, whereas the realization of nondual awareness leads to the liberation of a distinct stream of consciousness. The expansion of cognition is a function of the bodhisattvas' universal compassion, which propels these beings to acquire every conceivable resource that supports their vision of universal awakening.

In *Radiant Mind*, we keep shy of the Mahayana commitment to universal awakening. Our focus is on accessing, recognizing, and gaining more and more familiarity with nondual awareness while in relationship with others. We leave it to each participant to create the framework and context within which they cultivate nondual awareness. *Radiant Mind* emphasizes the wisdom aspect of Mahayana nondualism.

Non-meditation

The second extraordinary yoga and the final yoga of Gampapo's four links is "non-meditation." Non-meditation refers to the space in which the fruition of meditation has been realized (nondual awareness) and can't be interrupted by any activities or events. We're no longer meditating. Whatever meditation has meant to us, it is no longer happening. Nothing is happening! This is why it's called "non-meditation." We might be sitting still looking like we are meditating, but we aren't doing anything. No goal-oriented activity is inserted in our condition because there is nowhere further to go.

We might even be reciting a mantra or imagining extending light-energy throughout the universe, but at the same time no one is doing anything. If practice is happening, it's simply the organic, agentless functioning of our conditioning. There's no meditator and no meditation. We don't need to be doing what we are doing. And when we move from being still, and engage in our daily activities, nothing changes because there is nothing to lose, or sustain, and no one being still or active. This is called transcending or dissolving the difference between meditation and post- (meditative) attainment. At this level meditation can't be defined or identified. Other names that are used for this state are, no-mindfulness (*dran med*), being mentally disengaged (*yid la mi byed pa*), nothing but inactivity (*byas med tsam*), and non-contrivance (*bcos med*).

A quote from the *Tantra of the King of Secret Nectars* summarizes much of this:

> By meditating on the [natural mind's] real nature—emptiness and clear light—there is nothing to attain. By not meditating there is nothing to attain. Meditation is a false concept. Non-meditation is a false concept too. There isn't even the slightest cause to meditate, nor [the slightest] movement of distraction. (Brown, 2006: 396)

In *Radiant Mind*, we bring people to the point where they can't say whether they are meditating or not. It feels like meditation except that people aren't doing anything. There's no objective. They may be sitting still with their eyes closed, or have their eyes open, taking in other people, even talking and relating with them. It doesn't make any difference. We sometimes ask people what they are doing and they can't say. They don't know. There's no reference point to say what is happening. Often people will say, "I'm not meditating, but it is just happening. It's like super-smooth meditation, but I'm not doing anything, and there's full awareness of this space."

Their state is completely stable, yet movement and speaking can be happening. It seems that nothing is being asked of us, that nothing is prohibited or being encouraged. There is no pressure, just pure, effortless being.

The extraordinary understanding of non-meditation is simple yet far reaching. It's the possibility of abiding in nondual awareness without any interruption and across all activities.

In *Radiant Mind*, we speak about this as the duration of abiding in nondual awareness. At the result level, when resting in nondual awareness, there is no duration because we're no longer in time. At the pure unconditioned level nothing is happening through which to measure time. There's no past, future, or present.

When the seamless continuity of non-meditation is combined with unrestricted cognition, this is the full and complete awakening of buddhahood.

Dzogchen

In contrast to path-oriented forms of spirituality, Dzogchen begins and continues unceasingly at the level of the result. It takes away the whole notion of a path and destination. It directly reveals an open panorama in which an ever-changing display of phenomenal appearances (forms, colors, tastes, feelings, thoughts, etc.) is identical with infinite, contentless awareness. Through a vision that spontaneously dissolves all structures that separate reality into experiences of the sublime and mundane, pleasure and pain, Dzogchen masters abide in a radically natural and uncontrived way of being in the world, without any sense of personal accomplishment. They are the nature of reality itself. In Dzogchen, this is spoken about as the uncontrived realization of things-as-they-are (*dharmata*).

Dzogchen is a spiritual perspective that has been tapped into from beginningless time by sage-philosophers as they transcend any need to escape from, or indulge in, anything. From within this sphere of perfect completion, there is nothing to avoid and nothing to create. This tradition sources its origins to a primordial possibility that transcends limited and seductive interpretations of human existence offered by different religious and philosophical systems. This possibility is realized as the inseparable coincidence of forms and contentless wisdom that's completely untouched by the fears of suffering, or hope of liberation.

Dzogchen differs from the other approaches because of the rigor with which it speaks from the result or fruition level. In Dzogchen there's no territory to traverse. Nor do we arrive at the culmination of the spiritual journey. In this tradition the doctrinal structure of Buddhism and all paths deconstruct. This tradition removes the experience of being on a path, going somewhere. As a result, there's nothing to achieve (i.e., no *nirvana*), no practice to perform, and neither teachers nor students. (Neumaier-Dargyay, 1992: 1) There is nothing to gain or lose because this space transcends the need to avoid suffering, or achieve liberation. Nothing contradicts or threatens this sphere of being since everything that is ever thought, done, or witnessed is an expression of a state of complete fulfillment.

By connecting with pure, immutable awareness, Dzogchen masters gain the ultimate freedom to be exactly who they are without any need to consolidate, or avoid, their personalities. They live in the world without any contrivance, or self-gratifying agenda. They abide as awareness itself: natural, effortless, and imperturbable. All experience, even death itself, is a bliss-filled non-event.

Origins

Dzogchen emerged in visible form in North Western India and Tibet in the eighth to ninth centuries. This tradition was first brought forth by the master Vajraprahe (Tib. Garab Dorje) and then transmitted through various Indian masters, such as Manjushrimitra, Vairochana, Padmasambhava, Vimalamitra, Shrisimha, and Jnanasutra. In Tibet it was primarily transmitted within the Ancient School (Nyingma), which is the oldest school of Buddhism in Tibet, through a lineage that includes such illustrious masters as Yeshe Tsogyal, Longchenpa, Jigme Lingpa, Patrul Rinpoche, and Dilgo Khyentse Rinpoche. (Thundup, 1996)

These and other famous masters emerged on the historical landscape with such power and time-liness that they permanently transformed the shape of esoteric spirituality in India, China, and Tibet. Their wisdom impacted entire spiritual traditions. In the last twenty years, this form of nondual wisdom has begun to reshape Western understandings of freedom and fulfillment.

In Tibet and China many Dzogchen masters were spiritual educators, politicians, and adminis-trators. Their actions displayed the radical precision and bold spontaneity that naturally issues forth when one is no longer controlled by fear and fantasy.

Other adepts lived most of their lives in caves, their minds inseparable from the vistas of moun-tains and voyages of the stars through the heavens. Others lived in villages blending with their communities, bringing up families with a sense of unceasing joy, ease, and spontaneity. In Tibet many masters also lived in nomadic communes, caring for their extended families and tending herds of yaks on the high steppes of the Tibetan plateau. In the course of their lifetime, they might transmit the essence of their realization to just one or two students.

While some masters retained a notional affiliation with Buddhism, others belonged to no partic-ular tradition. It was impossible to say they were Buddhist, for nothing they said or did identified them with any particular philosophy. They moved beyond the need for symbolic paraphernalia or affiliation with any tradition or community. Their wisdom didn't depend on what they did, or believed. Instead it rested on being fully at ease with who they were.

More than any other tradition, Dzogchen cuts across religious, economic, and gender divisions due to its emphasis on integrating a state of realization into everyday living. It naturally steers away from the standardized practices that define any institutional culture. In traditional patrilineal cultures, it catered to women because it was non-monastic and communal.

Even though Dzogchen has very close historical links with Buddhism, it has also existed outside of Buddhism. In Tibet it manifested within the indigenous, pre-Buddhist religion called Bön. (Wangyal, 1993) It also shares historical and philosophical affinities with Chinese Ch'an Buddhism and the Hindu Shaivite tradition. (Norbu, 1984)

Dzogchen was little known in the West even twenty years ago. One reason being that it is invisible and inaccessible to those who believe that spiritual practice is a "means" for liberation. Paradoxically, it's perhaps the most profound, yet least distinctive of the world's spiritual traditions, since it cannot be located by pointing to any text, belief, teacher, ritual, or institution. For this reason, it is also easily misinterpreted and misrepresented.

Whatever we could "hope" to achieve by engaging with this tradition, it can't be the culmination of Dzogchen. As the great Indian master Manjushrimitra says: "The state of pure and total presence of the Joyful One does not exist. It is a magical apparition of that state that appears to those who are deluded." (1987)

Dzogchen can be aligned with every spiritual and psychological system, and even exist quite independently of any system or institution, because it isn't defined by values and beliefs. Dzogchen is all inclusive, since it is awareness-as-such. While our "understanding" of awareness can be threatened or supported by alternative interpretations of the "phenomenon," awareness-as-such has nothing to do with what we think about it. In fact, from the Dzogchen perspective, there is no such thing as a competing system or orientation since there is no "thing" for other systems to compete against. Similarly, there is nothing to be protected or to promote.

In Tibet, Dzogchen became differentiated into two phases called Cutting Through (*thregs chod*) and Leaping Over (*thog rgyal*). Cutting Through is the instantaneous dissolution of reference points, particularly those that create the sense of subject and objects, inside and outside. Cutting Through directly reveals the primordial or alpha purity of all reality (*ka dag*). Leaping Over is, on the other hand, an extremely esoteric level of Dzogchen that enables practitioners to gain total mastery of a psycho-cosmology in which fractal universes are created, dissolved, and recreated as a spontaneous display of appearances that indivisibly unifies the outmost reaches of the universes with the innermost realities of the psyche. This level of accomplishment is way beyond the reach of *Radiant Mind*.

Radiant Mind is deeply inspired by the Cutting Through transmission in Dzogchen. We take the Result level as the starting point and only move back into time, contingencies, and causation when people can't see that the present moment always delivers absolutely everything that we need. We also feel aligned with the non-institutional flavor of Dzogchen. We allow our work to emerge and grow organically, tending to where there is interest and appreciation, but without trying to grow it like a manicured garden. Also, *Radiant Mind* cuts across religious and spiritual affiliation and gender biases. We have people from all major religions participating in *Radiant Mind*, and there is no such thing as a gender-defined form of *Radiant Mind*.

The psychotropic terminology of Dzogchen and Mahamudra

We mentioned earlier that the Indian siddhas of the eighth to twelfth centuries were able to transport people to a recognition of their real nature through songs and poetry. The language of these traditions, especially when it's describing the ultimate state of spontaneous, carefree, embodied existence, opens us to the nondual simply through listening, without having to do anything from our own side.

Dzogchen and Mahamudra masters spent centuries crafting a distinctive language that describes the super-refined states of consciousness in which they live, teach, and play. The language they use is paradoxical. In one way, it is intelligible. What they write makes grammatical sense. The words and sentences of these masters are woven in a way in which they appear to be saying something, but in reality their words are self-referential. They have nothing to do with what they are talking about. If we try to grasp a meaning, it slips through our mind leaving us in a pristine state of non-referential awareness.

Keith Dowman describes the intended function of Dzogchen literature in a very illuminating way. He writes that the Dzogchen dialectic is:

> …self-referential, its letters, sounds and meanings always pointing at their luminous, joyful essence, its dialectic relentlessly and consistently referring back to the unstructured light or gnosis, and insofar as language is inseparable from our experience, we are constantly thrust into the reality that the Dzogchen exposition evokes. Its incessant self-reference, giving not an iota of validity to the perceptual and intellectual functions of our ordinary mind, dissolves all concrete points of reference and leaves us in the spaciousness of ineffable being…. There is no time lag between the momentary perception of the words of the poem and its consummation…. Far from being an objective philosophical description of the world at large, or a soteriological blueprint, the exposition is a magical psychotropic poem. (Longchenpa, 2006: xxiii)

The mere terminology of Dzogchen and Mahamudra is elevating, expanding, and freeing, even when people don't understand the specific, and often technical, context in which terms are used. In fact, the result-level writings in Dzogchen and Mahamudra are often a series of concepts, images, and metaphors that are strung together with little need for logical development. As Longchenpa, the famous fourteenth-century Tibetan Dzogchen master says, his own compositions "are like garlands of clouds [on a mountain], draped like a beautiful necklace that satiates fortunate ones with the nectar that showers down."

In recent years Western practitioner-translators have been drawing on the breadth and richness of European languages and really bringing Dzogchen teachings alive in their capacity to draw us into a sublime state of complete fulfillment that transcends transient beliefs, feelings, and perceptions.

The following is a description of the ultimate state by Longchenpa. The translation is by Keith Dowman who pushes his translations to the current limits of the English language. (Longchenpa, 2006: 4-5)

> In total presence, in the indeterminate nature of mind, lies the timeless pristine awareness of nondual perception; in sheer naked, non-contingent gnosis, lies the nondiscriminatory seed; in the holistic transparence of zero-dimensional gnosis, lies the contemplation of *dharmakaya* Samantabhadra; in essential absence, the intrinsic gnosis of total presence, non-referential, immaculate contemplation is shining.

> In the absence of outside and inside, subject and object, intrinsic gnosis, being out of time and space, supercedes all finite events that seemingly begin and end; pure as the sky, it is without signposts or means of access. And specific insight into gnosis is always deluded, so that any spiritual identity, always delusive, is abandoned; and convinced that the space of undifferentiated Samantabhadra is the all-encompassing super-emptiness of all *samsara* and *nirvana*, the natural state obtains as the reality without transition or change. Breaking out of the brittle shell of discursive view into the hyper spaciousness that is nowhere located, in the experience of absence the crux of the matter is fully disclosed.

Simple sign posts

The natural state of primordial awareness transcends all biases and fixations. Dzogchen identifies the primary dualistic biases in their behavioral, affective, and cognitive manifestations. Our natural mode of being, the sphere of being itself, is free of:

- Attachment and aversion.
- Hope and fear.
- All ideas about being trapped or being free.
- Any impulse to prevent (*dgag*) or make anything happen (*sgrub*). [We can equally understand this cognitively as transcending the tendency to validate and invalidate beliefs and experiences. It has both meanings in Dzogchen.]

These are some of the psychological tendencies and predispositions of our goal-oriented body-mind. They are habits that keep us locked into levels of experience that produce stress, frustration, anger, disappointment, and suffering.

I see many readers of Dzogchen and Mahamudra texts encountering these descriptions of the awareness itself and saying (or thinking), "Wow, how wonderful to be free of attachment and aversion! How amazing not to be gripped by fear and expectation! Imagine, letting go of all need to try to make some things happen, and avoid others! That would be real freedom."

It's easy for people to think that this state is beyond their reach, that it's nearly impossible to attain a state that's free of all preferences, judgments, contrivance, and manipulation. In Dzogchen texts, these biases are normally presented as tendencies that are absent in the state of pure awareness. Instead of focusing on pure awareness—our natural state—as a goal, we let the manifestation of these energetic and cognitive biases and tendencies come to the forefront of awareness. This way they provide signage into nondual awareness.

In *Radiant Mind*, we work with these biases. Giving attention to just one of these sets of biases, for example, validation and invalidation, can create a powerful opening to the essential unconditioned nature of mind. It's very easy to detect when we fall into the modes of agreeing and disagreeing with what we see and hear. All we need to do is to listen to the nature of our thoughts. The thoughts "That's right," "I agree," "That's reasonable," all signal agreement. They are a form of validation. "That's wrong," "That's ridiculous," etc. are forms of invalidation. It isn't difficult to discover a way of listening that's free of the tendency to agree and disagree. We listen and receive free of the tendencies to validate or invalidate what's happening. This is developed in *Radiant Mind* through the practice of "pure listening."

Working with attraction and aversion can be more difficult. But it's simple to begin. Attachment and aversion are easy to detect. We look to our thoughts and body sensations. If we would like to be somewhere else, aversion is manifesting. If we are bored, uncomfortable, looking for a way to change what's happening, this is aversion. If we'd like what's happening to continue, if we're comfortable, thinking this is great, interesting, fun, "I enjoy being here," etc., this is attraction. Once we recognize these energies, we learn to experience them as thoughts and sensations in the body that don't need to translate into actions.

The principle of not trying to avoid anything or make specific things happen is also extremely powerful. Exploring these principles for just a few hours a week expands our capacity to receive whatever is arising without judgment or preference. We become an open, centerless clearing through which thoughts, feelings, and sensations flow without producing any perturbation or stimulating any need for corrective action.

Auto-liberation or natural release

In Dzogchen reactive emotions and burdensome thoughts release themselves. As Longchenpa says, "We do not contrive or condition (our mind) by suppressing (experiences), or (applying) remedies, but rather let (the mind) rest naturally in whatever (condition we find it)." (1974: 67) The contemporary Complete Fulfillment master, Namkhai Norbu Rinpoche, explains this process more fully. (1984b: 30) He writes:

When we speak of the path of self-liberation, there is neither a concept of renunciation, because if it is always my energy manifesting, then it can manifest in many different ways; nor is there a concept of transformation, because the principle here is that I find myself in a state of pure presence, of contemplation. If I find myself for an instant in a state of contemplation, then from that point of view, wrath and compassion are one and the same. Good and evil are one and the same. In that condition there is nothing to do; one liberates oneself, because one finds oneself in one's own dimension of energy without escaping and without renouncing anything. This is the principle of self-liberation.

Self-liberation, or the spontaneous release of reactive emotions, occurs as a natural consequence of identifying with awareness-as-such. When our awareness ceases to be conditioned by the act of compulsively or intentionally engaging and disengaging with different sensations, then thoughts and feelings float through our awareness like clouds in the sky. Emotions dissolve like snow falling on the warm water of our panoramic awareness.

The ability to spontaneously liberate constricting emotions and compulsive thoughts occurs because we neither grasp onto, nor suppress, any arising thought, feeling, or perception. As Longchenpa writes,

> We don't discard [some experiences] and cultivate [others]. [Whether our experiences] are dynamic or stable we should let them go wherever they want to go.... When the mind is in a diffusing or dynamic state we aren't discouraged, and when it is calm and stable we desist from wanting [it to continue in that state)] (1974: 68 and 69)

Consequently, we don't judge some experiences to be sublime and others profane. We don't make more out of our experience than what is immediately given. We don't enhance or accentuate our experience as we do in Tantra, nor do we trivialize it or devalue it. Basically, we don't intervene, or meddle in our experience, in any way at all. Our experience is natural, unaffected, unmanipulated, and free from contrivance. This practice is called "leaving what appears just as it is."

In Dzogchen there is no deliberate attentiveness because this conditions our experience. Nor is there a need to refute, or establish any truths or theses, because the experience isn't influenced by our beliefs. In this way we become free from the duality of cognitions and a cognizer, and thus remain in a free state of non-appraisal.

In this tradition it isn't necessary to remove thoughts or emotions in order to achieve freedom. What is required is that we are no longer conditioned by thoughts and emotions. As Namkhai Norbu Rinpoche writes:

> One's passions only grow powerful because one is ignorant of the state of pure presence, and so consequently one follows after one's passions. But when one finds

oneself in the state of the pure presence of the passions, one is not dominated by them nor does one have to suppress them because they are like the ornaments of one's primordial state. Thus one's passions are self-liberated into their own condition whenever they arise. (1984a: 30)

When bare awareness has been activated, thoughts and emotions are no longer a conditioning agent. Even though we may engage in thinking and be subject to emotional responses, thoughts and emotions no longer cause or condition our present and future mental states. Thoughts and feelings arise, but are freed in the sense that they are merely a presence or happening occurring within the real dimension of our being.

In this tradition the only discipline is to stay in a natural and unfabricated state of bare awareness. The single commitment on this path is to be aware, knowing both that we cannot do this and that awareness itself is not an existing thing. We see that all the effort we have applied to gain this experience has neither contributed to, nor detracted from, its occurrence, since it is the primordial and unconditioned nature of being as such.

Pointing out events

In Dzogchen the nature of reality itself, which is mind-as-such, is pointed to in much the same way as reality is revealed in Essence Mahamudra. The teacher points without pointing to any thing. This is a unique pointing since there is no directionality; there is nothing to see or identify. In fact, a successful pointing out event by definition reveals nothing (*med pa*): "that" which neither is nor is not.

The two realities: alternating and simultaneous cultivation

Nondual systems often find it useful to speak about two levels of reality: the consensual or relative, and the ultimate. We do this in *Radiant Mind* as well. At the beginning we speak about conditioned experience and unconditioned awareness as though they are different. The conditioned reality is known through our body and mind—it's everything that can be felt, seen, or thought about. The unconditioned dimension is open, invisible, and unstructured. In Buddhism, this is the difference between form and openness. From one perspective the two are radically different.

However, in the ultimate realization the two realities fuse in a state in which form and openness are neither different nor the same. Because the unconditioned has no characteristics, we cannot say that it is the same as, or different from, anything else, since no comparison is possible. This is spoken about as the co-emergence of openness and appearances. Nondual systems approach the path to this state differently. Some systems offer two distinct forms of practice for realizing each of the two realities. The practices progressively merge as people move along a path. Classical Madhyamika uses this approach.

Alternating cultivation

In Madhyamika practice, access to the unconditioned level occurs mainly during formal meditation sessions using unfindability analyses to generate non-residual experiences of openness. These analytical contemplations begin with an empirical content, such as a feeling, thought-form, body image, or self-concept. Yogis take these contemplations through to a stage where the sense-base (the form they are investigating) recedes from awareness. At this point they rest in unconditioned awareness that's unrelated to conditioned phenomena. Non-residual means that there is no empirical residue remaining in this state. This is also called a "space-like equipoise." The rationale in this approach is that it is easier to access unconditioned awareness if there is no, or at least very minimal, stimulation in the form of thoughts, feelings, and sensory images.

Realization of the conditioned reality mainly refers to understanding the consequences of being embodied. The practice is to understand how the conditioned world functions, especially in terms of how we create incompletions (*karma*) that block recognition of unconditioned awareness. This information allows practitioners to modify their action to create a stronger foundation for resting in nondual awareness. An appreciation of the structural interdependencies with our conditioning is mainly cultivated outside of formal sitting meditation. The post-meditational practice also consists of diluting and dissolving the energy of attachment and aversion to thoughts, feelings, and sensations by seeing that these are illusory: that everything is interdependent and exists as a function of concepts and deep-seated beliefs.

In this way, Madhyamika yogis suffuse their experience of phenomena with the realization of openness. Then, within their space-like meditations on openness, they begin to allow the image of the object that acted as a springboard for their realization of openness to remain in their awareness alongside the emerging experience of openness. In time, the experiences of form and openness become inseparable—one cannot be had without the other.

A consequence of pursuing the realization of two realities independently of each other is that they need to be subsequently integrated in a way of being that seamlessly blends the freedom of unconditioned awareness with the complexities of living in a conditioned world.

A further consequence is that one can emphasize one or other of the two realities, and thus be led into the distortions that over- and under-negate the conditioned experience. For example, if one cultivates an experience of openness that is like space, but neglects to respect the power of thoughts, speech, and actions to condition subsequent experiences, people can lose their connection with the empirical world. People could become spaced out and lose their ability to operate safely and effectively in the physical world. Focusing exclusively on the unconditioned dimension can lead people to misinterpret contentlessness as nonexistence. This is called "falling to the nihilistic extreme," and it can have damaging consequences for people's evolution. This error can make people foolhardy and careless, and a danger both to themselves and to others. In current spiritual circles this is called "spiritual bypassing."

Conversely, if one cultivates the relative reality while ignoring the ultimate reality, one falls into the realist extreme. While one might take meticulous care with one's behavior and gain real control over the capacity to filter out negative experiences, one fails to gain the unconditional freedom that comes from realizing that nothing is solid and fixed, including any connection between behavior and what is experienced. By believing that karma is a real and invariant phenomenon, one becomes trapped by the need to constantly monitor and control behavior. Philosophically, this is falling to the extreme of believing that "reality" has a real or intrinsic existence. A consequence of this error is that spiritual practice becomes a very serious and unforgiving endeavor. It can become difficult or impossible to transcend causal conditioning.

Thus, while the theory of two distinct levels of reality is designed to assist our evolution, from a practical angle it can be misused in such a way that it gives license and support to the innate human impulse either to seek happiness and freedom by manipulating the empirical world, or to disconnect from the physical world in an effort to be free of suffering.

Even so, in *Radiant Mind* it is often useful to distinguish unconditioned awareness as something that is completely different from the world of conditioned experience. In order to initially reveal nondual awareness, we point out that "it" has nothing to do with what we think of as our everyday experience. It is totally unrelated to the world that is revealed through our senses and thoughts. It's also important to do this whenever people become captured by the sense- and thought-worlds. In terms of *Radiant Mind* practice, we also sometimes reveal nondual awareness within a contemplative state with eyes closed and nothing to think about in order to rest in a state of unconditioned awareness that is accompanied by minimal levels of thoughts and imagery.

The cycle of practice consists of distinguishing the state of unconditioned awareness from everyday experience, then collapsing the two as indistinguishable, again and again, until people are stabilized in a state wherein they cannot say that this conditioned moment is the same as, or different from, the transpersonal, transcultural, contentless dimension.

Simultaneous cultivation

Dzogchen offers an approach that doesn't split reality into conditioned and unconditioned dimensions. The notion of two realities is seen as a purely intellectual construction. This is also the final position of nondual Mahayana and Madhyamika. The bodhisattva Subhuti says, "Absolute openness and relative functioning are not divided. They are not two alternative dimensions, but utter simplicity." Dzogchen invites people to appreciate right from the outset that their own unique condition and process of embodiment is a pure and complete expression of unconditioned transcendence.

In Dzogchen there aren't two different sets of practices that need to be assimilated or integrated. *Radiant Mind* finds value in both approaches, but tends to follow the Dzogchen approach. The personal and transpersonal dimensions of the spiritual life are integrated right from the very outset. There is never any need to recover from an artificial split that is conditioned by segmenting practice into separate meditational and post-meditational phases. Dzogchen and *Radiant Mind* systematically deconstruct the predisposition to segment the path into meditative and post-meditative periods.

In Radiant Mind we notice how when silence emerges, this can sometimes devolve into meditation. This happens more with people who are experienced meditators. When they don't know what's happening they can fall into meditation because this is something they know, with which they are familiar and comfortable. We then give subtle, non-verbal signals and cues that "This" is not formal meditation.

This integrated approach has the advantage of eliminating, or at least reducing, the possibility of producing extreme and potentially dangerous spiritual realizations. It automatically corrects any personal bias that might lead people to disconnect from the physical reality, or believe that they are nothing more than an embodied mind. It is difficult to skew Dzogchen toward either the relative or the ultimate extremes, since the perspective to be cultivated is one in which we begin to connect with a disclosive space that allows all things to be just as they are. Spiritual bypassing is impossible in this approach.

Hindu Advaita

In Hinduism nonduality is transmitted through the nondual form of Vedanta. Vedanta means the culmination of the Vedas. The three forms are: Dualistic Vedanta, Qualified Nondual Vedanta, and Nondual Vedanta.

Nondual Vedanta

The South Indian saint Shri Shankaracharya (788–820 CE) is sometimes cited as the first Advaita master. In the space of little more than a decade, he established intuitional structures throughout India and wrote numerous independent texts and copious commentaries on important Hindu texts, interpreting them consistently from a nondual perspective. He is credited with the renaissance of Hinduism in India at a time when Buddhism was being extinguished in India at the hand of Muslim invasions. Shankara's teachings are based on the unity of the Self and ultimate reality, which is free of all characteristics.

Nondual (Advaita) Vedanta has captured the interest of Western seekers in the last 40 years, mainly through the transmissions offered by Shri Ramana Maharshi (1879–1950) and his disciple Shri H.W.L. Poonjaji (1910–1997), and Nisargadatta Maharaj (1897–1981) and his disciple Ramesh Balsekar (1917–2009). The latter three in particular have spawned a large number of Western-born nondual teachers.

The term "nondual" is a translation of the Sanskrit Advaita, or "not two." Exactly the same term is used in Mahayana Buddhist texts when talking about nondualism. It is found throughout the Perfect Wisdom (*Prajnaparamita*), Zen, Madhyamika, Dzogchen, and Mahamudra texts.

Contemporary polemics

Some people think that the Advaita form of Hinduism is the only real nondual tradition. They feel that Mahayana Buddhism, for example, compromises the nondual transmission because it is loaded up with practices and spawned many different philosophical systems. What must be recognized here is that Mahayana is a world religion with perhaps 400 million followers, whereas Advaita is a specialist tradition lived in its purest form by just a few million people. So there is no real comparison here.

Very briefly, Mahayana Buddhism lays out many different ways for pointing to nondual awareness. The variety is an expression of the Buddhist notion of skillful means. Skillful means invites teachers to construct hundreds of different pathways into nondual awareness, each one tailored to the preferences and predispositions of the student. Some Advaitans see this emphasis on skillful means as obscuring the nondual by conditioning the relative reality. Advaita, on the other hand, claims to focus on the direct path. It has been called a "leap philosophy" because it teaches that there is no path, no finite self, no lineage, just the immutable reality of Brahman.

In reality, it's not nearly as simple and clear-cut as this. Some nondual Buddhist teachers offer transmissions that come nearly exclusively from the nondual—meaning from the result level. Many Advaitans offer paths and dualistic models, suggesting, for example, that we need to see the illusory nature of conditioned reality, remove the veils of ignorance, or inquire into the nature of the self.

Right now a certain polarization is creeping into the contemporary nondual scene, with some teachers grouping themselves as Advaitans or Neo-Advaitans and others as Buddhist nondual teachers. There are legitimate lineage reasons for doing this, but there's also a certain amount of politics in it as well. In fact, the same points that differentiated Advaita and Mahayana are coming through in Western expressions of these traditions. For example, Mahayana teachers sometimes say that Advaita nondualism is nihilistic because it negates the self, but doesn't go on to negate the negation. Conversely, some Neo-Advaita teachers reject the emphasis that one finds—even in pristine traditions such as Dzogchen—on a linkage with a teacher (guru yoga) and the need to prepare oneself, perhaps for decades, prior to direct transmission. These beliefs and practices transgress the fact that nothing is needed to be here now in the radiance of the unconditioned.

In *Radiant Mind*, we find inspiration in all nondual traditions, Mahayana Buddhism and Advaita in particular. For us, Advaita is a space—a way of being—that transcends religion, psychology, and philosophy.

Gaudapada

The origins of Hindu Advaita, in fact, go back to the teacher of Shankara's guru, a saint by the name of Gaudapada (seventh-century CE). Shankara himself acknowledges that Gaudapada recovered the nondual essence of the Vedas. Gaudapada's summary of nondualism is contained in a clear and succinct set of verses on the *Mandukya Upanishad*. The Upanishad itself has only thirteen prose sentences. The central teaching is that the Self (*atman*) is the ultimate reality (*Brahman*).

The intriguing thing about Gaudapada is that while he introduced nondualism into Hinduism, we can't be certain that he was a Hindu. He has often been called a crypto- or clandestine Buddhist. In other words, a Buddhist who disguised himself as a Hindu in order to infiltrate and influence Hindu ideas. The well-respected, twentieth-century Hindu philosopher, Surendranath Dasgupta, writes that "I believe that there is sufficient evidence in his *karikas* for thinking that he [Gaudapada] was possibly himself a Buddhist."

What is clear is that his philosophy of nondualism is derived from Nagarjuna. He acknowledges the Buddha and is obviously familiar with Nagarjuna's *Fundamental Verses* because many of his own verses follow exactly the same content and deconstructive inquiry as Nagarjuna. What I like about the enigma surrounding Gaudapada is that it shows how nondualism can't be contained within, or defined by, a particular tradition. We don't know what Gaudapada was. And how appropriate that is! The very need to identify Gaudapada as Hindu or Buddhist misses the point, since if we try to find who Gaudapada "really" was, we won't find anyone! If we try to find the essence of his teaching, it too will be unfindable.

Like Nagarjuna, Gaudapada sees that the ultimate state is beyond causal conditioning. In order to transcend suffering, we need to transcend the causal states. This occurs through the recognition that there is a fourth state that subsists through, yet which is unconditioned by, the other three states known to us—waking, dreaming, and sleeping. Unlike the waking, dreaming, and sleeping states, the fourth state cannot be characterized. Here Gaudapada uses the language of pure negation to identify this state. It is invisible, ungraspable, beyond the reach of thought, indescribable, and nondual. It is neither produced nor destroyed. From within this reality there is no one who is trapped, no one who struggles, and no one who is liberated. This is the "not this, not that" (*neti neti*) language that is very often used in Advaita to point to the unconditioned.

Like Mahayanists, Gaudapada often uses the language of "neither...nor" in order to dismantle anything we could possibly think about this state. In reality, the things of this world are neither real nor unreal, neither existent nor nonexistent. The ultimate reality is a unique bliss (*ananda*) that transcends pleasure and pain.

Shri Ramana Maharshi

Ramana Maharshi inspires *Radiant Mind* through the way he uses a conversational form of deconstructive inquiry. This form of conversational inquiry has been used for centuries, probably millennia. While his teachings weren't recorded, we know that the written transcripts accurately reflect the structure of his conversations with his disciples. In contrast to the highly-concentrated and precisely-executed deconstructive analysis of the Madhyamikas that rocketed them into long *samadhi*-like contemplations on emptiness, Ramana Maharshi's inquiries into the Self are continually adapting to the questions and input from his students.

Satsang

He used a *satsang* setting for his transmission. *Satsang* means "gathering in truth," in other words, coming together for the purpose of directly presencing nondual awareness. It is much like a workshop setting. Students gather around a teacher in a mood of respect, with more or less formality, and engage in conversation and contemplation, asking questions about the role of practice, the goal of the path, the nature of reality, and so on.

Satsang offers us a very rich structure through which to offer nondual transmission in a group setting and is very flexible. Ideally, *satsang* centers around a so-called "fully awake being" like Ramana, who at the age of sixteen realized that he was formless, immanent consciousness that is neither born nor dies. He lived and died in this state. Unlike most people, his realization was final and irreversible. He became what is called a *jivanmukta*, someone who is fully liberated while still living. From that moment on, Ramana Maharshi never experienced any more fear, anxiety, ambition, or lust. Students recount that during one *satsang* a cobra crawled over his legs. While everyone around made a stir and commotion, for Ramana nothing unusual was happening at all. He kept on teaching as though a cat had curled up in his lap.

For the last two years of his life, Ramana Maharshi suffered from cancer. The effects of the cancer were very visible. He hobbled around with great difficulty using a cane. Even though he must have been experiencing great physical pain, he maintained the same serene poise and beatific smile that we see in all photos of him. We are told that one disciple, on seeing him, ran away crying because he couldn't bear to see his master in pain. Ramana just smiled and spoke to a disciple nearby. "He is crying because he thinks I am suffering agonies! My body is suffering, but I am not suffering. When will he realize that I am not this body?"

While it might be wonderful (or excruciating) to sit with a fully-realized master and engage with her directly, from the viewpoint of nondual transmission, there is only now. It's not necessary for the teacher to be fully realized in order to function periodically as a vehicle for effective transmission. All that's needed is that they are realized when transmission, "pointing-out," or inquiry is happening.

Some people think they aren't qualified to offer nondual transmission unless they abide permanently in the nondual. This is a limiting way to think. It stops us from making a vital contribution to people who are open to enter the field of our centerless awareness. The question of where we've come from, or where we're going, is irrelevant because in the moments of transmission there is no time, no coming or going.

Self-inquiry

Ramana is famous for simplifying self-inquiry (*atma-vichara*) and presenting it in a form that works without any need to be versed in the technical terminology of philosophical Advaita. Whereas Shankara wrote for philosophers and metaphysicians, Ramana brought jnana- or wisdom-yoga to the earnest lay seeker. His dialogs are free-flowing and wide-ranging, but he recursively and predictably comes back to the question of "Who is asking?" The questions posed by students are returned to his disciples as opportunities to contemplate "Who suffers?" "Who seeks?" "Who feels trapped in *samsara*?" "Who needs to practice?" etc.

Self-inquiry is woven into Ramana's understanding of concepts such as practice, devotion, the need for a guru, or the integration of realization in daily life. Sometimes Ramana teaches from the result level, saying exactly how it is from the space of nondual liberation. At other times he creates a context for practitioners.

Nisargadatta Maharaj

Unlike Ramana Maharshi, Nisargadatta doesn't necessarily fit with many preconceptions about a master who has gone beyond all desires and preferences. I mention him here because he manifested quite a different form of *satsang* than Ramana.

Nisargadatta's roots lie in the less well-known nondual tradition called Navnath Sampradaya. Nonetheless, his transmission is pure Advaita. He draws nearly exclusively on one of the famous "great sayings" of the Upanishads, namely, "I am that." Meaning, the "I" (which cannot be found as a subject) IS the universe (*Brahman*). Nisargadatta accomplished incredible amounts just with two words, "I am." He was able to deliver spontaneous, pith instructions with a force and velocity that catapulted people into a recognition that they at source are unbounded awareness itself. He blew out the seeking mind. Nisargadatta said, "Immortality is freedom from the feeling 'I am.' To have that freedom remain in the sense 'I am.' It's simple, it's crude, yet it works."

His style was provocative, confrontational, spontaneous, and even dismissive and rude. At times he would seem to be agitated, even annoyed and intolerant toward people. His *satsang*s cut to the chase. He didn't waste time with courtesies and didn't offer bandaids and platitudes. If he was done with someone, he might order him or her to leave the upper room of his small apartment in suburban Mumbai, to "get out" and never come back! Jack Kornfield describes him as "a combination of Krishnamurti and Fritz Perls." "Nisarga" means natural and uncontrived.

Nisargadatta offered the "direct way" for knowing ultimate reality by becoming aware of our original nature through a process of mental discrimination. He taught that liberation was available here and now. All we have to do is grasp it. The Navnath Sampradaya tradition contrasts the "bird's way" with the "way of the ant." The "bird's way" of gaining freedom is to grasp self-knowledge in one swift action, just as a bird swoops down from afar and catches its prey. Ants, on the other hand, follow a slow, gradual, and circuitous path that requires a lot of diligence and hard work. He taught that "There is nothing to practice. To know yourself, be yourself. To be yourself, stop imagining yourself to be this or that. Just be. Let your true nature emerge. Don't disturb your mind with seeking."

Awareness is the source of, but different from, individual consciousness, which is related to the senses and physical body. Awareness exists prior to the mind and memory and is beyond all concepts. He says, "Awareness is my nature; ultimately I am beyond being and non-being." Like Ramana Maharshi, he taught that it is only the belief that we are the body that keeps us from our true, transpersonal essence, the *atman*. This essence is pure, free, and untouched by anything that occurs. It is a silent witness that sees all, yet is unmoved, either to pleasure or pain, based on what it sees. This leads to the notion that there is no such thing as a "doer." We, as pure awareness, do nothing. The mind and body act of their own accord. We are the immutable witness of them. As Nisargadatta says, "You are the timeless, spaceless witness. And even if the mind tells you that you are the one who is acting, don't believe the mind. The [mind-body] apparatus which is functioning has come upon your original essence, but you are not that apparatus."

Nisargadatta taught in the vernacular. There were no fancy philosophical concepts in his transmission. His *satsang*s are a treasure trove of priceless pith instructions that are easily digested, simple, and incontrovertible.

> The very search for pleasure is the cause of pain.

> You will receive everything you need when you stop asking for what you do not need.

> You always want what you cannot have and don't want what you have. To be self-realized just reverse it.

> When I see I am nothing, that is wisdom. When I see I am everything, that is love. My life is a movement between these two.

What I appreciate about Nisargadatta is the unorthodox and uncompromising way he offered nondual transmission. He didn't please people or stroke them in any way at all. Nisargadatta taught without any regard for how he was perceived. He was unaffected by conventions. He didn't prepare the field, make people feel comfortable, or "create the right conditions" for people to receive his transmission. He had a natural sense of efficiency that could manifest in undiplomatic and unexpected ways.

Nisargadatta also showed how "no one doing nothing" doesn't necessarily mean that practices drop away. Nisargadatta continued to make ritual offerings to his lineage gurus, sing bhajans, and meditate throughout his life. If practice has been conditioned into our brain, blood, and bones, actions such as meditation, ritual singing, and praying, will still come through, after the point where practice has no more spiritual function.

I imagine that Nisargadatta would see *Radiant Mind* as far too complex and unnecessarily nuanced. It caters to people's need for change, variety, progress, and entertainment. It gives people too much to think about and do. This *Guide* is an anathema to the simplicity of Nisargadatta's transmission.

Appendix 2

The Heart of Liberating Wisdom

Thus have I heard: the blessed awakened one, the Buddha, was dwelling on Vultures' Peak in Rajagriha together with a great community of monks, nuns, and awakening beings. At a certain moment the Blessed One entered into a state of deep contemplation on the nature of things, called "profound illumination." In this same moment, the great exalted awakened being, known as "Loving Eyes," entered the deepest state of perfect wisdom, wherein he clearly saw the insubstantiality and transparency of all sensory and mental structures. Within the Buddha's transformational field, a monk named Shariputra turned and asked Loving Eyes, "How should the daughters and sons of the exalted lineage proceed in the perfection of liberating wisdom?" This is how the great exalted awakened being, Loving Eyes, answered Shariputra.

Shariputra, the sons and daughters of the exalted lineage who aspire to cultivate the profound perfection of wisdom see that all material forms and conscious states are void of any essence or self-nature. Your physical form is no different from the state of pure, open transparency. And pure transparency isn't different from your physical form. The same is true for your feelings, concepts, volitional energy, and mind-itself.

Shariputra, every structure of existence is clear and transparent. Nothing has any identifying characteristics. Nothing ever begins or ceases. Nothing is ever impure or pure. Nothing ever decreases or increases. And so, Shariputra, within the field of pure transparency there are no physical forms, feelings, concepts, volitional energy, or even the mind. There is no organ for sight, hearing, smelling, tasting, touching, or mind-organ. There is nothing to see, hear, smell, taste, touch, or think about. There is no visual field or sphere of consciousness.

Reality is never veiled by ignorance. So there is never a cessation of ignorance. There is no process of aging and dying, and so, there is no possibility of stopping these either. There is no suffering whatsoever, and hence, nothing can make you suffer. Consequently, there's no process of overcoming suffering and suffering never stops.

There is no primordial wisdom. There is nothing whatsoever to attain and equally nothing not to attain. And so Shariputra, awakened beings attain nothing, and this is why such beings are able to dwell in perfect wisdom. Their entire mindstream transcends the veils that obscure pure perception, and they are free of all traces of fear and anxiety. They thereby reach the ultimate state of unconditioned freedom. The fully awakened beings of the beginningless past, open future, and present time manifest perfect wisdom and thus bring themselves to the peerless state of the fully awakened buddhas.

So you should know that the perfection of liberating wisdom is contained in the syllabic sound of the miraculous, unequalled, and unsurpassable mantra that instantly and finally eliminates all suffering. This is the mantra that invokes the ultimate reality—the reality that lies beyond all fictions and falsehoods. It is like this:

> Pure presence is transcending, ever transcending, transcending transcendence, transcending even the transcendence of transcendence. This is full awakening. So it is.

This, Shariputra, is how great awakened beings proceed in the profound perfection of liberating wisdom.

Then the Blessed One arose from his deep absorption and praised the great exalted awakened being Loving Eyes saying, "Wonderfully expressed, wonderfully expressed, son of the lineage, so it is. One should follow the profound perfection of wisdom exactly as you have explained it." All those who had realized suchness rejoiced. When the Blessed One spoke thus, the young Shariputra filled with joy, and the great exalted awakened being Loving Eyes was also filled with joy. The assembly of followers and the entire world of celestial beings, humans, and spirits were overjoyed and united in their praise of this transmission from the Blessed One.

Appendix 3

Verses on the Realized Mind

by Sosan Zenji
Third Patriarch of Zen

The Supreme Way is not difficult for those who are impartial and without preferences.
When love and hate are both absent everything is revealed as clear and transparent.
Yet, the moment we distinguish this as "it," heaven and earth are set infinitely apart.
If you want to experience the Way then do not set up opinions for or against anything.
To set up what you like against what you dislike only produces mental disturbance.
In the absence of this deep and profound principle it is futile trying to pacify the mind.

The Way is perfect like vast space where nothing is lacking and nothing is in excess.
Indeed, it is due to our grasping and rejecting that we miss seeing the real nature of things.
Live neither in the entanglements of outer things, nor in the inner feeling of emptiness.
Be serene in the uniform nature of everything and your fixed views will dissolve by themselves.

When you try to be still through stopping activity your very effort makes you more active.

As long as you remain in one extreme or the other, you will never experience oneness.

Those who do not live in the Way flounder in their actions to achieve stillness through assertion and denial.

If you think that things are unreal, you miss their functional existence.

If you assert that things are empty, you also miss their reality.

To perpetually talk and think about "it" only leads you further away from harmony with the primordial reality.

If you investigate talking and thinking there is nothing you cannot penetrate.

To pursue appearances is to miss the source. Instead, return to the source of all appearances and discover the real meaning of the primordial principle.

In the moment of inner awakening one goes beyond appearances and emptiness.

The changes that occur in this empty world only appear to be real due to our ignorance.

Do not seek this primordial reality, merely drop your cherished beliefs and opinions.

Do not abide in dualistic positions and take care not to pursue them.

If there is even the slightest trace of this and that, of right and wrong, the mind-essence will be lost in confusion.

Although all experience arises from within the unified field (of awareness), do not become fixated even on this.

When the mind exists undisturbed in the Way, nothing in the world can disturb us. And when things are no longer a problem, they cease to exist in their usual way.

When no discriminating thoughts arise, the conditioned mind ceases to exist.

When objects cease to be experienced as external, the experience of being a separate subject also ceases. Likewise, if the experience of subjectivity ceases, so too does the experience of the world as a separate entity.

(Yet, in this experience of nonduality) things continue to exist because there is a mind to perceive them, and the mind continues because there are objects to be perceived.

Understanding the relativity of these two is the unity of emptiness.

In this emptiness perceiver and perceived are indistinguishable, and each contains within itself the other.

If you do not discriminate between coarse and subtle you will not be tempted to formulate biased positions.

To live in the Supreme Way is neither easy nor difficult.

Those with limited views experience fear and doubt.

Their haste to achieve liberation only slows them down.

Trying to grasp "it" with your mind will lead you further astray.

So just let things be in their own natural way and there is neither coming nor going.

When you live in accord with the nature of things, everything unfolds freely and without disturbance.

If your thinking is narrow and compulsive, reality will remain hidden because everything will
	be obscure and confused.
The burdensome practice of comparing and judging only produces frustration and fatigue.
What benefit can come from making arbitrary distinctions and false separations?

If you wish to enter the one Way, do not reject the world of senses and ideas.
Indeed, to accept them fully is identical with true awakening.
The wise have no goals or aspirations, but fools bind themselves (with hopes and fears).
There is one truth, not many. Arbitrary distinctions arise as the fixations of the deluded mind.
To seek the primordial mind with a clinging intellect is the greatest of all mistakes.

Rest and unrest derive from illusion. For the awakened mind there is no attraction or aversion.
Dualistic perceptions arise from mistaken discriminations, and like dreams or illusions of
	flowers in the sky, it is foolish to try to grasp them.
Thoughts of loss and gain, right and wrong, should be discarded, once and for all.

If the eye never sleeps, your dreams and fantasies will naturally dissolve by themselves.
When the mind ceases to make arbitrary discriminations, the infinite variety of things in the
	world will manifest in the nature of their true suchness.
By realizing the essenceless essence of this profound suchness, you will be released from all
	entanglements.
The timeless essence of being is realized when all things are seen equally (as neither the same
	nor different).
In this causeless, relationless space, comparisons and analogies are simply not possible.

To become still is to put something in motion, and when something is in motion it achieves its
	own stillness. In this way both movement and stillness disappear.
When such dualistic perceptions cease to exist the experience of oneness itself ceases to be.
In this perfectly open and structureless state no principle or description can be applied.

For the unified mind that accords with the Way all grasping and self-preoccupation ceases.
All doubts and irresolutions dissolve and life unfolds in an authentically confident and genuine
	way.
With a single stroke we are freed from bondage. Nothing clings to us and we hold onto nothing.
Everything arises as empty, transparent and self-illuminating and there is absolutely no need for
	any effort or exertion.
This space cannot be felt, analysed or understood (because there simply isn't anything to grasp).
In the experience of the real essence of being, there is neither self nor other.

If doubt ever arises within this space it can be re-entered by simply inquiring into the real
	nature of nonduality.
In this nondual experience, nothing is separate and nothing is excluded.

No matter when or where someone awakens to the truth, "This" is the reality that they experience.

This space cannot be shortened or extended, or diminished or enhanced (because it does not exist as such). In it a single thought is as complete as ten thousand years.
Abiding nowhere yet everywhere, the totality of the universe is your very sphere of consciousness.
The infinitely large and the infinitely small exist within each other. The boundary between them is invisible.
Existence is this very emptiness, and emptiness is this very existence.
So don't waste time in doubts and arguments that have nothing to do with this.

Everything is this single, uniform reality, and the uniform is simultaneously everything. To live within this realization is to be free from all concern about non-perfection.
To live this realization is the road to nonduality, because nonduality is the realization of mind.

This Way is beyond words and interpretation, for here there is no yesterday, no tomorrow, nor even this very moment.

A contemporary reworking by Peter Fenner based on previous English translations, 1997, 2008.

Appendix 4

The Natural Freedom of Being

By Longchenpa

Introduction

The Natural Freedom of Being is one text of a trilogy by the famous fourteenth-century Tibetan Nyingma lama, Longchenpa. The text is essentially divided into two distinct parts. The first part presents the Dzogchen view and includes a critique of various goal-oriented forms of Buddhism, which Longchenpa sees as counter-productive to spiritual evolution. The second part details many of the very same methods that are critiqued in the first section, but presents them as legitimate and even necessary methods for realizing the nature of being itself. No attempt is made by Longchenpa to reconcile his critique of the very same methods he advocates, since it is self-evident that our self-perfected nature is completely consistent with the magical display of yogic identities.

For Longchenpa there is a total and seamless continuity between Dzogchen, Tantra, and Buddhism. Dzogchen doesn't represent a departure from the Buddhist teachings, but is a natural and inevitable consequence of taking Buddhist practice to its limit.

At the same time, it is immaterial whether Dzogchen can be squared with Tantra or any other form of Buddhism—and even whether it is Buddhist or not. We may define our path and say, "I am Buddhist" or "I am Christian." But to the extent that we define ourselves as Buddhists, we define ourselves as non-Christian, and vice versa, and so we become trapped by our label. And the more thoroughly we become locked into our definition, the more it becomes a form of tribalism.

As Longchenpa repeatedly emphasizes, it is futile to become enmeshed in philosophical disputation and to buy into a discussion of whether Dzogchen is compatible or incompatible with any other approach, since in Dzogchen there is nothing to reject or accept.

This Appendix includes a translation of the first chapter of Part One, together with a commentary. The translation was completed with Ven. Traleg Rinpoche and Lama David Christensen. Professor David Germano went through a near-final draft and clarified many uncertainties with meticulous precision. I have added a commentary. The commentary presents the experiential space of Dzogchen as free from all reference points. It also unpacks the philosophical viewpoints and methods that Dzogchen supercedes, at least when they are used with the intention of being someone different from who we are, or somewhere else than where we are right now.

THE TRANSLATION

Chapter One:
Freedom through Realizing the Foundation

I pay homage to the principle of Cosmic Wholeness. From the very beginning in a state of harmony, in the unoriginated clear light, the unmoving mind-itself is free of any fixation and is totally spacious. Within the Unsurpassed Spiritual Environment arise the three modes of being which spontaneously actualize and are totally blissful. Homage to the fundamental fulfillment which is immutable.

Although the nature of my own and all living beings' minds is (already) pure and expansive, we wander, alienated in our mundane existence, due to the influence of primal ignorance. For those who wish for liberation from this state, I shall herein elucidate the mode of the core teaching about what is essential and ultimately meaningful, namely the path of the noble chariot (i.e., the Dzogchen perspective).

My friends who are in this bottomless state of cyclic existence are shaken by the waves of all manner of suffering. Since the error of ego fixation has arisen as a function of primal ignorance, the remedy is to cherish the perspective that apprehends our real mode of existence.

In this manner, everything which comprises the states of cyclic existence and unconditional freedom—the (entire) phenomenal world—is from the very beginning uncreated. From beginningless time, it is in a state of harmony. This state of spaciousness, the (true) nature of being, is without boundaries, and is nondual. It does not come into being and cannot be destroyed. It neither endures nor decays, and neither comes nor goes. Within this space, the entire variety of phenomena appears distinctly; yet when they manifest, all phenomena are naturally devoid of complexity.

There are no real external entities—they are (just) the mode of the appearance of the mind. Nor are these appearances mental, for phenomena do not originate in the mind either. The appearances of the five sense objects are like the hairlines perceived by someone with a visual defect. Though these appearances don't really exist, they still appear. By apprehending reality dualistically, we become confused. These appearances are like the illusory elephants that appear in our dream when we see ourselves surrounded by a (mounted) army. Because we hold the dream to be external to us, we are afraid. But is the nature of the dream other (than us, i.e., external) or does it exist mentally? Because there is nothing whatever existing outside or inside, for those who know the real nature of things, their terror dissolves by itself at the point (where it arises).

Thus, when nonduality is apprehended dualistically, those who lack understanding apprehend things to be real. They are thereby confused by (the illusions of) worldly existence. Because the wise cognize dualistic appearances as nondual, the nature of cyclic existence is liberated into the state of unconditional freedom.

Alas! This manifold of phenomenal appearances is primordially unoriginated and nondual, just like an image reflected in a mirror. The nature of openness (*shunyata*) is not separate from phenomenal appearances, just as water and its quality of being moist are combined in a nondualistic condition. Free of the limits of illusion, like an imaginary city, the instant things manifest, they are in the condition of being primordially unborn.

Although the phenomenal world appears to be located (in time and space, in fact) it is the non-abiding dimension of being itself. The instant an appearance seems to disappear, it does not in fact cease, (since ultimately phenomena) neither increase nor decrease. Therefore, phenomenal appearances do not exist in the manner in which they appear.

No matter in what way we investigate things, they lack any intrinsic nature. Things cannot exist in the way (in which we construct them). (The phenomenal world) has been free from the beginning and exists in an ongoing state of integration and Cosmic Wholeness (Samantabhadra).

All these entities lack a foundation, a source, and an essence. We should not deliberately seize (on things) and say that they are "this" or "that," as (ultimately) things are unidentifiable. Just like space, no creator can be perceived, and actions are devoid (of any sense of agency). There is no mental orientation whereby we can take reality as something, everything, or a particular thing.

Although one may take sides and give allegiance to a philosophical system, or even cultivate the innumerable types of philosophical viewpoints, meditational methods, or traditions of action, still it is difficult to see the authentic meaning of the essential mind-itself. Through their different analyses of the selflessness of people and things, the disciples of the fully awakened teachers, those who have awakened by themselves (*Pratyekabuddha*), the Idealists (*Chittamatra*), and the Constructive Middle Pathers (*Svatantrika Madhyamika*), (all lose sight of) the real practice of view and meditation and get sidetracked in the four (types of diversions), such as getting spaced out, etc. By going astray in this way it seems that innumerable creatures (prolong the need to) practice.

Within the creation (*utpatti*) and fulfillment (*sampanna*) practices of the Tantric tradition, there are many methods for manufacturing change, since (transformation) is the real intention behind the practices of Action, Performance, Yoga, and the Unexcelled. But even with these, one doesn't approach the unfabricated, self-presencing, spontaneously established, and genuine (reality, because one is still) ensnared by the net of proliferating complexity.

Some say that the purification of the mind is the goal of view, meditation, and action. Some suppress their drives and feelings. Some say that cutting their connection with the three times is the unimpeded state of immediate awareness. Others note the arising and ceasing (of whatever appears in their awareness). They say these are the authentic aims (of practice, but here there are only) turbulent waves of proliferating conceptualization.

In exactly the same way, people say that the control of one's inner energies and (the practice of physical) coupling (i.e., the use of *karma-mudra*) to (respectively generate) clarity and bliss are the real point of practice, but in fact they (just) get caught by their libidinous fixations. As well as getting stuck in the net of oscillating between what is acceptable and unacceptable, they will never see the essential point. For them there is no possibility to be free. They remain trapped in worldly existence because in every case they are deluded by an intellectual construction.

Alas! Because these people do not know how to recognize the precious jewel, they appear to be searching for junk jewelry, having discarded the wish-fulfilling gem. By rejecting what is supreme—the genuine nature of the mind-itself—they become trapped in the snake-like nest of fabricated techniques based on hope and fear. One can never become free with an obsessive mind. The fault occurs in the seeker who seeks for the meaning of that which is sought after.

Listen! If one wants (to apprehend) the meaning of the nature of the mind-itself, what is the use of many investigations and analyses? Whatever appears "that" is it (i.e., the ultimate reality), so let it appear as it is, without becoming fixated upon it. When we are free of fixations and don't adopt any position, we have no need to accept or reject (anything at all). Because everything is beyond mental orientation, don't meddle or spoil it!

If the objects which appear to the mind exist in the mode of openness, then what need is there to look for so-called "openness"? (On the other hand) if appearances do not exist (in the mode of openness), then even though one looks for their openness, they cannot become open. Therefore, what is the use of engaging in the meaningless and arduous task (of actively seeking to cognize the openness of appearances)?

Similarly, there is no need to meditate on the essence of the creation and fulfillment (phases of Tantra). (When we have realized our natural state of being), it is easy to hold the things to be accepted and rejected in any way at all. If this is real (for you), then there is no need to exert yourself. If it isn't, then it is (still) pointless to exert yourself. It would be like coal becoming gold. (In the final analysis) things don't exist, as they are (merely) an intellectual construction. This being the case, you should not spoil that natural awareness with mechanically contrived antidotes (in the hope of bringing about some change). This is the essential meaning of the unsurpassable Indestructible Career (Vajrayana).

(Ultimately) there are no sacred recitations (*mantra*), no Tantric tradition, and no acceptable philosophical positions. (Reality) cannot be identified as "This" or "that," and there is no view, meditation, action, or result of these. Everything that exists is in perfect harmony in the form of a unified spiritual universe (mandala) in which philosophical systems, viewpoint, meditation, action, and result are all fulfilled. The states of cyclic existence and unconditioned freedom are equally fulfilled, and being itself becomes totally pervasive.

The (mind-itself) is uncontrived and has never been liberated because it has been fully awake from the very beginning. Within the state of the ultimate dimension of being (*dharmakaya*)—which is like an effortless king whose (wishes) are spontaneously fulfilled—there are various physical embodiments (*nirmanakaya*) which are its illusory display. The world of appearances, the three dimensions of being (*trikaya*) and wisdom (*jnana*) are (one) indivisible (reality). You cannot conceive of anything to be rejected or accepted, (since) everything is in a state of complete purity.

In this state everything is totally spacious and elevated. All phenomena are spontaneously fulfilled and exist in a state of harmony and balance. The unborn king (i.e., being itself) has no boundaries, center, or directions, and the meaning of authenticity is to be free from attachment to objects of perception and a perceiver. There is no need to reject or accept anything, or to refute or establish (any viewpoint, since reality is) unbiased. This—Dzogchen—is the optimum peak of all perspectives.

You should (also) know that the king who is free from intentionality (i.e., the mind-itself) has no fixations. All deliberate attentiveness is a constricting factor (too). If there is no attentiveness with respect to whatever arises, then this is real wisdom.

(Letting the mind) rest in its natural state—empty of itself and unspoiled—this is the authentic state. You should ascertain this perspective, free from fixations and without any position or biases.

Alas! The variety of appearances is a joke, so don't (bother to) investigate them—but if you do, do so in a light-hearted way, and (discover that) there is nothing to identify. (Likewise), if you examine things very thoroughly, they transcend the extreme of being substantially existent. If you look inwardly at the mind which differentiates, you cannot perceive any temporal extension, and so there is no arising, ceasing, or abiding. (The mind) is colorless and has no shape and, therefore, doesn't have an identifiable nature. When an appearance arises, there is no place it comes from, nor anyone creating it. (With the mind) there is no apprehension of an inside or outside, and it transcends the (artificial) boundary between objects of perception and the perceiver.

Even though the mind appears to go out toward an external object, there is no place toward which it can move. Rather, things merely arise for the mind. If the mind did move out (to an external location in order to contact an object), then when (we were perceiving an external object) we would be inanimate (since our mind would have left our body). In a single instant our present awareness would split into two aspects.

There is absolutely no basis for the reflections (that appear in the mind, since the mind) is primordially free, like space. The (reflections of the world) arise (in the mind, but) they are not two different things. They are like the reflection of images in a mirror. Just as the ocean and its waves (are indivisible), in an ultimate sense (phenomenal appearances and the mind) are nondual. The meaning of the Dzogchen is that there is no need to reject or accept (anything).

In actuality (the mind) is pure from the very beginning, (so it is already) fully awake. The appearances of the phenomenal world and the mind are primordially insubstantial. Today I have realized the teachings of my magnificent master.

Now, because you have ascertained that everything is the ultimate dimension of reality, there is no assertion or negation; you are free from all hesitation and misconception and no (longer need) to ask anyone about the real meaning of the mind-itself. Without doing anything, you have seen the genuine essence. At this time, the dynamic and static (manifestations arise as) the play of the ultimate dimension of being. There is no need to reject or accept (anything). Whatever arises is an ornament (for the mind). If (your mind) is settled—abiding in the unified state of the unmoving, ultimate dimension of being—then everything is spontaneously and automatically fulfilled without any change or transformation. Now, we have arrived at the wisdom mind of the Victorious Ones of the three times. (Your experience is) totally blissful and spontaneously and automatically realized when the basis (of your very existence) is fulfilled in the state of Cosmic Wholeness (Samantabhadra). Everything is equally free in the primordial level of existence because at all times, whether past, present, or future, there is no change or transformation.

Alas! For one whose mind is fixated with biased attitudes there is no possibility of liberation. The factor which binds one is just these biased attitudes. The meaning of nonduality occurs when you are free of opinions, and if you have transcended clinging to extremes. There is no other way of disclosing this. You cannot see it by looking for it. Nor can you find it through logical analysis. Calling it "This" doesn't reveal it, so in relationship to this natural state don't fetter, or liberate it, with a grasping mind.

Although people desire the nondual and limitless (awareness, they make a) limit out of that which is not limited (and thereby) constrict the essential mind-itself. Even though people desire (the realization of) both (the ultimate and relative) realities, they fall into an extreme understanding of these. Although they desire the union of the two realities, this is not the way things naturally are. No matter in what way you investigate, you are trapped in the cage of (conflicting) desires.

Due to the confusion (created by splitting experience into) objects of perception and one who perceives, we have been dissatisfied since time without beginning, and so we persistently investigate because we are trapped by our mental images. Alas! I grieve for the deluded mind.

If one identifies (the nature of the mind) as some particular thing, then this is not the correct perspective. One does not need the cage of proliferating conceptualization. Whatever arises in the non-strategic field of bare awareness is neither expanded nor contracted, and neither sublime nor mundane. So give up your libidinous fixations!

With respect to the appearances in the mind, there is a freedom from the mental orientation (that thinks) "It is this." Do not condition your mind by (trying) to suppress your experience, apply an antidote, or mechanically transform it, but let your mind fall naturally into whatever (condition you find it). This is the incontrovertible essence of what is ultimately meaningful.

In their own nature, all the varieties of entities are in a state of harmony, so whatever arises is the nondual wisdom. Do not conceptualize it, and drop any frantic searching with your egocentric mind! Do not become trapped by the objects of perception, and don't let your mind become tarnished by allowing it to function as a subject of cognitions. If you are without any objects of desire, then you will know that all phenomena are like space, and you will see them as equivalent to an illusion. This is the nature of nonduality—the supreme king of views. Being free from extreme views is the (real) gauge of your realization. How wonderful!

Bare awareness is devoid of the duality of mundane existence and transcendental peace. It is a state of complete openness. (When) you understand the nature of your own being (*rang ngo she pa*), (you see that) there is no substance, ground, or root to it. The (real) meaning of Dzogchen is the nonduality of being bound or free. The minds of all beings, without exception, constantly abide in this state. In order to see this profound reality, which transcends depiction but is revealed as the manifestation of immaculate light rays (*dri med 'od zer*), I urge you not to fixate on the mind and its appearances, but rather to comprehend this perspective of impartial awareness through the illusory display (of phenomena appearing in the mind).

THE COMMENTARY

Salutation

I pay homage to the principle of Cosmic Wholeness. From the very beginning in a state of harmony, in the unoriginated clear light, the unmoving mind-itself is free of any fixation and is totally spacious. Within the Unsurpassed Spiritual Environment arise the three modes of being which spontaneously actualize and are totally blissful. Homage to the fundamental fulfillment which is immutable.

Following the custom observed in Tibetan religious texts, Longchenpa begins his work with a salutation, paying homage to the Buddha Samantabhadra. However, this salutation is not to be regarded as a mere formality, for it is particularly rich in significance, and in many ways summarizes the most important principles of the Dzogchen perspective. Indeed, Longchenpa comes at once to the heart of the matter in his salutation by acknowledging Samantabhadra, the awakened one who embodies cosmic wholeness, as the source of the spiritual perspective which he discloses in this work.

In orthodox Mahayana texts, Samantabhadra symbolizes the timeless, formless, and self-sustaining aspect of spiritual awakening, the fundamental dimension of enlightened awareness that is constant no matter when or where it is activated and that is realized by everyone who has become fully aware (a *buddha*). This is the dimension of awakening that knows that awareness-as-such is indestructible, and is in itself unchanged by the historical and personal circumstances through which it is realized. It is that dimension of awareness that is not differentiated in dependence on different cultural settings or personality structures, that dimension of who we are that was already totally aware even prior to the formation of our identity. Thus, in embarking on this work, Longchenpa is tapping directly into this primordial level of awareness.

In the context of Dzogchen, Samantabhadra is free of any residual theocentric associations that it may have had in the Mahayana and becomes a name for the fundamental nature of our own mind, which is totally free and completely spacious, because it is unstained and unmodified by any intellectual fixations or emotional attachments.

Yet, even though awareness-as-such is unoriginated and immutable, it becomes localized in space and time, both at a concrete physical level (*rupakaya*) and in more subtle spiritual dimensions of experience (*sambhogakaya*). Hence, Longchenpa also praises the capacity for evolutionary growth to be expressed in the physical presence and psychic resonance of those who choicelessly and spontaneously embody and express the sheer bliss (*mahasukha*) of Samantabhadra's awareness.

The fundamental nature of mind

Although the nature of my own and all living beings' minds is (already) pure and expansive, we wander, alienated in our mundane existence, due to the influence of primal ignorance. For those who wish for liberation from this state, I shall herein elucidate the mode of the core teaching about what is essential and ultimately meaningful, namely the path of the noble chariot (i.e., the Dzogchen perspective).

Longchenpa now declares that he will reveal the path to liberation through the most essential and definitive spiritual perspective possible, namely, that of Dzogchen.

He begins with a synopsis of that perspective. Although our minds are already pure (*sangs*) and fully expanded (*rgyas*)—although we are, in other words, fully realized, for the Tibetan term *sangs rgyas* means just that—the pristine clarity of our consciousness has been obscured by primal ignorance. As a result, we experience a constant sense of isolation and loneliness as we are pushed and pulled through life, confused about who we are, how we got here, and what we should be doing. This sense of separation, in which we feel ourselves to be inside a particular personality structure and alienated from others, emerges in concert with the formation of the primordial bifurcation of reality into an experience of self and other. Once this dualistic structure is locked in place, we have a sense of being forced either to enjoy or to endure the experiences of having a particular body-mind located in a relatively fixed environment. From here on, we are thrown into the world of mundane existence, where our life's work is to cycle between, on the one hand trying to defend, and on the other to escape from, this fixed and limited conception of who we are.

If we are to realize, and consequently see through, the illusion of separation and privacy that predicates our lives, an adequate understanding of the term "ignorance" (*ma rig pa*) is essential. *Ma rig pa* literally means "a lack, loss, or absence of awareness." But it means much more than a diminution of our capacity to know what is happening in and around us. Rather, it signifies a primitive and powerful energy that compels us to block out the experience of choiceless awareness by constantly becoming caught up in the complexity and confusion of managing and maintaining an inherently vulnerable personal identity. Ignorance thus refers to the primordial impulse to turn away from the authentic and radical simplicity of having nothing to defend or avoid.

The nature of suffering

> My friends who are in this bottomless state of cyclic existence are shaken by the waves of all manner of suffering. Since the error of ego fixation has arisen as a function of primal ignorance, the remedy is to cherish the perspective that apprehends our real mode of existence.

Longchenpa now uses one of the key terms of Buddhism: suffering or *dukkha*, which figures in one of the earliest and most fundamental doctrinal formulations of Buddhism, the Four Noble Truths:

1. Suffering.
2. The origin of suffering.
3. The cessation of suffering.
4. The path leading to the cessation of suffering.

The First Noble Truth identifies the fundamental problem of existence—that it is characterized by *dukkha*. Although this term is often translated as "suffering," that translation fails to bring out the full force of the term. The literal meaning of *dukkha* is "that which is difficult to bear," and this certainly includes suffering of all sorts: physical, mental, and emotional. However, the term has a wider range and embraces all experiences which we would prefer not to have, such as being parted from things we enjoy, being forced to endure things we do not like, not getting what we want. *Dukkha*, then, refers to the totality of life's unsatisfactory aspects, from the grossest to the most subtle. The early texts also identify *dukkha* as inseparable from conditioned existence, the unenlightened state; and indeed, in a sense the most extreme form of *dukkha* is to continue in that state.

In speaking of his "friends," Longchenpa is referring to all those who are afflicted by the *dukkha* of non-realization; and in so calling them, he expresses his compassion. His writing of this text is among the manifestations of that compassion.

Longchenpa then isolates the fundamental root of *dukkha*, as enunciated in the Second Noble Truth: ego fixation, deriving from the energy of ignorance. The remedy to the various types of *dukkha* inherent in our lives, all of which stem from ignorance, is the cultivation of a perspective that directly apprehends our real mode of being (*gnas lugs*), which we discuss further in the following section. Longchenpa also makes indirect reference to the Third and Fourth Noble Truths, which respectively refer to the fact that there is an alternative to the state of *dukkha*, and describes the path leading to that alternative: namely, the various practices of Buddhism.

Our real mode of being

> In this manner, everything which comprises the states of cyclic existence and unconditional freedom—the (entire) phenomenal world—is from the very beginning uncreated. From beginningless time, it is in a state of harmony. This state of spaciousness, the (true) nature of being, is without boundaries, and is nondual. It does not come into being and cannot be destroyed. It neither endures nor decays, and neither comes nor goes. Within this space, the entire variety of phenomena appears distinctly; yet when they manifest, all phenomena are naturally devoid of complexity.

The Tibetan term *gnas lugs* literally means our "mode or way of abiding," and points to our way of "being in the here and now." It is similar to Heidegger's term *Dasein*, which refers to our "beingness" or existence at the most basic and fundamental level. Knowing our Being or *Dasein* means becoming fully aware of what it means to be an "existing person." It signifies the raw, lived, and immediate dimension of our experience, as distinct from our interpretations, which are but one dimension of the totality of our existence.

Our real mode of being includes both our experience of being a particular person, located in time and space, experiencing a unique reality, and the transcendence of these limitations through the very awareness of our own individual style of being in, and experiencing the universe. As Medard Boss says, "Transcendence and being-in-the-world are names for the identical structure of *Dasein*, which is the foundation for every kind of attitude and behavior." (May, 1983: 148) From this perspective, the more deeply we appreciate the specific limitations, textures, and nuances of our manifest mode of being (*rupakaya*), the more directly, lucidly, and unequivocally we disclose the transpersonal, infinite, and unlimited dimensions of being (*dharmakaya*).

In Dzogchen, there is absolutely no effort, struggle, or need to escape who we are as an experience in the here and now, since this is our unique expression of transcendence. In fact, were we disembodied, transcendence would be impossible.

We come to appreciate our own unique style of embodiment, without making it in any way special or significant. We open up so that we can experience the subtle and dramatic modulations of our thoughts, moods, feelings, and perceptions, at the same time realizing that this is just a freely evolving dance of light and energy. Instead of arming ourselves with a battery of techniques for running away from unpleasant experiences and seeking out those we approve of, we come to see that every aspect and dimension of our experience is an exquisite expression of absolute freedom and transcendence. In this way, Dzogchen bridges the traditional tension between physical embodiment and spiritual transcendence.

The Dzogchen view

> There are no real external entities—they are (just) the mode of the appearance of the mind. Nor are these appearances mental, for phenomena do not originate in the mind either. The appearances of the five sense objects are like the hairlines perceived by someone with a visual defect. Though these appearances don't really exist, they still appear. By apprehending reality dualistically, we become confused. These appearances are like the illusory elephants that appear in our dream when we see ourselves surrounded by a (mounted) army. Because we hold the dream to be external to us, we are afraid. But is the nature of the dream other (than us, i.e., external) or does it exist mentally? Because there is nothing whatever existing outside or inside, for those who know the real nature of things, their terror dissolves by itself at the point (where it arises).

There are various methods of classifying the numerous schools and traditions of Buddhism, such as the broad distinction commonly drawn between Mahayana and Hinayana, or between Mahayana and Tantra.

In Indo-Tibetan Buddhism, a widely used approach to classifying Buddhist teachings rests on the trilogy of view (*lta*), meditation (*sgom*), and action (*spyod*), to which is sometimes added a fourth category, "result" (*'bras*). In each tradition a particular perspective or philosophical outlook—the view—is cultivated through a particular program of practice—the meditation—and a particular mode of behavior or conduct—the action. If the fourth category is used, the "result" defines the outcome that is to be expected. For example, Mahayana Buddhism is defined by the view of *shunyata*, the practice of the six perfections and the action of ethical behavior, resulting in the liberation of all beings.

Longchenpa is here concerned to enounce the perspective or "view" of Dzogchen, which at first sight appears to differ very significantly from that of other Buddhist traditions. As noted, the view of Mahayana Buddhism is that all phenomena are of the nature of *shunyata*; that is, they are open-ended, devoid of any essential own-being. In contrast, the view of the higher Tantras is that phenomena are inseparable from the nature of reality itself (*dharmata*). In Dzogchen, however, these perspectives, these "views," are regarded as artificial: they are mental constructs that we apply to the pristine nature of reality, and as such they do not promote our realization.

The view of Dzogchen is one of "no view." In fact, viewlessness can be found in the earliest Buddhist scriptures which portray the Buddha Shakyamuni himself as having no view, even on as crucial a topic as the existence of the self or *Atman*. The Pali Canon tells how a wandering holy man called Vacchagotta approached the Buddha and asked whether there is such a thing as a self, but the Buddha declined to commit himself to a view. (*Kindred Sayings*, 1950: IV.398-400)

Vacchagotta then framed his question slightly differently: "How, then, Master Gautama, is there not a self?" Again, the Buddha declined to answer, and Vacchagotta dropped the matter and left.

The Buddha later commented:

> When Vacchagotta asked, "Is there a self?" if I had replied, "Yes, there is," I would have been siding with the eternalists. But then when he asked, "Is there not a self?" to say that it does not exist would have been siding with the nihilists.... And when Vacchagotta asked, "Is there not a self?" if I had replied that there is not, it would have caused more bewilderment for the bewildered Vacchagotta. For he would have said, "Formerly, I had a self, but now I do not have one any more."

In Dzogchen, to return to our text, the perspective to be cultivated is one in which we begin to appreciate that all possible experiences—from the depths of torment to the blissful freedom of *nirvana*—are merely modulations of phenomena occurring within a disclosive space that allows all things to be no more and no less than just as they are. In our usual way of living, we relate to the flux of our experience in strictly bipolar terms, rejecting our pain and becoming addicted to pleasure. The alternative is to be a centerless, disclosive space within which we and the universe appear as processes that come into existence, endure, and decay. This disclosive space is not the same as the space that allows physical phenomena to subsist. It is the space that allows physical space to be where and as it is, and precludes its being where it is not. It is also the space that allows thoughts and emotions to emerge and subside as they do. As Longchenpa says, it is an ongoing state or condition of spaciousness that is nondual and without limitations or boundaries, in the sense that it does not favor or condition any particular phenomenal or transcendent construction. For example, it does not push the universe in the direction either of wholeness or of disintegration. It is not a teleological principle or force, but neither is it purposeless or adventitious. Instead, it is an unstructured and undefined matrix of possibility within which spiritual, mental, and physical phenomena evolve precisely as they do, without this evolution being forced or retarded in any way whatsoever. And, as a window of unlimited possibility, it neither endures nor decays; for were it to do either, it would support either stability or change and so would no longer be limitless. This state of spaciousness has no purpose or function. At root, it is simply the nature of being.

Furthermore, when we begin to relate to our experience as a disclosive space, we see that it is the very nature of what we are experiencing. That which is disclosed by the forms of our experience *is* the disclosive space itself. In fact, outside of what is disclosed, there is no disclosive space. Similarly, the very structure of our personality reveals the transpersonal nature of being itself. When we begin to experience the world as this disclosive space, the modulations of our thoughts and emotions, and the changes in our physical environment, become balanced and harmonized. Our experience becomes simple and uncomplicated, yet without any compromise in the full richness of its texture and distinctiveness.

The nature of appearances

Longchenpa now presents the truly radical nature of Dzogchen ontology. He begins by rejecting the notion that the world is an external, independent reality, suggesting instead that such is merely its mode of appearing to our minds. To begin with, it seems that he is about to align Dzogchen with the Idealist or Mentalist tradition (Vijnanavada/Chittamatra) of Buddhism, which denies any validity to the external universe. The thrust of Chittamatra thought is that what appears to exist as external to ourselves is no more than a mental projection, in some ways comparable to the hostility that a paranoid projects onto others' actions, whether intended as friendly or as purely neutral.

There are various complex threads within the Chittamatra tradition, but we need not disentangle them here. All agree in maintaining that phenomena are a manifestation of the mind, a flux of sensory impressions on the basis of which we infer the existence of an external reality. There is no evidence, according to this tradition, that the reality which we so construct has any objective existence. If it did, the argument goes, then it should exist independently of the observing mind, from which it should follow that all perceptions are objective and irrefutably factual. However, this is not so, as the subjectivity of perception demonstrates. The mere fact that different individuals differ in their perceptions of the same event demolishes the argument that perception is in any sense objective. Again, the case of the paranoid has a certain relevance.

However, Dzogchen is not seduced by this or any other philosophical position, as Longchenpa now shows; for having dismissed the idea that the world is an external reality, he at once parts company with the Chittamatra by rejecting also the postulate that appearances are merely mental fictions. In distinction to our ordinary understanding of dreams, he says, appearances do not originate in the mind. If they did, then they would depend on the mind: they would change as the observer changes; they would be absent when the observer is absent, and so on. From the Dzogchen perspective, the everyday forms we experience—the people we see and communicate with, the food we eat, and the clothes we wear—do not correspond to an external reality, but neither are they the dreamlike projections of our minds. In other words, our perceptions are *neither* objective nor subjective because the frameworks from which those categories derive—the realist and the idealist perspectives—equally distort the real status of sensory phenomena. Objectivity and subjectivity are equally invalid as indices of the veridical, for both are mental constructs.

A corollary of this perspective is that there is no substantive difference between the waking and dream experiences, since experience per se cannot be characterized as either objective or subjective. Dreams are not subjective. The most that can be said is that our baseline experience of relative stability and predictability (which we call "being awake") is periodically punctuated by unstable and unpredictable experiences (which we call "dreams").

Dzogchen invites us to experience the sensory world, which includes our own body, as a flux of wafer-thin, ephemeral appearances lacking any solidity or depth, but to do so without sliding into the trap of viewing them as non-physical—that is, without buying into any of the various interpretations of reality which Buddhist and non-Buddhist traditions have offered, however sophisticated they may be. This may sound impossible, since the extremes of realism and idealism (or variations of these) exhaust the ways in which the sensory world can exist. To put it at its simplest, surely the world either is, out there, factually and demonstrably, or it is merely our own invention. There seems to be no middle ground, or at least none which is logically defensible.

But this "non-perspective," as it were, is precisely the perspective of Dzogchen, which avoids all philosophical positions and excludes every possible way in which sensory phenomena can exist, without denying the fact that we can experience them. It is a perspective that invites us to release all tendencies to take a fix on our experience by interpreting it as either objective or subjective, real or unreal, caused or uncaused.

In order to ease us into this perspective, Longchenpa introduces the metaphor of the visual filaments that can be experienced by someone suffering from an optical defect. These filaments, which seem to hang in space in front of the affected person, undoubtedly appear; yet they are unreal, in the sense that there exists nothing external to the perceiver which corresponds to their appearance. In a similar way, phenomena can be likened to the illusory images that appear in our dreams; they have the capacity to stimulate our emotions, but do not correspond to any objective, external reality.

Another way into this perspective is to ask the question Longchenpa poses: "Is the nature of sense images external, or do they exist mentally?" However, asking this question does not entail the usual expectation of finding a neat and comforting solution. We do not simply scan our thoughts and derive an answer from our belief systems. Instead of superimposing our own feelings about whether our experience is objective or subjective, we let the phenomena we are experiencing reveal their own status to us. We decide that we will stay with this question and be present to our experience for as long as it takes for phenomena to reveal their own status. If we do this in an unhurried way, we discover that phenomena do not reveal their status in terms of being either real or unreal. Our experience isn't marked in such a way that it proclaims its objectivity or subjectivity. Instead, things reveal themselves as they are—which is that they are *neither* objective *nor* subjective. We discover that the distinction between illusion and reality is merely the grist for philosophical and psychological elaboration.

Longchenpa here also makes reference to one of the central experiences of Dzogchen, *rang sar grol* (often abbreviated to *rang grol*). This term, the importance of which is signalled by its use in the title of the text itself, *Chos nyid rang grol*, allows for various translations, depending on the context in which it occurs. In the title of this work, we have rendered it as "natural freedom," for in this case it signifies the inherent freedom of our natural condition. In the present context, however, it might be translated as "natural release," for it refers specifically to the phenomenon of limiting thoughts and conflicting emotions spontaneously transforming into the state of unconditional liberation the instant they are disclosed through uncontaminated, bare awareness (*rig pa*). Hence, in this section of the text, Longchenpa says that the terror that we can experience when confronted by threatening situations dissolves (*grol*) on the spot (*sar*) and by itself (*rang*) when we transcend the need to believe that our experience is caused or uncaused.

Spiritual systems

> Thus, when nonduality is apprehended dualistically, those who lack understanding apprehend things to be real. They are thereby confused by (the illusions of) worldly existence. Because the wise cognize dualistic appearances as nondual, the nature of cyclic existence is liberated into the state of unconditional freedom.

Longchenpa now moves on to speak of certain aspects of the experiences of duality and nonduality. These terms will perhaps require some clarification.

"Nonduality" is shorthand for an experience of reality that transcends the descriptors "one" and "many." As such, it does not refer to an undifferentiated experience in which all distinctions are absorbed into a uniform mystical experience. Rather, it refers to a sourceless experience that cannot be characterized as either one or many, finite or infinite, transcendent or immanent. Similarly, "duality" is shorthand for an experience that includes both the multiform nature of our everyday experience and mystical absorptions that transcend the experience of a multiplicity.

These distinctions are important, for in their absence Dzogchen can be misinterpreted as a philosophical monism. In expansion of this point, it will be appropriate to dwell briefly on the Buddhist view of spiritual systems.

In general terms, spiritual systems can be categorized using a Buddhist hermeneutical device, the "four alternatives" (*chatushkoti*). This device systematically distinguishes four different ways of describing the fundamental nature of reality, namely:

1. Using affirmative characteristics.
2. Using negative characteristics.
3. Affirming and denying the same characteristics.
4. Neither affirming nor denying any characteristics. (Chandrakirti, 1979: 180-181)

Most spiritual systems describe reality in the first way. For example, theistic spiritualities posit the existence of a divine being who is the source and caretaker of all creation and has a distinct set of attributes, such as compassion, love, wisdom, and so on.

Other spiritual systems posit an ultimate reality in the second way, by implicitly affirming its existence and then denying that it can be defined or categorized. In Western philosophical theism, this method is called the *via negativa* or "negative path," and in Hinduism, *neti neti*. For example, the ultimate reality of Advaita Vedanta is often said to be form*less*, color*less*, *a*temporal and *non*dual.

The third approach, in which the same characteristics are affirmed and denied at the same time, is less common. This method can be found in certain Hindu and Buddhist texts. For example, the Hindu foundational reality, *Brahman*, is sometimes said to be both one and many.

The fourth device (technically known as a "bi-negative disjunction") distinguishes Buddhist systems like Dzogchen and Madhyamika from other spiritual perspectives. Thus, when Longchenpa says that empirical reality is nondual, this is understood by practitioners to mean that at its core, sensory experience *neither* has *nor* lacks any internal or external boundaries. And when he says that those who lack understanding apprehend reality dualistically, he means that they become entangled in the whole system of distinguishing, preferring, and pursuing different materialistic and spiritual perspectives. People neurotically pursue the dualistic goals of materialistic and theistic philosophies; or conversely, they reject the phenomenal world in favor of self-absorption in a transcendent absolute.

In stating that dualistic appearances are liberated into the nondual state of unconditional freedom, Longchenpa means that Dzogchen frees people from extreme fixations wherein they compulsively attempt to consolidate a fragile identity through wealth, reputation, and worldly pleasures, or obliterate themselves through sleep, stupor, death, or spiritual trance.

An image in a mirror

Alas! This manifold of phenomenal appearances is primordially unoriginated and nondual, just like an image reflected in a mirror. The nature of openness (*shunyata*) is not separate from phenomenal appearances, just as water and its quality of being moist are combined in a nondualistic condition. Free of the limits of illusion, like an imaginary city, the instant things manifest, they are in the condition of being primordially unborn. Although the phenomenal world appears to be located (in time and space, in fact) it is the non-abiding dimension of being itself. The instant an appearance seems to disappear, it does not in fact cease, (since ultimately phenomena) *neither* increase *nor* decrease. Therefore, phenomenal appearances do not exist in the manner in which they appear.

Longchenpa continues to dismantle our everyday way of experiencing and interpreting the world. He now forthrightly rejects our habitual, commonsense experience of being located within a universe, since within the disclosive space that constitutes Dzogchen, there is no perceiver or perceived, no experience of distance, and *neither* motion *nor* absence of motion.

We will attempt to unpack these dimensions of the natural freedom of being, for they help in understanding the radical immediacy of the Dzogchen experience.

In order to explain how our sensory experience is uncreated and indivisible, Longchenpa introduces the analogy of a mirror-image. This is a recurring image in almost all Buddhist traditions, and illustrates how our experience lacks any discrete and irreducible properties. An image seen in a mirror seems to be composed of separate elements, discrete entities; yet in reality, it is a single and indivisible whole. We cannot isolate what seem to be the reflection's individual components and reassemble them in any other way. The apparent boundary between one feature and the next signifies nothing—there is no change in constitution to differentiate one feature from another. Even if the image is moving and changing, it cannot be broken up into separable parts.

From the Dzogchen perspective, the sense-world is no different from the mirror image. While it appears to be divisible and manipulable, like a set of building blocks, the idea that we can isolate one element of our experience and move it around or replace it with another is an illusion based on our habits of language and our tendency to believe and reify them—a linguistic artifact, in other words. In particular, the sense-world is created through that language which attributes choice and agency to ourselves and others. The language of human agency produces the appearance of control and manipulation; we learn to claim responsibility when certain, often repetitive, actions occur in predictable ways. For example, when our body moves as we stand up from a chair, we say we have "chosen" to do this.

At a more profound level, the image of a reflection in a mirror also illustrates the inseparability between a perceiver and that which is perceived. According to Dzogchen, the concepts of a perceiver on the one hand and objects of perception on the other are theoretical abstractions which have no basis in the domain of being. In the same way that an image in the mirror is inseparable from the mirror itself, we do not exist as something different from the universe that we experience.

This is an extension of the idea that is now commonly accepted in the natural and human sciences, that our experience is "theory-laden." In other words, our perceptions are shaped and influenced by the beliefs, theories, and structures which we have developed in order to interpret the world. However, the Dzogchen tradition applies this discovery in a far more radical way by demonstrating that even the most obvious and palpable dimensions of our experience, such as the feeling of being different from the things we experience, are no more than structures of interpretation.

For example, right now we think that we are seeing a real piece of paper in front of us, as opposed to a reflected image. We believe this is real because we don't see a gestalt that we call "ourselves" looking right back at us. But from the Dzogchen perspective, the familiar image that recurrently stares back at us isn't a reflection at all, since, in terms of the evidence immediately available to us, we do not have a face. On the basis of what I can "directly see," my face is invisible, in just the same way that I cannot see what is "behind me." In terms of the raw phenomena that we are presented with when looking into a mirror, there is "nothing" looking at what I consider to be a reflection of my head.

The late British sage Douglas Harding presented the visual dimensions of this disclosive space in a particularly accessible way through his notion of "having no head." As Harding demonstrates, both in his writings (Harding, 1986) and through simple practical exercises (Harding, 1993), we never experience our own head in the same way that we experience those around us. In place of our head is a space that is the universe we experience. As Harding writes, "This is not a matter of argument, or of philosophical acumen, or working oneself up into a state, but of simple sight…. Present experience, whatever sense is employed, occurs only in an empty and absent head." (1986: 9) Our own head, in other words, is a theoretical construct, inferred on the basis that we are like the people who show up within the field of our experience.

Though our limbs and torso are often revealed within this field, our head is never revealed as a direct object of perception. Were it ever to be where we "think" it is, it would preclude the possibility of experiencing anything else. If our head were where we "imagine" it is, the universe would disappear. As Harding says, "There is one place where no head of mine can ever turn up, and that is here on my shoulders, where it would blot out this Central Void which is my very life-source." (1986: 11)

Of course, we might say that the existence of our head as the gateway for our visual, auditory, and olfactory perception can be confirmed simply by reaching out and touching a mass that seems to rest on our shoulders. But as Harding says, "When I start groping around for my lost head, instead of finding it here I only lose my exploring hand as well: it, too, is swallowed up in the abyss at the centre of my being." (1986: 8) What we think is our hand is absorbed in the unseeable void we think is our head.

In the place where our head would be is a space that is the universe as we experience it. Consequently, from this perspective we ourselves are the universe. As Harding puts it: "It is absolutely Nothing, yet all things; the only Reality, yet an absentee…. There is nothing else whatever. I am everyone and no one…." (1986: 19)

Returning to Longchenpa, the section of the text we are now considering employs the term "openness" (*stong pa nyid, shunyata*) for the first time, thus connecting Dzogchen to the broad and powerful river of Buddhist thought contained in the Perfect Wisdom (*Prajnaparamita*) tradition. In language reminiscent of the famous Buddhist text, the *Heart Sutra* (*Prajnaparamita-hrdaya Sutra*), Longchenpa writes that "the nature of openness isn't separate from phenomenal appearances." The *Heart Sutra* itself says, "Form is openness and openness itself is form. Openness does not differ from form, and form does not differ from openness. Whatever is form, that is openness. Whatever is openness, that is form. The same is true of feelings, perceptions, drives, and consciousness."

The point made here is that there is no separation between that which is disclosed (the phenomenal world) and the disclosive field that makes the disclosure of any universe possible. A disclosive space is the field within which all things manifest, persist, and decay, exactly as they do. Ultimately, that space is indistinguishable from the experiential field; it is itself the occurrence of that which occurs in it. As Harding says, "The Space is the things that occupy it." (1986: 60) This disclosive space cannot be created, since this would be tantamount to creating the universe. Further, to the extent that there is never a time when there is no disclosive space (since time is an occurrence within it), that space is a vacuous concept. In fact, the disclosive space that is disclosed does not exist, which is why Buddhist philosophers such as Nagarjuna and Chandrakirti continued to emphasize that the experience of openness is itself open and insubstantial.

A consequence of this level of immediacy is that we don't see through our eyes. Nor do we hear through our ears or feel with our skin. In fact, there is no act of perception at all. As the *Heart Sutra* also says, "In the sphere of openness there is no eye, ear, nose, tongue, body, or mind, and there are no forms, sounds, smells, tastes, touchables, or objects of mind." Rather, there is a disclosive space within which the perceptual organs of others show up, from which we infer that we see with eyes, hear with ears, etc.

Because there is no perception, there is likewise no perceiver, or object of perception. As Harding writes, "…these coloured shapes present themselves in all simplicity, without any such complications as near or far, this or that, mine or not mine, seen-by-me or merely given. All twoness—all duality of subject and object—has vanished: it is no longer read into a situation which has no room for it." (1986: 6) It is meaningless to say that the world is either out there or in here, because disclosive space is *neither* inside *nor* outside. There is nothing it doesn't disclose, so it can't be inside since there is no outside; outside only exists if there is inside as well. Nor can there be an outside because whatever could be known as outside is by definition within the disclosive space. Also, because there is no inside or outside, this space can't be said to be small or large, expanded or contracted, hidden or revealed, here or there.

Moreover, because there is no sense of "here" or "there," there is no experience of distance within this disclosive space. The feeling that we are closer to some things and further away from others is an illusion created by the beliefs that things remain constant in size, even when they change their dimensions, and that things can preclude each other. It follows that we aren't located within this space, because we are the space itself. For example, when we sit in a room, we believe that the room is located within a house which is within a city or town, but this isn't given in our experience at all. That our room is located in a country on planet Earth is an interpretation that is seemingly substantiated by memories.

"Perhaps that is so," you might say, "but I still have the experience of being located in this room." You might say you are sitting near the west-facing wall, or standing in the middle of the room. But, if we say we are located near the west wall, we do so on the basis of a belief that the room exists in a larger universe. This sense of location is derived, not from our experience, but from the belief that things exist "on the other side" of our experience. If we say we are in the middle of a room, we believe that things can be either more or less distant from us, and that belief in turn is based on the belief that phenomena have stable dimensions, even when they shrink or enlarge within our field of experience.

Since in Dzogchen the experiences of distance and location deconstruct, it follows also that there is no experience of motion or stillness. The phenomena of walking or driving are completely consistent both with our moving through a stationary landscape, and with the landscape moving through us. In the absence of an arbitrary framework of interpretation, there is absolutely no way of distinguishing whether we are moving, or phenomena are moving, through the clearing that we identify as the locus of our head. Consequently, we are *neither* still *nor* moving. From the Dzogchen perspective, there is simply "an experience" of colors and shapes that modulate like reflections on water.

This thing that we call our "body" is not the locus of our identity. It is simply the most constant gestalt that occurs in "our" experience. Many of our visual experiences are accompanied on the lower periphery by an inchoate sensation that frequently transforms into an experience of hands, arms, and sometimes legs. We identify these sensations as our body because they invariably show up wherever we think we are. We think we are there because these limbs consistently display the same markings in terms of color, shape, size, weight, etc. But, if another set of limbs showed up with predictable constancy around the bottom half of our visual field, we would think that we were there.

We interpret that we are walking when certain changes occur in our visual, auditory, and tactile fields. In fact, we simply witness modulations in our experience similar to those which can, to a certain extent, be replicated using virtual reality technology. The difference between virtual reality and the Dzogchen perspective is that virtual reality creates an impression of movement *while we are stationary*. This is partially a limitation of virtual reality technology itself, which cannot yet replicate the pixel resolution of human vision, or simulate the muscular activity involved in actions like walking. But to a more significant degree, the difference is attributable to the memories we have of stepping into a virtual reality unit. Unlike virtual reality, however, the Dzogchen perspective does not condition the experience of being in a fixed location with images changing around us. In other words, although the experience of real motion dissolves, it does not produce the sensation of being stuck in the same location. Spatial location and dislocation both dissolve in this perspective. From the Dzogchen perspective, reality is always a virtual reality. In other words, what we call "real" is only ever an appearance of reality.

Intrinsic nature

No matter in what way we investigate things, they lack any intrinsic nature. Things cannot exist in the way (in which we construct them). (The phenomenal world) has been free from the beginning and exists in an ongoing state of integration and Cosmic Wholeness (Samantabhadra). All these entities lack a foundation, a source, and an essence. We should not deliberately seize (on things) and say that they are "This" or "that," as (ultimately) things are unidentifiable. Just like space, no creator can be perceived, and actions are devoid (of any sense of agency). There is no mental orientation whereby we can take reality as something, everything, or a particular thing.

Longchenpa concludes what may be regarded as his introductory comments by taking up a point fundamental to all Buddhist thought, namely, the inadequacy of substantialist theories—those theories which hold that there exists such a thing as an intrinsic nature. The Buddhist refutation of such theories takes two principal forms: the *anatmavada* teaching of early Buddhism, which points to the impossibility of isolating anything in the individual which could be described as a "soul," "self," or "intrinsic nature," and the *shunyata* teaching of Mahayana, which applies that same principle to the entire phenomenal universe and carries it to the furthest reaches of its implications. It will be appropriate here to give a brief summary of these two teachings in order to set Longchenpa's remarks within their proper context.

Anatmavada

Early Buddhism analyses the components of embodied existence into five categories known as the five *skandhas*, literally meaning "heaps:" form, feeling, perception, consciousness, and karmic formations. The category of form subsumes corporeality, as well as cohesion, heat, and vibration. This category is thus a little broader than the word "form" might suggest. "Vibration," for example, embraces energy, and hence movement and stability, while "cohesion" embraces those forces which hold matter together. The *form* category thus comprises the body and all its members and organs, as well as its ongoing presence as an identifiable entity. The category of *feeling* includes bodily and emotional feelings, whether pleasant, painful, or neutral, and thus comprises physical sensations such as taste and sight; it also includes affective states such as happiness, boredom, and depression. The category of *perception* includes the recognition by the sense organs of their respective fields (taste, sound, odor, etc.). To the five sense organs recognised in the West, Buddhist thought adds a sixth: the mind, whose field comprises the mental contents. The *perception* category therefore comprises the discernment of each of the five sense fields, plus the discernment of mental contents. The category of *consciousness* subsumes the awareness of the various sense objects—awareness of taste, smell, and so on—while the category of *karmic formations* comprises the propensities and volitional impulses resulting from past actions.

The teaching of the five *skandhas* can be analysed at considerably greater length, but for our present purposes its conclusion is more important than the details: none of the *skandhas* has any intrinsic existence, or any quality that could be called an immortal self. It follows that the whole, which is made up of these qualities, must likewise be devoid of any intrinsic existence. This teaching, one of the cornerstones of early Buddhism, is known as *anatman*, literally "no self." A simile used in Buddhist scriptures in further illustration is that of the chariot. If a chariot is dismantled into its components parts—wheels, axle, and so on—there is nothing left to which the name "chariot" can be applied. None of those parts, moreover, has any specific "chariotness." Similarly, if an embodied being is reduced to its component parts—the five *skandhas*—there is no special "beingness" about any of them.

Shunyata

In Mahayana Buddhism, the analysis of the five *skandhas* is applied universally: no phenomenon whatsoever has any intrinsic identity; the only characteristic we can identify in phenomena is their lack of any characteristic. Since we cannot find any characteristic in any phenomenon, this lack of characteristic must itself be the nature of phenomena. This lack of intrinsic nature is known as *shunyata*, literally meaning "emptiness." *Shunyata* does not, however, refer to a state of vacuum or nothingness, but rather to the proposition that phenomena are entirely open-ended.

The teachings of *shunyata* have their origin in the various texts of the *Prajñaparamita* or Perfect Wisdom scriptures, of which perhaps the best known in the West are the *Heart Sutra* (*Prajnaparamita-hrdayasutra*) and the *Diamond Sutra* (*Vajracchedikasutra*). However, it is in the Madhyamika teachings that the implications of *shunyata* are most fully worked out. Madhyamika, as a whole, is based on the work of the second-century thinker Nagarjuna and was further elaborated by a number of later logicians, such as Shantideva and Chandrakirti. The system of analysis which these thinkers evolved is properly known as Deconstructive Madhyamika, in contrast to Constructive Madhyamika.

According to Deconstructive Madhyamika, if things had an intrinsic nature—something that really made them what they are—we would be able to discover that "something" by close and careful examination, without the need to rely on any assumptions or presuppositions of our own. Indeed, the more thorough and rigorous the examination, the more obvious will the nature of phenomena become. If the world exists independently of us, for example, a close investigation of its condition will reveal this to be so. Similarly, if we really exist as distinct and independent identities, we should be able to confirm this by closely examining the phenomenon that we are.

However, as Madhyamika philosophers show, close examination of phenomena fails to reveal a foundation (*gzhi*), a source (*rtsa*), or an essence (*dngos po*). Whenever we rigorously investigate things, we discover that they cannot be found—they are empty of an intrinsic nature. In the language of Madhyamika, they are "analytically unfindable."

Returning now to Longchenpa, while he does not advocate the Madhyamika approach to realizing insubstantiality (*nihsvabhava*), which relies on powerful meditative analysis (*vichara*), he acknowledges the validity of the Madhyamika discovery that reality is analytically unfindable. A consequence of this realization is that we no longer lock up our experience of reality by fixating on things as being "this" and "that." We don't adopt a rigid and inflexible mental orientation, but instead allow our experience to unfold freely in a way that transcends the illusion of effort and struggle.

The critique

Although one may take sides and give allegiance to a philosophical system, or even cultivate the innumerable types of philosophical viewpoints, meditational methods, or traditions of action, still it is difficult to see the authentic meaning of the essential mind-itself. Through their different analyses of the selflessness of people and things, the disciples of the fully awakened teachers, those who have awakened by themselves (*Pratyekabuddha*), the Idealists (*Chittamatra*), and the Constructive Middle Pathers (*Svatantrika Madhyamika*), (all lose sight of) the real practice of view and meditation and get sidetracked in the four (types of diversions), such as getting spaced out, etc.

> By going astray in this way it seems that innumerable creatures (prolong the need to) practice.

At this point, Longchenpa changes direction. Thus far, he has presented a concise account of some of the main features of the Dzogchen view, but he now embarks on a critique of the goal-oriented perspective of certain Buddhist traditions, which he regards as a hindrance to spiritual practice. As a consummate practitioner and scholar, Longchenpa was, of course, intimately familiar with both the practices of these traditions and their philosophical views; he was acquainted also with the arguments—or in some cases the polemic—which the proponents of each tradition have brought to support their position. He assumes a comparable degree of experience and knowledge in the reader, and sometimes uses only a couple of key words to refer to a point whose full expansion would require lengthy exposition. Thus, in order to follow his critique, we shall find ourselves involved with points of Madhyamika logic, Tantric metaphysiology, Zen crypticism, and various other matters.

Longchenpa opens his critique with the assertion that it is impossible to understand the mind-itself (*sems nyid*) by relying on any philosophical system or meditative method, whether Buddhist or non-Buddhist. By "mind-itself," Longchenpa means the mind as distinct from mental activities, such as thinking and perceiving. Mind-itself is unconditioned and unstained by thought activity. It is likened to a mirror which reflects the world just as it is, without preferring any precept over any other one. The mind-itself is the Zen no-mind.

From the large range of Buddhist philosophical systems, Longchenpa specifically targets Idealism (*Chittamatra* or *Yogachara*), whose views I mentioned, and Constructive Madhyamikas (*Svatantrika Madhyamika*).

The importance of Madhyamika, as it originally evolved, does not lie in the realm of theory or doctrine, but in the uncompromising and thoroughgoing application of the most rigorous logic to the dismantling of all positions, the deconstructing of all theories and views. In its original form, Deconstructive Madhyamika has no position of its own, has no theories or dogmas, for if it had any, it would have to use its own weapons on itself and take them apart. Madhyamika, then, is not a school of thought, but an analytical procedure.

In the course of time, however, there arose a variant form of Madhyamika known as Svatantrika or Constructive Madhyamika, so called because its followers propounded or constructed their own views (*svatantra*), rather than adhering to the strictly non-positional approach of Deconstructive Madhyamika. Thus, for example, they held that while phenomena lack an independent existence (*svabhava*) at the highest level of reality (*paramartha-satya*), they exist independently at the empirical level (*samvrti*). In short, the Constructive Madhyamikas simply perpetuated their own intellectual fixation; in their hands, Madhyamika is no longer an analytical tool, but has deteriorated into precisely the sort of mental construct which that tool was intended to demolish.

According to Longchenpa, the very meditations which Constructive Madhyamika claims to be effective in reversing conceptual proliferation (*prapanca*), in fact lead meditators astray. Those meditations operate in a self-sustaining circle; rather than leading to liberation from the cycle of rebirth, they lead only to more of the same—the need for more and more meditation practice—because they perpetuate the thinking process. Thus, even though these practitioners have a sophisticated and detailed philosophical understanding of selflessness, when they get to the heart of the practice, they miss the essential point, which is the nature of the mind-itself.

An identical assessment of the negative value of traditional spiritual methods was voiced earlier by powerful exponents (*mahasiddha*) of the Mahamudra tradition, such as Saraha, who boldly proclaimed that, "Mantras and tantras, meditation and concentration are all a cause of self-deception. Do not defile in contemplation thought that is pure in its own nature, but abide in the bliss of yourself and cease these torments." (Snellgrove, 1964: 227)

In Zen, too, we can find similar declarations. The eighth-century Chinese master Mazu, for example, wrote that "To grasp the good and reject the bad, to contemplate emptiness and enter concentration, is all in the province of contrivance—and if you go on seeking externals, you get further and further estranged." (Cleary, 1989: 1) Similarly, Yuanwu, a Chinese master from the East Mountain School of Zen, wrote that "To study Zen conceptually is like drilling in ice for fire, like digging a hole to look for the sky. It just increases mental fatigue. To study Zen by training is adding mud to dirt, scattering sand in the eyes, impeding you more and more." (Cleary, 1989: 37) The ninth-century master Huang Po is even more outspoken: "It is obvious that mental concepts and external perceptions are equally misleading, and that the Way of the Buddhas is as dangerous to you as the way of demons." (Blofeld, 1958: 75)

Longchenpa mentions in passing that traditional methods for contemplating egolessness can easily sidetrack people into certain types of diversion. According to the eighteenth-century Tibetan master 'Jigs med gling pa, there are three types of diversion (*gol ba gsum*), which arise through becoming attached to the bliss, clarity, and non-conceptuality, that arise from practice. Attachment to bliss leads to rebirth in the desire realm; attachment to clarity projects one's consciousness into the realm of form; and addiction to non-conceptuality causes rebirth in the formless realms. 'Jigs med gling pa also talks about the four ways of getting lost. These are: (1) by viewing openness as having the nature of knowability, i.e., viewing it as a thing that can be known or cognized; (2) by construing openness as a path; (3) by viewing openness as a remedy; and (4) by branding things with openness—superimposing the concept of openness on things, rather than letting it arise as their natural condition, i.e., talking oneself into believing that reality is open, as opposed to letting it self-disclose its insubstantiality.

Tantra

Within the creation (*utpatti*) and fulfillment (*sampanna*) practices of the Tantric tradition, there are many methods for manufacturing change, since (transformation) is the real intention behind the practices of Action, Performance, Yoga, and the

Unexcelled. But even with these, one doesn't approach the unfabricated, self-presencing, spontaneously established, and genuine (reality, because one is still) ensnared by the net of proliferating complexity.

Longchenpa now switches his criticism away from the scriptural (*sutra*) traditions of Buddhism and directs his attention to the systems of Tantra, which he regards as no less counterproductive in compounding mental constructs.

In the *sutra* traditions—Theravada and most forms of Mahayana—liberation is conceived as a result to be attained by diligent practice of meditation and ethics. Thus, for example, the Theravada monk observes the rules of monastic discipline and practices certain forms of meditation, while the Mahayana practitioner passes through the various stages of the bodhisattva path with their corresponding practices. For this reason, the *sutra* tradition as a whole is also known as the "vehicle of cause"— liberation is caused by practice.

Tantra, on the other hand, is known as a "vehicle of fruition," meaning that tantric practitioners attempt to simulate the state of realization with the objective of finally reaching the point at which the simulation becomes a reality—in a sense, liberation is caused by liberation. Within the Tantric tradition, there is a series of practice levels, known as the "creation" and "fulfillment" stages, which begin with the meditator visualizing an ideal spiritual being as external and conclude with the meditator radically transforming his or her own self image so that it is identified with the physical and mental attributes of the exalted being. (see Hopkins, 2009) These, Longchenpa says, miss the point, for they do no more than lock the practitioner into another self-sustaining cycle.

Not even the highest tantras escape Longchenpa's strictures; even the most esoteric and sophisticated methods of Tantra miss the mark, because they trap the meditator in a complex system that only serves to proliferate conceptual activity rather than leading to the experience of mind-itself. Whether any practices at all could lead to that experience is a matter that Longchenpa takes up later.

Trance

Some say that the purification of the mind is the goal of view, meditation, and action. Some suppress their drives and feelings. Some say that cutting their connection with the three times is the unimpeded state of immediate awareness. Others note the arising and ceasing (of whatever appears in their awareness). They say these are the authentic aims (of practice, but here there are only) turbulent waves of proliferating conceptualization.

In these lines, Longchenpa singles out for criticism meditations that are designed to produce a trance-like experience, including even the time-honored method of mindfulness meditation (*satipatthana*), advocated by the Buddha Shakyamuni himself, in which we note the arising and ceasing of different feelings and sensations, such as our breath. He also notes that the suppression of emotions, generally recommended in monastic traditions, precipitates rather than attenuates conceptual activity.

Longchenpa isn't saying that these methods are in themselves misguided. His aim is to point out that the practices themselves are not the goal. He is warning against getting caught up in techniques and becoming conditioned by them to the point that we can actually inhibit the development of our awareness, and so reduce our spontaneity and freedom. If we allow ourselves to fall into this trap, the very techniques which are meant to reveal a more fulfilling dimension of experience can have precisely the opposite effect, in that they can constrict and limit us. Longchenpa wishes us to bear in mind, in other words, that the methods we use are for increasing our awareness, and not for further conditioning ourselves.

Longchenpa also criticizes those who claim that our ordinary, everyday way of experiencing the world is the open dimension that spiritual seekers desire. Although that impression seems to be conveyed in some of the literature of Dzogchen and other "unorthodox" Buddhist traditions, such a reading involves a confusion of category. To put it at its simplest, Zen masters have been known to beat their students, but beating people does not make one a Zen master. Similarly, to the enlightened perception, everyday experience is no different from realization; but that perception does not arise simply by declaring that it is so.

Discipline

> In exactly the same way, people say that the control of one's inner energies and (the practice of physical) coupling (i.e., the use of karma-mudra) to (respectively generate) clarity and bliss are the real point of practice, but in fact they (just) get caught by their libidinous fixations. As well as getting stuck in the net of oscillating between what is acceptable and unacceptable, they will never see the essential point. For them there is no possibility to be free. They remain trapped in worldly existence because in every case they are deluded by an intellectual construction.

Longchenpa now targets some of the most elevated practices in the Tantric tradition. In certain Tantric practices, meditators attempt to control the energies in their nervous system by visualizing a network of meta-physiological channels (*nadi*) and energies (*prana*) which give vitality to the body and provide a subtle physical basis for emotional, mental, and spiritual processes. By controlling the flow of the energies within the channels, meditators attempt to control their conceptualizing activity. Advanced Tantric meditators may also use sexual intercourse as a yogic practice, in conjunction with visualization and control of the vital energies (*prana*), to produce experiences of pure bliss (*mahasukha*). The underlying idea here is that an experience of bliss is the best foundation upon which to realize the lucid or clear-light nature of reality (*prabhasvara*), since there is no emotional objection or resistance to what one is experiencing. However, according to Longchenpa, such practices merely stimulate emotional entanglement.

Such practices stand in contrast to the highly-regulated and disciplined behavior of monks and nuns, which are controlled by a detailed set of precepts, the Vinaya, which lays down in great detail how monks and nuns are to live. Thus Theravada monks, for example, are required to observe some 227 rules, which govern every aspect of their lives, from when and how they may eat and what they may wear to the most minute details of personal conduct. The purpose of these behavior controls is to filter out intense feelings of desire and aversion, thereby supporting the practice of meditation. According to the Dzogchen perspective, however, this discipline carries the danger of fixation; rather than using the rules as a tool, monks easily reify them and become trapped by them, and once again become locked into a self-sustaining cycle in which mind-as-such is obscured. Thus they forfeit the spontaneously arising and ever-present capacity to realize their natural state.

Longchenpa here also warns against a morality which is governed solely by rules or precepts. Rather, people's behavior should be authentic, in the sense of both arising from and promoting their awareness.

Something's missing

> Alas! Because these people do not know how to recognize the precious jewel, they appear to be searching for junk jewelry, having discarded the wish-fulfilling gem. By rejecting what is supreme—the genuine nature of the mind-itself—they become trapped in the snake-like nest of fabricated techniques based on hope and fear. One can never become free with an obsessive mind. The fault occurs in the seeker who seeks for the meaning of that which is sought after.

Having emphasized the pitfalls inherent in these practices, Longchenpa now comes to the heart of the problem. The assumption in all the methods of spiritual practice so far mentioned is that our present condition is inadequate and impoverished, and that things shouldn't be this way. All these practices are predicated, in other words, on the belief that "something is missing," and if we want to make any progress on the spiritual path, we absolutely must have that something as soon as possible. Thus, if we follow Theravada, we lack experience of the eight progressively subtle states of meditative absorption, the *jhanas*, without which no further progress is possible. If we are involved in Zen, we still don't have the breakthrough illumination of *satori*, which is the objective of the intensive koan and zazen practice which Zen practitioners undertake and without which, again, no progress is to be looked for. If we practice the techniques of Madhyamika, we are still waiting for the insight (*prajna*) that corrects our fundamental ignorance, and we cannot expect to get any further until we've got it. And if we are practitioners of Tantra, we need the pure vision that transforms our mundane and contaminated perception into the world-view of a fully awakened being, and there is no hope whatever that we will get anywhere at all unless we keep applying the *mantras* and the *mudras* with all diligence until we have that view firmly established in our consciousness.

The methods of these traditions are all designed to bring forth whatever is thought to be missing. Because the assumption that "something is missing" is so pervasive and constant, Longchenpa refers to it as the "obsessed mind." This problem is inherent in the identity of the "seeker," who is driven by the belief that there is something of value to find. Yet, for as long as practitioners are "seekers," they are doomed to be dissatisfied, since they have not reached the goal they seek. Hence, Longchenpa writes that "The defect lies in the seeker who seeks for the meaning of that which is sought after."

Centuries earlier Saraha made the same point—that reality is present and available, yet elusive if deliberately sought, "The nature of the sky is originally clear but by gazing and gazing the sight becomes obscured. Then when the sky appears deformed in this way, the fool does not know that this is the fault in his own mind." (Snellgrove, 1964: 229) The ninth-century Chinese Zen master Linji makes the same observation, "When you look for it [enlightenment] you become further from it, when you seek it you turn from it all the more." (Cleary, 1989: 6)

Just as it is

> Listen! If one wants (to apprehend) the meaning of the nature of the mind-itself, what is the use of many investigations and analyses? Whatever appears "that" is it (i.e., the ultimate reality), so let it appear as it is, without becoming fixated upon it. When we are free of fixations and don't adopt any position, we have no need to accept or reject (anything at all). Because everything is beyond mental orientation, don't meddle or spoil it!

In the Dzogchen view, as we have seen, there is no effort to turn ourselves into something else or to deny what we are in the here and now. Similarly, as Longchenpa now emphasizes, we should not make more out of our experience than what is immediately given—we should not under-value, trivialize, or suppress our experience, but allow it to remain unaffected, unmanipulated, and free from contrivance.

Longchenpa dismisses the Madhyamika claim that conceptuality can be deconstructed and that a cessation of thought can be accomplished through logical analysis—the Madhyamikas are just living in hope if they believe that these methods can precipitate a non-conceptual experience of reality. The same can be said of Zen practitioners who work with koans; and although mainstream Rinzai Zen practitioners rely on koans to achieve satori, some Zen masters have criticized their use. The seventeenth-century Japanese master Bankei rejected both sitting meditation (*zazen*) and koan practice, calling them "tool Zen." He is quoted as saying that:

> Zen masters of today generally use "old tools" when they deal with pupils, apparently thinking they cannot raise the barriers [to enlightenment] without them. They do not teach by thrusting themselves directly forward and confronting their students without their tools. These men who teach with tools and cannot do without them are the blind men of Zen. What is more, they tell their students that there can be no

progress in Zen unless they raise a "great ball of doubt," and then break through this doubt. So, first of all, they have them raise a ball of doubt by any means possible; they do not teach them to live by the unborn buddha mind. Those who have no ball of doubt themselves, they saddle with one, causing them to change their buddha mind into a ball of doubt. That is a mistake. (Waddell, 1974: 147)

Bankei explains the fallacy of using methods like a koan:

Cutting off occurring thoughts is like washing blood off with blood. The original blood might be washed off, but you're still defiled by the blood you wash in. You can wash it as much as you like, the bloodstains won't go away. You don't know that your mind is originally unborn and undying, that it is free of illusion, and you think that thoughts really exist, so you revolve in the cycle of birth and death. You must realize that thoughts are temporary, changing appearances, and neither seize on them or hate them, just let them occur and cease of themselves. It's like the image reflected in a mirror. The mirror is clear and bright and reflects whatever is placed before it. But the image does not stay in the mirror…. (Waddell, 1974: 114)

The non-aligned teacher U. G. Krishnamurti was an outspoken critic of all forms of spiritual and religious practice. According to him:

If you practice any system of mind control, automatically the "you" is there, and through this it is continuing…. Nor can you practice mindfulness, trying to be aware every moment of your life. You cannot be aware; you and awareness cannot co-exist. If you could be in a state of awareness for one second by the clock, once in your life, the continuity would be snapped, the illusion of the experiencing structure, the "you," would collapse, and everything would fall into the natural rhythm. In this state you do not know what you are looking at—that *is* awareness. (1982: 62)

The reason why we can't reverse the thinking process is that thought only moves in the direction of producing more thought. Hence, if a reversal of the thinking process is ever to occur, it must be acausal, since every attempt to cause it to invert will only guarantee its continuation. It is impossible to willingly stop thinking, since every effort to do so only adds momentum to conceptual activity. In other words, we cannot *think* our way to the end of thought. Krishnamurti explains:

We are all talking of thought. Is it possible for you to look at thought? No, there is another thought which is looking—that is the tricky part, you see—it divides itself into two—otherwise you can't look at thought…. So, what creates the division? The division is created by thought—that is the beginning of your thinking. It is a very tricky process. It is one movement, and what is looking at what you call "thought" is all the definitions you have of thought…. So all the tricks you are playing—that if you look more carefully, with total attention—all this is only deception, because all you are doing is clarifying your thinking…. (1982: 95 and 149)

The assumption here is that all spiritual theories and methods, despite their stated aim, result in perpetuating the practitioner's independence and individuality. It doesn't matter whether we are controlling our thoughts or letting them be, intensifying our emotions or releasing them, since all the experiences that arise are appropriated by the ego.

The Dzogchen tradition contrasts the mind that obsessively seeks to maintain its existence with the natural mind, which simply allows whatever is there to be there, without fixation or preference. This mind does not seek to determine whether what one is experiencing should or shouldn't be there. It does not accept some aspects of experience and reject others, but simply allows what is present to be present just as it is, without bias or fixation.

Searching for openness

If the objects which appear to the mind exist in the mode of openness, then what need is there to look for so-called "openness"? (On the other hand) if appearances do not exist (in the mode of openness), then even though one looks for their openness, they cannot become open. Therefore, what is the use of engaging in the meaningless and arduous task (of actively seeking to cognize the openness of appearances)?

You are more familiar now with the process of deconstructive contemplation. According to many Madhyamikas, the direct realization of openness is only possible through their form of contemplation.

Longchenpa, however, asserts that such practice is entirely futile. If objects are empty, he says—that is, if they lack an intrinsic existence—then that is how they are, and they will remain that way whether we search for their emptiness or not. So why go searching for something that is already there? It would be like searching for your house when you are sitting in it. On the other hand, if things are not empty of intrinsic or inherent characteristics, then no amount of searching will reveal their emptiness, and no amount of effort will transform them. Saraha, whom we quoted earlier, says much the same: "If it's already manifest, what's the use of meditation? And if it is hidden, one is just measuring darkness." (Snellgrove, 1964: 226)

No exertion

Similarly, there is no need to meditate on the essence of the creation and fulfillment (phases of Tantra). (When we have realized our natural state of being), it is easy to hold the things to be accepted and rejected in any way at all. If this is real (for you), then there is no need to exert yourself. If it isn't, then it is (still) pointless to exert yourself. It would be like coal becoming gold. (In the final analysis) things don't exist, as they are (merely) an intellectual construction. This being the case, you should not spoil that natural awareness with mechanically contrived antidotes (in the hope of bringing about some change). This is the essential meaning of the unsurpassable Indestructible Career (Vajrayana).

Longchenpa now returns to Tantra and reiterates that the elaborate practices of development and fulfillment stages are equally futile.

He also makes the further point that exerting ourselves to achieve an understanding of the ultimate reality effectively places the ultimate beyond our experience. It doesn't matter if this is an all-out struggle to achieve spiritual awakening, or just a gentle change in our perspective designed to cultivate a more accurate perception of reality. The very notion of exertion implies that we are trying to achieve or gain something that we don't already have; and according to Dzogchen, we cannot have more or less of what we already have, since this would mean that things can be different from how they are. The fourteenth-century Zen master Yuansou explains this well, "In Buddhism there is no place to apply effort. Everything in it is normal—you put on clothes to keep warm and eat food to stop hunger—that's all. If you consciously try to think about it, it is not what you think of. If you consciously try to arrange it, it is not what you arrange." (Cleary, 1989: 78) Ying-an, a master from the East Mountain School of Zen, writes similarly: "If you have a single thought of eagerness to attain Zen mastery, this burns out your potential, so you cannot grow anymore." (Cleary, 1989: 69)

Statements of this sort seem to fly in the face of such venerable Buddhist categories as "right effort," the sixth member of the Noble Eightfold Path, which is itself among the core teachings of Theravada Buddhism. But what Longchenpa and the Zen masters are here warning against is a goal-oriented attitude to practice, the view that spiritual endeavor is mechanistic—push the right button with the correct degree of force and the desired result is guaranteed. Thus Huang Po says:

> Though you perform the six paramitas for as many eons as there are grains of sand in the Ganges, adding also all the other sorts of activities for gaining Enlightenment, you will still fall short of the goal. Why? Because these are karma-forming activities and, when the good karma they produce has been exhausted, you will be born again in the ephemeral world. (Blofeld, 1958: 68)

U. W. L. Poonja connects the application of effort with the creation of time: "If you make any effort or use any method of trying to achieve something at some distant future, this will bring you into time. And time is mind. So this will be the play of mind only. But your original nature is empty." (1992: 66) Some spiritual traditions, both Buddhist and non-Buddhist, have spoken of realization in terms of a realm of timelessness. However, as we suggested above, the concept of a timeless realm turns out to be just another of the ego's stratagems for its own perpetuation—"the play of the mind." One of the ways to enter this timeless realm is said to be to live only in the present moment, to "be here now." But this is also problematic, for living entirely in the present involves cutting ourselves off from two-thirds of our experience; whereas the stated aim of Buddhism and other spiritual traditions is not to curtail our experience, but to bring about a heightened awareness, culminating in the total experience which is realization. Furthermore, the moment we recognise that we are living in the present, we automatically leave the realm of the timeless; since timelessness only exists in relation to time, the recognition of timelessness can only occur alongside a recognition of time.

Thus time and effort converge at a place where the mind is still involved in the elaboration of fictions.

No Tantra

(Ultimately) there are no sacred recitations (*mantra*), no Tantric tradition, and no acceptable philosophical positions. (Reality) cannot be identified as "This" or "that," and there is no view, meditation, action, or result of these. Everything that exists is in perfect harmony in the form of a unified spiritual universe (*mandala*) in which philosophical systems, viewpoint, meditation, action, and result are all fulfilled. The states of cyclic existence and unconditioned freedom are equally fulfilled, and being itself becomes totally pervasive.

Here again, Longchenpa echos the *Heart Sutra*, which teaches that from the perspective of openness there is no perception and no object of perception; similarly, Longchenpa teaches that from the perspective of mind-as-such, there is no mantra and no Tantra. That is to say, in the effortless and uncontrived state of total beingness, such matters as the view, meditation, and action of Tantra are no more than mental constructs and as such act as obstacles to realization.

Longchenpa goes on to say that view, meditation, action, and result are all fulfilled (*rdzogs*). Here he is trading on two slightly but significantly different uses of the word *rdzogs*, which means both "to complete," and "perfect" or "fulfilled;" not only do these practices reach completion, they also fall away because they are no longer relevant and so are fulfilled.

From this point on, Longchenpa begins to distinguish the state of being that is naturally attuned to the way things are (*chos nyid*), as opposed to the spiritual life that is lived in the pursuit of a goal, such as enlightenment or *nirvana*. From the perspective of Dzogchen, *nirvana* is no more intrinsically preferable than *samsara*. Bondage and liberation are co-emergent (*sahaja*) and interdependent, and because of this they lack any real existence. Hence, to seek one and reject the other only compounds our suffering.

No liberation

The (mind-itself) is uncontrived and has never been liberated because it has been fully awake from the very beginning. Within the state of the ultimate dimension of being (*dharmakaya*)—which is like an effortless king whose (wishes) are spontaneously fulfilled—there are various physical embodiments (*nirmanakaya*) which are its illusory display. The world of appearances, the three dimensions of being (*trikaya*) and wisdom (*jnana*) are (one) indivisible (reality). You cannot conceive of anything to be rejected or accepted, (since) everything is in a state of complete purity.

In the state of Dzogchen, all communication and social activity unfold effortlessly and with exquisite precision. Those who embody this realization find that every dimension of their lives is automatically and totally fulfilling, because fulfillment is not contingent upon satisfying specific desires, or even fulfilling the overarching need for peace and contentment.

Totally spacious

In this state everything is totally spacious and elevated. All phenomena are spontaneously fulfilled and exist in a state of harmony and balance. The unborn king (i.e., being itself) has no boundaries, center, or directions, and the meaning of authenticity is to be free from attachment to objects of perception and a perceiver. There is no need to reject or accept anything, or to refute or establish (any viewpoint, since reality is) unbiased. This—Dzogchen—is the optimum peak of all perspectives.

Here Longchenpa is essentially summarizing a number of the points he has already dealt with.

No fixations

You should (also) know that the king who is free from intentionality (i.e., the mind-itself) has no fixations. All deliberate attentiveness is a constricting factor (too). If there is no attentiveness with respect to whatever arises, then this is real wisdom.

Longchenpa now moves on to identify some of the aspects of fixation. The energy of fixation, he says, is characterized by a particular focus of our attention on just one element or dimension of our experience. When we are fixated, our minds become preoccupied by particular thoughts, feelings, or sensory stimulants, either because we are trying to indulge them, or because we wish to avoid them.

In general, there are two ways in which we become fixated. Sometimes the focus of our attention seems to be captivated, and so determined, by the phenomenon we are experiencing. It is as though we become glued to a particular thought pattern, feeling, person, sound, etc. through no choice of our own, as though we were mesmerized. If we try to divert our attention, the object that has caught it drags us back, like a magnet. At other times, we choose to focus on a restricted area of interest; we deliberately fix our attention on the particular task at hand. Driven by the desire to alter or maintain our experience, our awareness becomes purposive or intentional. We become obsessively focused on what we are thinking about, or doing, and view other sensations as unwelcome, or even annoying intrusions. (Spiritual practice, as Longchenpa has already pointed out, can easily take on this obsessive character.)

In both cases, we are unable to come to an unbiased experience of the panorama of sensations. We find ourselves caught in a vortex of energy that distorts our ability to see things clearly and in perspective. But when our attention is not fixated in this way, our minds rest evenly and impartially on all aspects of our experience; and this, according to Longchenpa, is the hallmark of real wisdom.

Empty or empty?

> (Letting the mind) rest in its natural state—empty of itself and unspoiled—this is the authentic state. You should ascertain this perspective, free from fixations and without any position or biases.

Here it seems that Longchenpa is making an implicit reference to two interpretations of the word "empty" (*stong, shunya*) as used in Buddhist texts: namely "empty of itself" (*rang stong*) and "empty of other" (*gzhan stong*), a distinction which has been the focus of a good deal of debate within the schools of Tibetan Buddhism, and continues to be controversial. (see Hookham, 1991)

Briefly, "empty" may be taken to refer either to phenomena or to the state of realization—that is, to the relative or the absolute view. In the first case, "empty" means that phenomena are devoid of own-nature: they have no essential essence of their own, and their apparent uniqueness is a mental construct, an illusion. This is the "empty of itself" interpretation. Alternatively, if "empty" is understood as referring to the state of realization, it means that realization is "empty" of all opposites and all conceptualizations, free of all defilement or limitation—"empty," indeed, of all qualities whatsoever. This is the "empty of other" interpretation.

Although Dzogchen is usually identified with the "empty of other" view, Longchenpa makes it clear that when he talks about the mind being "empty," he means that it is "empty of itself." In other words, the mind is empty in the sense that it is unfindable by virtue of lacking any intrinsic essence or core, and there is no need to remove mental defilements in order to be liberated. All that is needed is to discern that the mind already lacks any reality by letting it rest in its natural state. When we appreciate this, defilements spontaneously dissolve and the mind manifests in its original, unspoiled condition. Longchenpa's use of the term "empty of itself" is significant here because it implicitly indicates that in Dzogchen, the relative and ultimate realities are not different, since the ultimate reality (i.e., openness) is the reality realized through letting the mind rest in its natural state. In other words, the authentic view can accommodate all views without bias or fixation.

A joke!

> Alas! The variety of appearances is a joke, so don't (bother to) investigate them—but if you do, do so in a light-hearted way, and (discover that) there is nothing to identify. (Likewise), if you examine things very thoroughly, they transcend the extreme of being substantially existent. If you look inwardly at the mind which differentiates, you cannot perceive any temporal extension, and so there is no arising, ceasing, or abiding. (The mind) is colorless and has no shape and, therefore, doesn't have an identifiable nature. When an appearance arises, there is no place it comes from, nor anyone creating it. (With the mind) there is no apprehension of an inside or outside, and it transcends the (artificial) boundary between objects of perception and the perceiver.

"The variety of appearances is a joke," Longchenpa says. Here he states that the emptiness or non-intrinsic identifiability of reality can be realized either by looking at things in a relaxed way, free from compulsion and necessity, or by investigating them in a structured and disciplined way, specifically using the analyses supplied by Madhyamika. The first method is specifically a Dzogchen approach, while the second is used by Deconstructive Madhyamika (*Prasangika-madhyamika*).

Longchenpa's point is that to examine things in an unstructured and undisciplined way, without the epistemological commitment and control of deconstructive analysis, is to give rein to an unbridled and uncontrolled conceptuality which simply consolidates and confirms the intrinsic existence of things and concretizes our fixations.

The movement of the mind

> Even though the mind appears to go out toward an external object, there is no place toward which it can move. Rather, things merely arise for the mind. If the mind did move out (to an external location in order to contact an object), then when (we were perceiving an external object) we would be inanimate (since our mind would have left our body). In a single instant our present awareness would split into two aspects.

As suggested earlier, from the Dzogchen perspective there is no distance between the mind and what it experiences. The sense of spatial separation between the perceiver and the perceived is only an appearance for the mind, which in itself has no spatial dimension. Ultimately, there is no sense of an "inner" or "outer."

Thus, Longchenpa here points to the absurdity of the view that consciousness must leave the cognizer in order to contact putative external objects. In the first place, if our consciousness departs when we are perceiving the external world, then our body would become insentient—it would be no different from a corpse. If we object to this reasoning and maintain that consciousness does indeed leave the cognizer in knowing the external world, while the cognizer does not become inanimate, then we have the alternative absurdity that consciousness would adopt two radically different characteristics: on the one hand, there would be a type of consciousness that could leave the cognizer; and on the other, a consciousness that remained with the cognizer in order for the cognizer to be aware of the consciousness that had contacted the external world. This latter type of mind would have to remain unlocated (or retain its original location) in order to know that the moving mind had contacted the object. These same objections were made much earlier in the *Surangama Sutra*. (Teschner, 1981)

Buddha nature

> There is absolutely no basis for the reflections (that appear in the mind, since the mind) is primordially free, like space. The (reflections of the world) arise (in the mind, but) they are not two different things. They are like the reflection of images in a mirror. Just as the ocean and its waves (are indivisible), in an ultimate sense (phenomenal

appearances and the mind) are nondual. The meaning of the Dzogchen is that there is no need to reject or accept (anything). In actuality (the mind) is pure from the very beginning, (so it is already) fully awake. The appearances of the phenomenal world and the mind are primordially insubstantial. Today I have realized the teachings of my magnificent master.

In this section, Longchenpa makes his first explicit reference to a principle fundamental to Dzogchen, namely, that our minds are already pure and totally awake—in Tibetan, *sang rgyas*, which, as we noted earlier, means no more and no less than buddha. Here Longchenpa is saying that there never has been a time when we were not buddhas. When we realize the true nature of reality (*chos nyid, dharmakaya*), we see that we and everyone else possess the same ultimate nature of the mind (*sems nyid*). In a sense, we already are all the qualities needed to be liberated; we simply don't experience it.

The idea that we are—or have the innate potential to become—buddhas has been explored in many different Buddhist traditions, perhaps most notably Zen, and its underpinning is found in the concept of "buddha nature" (*tathagatagarbha*), which in Mahayana Buddhism is held to be a property of all sentient beings. Some schools have interpreted this to mean that all creatures have the potential—the spiritual genes, as it were—to mature into buddhas under the right conditions. With skillful spiritual practice, in other words, our capacity for spiritual growth will inevitably lead us to the goal of full awakening. Other schools have a more radical interpretation and hold that we are *already* fully awake and aware, but fail to experience that we are buddhas because our minds are contaminated by dualistic beliefs and conflicting emotions.

In Zen, these two positions find expression in the legendary verse-exchange recounted in the *Platform Sutra*. (Yampolsky, 1967: 130 and 132) The monk Shen-hsiu wrote,

> The body is the Bodhi tree,
> The mind is like a clear mirror.
> At all times we must strive to polish it,
> And must not let the dust collect.

This enunciates the view of "orthodox," goal-oriented forms of Buddhism: the natural mind is contaminated and needs to be purified, whence realization is something lying in the future, something to be striven for. Hui-neng replied with this verse,

> Bodhi originally has no tree,
> The mirror also has no stand.
> Buddha nature is always clean and pure;
> Where is there room for dust?

This verse states the view which has become normative for Zen Buddhism, namely, that we are already enlightened. The natural mind-itself is buddha nature, pure, and undefiled.

Over the centuries, Buddhist philosophers have applied considerable effort to debating their differences on these matters. But from the Dzogchen perspective, it is naive and misguided to engage in such disputes with the intention of accepting or rejecting any particular point of view. Dzogchen practitioners relate to theories and doctrines in a very light manner—they aren't given to vigorous philosophical disputation. The real issue is not whether we are or are not already enlightened, but rather to appreciate that there is no solid obstruction to the natural clarity of our awareness. If we try and find any hindrance or barrier, all we ever discover is a naturally arising thought or feeling that we believe shouldn't be there.

Nothing to know

Now, because you have ascertained that everything is the ultimate dimension of reality, there is no assertion or negation; you are free from all hesitation and misconception and no (longer need) to ask anyone about the real meaning of the mind-itself. Without doing anything, you have seen the genuine essence. At this time, the dynamic and static (manifestations arise as) the play of the ultimate dimension of being. There is no need to reject or accept (anything). Whatever arises is an ornament (for the mind). If (your mind) is settled—abiding in the unified state of the unmoving, ultimate dimension of being—then everything is spontaneously and automatically fulfilled without any change or transformation. Now, we have arrived at the wisdom mind of the Victorious Ones of the three times. (Your experience is) totally blissful and spontaneously and automatically realized when the basis (of your very existence) is fulfilled in the state of Cosmic Wholeness (Samantabhadra). Everything is equally free in the primordial level of existence because at all times, whether past, present, or future, there is no change or transformation.

Longchenpa is here concerned to make the point that when one has realized the ultimate dimension of being (*dharmakaya*), there are no more questions to ask. There is nothing more one needs to do, nothing more one needs to know, because this mode of existence transcends all limitations. There is no knowledge to acquire, nor any ignorance to remove. Since there is nothing to be appropriated and nothing to be rejected, all experiences arise as the dynamic and free-flowing expression of the wisdom-mind. Thus, even when the mind is subject to turbulent and potentially unsettling change, it remains undisturbed, because at its source the mind is experienced as the unique and uniform dimension of being itself. An image commonly used in Dzogchen writing compares such turbulence to clouds scudding across the sky, for clouds do not change the fundamental nature of the sky itself. Indeed, in another Dzogchen image, all thoughts and feelings are seen as ornaments of the mind, just as clouds can be seen as enhancing the beauty of the sky.

Moreover, when one has realized this ultimate dimension of being, there is no hesitancy in one's behavior because there is no fear to overcome, no doubt to be removed. There are no enemies, either real or imagined, because there is nothing to protect or defend. However, this does not give rise to any egoistic feeling of invincibility, because the Dzogchen adept also deconstructs any feeling of attainment.

Reality presents itself

Alas! For one whose mind is fixated with biased attitudes there is no possibility of liberation. The factor which binds one is just these biased attitudes. The meaning of nonduality occurs when you are free of opinions, and if you have transcended clinging to extremes. There is no other way of disclosing this. You cannot see it by looking for it. Nor can you find it through logical analysis. Calling it "This" doesn't reveal it, so in relationship to this natural state don't fetter, or liberate it, with a grasping mind.

Once again, Longchenpa emphasizes that we cannot see reality by looking for it. If we try to search out and discover reality in a very deliberate, intelligent, and self-conscious way, it eludes us. But if we relax into our natural condition, reality presents itself in a simple and completely uncomplicated way. In fact, there is no need to look for it because it is already there—wherever we are—as Saraha says, "Though the house-lamps have been lit, the blind live on in the dark." (Guenther, 1968: 63)

The limits of the limitless

Although people desire the nondual and limitless (awareness, they make a) limit out of that which is not limited (and thereby) constrict the essential mind-itself. Even though people desire (the realization of) both (the ultimate and relative) realities, they fall into an extreme understanding of these. Although they desire the union of the two realities, this is not the way things naturally are. No matter in what way you investigate, you are trapped in the cage of (conflicting) desires.

Throughout the ages, mystic philosophers and metaphysicians have contrasted the limited, deceptive, and impermanent reality that we experience through our senses with a limitless, transcendent, mystical reality—which has been called the Godhead, Brahman, Tao, Emptiness, and many other names. However, from the Dzogchen perspective, these realities are themselves limited; they are limited to precisely the same extent that they are distinguished from that which is limited. In other words, as soon as limitlessness displaces that which is limited, it assumes its own limits and restrictions.

It is against this background that Longchenpa points to the dangers of limiting ourselves by becoming fixated on the limitlessness of the mind-itself. Having distinguished the nature of the mind-itself as fundamentally different from mental phenomena, such as thoughts and feelings, one can become intellectually and philosophically captivated by the "idea" that the mind is limitless. But in so doing, one falls into a fixed and extreme understanding of the Dzogchen perspective. The Chinese East Mountain Zen master Foyan makes the same point, "You shouldn't set up limits in boundless openness, but if you set up limitlessness as boundless openness, you've trapped yourself." (Cleary, 1989)

This type of fixation is based on drawing a distinction between appearance and reality. In orthodox Buddhism and mystical philosophies, such as Hindu Advaita, this is formalized as a theory of two levels of reality (*satyadvaya*): the social (*vyavahara*) or relative (*samvrti*), and the ultimate (*paramartha*). (see Swanson, 1995; Newland, 1992; Eckel, 1987) In Buddhism, this differentiation reflects a division between form and openness. The relative reality (form) corresponds to the world of that which is known through our body and mind—everything that can be felt, seen, or thought about. The ultimate reality corresponds to the open, unmarked, and insubstantial reality that underlies the existence of everything. In Buddhism, this is called openness or emptiness. This difference also corresponds to a fundamental divergence in practice between orthodox Buddhism and Dzogchen.

One of the most profound features of Dzogchen is the way in which reality is never split into different dimensions—the ultimate and relative, the spiritual and worldly, or the transpersonal and personal. Right from the very outset, reality is revealed in a way that doesn't privilege any state over another one. Every conceivable reality is seamlessly integrated in the fundamental space of "being as such." What this means is that nothing needs to be changed or altered in order to realize the nature of mind-itself while fully immersed in our embodied existence.

Perception and perceived

Due to the confusion (created by splitting experience into) objects of perception and one who perceives, we have been dissatisfied since time without beginning, and so we persistently investigate because we are trapped by our mental images. Alas! I grieve for the deluded mind.

Once again, Longchenpa stresses the negative effects of earnest and well-intentioned spiritual practice.

The thicket of views

If one identifies (the nature of the mind) as some particular thing, then this is not the correct perspective. One does not need the cage of proliferating conceptualization. Whatever arises in the non-strategic field of bare awareness is *neither* expanded *nor* contracted, and *neither* sublime *nor* mundane. So give up your libidinous fixations!

Here Longchenpa emphasizes the trap which is inherent in any opinion about the nature of the mind. The moment we impute even the simplest of characteristics to the mind, we set the stage for developing a full-fledged theory about the nature and workings of mental phenomena, and we thus find ourselves trapped in what the Buddha Shakyamuni describes in several of the earliest Buddhist texts as "a thicket of views, a wilderness of views, a contortion of views, a vacillation of views, a fetter of views." For example, if we say that the mind has a form, or doesn't have a form, various questions automatically present themselves, such as: How does the mind relate to the body and emotions? Is there one mind or are there many minds? and so on. Similarly, if we say that the mind is pure, or that it is defiled, we need to explain why this is so. We also need to spell out the consequences of our assumptions for our spiritual practice. If the mind is defiled, for example, how are we to set about purifying it? Moreover, having established a position, we soon find ourselves having to defend it against those who hold differing positions: we have to add more detail, more texture to our theories; we have to refine them with conditions and riders; we have to refer to philosophical and textual authorities, and so on. This, of course, is the impulse behind philosophers' and psychologists' efforts to develop complex, competing theories about the relationship between cognition and perception, perception and feelings, thinking and behavior. And if our theories become indefensible, we must either modify them or revoke them in favor of more adequate theories. As Longchenpa says, we get caught in the cage of proliferating conceptualization (*prapanca*).

Bound hand and foot

With respect to the appearances in the mind, there is a freedom from the mental orientation (that thinks) "It is This." Do not condition your mind by (trying) to suppress your experience, apply an antidote, or mechanically transform it, but let your mind fall naturally into whatever (condition you find it). This is the incontrovertible essence of what is ultimately meaningful.

Longchenpa here further develops the theme that one should not become fixated about how things are. This applies equally to the mundane and the sublime. In fact, the very distinction between these only serves to trap us, since it can lead us into believing that we have understood what the spiritual search is all about, whereas all we have done is to erect further edifices of conceptualization. As Foyan says, "The minute you fixate on the recognition that "This is 'it,'" you are immediately bound hand and foot and cannot move around anymore." (Cleary, 1989: 44)

The king of views

In their own nature, all the varieties of entities are in a state of harmony, so whatever arises is the nondual wisdom. Do not conceptualize it, and drop any frantic searching with your egocentric mind! Do not become trapped by the objects of perception, and don't let your mind become tarnished by allowing it to function as a subject of cognitions. If you are without any objects of desire, then you will know that all phenomena are like space, and you will see them as equivalent to an illusion. This is the nature of nonduality—the supreme king of views. Being free from extreme views is the (real) gauge of your realization. How wonderful!

According to the Dzogchen tradition, there is no distinction between appearance and reality, or between confusion and wisdom. There is nothing other than what is present for us in any moment. There is no such thing as an "obstruction" or "hindrance" to enlightenment, for such a thing would presuppose that one experience can displace another.

Hence, Longchenpa claims that thoughts themselves are the nondual and non-conceptual wisdom, and similarly, that phenomena themselves are the very medium that they displace—this is the "king of views." The test of one's realization is whether one has the capacity to see and experience the transcendental field of being as indistinguishable from the sense-world as it manifests each moment. Indeed, it is misleading to talk in terms of finding the two indistinguishable, for this is not a question of infusing sense experience with the qualities of super-sensory spiritual experiences; rather, they mutually express each other in the sense that each discloses the other.

From this point of view, spiritual goals such as enlightenment are a full-scale distraction from being just as one is. Enlightenment becomes a possibility the instant we declare that human existence is limited or unsatisfactory. And for as long as we seek to escape from that which is now unsatisfactory, human existence continues to be limited and painful. Dzogchen is forsaken the moment we buy into the "myth of spiritual liberation."

The meaning of Dzogchen

> Bare awareness is devoid of the duality of mundane existence and transcendental peace. It is a state of complete openness. (When) you understand the nature of your own being (*rang ngo she pa*), (you see that) there is no substance, ground, or root to it. The (real) meaning of Dzogchen is the nonduality of being bound or free. The minds of all beings, without exception, constantly abide in this state. In order to see this profound reality, which transcends depiction but is revealed as the manifestation of immaculate light rays (*dri med 'od zer*), I urge you not to fixate on the mind and its appearances, but rather to comprehend this perspective of impartial awareness through the illusory display (of phenomena appearing in the mind).

Longchenpa completes this chapter by reiterating the point that the state of Dzogchen cannot be equated with the common spiritual ideals of peace and quietude, or a feeling of being free to do, or create, whatever we wish. The real meaning of Dzogchen lies in an impartial awareness that transcends all preoccupation with loss, or gain.

Bibliography

General Introductions

Fenner, Peter (2002). *The Edge of Certainty: Dilemmas on the Buddhist Path*. Newburyport, MA: Nicolas-Hays.

Katz, Jerry (2007). *One: Essential Writings on Nonduality*. Sentient Publications.

McLeod, Ken (2001). *Wake up to Your Life: Discovering the Buddhist Path of Attention*. New York: HarperCollins.

Ray, Reginald A. (2000). *Indestructible Truth: The Living Spirituality of Tibetan Buddhism*. Boston: Shambhala Publications.

Ray, Reginald A. (2002). *Secret of the Vajra World: The Tantric Buddhism of Tibet*. Boston: Shambhala Publications.

Perfect Wisdom (*Prajnaparamita*)

Brunnholzl, Karl (trs.) (2014). *Gone Beyond*: The Prajnaparamita Sutras, The Ornament of Clear Realization, *and Its Commentaries in the Tibetan Kagyu Tradition (Volume 1)*. Ithaca, NY: Snow Lion.

Diamond Sutra. (2002). *The Diamond Sutra*, trs. and comm. by Red Pine (Bill Porter). Berkeley, California: Counterpoint.

Heart Sutra. (2004). *The Heart Sutra: the womb of the Buddhas*, trs. and comm. by Red Pine (Bill Porter). Berkeley, California: Counterpoint.

Hixon, Lex (1993). *Mother of the Buddhas: Meditation on the Prajnaparamita Sutra*. Wheaton, Ill.: Quest Books.

Tanahash. Kazuaki (2014). *The Heart Sutra: A Comprehensive Guide to the Classic of Mahayana Buddhism*. Boston: Shambhala.

Vimalakirti. *Vimalakirti Nirdesha Sutra*. (1976). [Trs. by Robert A. F. Thurman as *The Holy Teaching of Vimalakirti: A Mahayana Scripture*.] Pennsylvania State University Press.

Madhyamika

Chandrakirti. (1979). *Lucid Words*. A partial translation of (*Prasannapada*) by Mervyn Sprung, Boulder: Prajna Press.

Chandrakirti. (1991). *Introduction to the Middle Way (Madhyamikavatara)*. [Trs. in Peter Fenner *The Ontology of the Middle Way*.] Dordrecht, Holland: Kluwer.

Chandrakirti. (2005). *Introduction to the Middle Way: Chandrakirti's Madhyamikavatara with Commentary by Ju Mipham*. Boston: Shambhala Publications.

Duerlinger, James (2013). *The Refutation of the Self in Indian Buddhism: Candrakirti on the selflessness of persons*. London and New York: Routledge.

Nagarjuna and Lama Mipham. (1975). [Trs. by Leslie Kawamura, *Golden Zephyr: Nagarjuna's A Letter to a Friend (Suhrllekha)*]. Emeryville, California: Dharma Publishing.

Nagarjuna. (2001). [Trs. by Stephen Batchelor, *Verses from the Center: A Buddhist Vision of the Sublime*.] Riverhead Trade; Reissue edition, 2001.

Nagarjuna. (2005). [Trs. by Erik Hoogcarspel. *The Central Philosophy: Basic Verses*.] Olive Press, Amsterdam.

Shantideva. (1997). [Trs. by Vesna and B. Alan Wallace, *A Guide to the Bodhisattva Way of Life (Bodhicaryavatara)*]. Ithaca, N.Y.: Snow Lion Publications.

Siderits, Mark and Shoryu Katsura (2013). *Nagarjuna's Middle Way (MulaMadhyamikakarika)*, Boston: Wisdom Publications.

Thurman, Robert (1984). *Tsong Khapa's Speech of Gold in the Essence of True Eloquence: Reason and Enlightenment in the Central Philosophy of Tibet*, Princeton, New Jersey: Princeton University Press.

Tsultrim Gyamtso, Khenpo (2003). *The Sun of Wisdom: Teachings on the Noble Nagarjuna's Fundamental Verses of the Middle Way*, Shambhala, Boston and London.

Tyler Dewar (trs.) (2008). *The Karmapa's Middle Way: Feast for the Fortunate, the Ninth Karmapa, Wangchuk Dorje*, Ithaca NY: Snow Lion.

Advaita

Ashtavakra Gita. (2001). [Trs. by Thomas Byrom, *The Heart of Awareness: A Translation of the Ashtavakra Gita.*] Boston: Shambhala.

Maharshi, Ramana (1988). *The Spiritual Teaching of Ramana Maharshi*, Boston: Shambhala.

Maharshi, Ramana (1989). *Be as You Are: The Teachings of Sri Ramana Maharshi.* Edited by David Godman. Penguin.

Nisargadatta (1990). *I am that I am: Talks with Shri Nisargadatta.* North Carolina: Acorn.

Waite, Dennis (2007). *Back to the Truth: 5000 years of Advaita.* Berkeley, California: O Books.

Zen

Cleary, Thomas Trs. (1989). *Zen Essence: the Science of Freedom.* Boston: Shambhala.

Cleary, Thomas Trs. (1998). *Book of Serenity: One Hundred Zen Dialogues.* Boston: Shambhala.

Leighton, Taigen D. Trs. (1991). *Cultivating the Empty Field: the Silent Illumination of Zen Master Hongzhi.* San Francisco: North Point Press.

Merzel, Dennis G. (1991). *The Eye Never Sleeps: Striking to the Heart of Zen.* Boston: Shambhala.

Mumonkan. (1998). [*The Gateless Gate.* Trs. by Eiichi Shimomissé.] www.csudh.edu/phenom_studies/mumonkan/mumonkan.htm .

Sekida, Katsuki (2005). *Two Zen Classics: The Gateless Gate and the Blue Cliff Records.* Boston: Shambhala.

The Lankavatara Sutra. (2013). *The Lankavatara Sutra*, trs. and comm. by Red Pine (Bill Porter) California: Counterpoint.

The Surangama Sutra. (2009). *The Surangama Sutra.* With Excepts from the Commentary by the Venerable Master Hsuan Hua, Buddhist Text Translation Society, 2009

Taigen Dan Leighton (2011). *Zen Questions: Zazen, Dogen, and the Spirit of Creative Inquiry.* Boston: Wisdom.

Tanahashi, Kazuaki and Peter Levitt (eds.) (2013). *The Essential Dogen: Writings of the Great Zen Master.* Boston: Shambhala.

Mahamudra

Brown, Daniel (2006). *Pointing Out the Great Way: The Stages of Meditation in the Mahamudra Tradition*, Boston: Wisdom Publications.

Dorje, Wangchug (1978). *The Mahamudra: Eliminating the Darkness of Ignorance.* Trs. by Alexander Berzin. Dharamsala: Library of Tibetan Works and Archives.

Guenther, Herbert V. (Trs.) (1993). *Ecstatic Spontaneity: Saraha's Three Cycles of Doha*, Berkeley. Calif.: Asian Humanities Press.

Jackson, Roger R. (2004). *Tantric Treasures: Three Collections of Mystical Verse from Buddhist India.* Oxford: Oxford University Press.

Jinpa, Thupten (ed.) and Peter Alan Roberts (trs). (2014) *The Mind of Mahamudra: Advice from the Kagyu Masters.* Boston: Wisdom Publications.

Khamtrul Rinpoche and Gerardo Abboud (trs). (2014). *The Royal Seal of Mahamudra: Volume One: A Guidebook for the Realization of Coemergence.* Boston: Shambhala.

Milarepa (Nicole Riggs, Trs.) (2003). *Songs on the Spot.* Eugene, Oregon: Dharma Cloud.

Nyenpa, Sangyes and David Molk (trs). (2014). *Tilopa's Mahamudra* Upadesha: The Gangama Instructions *with Commentary.* Ithaca: Snow Lion. Schaeffer, Kurtis R. (2005). *Dreaming the Great Brahman: Tibetan Traditions of the Buddhist Poet-Saint Saraha.* Oxford: Oxford University Press.

Tashi Namgyal, Dakpo (2001). *Clarifying the Natural State: A Principal Practice Guide for Mahamudra.* Translation of *gNyug ma'i de nyid gsal ba* by Erik Pema Kunsang, Boudhanath, Nepal: Rangjung Yeshe.

Thrangu Rinpoche, Khenchen (2006). *A Song for the King: Saraha on Mahamudra Mediation,* Wisdom Publications.

Dzogchen

Anyen Rinpoche (2009). *Momentary Buddhahood: Mindfulness and the Vajrayana Path.* Boston: Wisdom Publications.

Dowman, Keith (trs.) (2014). *Spaciousness: The Radical Dzogchen of the Vajra-Heart: Longchenpa's* Treasury of the Dharmadhatu. Kathmandu: Vajra Publications.

Duff, Tony. Trs. (2008). *Alchemy of Accomplishment.* Kathmandu: Padma Karpo Translation Committee.

Garab Dorje (1996). *The Golden Letters.* Trs. by John M. Reynolds. Ithaca, NY: Snow Lion Publications.

Hatchell, Christopher (2014). Naked Seeing: *The Great Perfection, the Wheel of Time, and Visionary Buddhism in Renaissance Tibet.* Oxford: Oxford University Press. Longchen Rabjam (1998). *The Precious Treasury of the Way of Abiding,* Junction City, California: Padma Publishing.

Khenpo, Nyoshul and Surya Das (2008). *Natural Great Perfection: Dzogchen Teachings and Vajra Songs.* Ithaca: Snow Lion,

Khenpo, Nyoshul and David Christensen (trs.) (2015). *The Fearless Lion's Roar: Profound Instructions on Dzogchen, the Great Perfection.* Ithaca: Snow Lion.

Klein, Anne Carolyn and Geshe Tenzin Wangyal Rinpoche (2006). *Unbounded Wholeness: Dzogchen, Bon, and the Logic of the Nonconceptual.* Oxford: Oxford University Press.

Longchen Rabjam (2001). *A Treasure Trove of Spiritual Transmission,* Junction City, California: Padma Publishing.

Longchen Rabjam (2001). *The Precious Treasury of the Basic Space of Phenomena,* Junction City, California: Padma Publishing.

Longchenpa (2000). Trs. by Kennard Lipman. *You are the Eyes of the World.* Ithaca, NY: Snow Lion Publications.

Longchenpa (2006). *Radical Dzogchen: Old Man Basking in the Sun.* [Trs. of Longchen Rabjampa's *Treasury of Natural Perfection* by Keith Dowman.] Kathmandu, Nepal: Vajra Books.

Manjushrimitra (1987). Trs. by Kennard Lipman and Namkhai Norbu, trs. *Primordial Experience: an Introduction to rDzogs-chen Meditation.* Boston & London: Shambhala.

Ponlop, Dzogchen (2003). *Wild Awakening: The Heart of Mahamudra and Dzogchen.* Boston: Shambhala.

Reynolds, John M. (1989). *Self-Liberation through Seeing with Naked Awareness.* Barrytown, New York: Station Hill Press.

Psychotherapeutic and psychodynamic sources

Blackstone, Judith (2007). *The Empathic Ground: Intersubjectivity and Nonduality in the Psychotherapeutic Process* (S U N Y Series in Transpersonal and Humanistic Psychology). Albany, NY: SUNY.

Blackstone, Judith (2012). *Belonging Here: A Guide for the Spiritually Sensitive Person,* Boulder: Sounds True.

Bodian, Stephan (2014). *Beyond Mindfulness: The Direct Approach to Lasting Peace, Happiness, and Love.* Waterfront Digital Books.

Brazier, David (1995). *Zen Therapy: Transcending the Sorrow of the Human Mind.* NY: John Wiley and Sons.

Cayton, Karuna (2012). *The Misleading Mind: How We Create Our Own Problems and How Buddhist Psychology Can Help Us Solve Them.* California: New World Library.

Foster, Jeff (2012). *The Deepest Acceptance: Radical Awakening in Ordinary Life*. Boulder: Sounds True.

Griggs, Carole (2013). *Space to See Reality: A New Model for Professional Coaches.*

Olendzki, Andrew and John Tarrant (2010). *Unlimiting Mind: The Radically Experiential Psychology of Buddhism*. Boston: Wisdom Publications.

Preece, Rob (2014). *Feeling Wisdom: Working with Emotions Using Buddhist Teachings and Western Psychology*. Boston: Shambhala.

Prendergast, John J. (2015). *In Touch: How to Tune in to the Inner Guidance of Your Body and Trust Yourself*. Boulder: Sounds True.

Prendergast John J., Peter Fenner, and Sheila Krystal (eds.) (2003). *The Sacred Mirror: Nondual Wisdom & Psychotherapy*. St.Paul, MN: Paragon House Publishers.

Prendergast, John J. and Ken Bradford (eds.) (2007). *Listening from the Heart of Silence*. St.Paul, MN: Paragon House Publishers.

Safran, Jeremy D. (ed). (2003). *Psychoanalysis and Buddhism: An Unfolding Dialogue*. Boston: Wisdom Publications.

Rosenbaum Robert (1999). *Zen and the Heart of Psychotherapy*. Philadelphia: Taylor and Francis.

Tzu, Gary (2014). *Awakening in the Paradox of Darkness*. Victoria, BC: Friesen Press.

Unno, Mark (ed.). (2006). *Buddhism and Psychotherapy Across Cultures: Essays on Theories and Practices*. Boston: Wisdom Publications.

Welwood, John (2000). *Towards a Psychology of Awakening: Buddhism, Psychotherapy, and the Path of Personal and Spiritual Transformation*. Boston: Shambhala.

References

Alexander, H. G., ed. (1956). *The Leibniz-Clark Correspondence.* New York: Manchester University Press.

Blofeld, John, Trs. (1958). *The Zen Teaching of Huang Po.* London: Rider.

Candrakirti (1970). *Madhyamikavatara et Bhaysa par Candrakirti* [Ed. and Trs. by Louis de la Vallée Poussin]. Osnabrück: Biblio Verlag.

Chandrakirti (2002). *Introduction to the Middle Way* [Candrakirti's *Madhyamikavatara* with *Mipham Rinpoche's Commentary* Trs. by Padmakara Translation Group]. Shambhala.

Chandrakirti (2003). *Introduction to the Middle Way.* [Chandrakirti's *Madhyamikavatara* Trs. Dzongsar Jamyang Khyentse Rinpoche, Ed. Alex Trisoglio] Khyentse Foundation.

Cleary, Thomas (2000). *Zen Essence: The Science of Freedom.* Boston: Shambhala.

Conze, Edward (1972). *Buddhist Wisdom Books: the Diamond Sutra and Heart Sutra.* New York: Harper and Row.

Conze, Edward (1975). *The Large Sutra on Perfect Wisdom* [Trs. of *Pañcavimshatisahasrika-prajñaparamita-sutra*]. Berkeley: University of California Press.

dGe-'dun-grub (nd). *dBu-ma-la 'jug-pai-bstan-bcos-kyi-dgongs-pa rab-tu gsal-ba'i-me-long.* In *The Collected Works (gSung-'bum) of dGe-'dun-grub-pa.* Sikkim, Gangtok: Dondrup Lama, Deorali Chorten.

Eckel, Malcolm D. (1987). *Jnanagarbha's Commentary on the Distinction between the Two Truths: an Eight Century HandBook of Madhyamika Philosophy,* Albany, New York: State University of New York Press.

Fenner, Peter (1990). *The Ontology of the Middle Way.* Dordrecht, Holland: Kluwer.

Guenther, H.V., Trs. (1968). *The Royal Song of Saraha: a Study in the History of Buddhist Thought.* Seattle and London: University of Washington Press.

Guenther, Herbert, Trs. (1993). *Ecstatic Spontaneity: Saraha's Three Cycles of Doha.* Berkeley, California: Asian Humanities Press.

Harding, Douglas E. (1986). *On Having No Head: Zen and the Rediscovery of the Obvious.* London: Arkana.

Harding, Douglas E. (1993). *The Near End: The Science of Liberation and the Liberation of Science.* Shollond, Ipswich.

Hookham, S. K. (1991). *The Buddha Within: Tathagatagarbha Doctrine According to the Shentong Interpretation of the Ratnagotravibhaga.* Albany, New York: State University of New York Press.

Hopkins, Jeffrey (1996). *Meditation on Emptiness.* Boston: Wisdom Publications.

Hopkins, Jeffrey (2009). *Tantric Techniques.* Ithaca, New York: Snow Lion Publications.

Huntington, C.W. (1989). *The Emptiness of Emptiness.* Hawaii: University of Hawaii Press.

Kawamura, Leslie (1975). *Golden Zephyr* [Trs. of *Suhrllekha* with commentary by *Mi-pham*]. Dharma Publishing.

The Kindred Sayings (Samyutta Nikaya) (5 vols). (1950). London: Luzac

Krishnamurti, U. G. (1982). *The Mystique of Enlightenment: the Unrational Idea of a Man called U.G.* (ed. Rodney Arms). Goa, India: Dinesh Vaghela Cemetile Co.

Latta, Robert, Trs. (1925) Leibniz,*The Monadology and Other Philosophical Writings.* London: Oxford University Press.

Longchenpa (1974). *Chos nyid rang grol.* Gangtok, Sikkim: Dodrup Chen Rinpoche. Manchester University Press.

May, Rollo (1983). *The Discovery of Being: Writings in Existential Psychology.* New York: W.W. Norton and Co.

Nagarjuna (1967). *MulaMadhyamikakarika.* [Trs by Frederick J. Streng] (1967). Nashville: Abingdon Press.

Neumaier-Dargyay, E.K. (1992). *The Sovereign All-Creating Mind: the Motherly Buddha.* Albany: State University of New York Press.

Newland, Guy (1992). *The Two Truths in the Madhyamika Philosophy of the Ge Luk ba Order of Tibetan Buddhism*. Ithaca, NY: Snow Lion Publications.

Norbu, Namkhai (1984). *The Cycle of Day and Night: Where one Proceeds along the Path of Primordial Yog*a. Oakland: Zhang Zhung Editions.

Norbu, Namkhai (Ed. Kennard Lipman) (1984b). *Dzog chen and Zen*. Oakland, Caifornia: Zhang Zhung Editions.

Poonja, H. W. L. (1992). *Wake Up and Roar*. Volume 1. Kula, Hawaii: Pacific Center Publications.

Shantideva. (1999). *The Way of the Bodhisattva*. Trs. *Bodhicharyavatara* by Padmakara Translation Group. Boston, Mass.: Shambhala.

Snellgrove, David, Trs. (1964). *"Songs for the People" from Saraha's Collected Songs (Dohakosha)*. In Edward Conze (Ed.). *Buddhist Texts through the Ages*. New York: Harper and Row.

Sprung, Mervyn (1979). *Lucid Verses on the Middle Way: the Essential Chapters from the Prasannapada of Candrakirti*. Boulder: Prajna Press.

Streng, Frederick J. (1967). *Emptiness: A Study in Religious Meaning*. Nashville: Abingdon Press.

Swanson, Paul (1995). *Foundations of T'ien T'ai Philosophy*. Fremont, California: Asian Humanities Press.

Teschner, George (1981). *"The Relation between Mind and Body in the Surangama Sutra."* Journal of Indian Philosophy (9).

The Kindred Sayings (Samyutta Nikaya). London: Luzac, 1950 (5 vols).

Thondup, Tulku (Ed. Harold Talbott) (1996). *Masters of Meditations and Miracles: the Longchen Nyingthig Lineage of Tibetan Buddhism*, Boston: Shambhala.

Thurman, Robert (1991). *Central Philosophy of Tibet* [Trs. Of Tsong kha pa's *Essence of the Eloquent*]. Princeton University Press.

Waddell, Norman, Trs. (1974). *"A Selection of Bankei's Zen Dialogs."* Eastern Buddhist (8).

Wangyal, Tenzin (1993). *Wonders of the Natural Mind: the Essence of Dzogchen in the Native Bon Tradition of Tibet*. Barrytown, New York: Station Hill Press.

Wittgenstein, Ludwig (1961). *Tractatus Logico-Philosophicus*. London: Routledge & KeganPaul.

Yampolsky, P., Trs. (1967). *The Platform Sutra of the Sixth Patriarch*. New York: Colombia University Press.

Index of Sections

About the author

Peter is a leader in the Western adaptation of Buddhist wisdom. He is a pioneer in the new field of nondual psychotherapy. He was a celibate monk in the Tibetan Buddhist traditions for nine years. He has a Ph.D. in the philosophical psychology of Mahayana Buddhism and has held teaching positions at universities in Australia and the USA.

His recent books include:
- *Radiant Mind: Awakening Unconditional Awareness,*
- *Radiant Mind: Teaching and Practices to Awakening Unconditioned Awareness* (7-CD set),
- *The Edge of Certainty: Paradoxes on the Buddhist Path,*
- *The Sacred Mirror: Nondual Wisdom and Psychotherapy* (ed. with John Prendergast and Sheila Krystal).

He has taught workshops at Naropa University, the California Institute for Integral Studies, Omega Institute, and other centers, and given invited presentations at JFK University, Saybrook College, Stanford Medical School, Columbia University, and internationally.

Peter's way of teaching is known for its dynamic and engaging deconstruction of all fixed frames of reference that block entry to unconditioned awareness, and for the purity and depth of natural, uncontrived silence that emerges in his work. He also has a unique capacity for sharing the skills and states of his transmission in a way that other's can easily understand and begin to replicate the nondual transmission.

CPSIA information can be obtained
at www.ICGtesting.com
Printed in the USA
BVHW050848141118
533112BV00014B/271/P

9 781896 559247